UNIVERSITY OF NOTTINGHAM

60 0372852 9

FROM THE LIBRARY

DATE DUE FOR RETURN

UNIVERSITY LIBRARY

27 JAN 2011

SeM

DATE DUE FOR RETURN

D1426410

The Brothers Karamazov is Dostoevsky's last and most complex novel. It represents the fullest expression of his quest to achieve a literary work which would express the dilemmas and aspirations of his time and also represent the eternal, absolute values he perceived in the Christian tradition. Diane Thompson's study focuses on the meaning and poetic function of memory in the novel, and seeks to show how Dostoevsky used cultural memory to create a synthesis between his Christian ideal and art. Memory is considered not only as a theme or subject, but also as a principle of artistic composition. Her interpretation identifies those aspects of cultural memory Dostoevsky incorporated into his novel, and analyses how he used them as significant components of his characters' memories.

CAMBRIDGE STUDIES IN RUSSIAN LITERATURE

The Brothers Karamazov and the poetics of memory

CAMBRIDGE STUDIES IN RUSSIAN LITERATURE

General editor MALCOLM JONES

Editorial board: ANTHONY CROSS, CARYL EMERSON,
HENRY GIFFORD, G. S. SMITH, VICTOR TERRAS

Recent titles in this series include:

Marina Tsvetaeva
SIMON KARLINSKY

Bulgakov's last decade
J. A. E. CURTIS

Velimir Khlebnikov
RAYMOND COOKE

Dostyevsky and the process of literary creation
JACQUES CATTEAU
translated by Audrey Littlewood

The Poetic imagination of Vyacheslav Ivanov
PAMELA DAVIDSON

Joseph Brodsky
VALENTINA POLUKHINA

Petrushka: the Russian carnival puppet theatre
CATRIONA KELLY

Turgenev
FRANK FRIEDEBERG SEELEY

*From the idyll to the novel: Karamzin's
sentimentalist prose*
GITTA HAMMARBERG

A complete list of books in this series
is given at the end of the volume.

THE BROTHERS KARAMAZOV AND THE POETICS OF MEMORY

DIANE OENNING THOMPSON

NOTTINGHAM UNIVERSITY LIBRARY

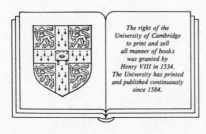

The right of the
University of Cambridge
to print and sell
all manner of books
was granted by
Henry VIII in 1534.
The University has printed
and published continuously
since 1584.

CAMBRIDGE UNIVERSITY PRESS

Cambridge
New York   Port Chester
Melbourne   Sydney

Published by the Press Syndicate of the University of Cambridge
The Pitt Building, Trumpington Street, Cambridge CB2 IRP
40 West 20th Street, New York, NY 10011, USA
10 Stamford Road, Oakleigh, Melbourne 3166, Australia

© Cambridge University Press 1991

First published 1991

Printed in Great Britain at the University Press, Cambridge

British Library cataloguing in publication data

Thompson, Diane Oenning
The brothers Karamazov and the poetics of memory. –
(Cambridge studies in Russian literature)
1. Fiction in Russia
I. Title
891.733

Library of Congress cataloguing in publication data

Thompson, Diane Oenning.
The brothers Karamazov and the poetics of memory / Diane Oenning Thompson.
p.   cm. – (Cambridge studies in Russian literature)
Includes bibliographical references
ISBN 0–521–34572–3
1. Dostoyevsky, Fyodor, 1821–1881. – Brat'ia Karamazovy. 2. Memory in literature.
3. Soviet Union – Civilization – 19th century – Fiction. 4. Christianity in literature. I.
Title. II. series.
PG3325.B73T49 1991
891.73'3–dc20   90–20044
CIP
ISBN 0 521 34572 3 hardback

600372852 9

To the memory of my Grandmother
Elise Helmine Eidsor Baer
Kristiansund, Norway 1881–1971 Chicago, Illinois

Contents

Preface

This book is an interpretation of *The Brothers Karamazov* based on a study of the meaning and poetic function of memory in the novel. Aristotle said in the *Poetics* that all people experience the 'greatest of pleasures' when contemplating a work of imitation because they are at the same time 'learning something', which he calls 'gathering the meaning of things'. Establishing, illuminating and ordering meanings is the primary goal of literary interpretation. An emphasis on poetics requires that we focus on the text of *The Brothers Karamazov* as a system of mutually connected elements in order to discover the aesthetic principles of their interrelation. Poetics and interpretation are in fact complementary activities. Poetics studies how an artistic text is constructed, interpretation strives to reveal its meanings.

Memory, in its broadest sense, is the general category of what remains of the past. The past is inscribed in memory, individual and cultural. Every individual retains in memory traces of his or her own past experience which can become the subject of an artistic representation. There are also supra-individual memories shared by all people in a given culture and extending over generations. This study attempts to identify those aspects of cultural memory Dostoevsky variously incorporated into his novel, to analyse how he used them as significant components of the individual memories he created for his characters, and to explore the dialogic interactions between them. It proceeds from two basic positions which have been convincingly argued by M. Bakhtin in his by now famous book on Dostoevsky's poetics, namely, that the novel is preeminently an artistic genre, and that Dostoevsky, notwithstanding his polemical involvement in the ideological issues of his day, was first and foremost an artist. Thus, I consider memory not only as a theme or subject, but as a principle of artistic composition. This means that we shall want to discover what is distinctive to those aspects of memory Dostoevsky selected to shape his poetic structures and give meaning to his novel.

The Brothers Karamazov has been approached from many avenues. Some have treated it as a philosophical work, others as a quasi-documentary reflection of socio-political reality, still others as a religious credo. Much valuable scholarly work has been devoted to tracing its literary and historical sources. The particulars of Dostoevsky's biography, his intellectual and publicistic preoccupations and his socio-historical milieu have also received the attention of many outstanding scholars. These investigations have contributed greatly to our understanding of the novel's diverse sources and the circumstances of its composition. By approaching *The Brothers Karamazov* through the concept of poetic memory, we may hope to see some of its meanings in a new perspective and to discover some of those aesthetic principles which unify the whole.

I was first drawn to the idea of analysing the poetic structure of *The Brothers Karamazov* from the point of view of memory after being struck by the multitude of references to memory in the novel, far exceeding that of all Dostoevsky's previous fiction. While there is rich material in his earlier work for a study of memory, it is in *The Brothers Karamazov*, his last novel, that we see him at full stretch in his creative uses of memory. Interestingly, it is also the work in which a word of hope for the future sounds most clearly.

Another general observation inspired me to concentrate on poetics. I had long been intrigued by the fact that people of the most diverse social, linguistic and cultural backgrounds, even those totally unacquainted with the Russian tradition, find that Dostoevsky's art speaks powerfully and significantly to them. This can only mean that *The Brothers Karamazov* is not entirely conditioned by, or dependent on, its cultural context for understanding or aesthetic enjoyment. This further suggests that there are universal themes and poetic properties in this work which transcend the concrete cultural and historical conditions in which it had its birth. Indeed, it would seem that the more poetic a text, the less it depends on its contemporary historical context, the more it creates its own world, at once unique and full of universal signifiers. In Dostoevsky, this search for universals was part of his major project to synthesise his Christian ideal with aesthetic form. To discover how Dostoevsky gave poetic expression to this quest through his artistic use of memory was one of the main impulses forwarding my work.

Memory has recently become a major theme in Russian literature and literary scholarship. This interest has arisen largely as a response to those Soviet policies which aimed to suppress and efface whole areas of Russian history and culture. However, it was not only the political leaders who were bent on distorting and extinguishing the Russian past. The avantgarde movement of Russian futurism, instead of relying on experience, also espoused a contempt for the past in its single-minded preoccupation with an abstract future utopia. We are now witnessing a genuine resuscitation of Russia's past, of its historical, cultural and literary memory. The study of the meaning and function of memory in a great work of the last century has acquired a new significance in this context.

Memory has now become topical in Russia but it is not new. The Symbolists and Acmeists, in particular V. I. Ivanov and O. Mandel'shtam, were deeply involved with cultural memory, both as poets and critics. In Russian literary scholarship we can trace a continuous interest in memory from V. I. Ivanov, one of Dostoevsky's early interpreters, to Bakhtin and to Lotman and Uspensky in the present. And not only the Russians have discovered fertile poetic possibilities in memory as both theme and structuring principle. Joyce and Proust used memory in profoundly creative though very different ways from Dostoevsky, and from each other.

My general concepts of poetics owe most to the theoretical ideas of Roman Jakobson, Jury Lotman, B. Uspensky, F. K. Stanzel and Mikhail Bakhtin. I have found Erich Auerbach to be a model of interpretative inspiration as well as a source for several indispensable ideas. The phenomenon of memory has long attracted the scrutiny of philosophers, theologians and, more recently, psychologists. With all this vast material I had to be very selective since comprehensive coverage was out of the question. For studies on Dostoevsky's poetics in general I am most indebted to Bakhtin's stimulating ideas, even though the reader will quickly see that I do not agree with him *in toto*. Studies on the poetics of *The Brothers Karamazov* which have proved most essential for my work are those of Jostein Børtnes, Nine Perlina and V. E. Vetlovskaia. Finally, 'Gérard Genette's study on Proust's poetic use of memory offered a very suggestive contrast to Dostoevsky. From all these sources, as well as many others, I have freely borrowed and adapted ideas which seemed most pertinent to *The Brothers Karamazov*. I have not found it possible or desirable to adhere unswervingly to any one of the many scholars, interpreters and thinkers who have guided my way. Without them, though, this book could not have been written.

One also needs to have dialogues with people. I should first like to record my grateful memory of the late Dr N. Andreyev who first took me on as a research student and whose lectures on Russian literature were a source of pleasure and inspiration for generations of students at Cambridge. Malcolm Jones and Sergei Hackel gave me the benefit of their comments and corrections. Ludolf Müller kindly allowed me to participate in his seminar on *The Brothers Karamazov* at the University of Tübingen. I was also fortunate in having a memorable discussion with V. E. Vetlovskaia. Conversations with Joseph Frank were invariably stimulating and informative. I should like to record my thanks to him and to Malcolm Jones for reading my chapter on the narrator. Robert Jackson read my chapter on 'Forgetting' and made several valuable comments. Nina Perlina read this as a thesis and gave me much appreciated encouragement. To Bobbie Coe, my thanks for her expert, cheerful and sustaining help in preparing the typescript. I should also like to mention my special gratitude to the late Bruno Bettelheim, friend and teacher, who gave me warm personal encouragement and advice. My daughter, Kari Carstairs, gave me the benefit of a non-specialist's reaction to most of my text, pointing out several obscurities. My husband, John Thompson, took on the exacting task of proofreading the whole typescript. I am most grateful to Jostein Børtnes who patiently saw this study through from its beginnings as a doctoral dissertation to its revision into book form. I thank him for his illuminating scrutiny of my work, for his generosity in reading through the whole typescript in an earlier draft version and for sharing with me his insights into Dostoevsky's art.

Note on the text

All translations are my own. The Russian text of *The Brothers Karamazov* used is that of the Academy of Sciences Edition, *Polnoe sobranie sochinenii v tridtsati tomakh*, volumes 14 and 15 (Leningrad, 1976), abbreviated as *PSS*, except I have restored all Dostoevsky's initial capitals for the divine names, pronouns and synonyms according to the *Polnoe sobranie sochinenii F. M. Dostoevskogo* (St Petersburg, 1911) and the YMCA-Press edition of *Brat'ia Karamazovy* (Paris, 1954). I have also adhered to Dostoevsky's capitalisation practice in my own text. Citations from the *PSS* text of the novel are enclosed in brackets with the volume number followed by the page number. My ellipses within quotations are indicated by pointed brackets.

The transliteration scheme is that of the Library of Congress, except the standard English equivalents for well-known names are used, so Dostoevsky, rather than Dostoevskii, Fyodor, rather than Fedor, etc.

Chapters 6 and 7 contain a few paragraphs, somewhat revised, from my article 'Poetic Transformations of Scientific Facts in *Brat'ja Karamazovy*', *Dostoevsky Studies*, 8 (1987), 73–85.

CHAPTER I

Memory and poetics

Mnemosyne is Eternal Memory. Here is another name
for that continuity of communion in spirit and force
between the living and the departed.

Vyacheslav Ivanov, *By the Stars*

One may well wonder what memory has to do with *The
Brothers Karamazov*, a novel whose story covers little more than
two months, more, whose narrated time is mainly compressed
into a mere six days. Yet, the interplay between cultural
memory and the individual memories of the author and reader,
narrator and characters has been so fully, subtly and variously
developed that it can be seen as a dominant means of organising this novel's artistic system, structurally, aesthetically and
semantically. For *The Brothers Karamazov* abounds in symbolic
imagery, generic styles and images of people engaging in many
strange conversations on manifold topics, each of which has its
own words laden with the semantic, contextual and stylistic
accretion of centuries. The Russian scholar, Leonid Grossman,
traced Dostoevsky's generic roots to the 'sacred drama of the
Eleusinian mysteries'.[1] Bakhtin also found that they 'go back
to deep antiquity', to 'the very sources of European literature'.[2]
The whole novel constitutes a great eschatological dialogue in
which, as Bakhtin put it, the questions of Dostoevsky's characters 'sound before earth and heaven'. And in the composition
of their sounds mingle all the muses in Dostoevsky's 'polyphonic' universe; the muses of history, comedy, tragedy, music,
astronomy and even dancing. Indeed, the idea that the origins
of art and knowledge lie in divine memory goes back to Greek

mythology where Mnemosyne, goddess of memory, gave birth
to the muses; and it later found its great philosophical elabor-
ation in the Platonic concept of anamnesis. Memory, as a
channel to the divine, was re-interpreted by Christianity and
symbolised in the eucharistic liturgy which recalls the sacrifice
of Christ in the anamnestic prayer. From this conception, we
shall discover a direct generic and thematic link to Dostoevsky's last novel.

In order to see *The Brothers Karamazov* as a poetic system of
cultural and individual memory, we require a theoretical
foundation. Roman Jakobson's ideas on the poetic function of
language as the 'focus on the message for its own sake' may
serve as our starting point because of their general applicabi-
lity to verbal art.[3]

In a novel read as a work of verbal art, the goal is not
primarily that of practical communication, but of building up a
fictitious universe. This focusing on the text entails recourse to
the traditional devices of poetry, especially metaphor, metonymy and symbol. Though different in important respects, all
share radical processes of transformation whereby what is said
becomes something more or something different. It is the
surplus meanings carried by these poetic figures, and the
ambiguities they generate, which map the domain of poetics.
Dostoevsky wanted, in *The Brothers Karamazov*, to say much
more than the ordinary, everyday use of language can bear.
These powerful poetic modes offered him the richest means for
extending the expressive possibilities of language. Each one he
used in subtly differentiated ways. This is where Jakobson's
ideas on the metaphoric/metonymic opposition in verbal art
come to the fore. Selection and combination are the two
fundamental operations involved in the composition of all
poetic utterances. A novelist selects words from the given stock
of language and combines them with others in building up a
discourse. Selection implies the possibility of substituting one
word for another, 'equivalent in one respect, different in
another'. This produces substitution sets whose words are
internally 'linked by various degrees of similarity, likeness,
contrast, analogy', and so on. Metaphoric processes juxtapose

elements from different or similar domains in order to highlight striking differences or similarities between them. Combination is based on external relationships of contiguity,
neighbourhood, successivity, causality, proximity, remoteness. Metonymic choices foreground one element in order to
suggest another to which it is related by contiguity, for
example, a part for the whole or vice versa (synecdoche). This
opposition, Jakobson finds, carries over to whole literary
trends. Metaphor is characteristic of symbolism and romanticism, while metonymy marks realistic prose. Every combination creates a context. The founders of Gestalt psychology took
as their fundamental tenet the idea that the whole is greater
than its parts. For whenever we select two or more things and
bring them together, we create something new. This is because
what we see is the interaction between them and the interaction is greater than, or different from, them in separation.

The metaphoric/metonymic opposition is very relevant to
memory. Identity and continuity are guaranteed by memory,
cultural and individual. To paraphrase William James: the
continuity of memory makes us unite what dissimilarity
(spatio-temporal) might otherwise separate; similarity makes
us unite what discontinuity in the memory might hold apart.[4]
In terms of Jakobson's poetics, the establishment of contiguity
(continuity) and similarity (metaphor) relations is the major
way in which memory imposes aesthetic unity on the multipli-
city and diversity of experience through time.

Since *The Brothers Karamazov* is an extensive work in prose, it
relies on larger poetic structures for unifying and organising its
diverse, manifold elements. Particularly important are parallel
patterning and prefiguration which link large textual segments
in subtle semantic and figurative networks. Mediating
between the novel's empirical and spiritual events is an all-
pervading symbolic code which stems from ancient prototypes
and resonates at the deepest levels of cultural memories. These
symbols are the most important avenue for the creative
evocation of memory in the novel.

Literary art is not a mere assemblage of abstract verbal
structures, but a rich bearer and retainer of information, of

messages or content. There are three basic types of retained information. The first is that held in every individual person's memory, the second is the intersubjective collective memory of social groups, while the third is the transpersonal storage of information held for culture. Between the three there is a continuous interaction. We first consider the broad phenomena of cultural and collective memory.

CULTURAL MEMORY

Lotman and Uspensky have recently formulated an interesting theoretical model of the relation between memory and culture which provides us with a very useful and apposite framework for analysing the function of cultural memory in *The Brothers Karamazov*.[5] Culture 'is a social phenomenon', a recording in the memory of a collective's past historical experience. In order for human experience to have meaning and not to be lost, it has to be codified and represented in forms which can be passed on to succeeding generations. Every culture consists of memories, coded survivals of past experience preserved in an enormous variety of forms, from writings, monuments and works of art, to social customs, rituals and traditions, what Lotman and Uspensky broadly call 'texts'. Culture as the 'non-hereditary' collective memory is a 'superindividual mechanism for the preservation and transmission of certain information (texts) and for the production of new ones'. This information is 'expressed in a definite system of interdictions and prescriptions', through signs combined according to certain rules or codes. 'The very existence of culture presupposes the construction of a system, of rules for the translation of direct experience into a text'. The systematic nature of memory is one of its fundamental attributes. In order to reconstruct our memories, we must have a system. For one memory calls forth another, with the help of some memories we can reconstitute others. Every cultural memory forms a context. Every context is part of a larger system of cultural memory (social, intellectual, religious), of a whole composed of interdependent parts joined according to some common idea or scheme. Religion is one of the most powerful systems we have for restoring and translating essential memories, individual and cultural. And just as one topic leads to another either through similarity (metaphor) or contiguity (metonymy), so will discourses developed from memory exhibit the same bipolar principle. Both serve very different but crucial poetic functions in *The Brothers Karamazov*.

A culture's long-term memory is defined by its complement of long-term texts and their codes. Together they make up the space of culture, the 'space of a common memory'. Texts of long standing contain certain semantic invariants which can be actualised and revived in the context of a new epoch. By a semantic invariant, Lotman means something which through all its varying interpretations retains 'an identity to itself'. Any invariant has by definition long been part of cultural memory. The idea of an invariant as a generator of variations will be fundamental for our study. As we shall see, Dostoevsky's art is strongly marked by his gift for creating an extensive register of variations on invariant motifs, ranging from imitations to subversions.

Depending on the kind of information they preserve, texts fall into two categories. The first Lotman calls texts of 'informative memory', that is, those texts which preserve the sum of a society's cognitive activity, its factual, scientific and technological information. Informative memory 'has a superficial character' since it is 'subordinated to the law of chronology. It develops in the same direction as the flow of time and in agreement with it'. For informative memory 'only the result is active', the latest fact is the most valuable. The second category comprises the texts of 'creative memory' which Lotman calls 'the memory of art'. For creative memory 'the whole corpus of texts' turns out to be 'potentially active'. They are all, so to speak, laid out before us not syntagmatically, but along a continuum where antique drama coexists with the latest detective thriller. Instead of the chronological newsreel of information memory, relentlessly rushing forwards consuming the past, the field of creative memory presents a great montage. When we speak of literary art we are concerned not so much with the storage of information about reality, but with transformations of reality by the individual imagination in its potentially creative alliance with cultural memory. This is one reason why the products of creative memory cannot be reduced to the idea that the 'newest is the most valuable'.[6] There are others.

Memory is at once a highly conservative and a highly creative mechanism. Therein lies its great significance for art. As a conservative mechanism, memory, remarks Lotman, is not only 'panchronic, but opposed to time'. From the point of view of creative memory when working with the great corpus of cultural information, 'the past has not passed'. On the other hand, texts which have attained the status of art or great cultural value 'cannot be passive depositories of constant information'. They are not just storehouses but 'generators'. For under the influence of new texts (and codes), the old texts change, a 'displacement of significant and insignificant elements' occurs. Conversely, old texts and their codes generate new ones (the Bible is a prime example). Thus, meanings in the memory of culture are not only preserved. They 'grow'. This is why 'historicism in the study of literature, in that aspect first created by the Hegelian theory of culture, and then by the positivist theory of progress, is in fact anti-historical since it ignores the active role of memory in the generation of new texts'.

Forgetting is also an essential part of the mechanism of cultural memory. Every culture, at any given moment in its history, determines its paradigm of what should be remembered and what should be forgotten. Thus, whenever a new fact, idea or event (text) is transformed into a cultural value and integrated into the system of memory, other elements are forgotten for awhile. There is no room to retain them all actively in the current volume of cultural memory. However, there are two types of forgetting, and the differences between them are crucial. The first we may call benign neglect and the other compulsory forgetting. Under benign neglect (or contempt), those texts declared inessential or irrelevant do not disappear but are stored away, 'deactivated'. They fall out of circulation and 'pass over to a potential' to be retrieved at a later date when the cultural paradigm changes. But as long as they remain stored, they are still integrated into the system of memory. Under compulsory forgetting, such as that imposed by a totalitarian state, certain memories are pronounced permanently inessential, irrelevant or harmful. They are to be liquidated, obliterated from the collective consciousness. The enforced suppression and annihilation of whole sets of cultural memories can disturb and even destroy a culture.

By a similar token, memory is also profoundly related to the future. Culture, as information about the past, is stored and codified according to a definite system of rules of behaviour, what Lotman and Uspensky called a 'programme'. Information and programme are two aspects of the same thing, only they face opposite directions. Any text can be interpreted as an actualisation of the past (of cultural memory) and as a programme for carrying that memory into the future. As soon as we use cultural information to predict or order the future, we are in fact transferring memory into a programme for shaping the future.

One consequence of the systematic nature of memory is that memories are often something we share with others. Sharing takes place within a social context, within a dialogue with others. People participate in various social, intersubjective groups, as well as transpersonal cultural systems which also provide a setting and context for their memories. Many essential memories are passed on from generation to generation by behavioural example through various social groups such as the family, and by traditions, customs, rituals, and so on. The remembrances of social groups and their traditions also form systems. Moreover, people forget people (family, friends, neighbours), places (home, country, native roots) and traditions. They also project their futures with social groups in mind (marriage, work and community), and some imagine future ideal societies.

In his sociological study of memory of 1925, Maurice Halbwachs introduced the term 'collective memory', by which he meant the aggregate remembrances of all the members of groups whose base is a coherent body of people. Halbwachs takes it as an axiom that 'a person remembers only by situating himself within the viewpoint of one or several groups and one or several currents of collective thought'.[7] In short, social contexts determine all our thoughts and memories. Halbwachs's absolute positivism and social determinism are open to philosophical and psychological objections, but his insights into the shared and social nature of many of our memories are germane to *The Brothers Karamazov*, where we find manifold social and economically stratified groups such as several families, the monastic brotherhood, landowners, servants, merchants, peasants and a gang of schoolboys. Thus, we shall want to consider what systems of cultural and collective memory provide the contexts for the memories represented in the novel. What paradigms of memory/amnesia are advanced, and what programmes for the future are promoted or implied by the paradigms? And finally, how does this heterogeneous material of cultural memory enter *The Brothers Karamazov*?

In an attempt to answer these questions, we turn to Bakhtin's study of Dostoevsky's poetics. We consider the question first from the general literary level of language, genre, themes and imagery. This we may call the metadiegetic plane of memory. Through the meanings created by the metadiegetical network of allusions, references and associations, Dostoevsky communicates with his readers, drawing on their cultural background, on that space of a common memory where the reader, author and his characters can meet.

Two ideas of Bakhtin concerning language and genre are particularly important for our theme because they point to two main ways by which cultural memory enters *The Brothers Karamazov*. Significantly, both ideas come from the second edition of his study on Dostoevsky's poetics, and both rest on his fundamental premise that the creative power (*energeia*) of the past never ceases to exist. What I call the 'memory of the word' derives from Bakhtin's thinking about the nature of human discourse. Words are carriers of cultural memory, of ideas, images, events and traditions from the past. Every word is at once stable and fluid, it comes to us with a context, and with a potential for entering a new context. While the novel preserves the lexical meaning of a word, it simultaneously renews and extends its semantic range by passing it through its own contexts. Bakhtin expresses this idea with eloquent precision:

The word is not a material thing, but rather the eternally mobile, eternally changeable medium of dialogic communication. It never gravitates towards a single consciousness, a single voice. The life of the word is contained in its transfer from one mouth to another, from one context to another, from one social collective to another, from one generation to another generation. In this process the word does not forget its own path and cannot completely free itself from the power of those concrete contexts into which it has entered. When a member of a speaking collective comes upon a word, it is not at all as a neutral word of language, free from the aspirations and evaluations of others, uninhabited by others' voices. No, he receives the word from another's voice and filled with that other voice. The word enters his context from another context, permeated with the interpretations of others. His own thought finds the word already inhabited.[8]

In *The Brothers Karamazov* Dostoevsky systematically transposed certain old words (ideas) into the sphere of new ones, never abstractly, to be sure, but only by embodying them as the viewpoints of living persons. (For the moment, though, we consider only the metadiegetic plane of memory.) Vitally important for this novel are those semantically charged and historically seminal ancient words – God, love, miracle, Christ, devil, hell, morality, Madonna, Jerusalem, paradise – all of which belong to the same complex of ideas, to the cultural system of Christianity. The more memories the reader has of these words' previous paths, the more the novel expands with their resonances, their accents and 'languages'. Dostoevsky forced these old words to interact with certain new ones (or re-accented old ones) – liberal, nerve ends, affect, ethics, ultramontanism, socialism, non-Euclidean geometry – that is, he brought the old ideas into an intense struggle with the new ideas and intentions threatening to supplant them. In the new context of *The Brothers Karamazov*, the old contexts of these ancient words become the novel's subtexts. Similarly, the new words undergo modification and re-accentuation, thanks to their dynamic interaction with the old. From the point of view of memory, though, the old words have the historical and poetic advantage, thanks to their greater semantic saturation over the ages. This is one reason why memory was so important for Dostoevsky. Indeed, we shall find that Dostoevsky was not trying to free his work 'from the power' of the memories of these old words. On the contrary, he filled them with his own aspirations and interpretations in order to reassert their power by revitalising their memories in a contemporary context.

And not only words carry cultural memory, but so do larger literary structures. Bakhtin's investigation into the generic sources of Dostoevsky's art may have led him to his concept of the 'memory of the genre', by which he meant the retention in a new work of the formal, stylistic and semantic features of older or archaic literary genres. Retention does not mean stasis. Bakhtin saw genre as 'a representative of creative memory <...> guaranteeing the *unity* and *uninterrupted continuity*' of 'literary development'. Whenever a discourse is organised by a particular genre, reminiscences of the genre's distinctive features will inevitably reverberate throughout that discourse. Genres, just as words, resound with their old contexts, thus allowing us also to speak of generic subtexts. This may be illustrated by the following quotation from Bakhtin:

A literary genre, by its very nature, reflects the most stable, 'eternal' tendencies in literature's development. Always preserved in a genre are underlying elements of the *archaic*. True, these archaic elements are preserved in it only thanks to their constant *renewal*, which is to say, their contemporisation. A genre is always the same and yet not the same, always old and new simultaneously. Genre is reborn and renewed at every new stage in the development of literature and in every individual work of a given genre. This constitutes the life of the genre. Therefore even the archaic elements preserved in a genre are not dead but eternally alive; that is, archaic elements are capable of renewing themselves. A genre lives in the present, but always *remembers* its past, its beginning.[9]

Here Bakhtin stresses the conservative function of memory, but he is saying very much the same thing as Lotman. Established genres never die only because they are being continually 'reborn'. And the fact that they are capable of simultaneously preserving and renewing themselves, and the cultural values they convey, no matter how many idiosyncratic transformations they undergo, points to certain formal and semantic invariants from which something new can be endlessly generated. Genre, in Bakhtin's theory, has to be understood in the widest sense. By a genre he means not just its formal features but the whole complex of elements which make up a genre as a distinctive, recognisable entity. Every genre has its characteristic themes and content, so we may also speak of the memory of themes. Dostoevsky incorporated into *The Brothers Karamazov* the richest array of genres in his *œuvre*. Among them are a criminal thriller, a saint's life, sermons, diatribes, résumés of essays, songs, poems, theatrical scenes, philosophical dialogues, courtroom proceedings, forensic and commemorative speeches, and so on. This generic abundance bears out Lotman's idea that generically heterogeneous texts are saturated with cultural memory, and consequently with manifold invariants. Genres also preserve the memory of great images of speaking persons from the past, historical and fictitious. Monks, Schiller, buffoons, a Grand Inquisitor, the Russian folk, Voltaire, drunkards, schoolboys, the saints of history and legend, the humiliated and downtrodden, landowners, an 'infernal woman', a chronicler and Christ, all intermingle in *The Brothers Karamazov*. The memory of the genres introduced by Dostoevsky is preserved by their forms and contents which are instantly recognisable thanks to their distinctive features. For example, perceiving that Lise's letter to Alyosha is a love letter, the reader will at once have certain expectations about its sender and receiver, its form and content. But these expectations could not arise were it not for our memory of the traditional features of this genre, whether our memory is based on previous literary examples (Tatyana's letter to Onegin) or on our personal experience. Thus the formal properties of a genre, exemplified in its previous models and invested with new content, are one aspect of the preservation and renewal of a genre's memory.

Imagery is another. The teachers of the ancient art of memory used images to reinforce a memory for words, thereby acknowledging the primary power of image-memory.[10] There are numerous nonverbal carriers of cultural memory which can be described in words but are not expressed in words. In *The Brothers Karamazov* Dostoevsky used language to create a prominent spatial dimension of visual imagery as well as an elaborated poetics of gesture which relies on that generally shared reading of the sign language of images, bodily movements and expressions. Gesture not only enhances the expressive force of words, but communicates feelings and thoughts for which language may be inadequate or even powerless. Dostoevsky frequently casts doubts on the truth value of his characters' words in favour of a 'natural' language of gesture and imagery, because it often expresses a truer language of meaning (Alyosha knows Mitya is innocent 'by his face'). Images from contemporary life are shot through with deeper older layers. Certain faces are reminiscent of older faces and cultural epochs. Fyodor, for example, likens his nose to the Romans of the 'decadent period', thereby calling up familiar associations of pagan debauchery as well as the concurrent waning of the classical world and the ascendancy of Christianity. It is most of all the religious imagery and ritual gestures (and their inversions) which derive from memory since they are a kind of *aide-mémoire* of ancient prototypes. The pervasive biblical images of the angel and the devil resolve into an angelic–demonic opposition which turns out to be central to this novel's poetic system. Religious ritual gestures such as bowing, blessing, crossing, hand kissing and kneeling in prayer are particularly prominent in the novel, and still very active in the Orthodox Church, among others. *The Brothers Karamazov* proves how gesture alone can become an important event. One of the most significant gestures in the novel is surely Christ's kiss of the Grand Inquisitor. Instead of speaking, Christ kisses him. No reader can forget this kiss, subsequently repeated by a correlate pair of 'living' characters when Alyosha kisses Ivan towards the end of their meeting. Thus, gestures and images offered Dostoevsky another rich field of cultural memory for creating new variations and gathering new semantic resonances.

Texts which have longest withstood the test of time within a culture occupy the highest hierarchical position, which 'is usually identical to a hierarchy of values'.[11] The various words and genres Dostoevsky incorporated into *The Brothers Karamazov* gradually establish an ideological hierarchy which corresponds to their cultural age. The saint's life, the sermon, and reminiscences of the mystery and morality play are major generic sources. But the most important ancient source by far is the Bible, especially the Gospels. The dominant themes and topoi of *The Brothers Karamazov* are from the Bible, which is itself a collection of stories, parables and teachings played out in actions and words. The master–disciple topos, for example, is enacted throughout the novel by two antonymous pairs, Ivan/Smerdyakov and Zosima/Alyosha. Ivan, as Fasting has shown, plays the Good Samaritan when he rescues the peasant from freezing to death.[12] Snegiryov, remarks Perlina, is a 'figural variation' of Job and Ivan of Cain.[13] The theme of 'fathers and children' becomes linked through a crime of parricide to the biblical idea of God the Father and His children (a radically different interpretation from that of Turgenev). Christ's parable of the sower is the master metaphor of the novel. While numerous other words and genres are 'remembered', while a great variety of other works are alluded to, there is not a single chapter of the novel which does not evoke, directly or indirectly, biblical motifs and teachings. Other works, other genres, appear sporadically or singly, but the Bible accompanies the novel from beginning (the Epigraph) to end (Alyosha's last speech). The all-pervasive presence of these ancient sacred sources in a modern, ostensibly realistic novel implies that Dostoevsky sought to bring an eternal message to the topical, to his contemporary epoch, and beyond.[14]

And if all these 'undying elements' are remembered, so are their basic meanings. True, some meanings have considerably faded, some Dostoevsky clearly wished to reject by compromising the image of a person who believes them. For example, the religious meanings represented by Father Ferapont are interpreted as moribund and superstitious because his faith expresses itself in an obsession with devils and a severance of dialogic contact with the world (his self-imposed silence rarely broken by his incoherent speech is symptomatic). Whereas the religious meanings represented by Father Zosima are interpreted as eternal, compassionate and life renewing because his faith brings him into a continuous, loving conversation with 'everyone and everything' (his eloquence is equally symptomatic).

Also important for *The Brothers Karamazov* is the way the memory of the genre itself becomes an integral part of the representation of the characters' personalities and worldviews. This forms one of the main metadiegetical links between individual and cultural memory. All the protagonists emanate one or more particular genres which are associated with them and become dominant features of their images. Ivan evokes the learned article, the philosophical tale and the modern utopian fantasy built on scientific progress; Mitya, the adventure novel and German Romantic poetry; Fyodor, the carnivalised genres of *parodia sacra* and salacious anecdotes; Alyosha, hagiography and the Gospels; Zosima, the didactic religious genres, hagiography and the Bible; Grushenka, the religious folk tale; Lise, the gothic sensational novel; Ilyusha and the Snegiryovs, the sentimental family novel; Kolya, the *Bildungsroman*; the narrator–chronicler, the biographical and memoire genres.

Still more arresting, and especially characteristic of Dostoevsky, is the way he leaves his protagonists to create images of themselves and their ideas through their own interpretations of cultural texts and their own compositions, written and spoken. Two of the brothers (Ivan and Alyosha) are authors, and the genres they choose are emblematic of their worldviews, of the emotional and intellectual colouration of their personalities and memories. This linkage of particular genres with particular characters is a major factor which makes their ideas and images larger than themselves. They are not contained by the concrete local conditions in which they have their being, but join up with a long tradition whose distinctive attributes they share by association, appropriation and identification. By creating such a variety of characters,

Dostoevsky was able to introduce a great variety of genre reminiscences into his novel, thus opening its provincial world into the great time and space of cultural memory.

Quotation is the main channel through which Dostoevsky introduced cultural memories into the consciousness of his characters. *The Brothers Karamazov* is a veritable cornucopia of direct and indirect quotations from other texts, both sacred and secular, ranging from the Bible to Voltaire, from Pushkin to popular songs. Perlina has recently revealed the enormous extent to which the novel relies on quotations for creating a context and subtext of hierarchically ordered poetic utterances.[15] Quotation is very much determined by the principle of memory. The characters' extra-textual references play a prominent role in shaping their ideological profiles as well as enlarging the novel's dialogical sphere and semantic scope. By their quotations we find out, to a large extent, what they remember, what they feel and think, and thus who they are. Important for interpretation are not only the contents of their cultural, collective memories, but the way they use this information, especially that held in sacred texts, in their 'here and now'. Zosima quotes the Bible accurately, Fyodor travesties it and Smerdyakov corrupts it. From informative memory we find many references to historical and scientific facts which ground the novel in the real world and thereby give the fictional characters a quasi-factual existence. Allusions to historical events greatly widen the role of cultural memory in *The Brothers Karamazov*. References to recent history (serfdom, judicial reforms, the emancipation of women, scientific discoveries, the Revolution of 1848) serve to make the novel topical, relevant and contemporary, a factor of great importance for Dostoevsky. For example, Rakitin, Kolya and Miusov approvingly paraphrase the words of Russian liberals and radicals (Herzen, Belinsky, Saltykov–Shchedrin) and the slogans of the French Revolution. Allusions to events from the deeper past bind the present and future with values of long duration. The narrator reverently invokes the Russian medieval monastic tradition, a theme which is later taken up by Zosima in his sermons with prophetic elaborations on the mission of Holy Russia. Fyodor invents history in telling false anecdotes about historical persons (Diderot). It is Ivan whose consciousness encompasses the greatest range of historical and cultural allusions in the novel (from the Spanish Inquisition to the latest discoveries in maths and science), and it is he who will use his knowledge in the most subtle and ambiguous ways.

The world of art and literature provides yet another domain in which the novel's characters intermingle their own memories with cultural memory. By their choices of the 'texts of art' and the way they allude to them, they reveal their deepest spiritual attitudes and aesthetic sensibilities, or lack of them. Fyodor invokes Voltaire and Diderot to mock the monks. Ivan alludes to Dante, a French medieval mystery play and a Russian apocrypha as a prelude to reciting his 'poem', the Grand Inquisitor. Mitya quotes Schiller and Goethe from memory and invokes the antonymous images of Sodom and the Madonna while wondering at the mystery of beauty. The narrator enlarges on Pushkin's interpretation of *Othello* and depicts a painting by Kramskoy. The devil is an admirer of Tolstoy's art. Mme Khokhlakova ludicrously identifies herself with Famusov when citing Griboyedov's *Woe from Wit*. Smerdyakov is impervious to art and despises literature (Gogol's stories are 'all untrue', a visit to the theatre leaves him 'displeased'). Thus, the literary discourse of *The Brothers Karamazov* senses other literary discourses; it 'remembers' the artistic memorials of the past and draws them into its new dialogue. And in so doing it joins the whole novel with the world of the collective imagination of European civilisation. In all these respects an individual's memories can be very old, can transcend his limited life span, since all people inevitably participate in social life, in language, and are the heirs of centuries of human culture.

The cultural and collective memories we have outlined were not totally under Dostoevsky's semantic control precisely because they have been long 'inhabited' by others' 'intentions'. When it came to creating personal memories for his fictional characters, he had a considerably freer inventive hand. Quotations and memories of the word and genre are not enough for composing images of people, except perhaps at the schematic level of allegory. At this point Dostoevsky joined the realist trend. For one of his greatest achievements was to integrate significant cultural memories into psychologically convincing human personalities, by turning them into inalienable components of their innermost preoccupations, their most pressing conflicts and dilemmas. Cultural memories are not organised as the memories of one's own past. Cultural memories are conceived or imagined memories, appropriated by individuals. In Halbwachs's terms, they are 'borrowed memories', 'symbols' passed down through time which 'are all that come to us from the past'.[16] Cultural monuments do not reminisce, but are reminiscent of something to someone. Only people have memories, only they reminisce or remember. Only they forget and prophesy.

Our threefold model of cultural memory, then, has to be translated into the mnemic activities of human beings. Remembering, forgetting and anticipating (foretelling) are three major modes of response to experience. In *The Brothers Karamazov* images of people remembering, forgetting and foretelling are the three cardinal facets of its poetic memory system. Together they play a fundamental role in organising the whole novel, aesthetically, formally and thematically. These three modes of memory will be the revolving focus of this study. Remembering is the base because it is from memory that one views the 'here and now' and goes into the future.

INDIVIDUAL MEMORY

Dostoevsky's hero is always a human being and never an idea 'in itself', as Bakhtin rightly maintains. A human being without memory is inconceivable. The very concept of ourselves as temporally extended subjects depends on recursive memory. Without it, we could have no coherent overview of our thoughts and activities, and thus no continuity of personal identity. Nor could we sustain any living links with others. Without memory we could not make any sense of our lives whatsoever. In fact, as I. A. Richards remarked, 'there is no kind of mental activity in which memory does not intervene'.[17] However, two main facets of individual memory must be distinguished. The first defines memory as the ability to retain traces of past experience, as that faculty by which one remembers. Memory is a disposition, whereas remembering is a mental, emotional activity that goes on at a particular time about particular things which happened in the past. In poetics we are not concerned with memory *qua* faculty, but with acts or performances of remembering which serve as material for an artistic literary representation. If, as Bakhtin said, the primary artistic task of the novel is to represent images of speaking persons, then as a corollary we may add that the novel can also represent images of remembering persons. This entails representing their concrete memories, whether directly in spoken dialogues or in the inner speech of their thoughts.

In epic fiction we usually encounter unique specific events reported in the past tense. If these events are explicitly designated as being remembered, then we can speak of the memory of these events. 'To remember' is a verb of inner action. Normally one can only remember one's own past. In *The Brothers Karamazov* Dostoevsky divided the memory discourses between the mimetic way, whereby the characters' report their memories in their own direct speech, and the diegetic way, where there is a narrator who tells us their memories. In verbal art an act of remembering and what is remembered form a double event because both the rememberer and his memories are depicted together. When a personalised narrator reports a memory confided to him, we receive yet a third image of a speaking person and hence a double plane of mediated memories (the narrator remembers Alyosha's memory of his mother). In this way Dostoevsky created triply embedded narrative events and thus imparted greater mnemic and temporal density to his text. Whoever reports a character's memories, the very fact that Dostoevsky made space for them implies that they are significant. And not only what the characters and the narrator remember, but the style in which their memories are reported is particularly revealing for a poetic interpretation. For one cannot report a

memory, personal or cultural, without expressing one's attitude to it. As Wittgenstein put it: 'The words with which I
express my memories are my memory-reaction.'[18]

Memory is bound to the particulars of human experience, it
always tends to individualisation. This is part of its dynamic
structure. Everyone retains a unique set of memories, of
experiential survivals which belong solely to that person. In
Dostoevsky's fiction, memories are not only individualised, but
highly personalised. We recall Bakhtin's insight that, for
Dostoevsky, ideas are never mere abstract objects of cognition,
but are always someone's ideas. Consequently, they are always
personalised because in Dostoevsky's art one cannot totally
detach an idea from the image of a person who speaks it. The
same is even more true of memories. In *The Brothers Karamazov*
every memory is always someone's memory and bears the
stamp of that person's experiences, evaluations. For, unlike
statements focused on an external referent (ratiocination, the
communication of information), memory statements must
include the self, they refer to something a person has learned,
perceived or experienced, and hence enter into the most
intimate bond with his life, views and personality. This is one
reason why the word of memory sounds different from other
words. It has its own deeply personalised accents, evaluations
and poetics. Thus, the creation of particular memories for
particular characters offered Dostoevsky exceptionally fertile
possibilities for building up artistic images of highly individuated personalities.

The main way a person becomes aware of the traces of his
past life is through remembering, the exercise of memory
which recalls past events to consciousness. In the process they
are reproduced and re-experienced, though in subtly altered
ways. When a person remembers something, what he perceives
in his mind is a present content which is unique and private to
him. A memory of a past perception or experience is not the
same thing as that original perception or experience, but a
likeness of it. We may take it further. A memory is a likeness of
one's view of that thing. An individual's personal memories are
not mere mechanical recapitulations of the past, but at the

same time intellectually and emotionally charged interpretations which reflect that person's evaluation of them. In fact, every memory is essentially an interpretation, every represented memory a re-interpretation. In this preference that memory gives to transformation over replication it is analogous to art.

Annexed to every memory is the perception that it refers to something that happened in the past. Present perception and anticipation are poor counters of time. It is through memory that we perceive time. Memories are ascribed to specific prior events and objects to which they owe their origins, thus anchoring our sense of time to reality. The task of constructing a concept of time in order to account for the phenomenon of memory is an exceptionally complex psychological and philosophical problem which goes far beyond our topic. For our purposes we shall rest with Wittgenstein's remark: 'Man learns the concept of the past by remembering.'[19] Analysing the way Dostoevsky's characters remember, we may discover how they conceive and evaluate the past, their own and the cultural past.

Since all works of fiction are products of the imagination, the distinction between memory and imagination only becomes important for poetics when a fictional discourse *explicitly* pretends to be a product of memory. The chief difference between imagined and remembered events or states is that the latter are held to represent something which actually occurred or existed, they are believed as representations of reality, of facts or truths, and thus function as an index of beliefs and knowledge. This is why memory has a much greater authoritative epistemological status than imagination. If a memory refers to an event, then, since every event has an inherent temporal order, a series of memories will usually arise. In *The Brothers Karamazov*, various remembered events are not always represented according to their actual temporal sequence. For interpretation it becomes interesting to ask why, in many instances, Dostoevsky chose the mode of memory over imagination, and how he ordered the remembered material.

An individual's personal memories are confined to his own

lifetime, and to those social and cultural contexts in which he has had his being. From what we have said about cultural and collective memory, it follows that every personal memory represented in *The Brothers Karamazov* is always part of a larger cultural whole, of one or more distinct systems of cultural and collective memory. One cannot have *a* memory. Every word, and particularly every word presented as a memory, has a context and belongs to a larger system of memory, whether to the family, community, national tradition or to the cultural systems of philosophy, religion, art, literature, and so on. The narrator presents a multitude of views. Each person in Dostoevsky's novel has a point of view, each individual memory is an interpretation of a particular larger context. In other words, each individual locates his memories in a particular socio-intersubjective or a cultural transpersonal system. Alyosha, for example, contextualises his memories in one way, Grushenka in another, Ivan in yet another, and so on. There can hardly be a mental activity more context sensitive than memory. How, then, does Dostoevsky contextualise his characters' memories, or, how do they contextualise their own memories? To which systems of cultural memory do they assimilate their memories, from which do they dissociate them? And how do their choices impinge on the novel's events?

But we need not take contextualisation as far as Halbwachs, who denies the very possibility of an individual memory which is not totally determined by its social context: Even 'our most personal feelings and thoughts originate in definite social milieus and circumstances'.[20] In *The Brothers Karamazov* they take place there, but they do not always originate there but rather in 'other worlds'. 'In reality we are never alone <...> since we always carry with us and in us a number of distinct persons'.[21] This is profoundly true of Dostoevsky's art. His heroes are endlessly conversing with the persons within them, but they are not always conventional 'persons'. Halbwach's insight has also to be qualified on general grounds. Individuals bring something of themselves to their experiences. An individual's memory is not just a passive receptacle for others' thoughts and memories but a creatively generating and transforming mechanism as well. For the others within us are not us, but come from outside us. We are not just simulacra of others. We make them our own by adding something that is innate to us, by projecting something uniquely our own onto them. Zosima is within Alyosha but Alyosha does not equal Zosima or anyone else. Alyosha's intrinsic need to love someone holy comes from within him and seals the bond between him and his elder. No one is the mere sum of others. As Bakhtin has shown, Dostoevsky's characters never coincide with others, or themselves. They all bring their 'own word' to their dialogues and in the interaction something new, and old, emerges.

And here it seems well to remind ourselves that the Karamazov brothers are very young men. They are at the crossroads of their lives, 'on the threshold', facing ultimate questions and decisions about their place in the world. Their ideological and personal allegiances are oscillating between various social groups and two opposing cultural, ideological systems, between the monastery and the world, Russia and Europe, God and atheism. In the dialogic process of internalising or rejecting their cultural tradition, they find out who they are and who others are. Their attitudes to memory, their own and cultural memory, will prove all-important in the resolutions, and unfinished resolutions, of their crises, and in the ways they affect others in the novel's world.

Memories lie deeper in the mind than will, reason or knowledge and are only potentially in the consciousness. It thus becomes essential for a poetic interpretation to ascertain what stimulates their revival in the characters' consciousnesses. Memories in general occur either voluntarily or involuntarily. Voluntary memory in the novel tends to take the extended form of reminiscence, either biographical or autobiographical, whereby a series of sequential memories are spun out into a narrative. There are a number of such retrospective narratives in *The Brothers Karamazov*, the largest being those of the narrator and Zosima. These discourses, because of their cohesive, chronologically ordered presentation, are forwarded by contiguity and form the realistic backbone of the novel.

Involuntary memories convey a very different aesthetic and

psychological impression and they are given ample play in *The Brothers Karamazov*. One need only recall the frequent occurrences of the adverbs 'suddenly' and 'unexpectedly'. Though often encountered in connection with the sudden occurrence of some thought or feeling, they also occur in conjunction with the welling up of a memory which present events or utterances have unaccountably aroused. Spontaneous memories impart a greater impression of freedom to the characters' mental processes, releasing them from the confines of the present. Such fragmentary, episodic memories break in upon consciousness suddenly, in a seemingly random, inexplicable fashion. Of course there is nothing random about them, since the author has deliberately shaped them to accord with his overall artistic design. Nevertheless, Dostoevsky could rightly claim that in presenting the sudden occurrences of involuntary memories as puzzling, enigmatic or mysterious, he is representing an authentic aspect of reality, even though he often interprets them in ways that go counter to conventional notions of reality. Both types, the voluntary and involuntary, are exceptionally telling.

Memory entails the contrary notions of presence and absence, since by memory we conceive of the absent as if it were present. In art, as in life, the primary function of memory is recuperative. A memory is a revival and a representation of something that was once present. Thus we shall want to enquire what presences are evoked by the characters' memories, personal and cultural, what images and voices are summoned forth by their very language. Of whom or what do their actions remind us? What numinous presences accompany them, or what absences haunt the margins of their thoughts, feelings and utterances? How does the presence/absence opposition function in the novel's poetics? In fact, the resurrectional function of memory will prove the most important facet of memory, individual and cultural, in *The Brothers Karamazov*.

Memory has great combinatorial potentials and this is another of its creative facets. Past experience retained in memory can freely combine with present events thereby giving rise to unexpected associations and striking juxtapositions.

Thus the workings of memory erupt the flat surface of sequential events, creating new associations, connotations and connections, thereby rendering the text polysemantic, multi-dimensional. According to Bakhtin, Dostoevsky's artistic vision was dominated by the spatial principles of simultaneity, coexistence and dialogic interaction. All the meaningful material in his world is dramatically counterposed in the 'cross-section of a single moment' and developed 'extensively'.[22] Thus, his well known affinity for the drama and temporal compression. Artistic principles of an 'evolving sequence', a unifying mind and environmental influences have virtually no place in Dostoevsky's fiction and are ideologically rejected. This is why Dostoevsky's characters 'remember from their own past only that which has not ceased to be present for them'. Bakhtin was evidently led to this view by his thesis that the main object of representation in Dostoevsky's art is consciousness, or self-consciousness. Neither memory nor consciousness strictly orders time or events linearly. From the standpoint of the individual memory and consciousness, all is current, or potentially so. Images from early childhood coexist with those in old age in the spatial 'cross-section of a single moment'. In this respect, the individual memory is analogous to the spatio-temporal continuum of creative memory where all coexists.

Life is transient, and 'everything transient' really 'is only a likeness', a set of fluctuating images, thoughts, feelings and silent voices surviving in each human soul. But some memories endure and instead of decaying with the passage of time, exhibit what Luria calls an 'enhanced reproduction'.[23] This enhancement is surely owing to emotional factors still active in a person's life. Enhancement implies a refining, sieving and highlighting of significant experiences. Here we are reminded of Zosima who has retained extraordinarily fresh and vivid memories from his childhood, but which he now interprets and re-experiences in a way that would have been totally impossible for him earlier in life. For Zosima, what endures is a semantic invariant (the spiritual essence of his brother's dying words) and a transformed affect (tears which have turned into 'quiet joy'). This points to two further intriguing and universal characteristics of memory, namely, our proclivity for suppressing negative traces and retaining positive ones, and for converting our experiences into meaningful life patterns. In this process our memories often assume narrative shape. They become saturated with various emotional colourations as well as vivid images and lingering words whose meanings continue to grow. All these mnemic processes of mental and emotional enhancement are aesthetic activities. In this sense, perhaps, our memories make artists of us all.

In *The Brothers Karamazov* there is also a word *about* memory which synthesises the novel's major themes. Significantly, Dostoevsky reserved this word for his narrator and his two positive heroes, Zosima and Alyosha.

Yet another factor which marks this text with a sense of *renvoi*, 'sending back', it that is was conceived as a memoir. *The Brothers Karamazov* is itself cast in the form of a fictional memoir which contains a complex variety of remembered and commemorative material. The whole novel takes place against the dialogising background of the narrator's discourses who sees all its events in retrospect.

CHAPTER 2

The fictional narrator

'It's a poor sort of memory that only works backwards',
the Queen remarked.

Lewis Carroll, *Through the Looking Glass*

In every work of narrative fiction someone is conducting the
narration, someone is playing the role of mediator in reporting
the fictional events. Every narrator is a mediator who stands in
varying degrees of proximity between the author, the story and
the reader. For the very act of imaginative writing puts a
distance between a living author and his fictitious creations. In
Stanzel's words, 'mediacy is the generic characteristic which
distinguishes narration from other forms of literary art'.[1] The
agent of mediation, whether a narrator or a reflecting
consciousness, is just as much a creation of the author's
imagination as are the characters and their world. In fact
Dostoevsky reveals his mastery of literary art very much in the
way he renders mediacy in his fiction. This distance induced
by mediacy is where our topic of memory comes to the fore. In
The Brothers Karamazov there are many characters who relate
their experiences and represent the speech of others. All the
novel's strands of direct and indirect narration make for
manifold points of view creating an intricate 'polyphony' of
individuated consciousnesses. Still there is one fixed launching
point for our discussion and that is the fictional narrator to
whom Dostoevsky encharged the telling of the novel as a
whole. The main point is the perspective from which the
narrator mediates the novel's events.

A narrator's physical distance from the events he relates is measured by space and time, his psychological distance by the degree of his involvement in what he is telling. As concerns his temporal location Dostoevsky's narrator is quite explicit, thus enabling us to trace with precision the temporal scheme he establishes for the entire novel with respect to his narrating position. We have an approximate idea of the narrator's spatial location, though we cannot fix it with the same exactitude because of his minimal embodiment within the novel. His psychological distance is a far more complex matter because his involvement is limited by his primary role as a narrating self. Yet he performs his narration in a voice of such subtle stylistic and intonational variety that we cannot fail to gain a marked impression of his personality, of his experiencing self. Dostoevsky uses his narrator most ingeniously to accommodate all the novel's discourses in a way that perfectly accords with his artistic and philosophical aims, namely, he doubles his narrator's perspectives by having him narrate in both the first- and third-person modes while retaining the single node of his memory through which he passes the narration of the novel as a whole. Each narrative mode offers certain advantages as well as imposes certain restrictions on constructing a narrative. By combining both modes Dostoevsky creates a complementary narrative system wherein he compensates for the limitations of the one with the advantages of the other and subordinates them to the principle of memory. It becomes most revealing for any interpretation to ascertain which discourses Dostoevsky allocates to one or the other type of narration.

The narrator's subject is the story of a 'catastrophe', a particular crime of parricide which took place in about 1867 in a provincial Russian town. The crime arises out of the tangled relationships within a family, or non-family, of the minor nobility, the Karamazovs, wherein normal family ties have broken down. The provincial setting of the story along with the inclusion of a large number of socially diverse characters who are residing permanently or temporarily in this town, widens the novel's social canvas so that we gradually gain a broad diversified image of the narrator's contemporary Russia, of its social, moral and spiritual problems, its historical dilemmas.

The telling of this story he conducts primarily in his third-person mode.

Third-person narration is generally perceived as being more objective and impartial owing largely to the external perspective from which it is conducted. This perception also seems to be rooted in the nature of third-person narration – someone, or something spoken of – which 'strongly involves the referential function of language'.[2] There are two main types of such narration relevant for *The Brothers Karamazov*, the mimetic and the indirect, depending on the degree of the narrator's presence. Mimesis is the chief characteristic of drama. Dostoevsky carries it over into the novel on a very large scale in order to give a dramatic presentation to the events of his story. The direct mimetic representation of people speaking and acting in their 'here and now', even though they are in fact located in the past, gives the reader the illusion that the action is taking place. This illusion of immediacy is essential for heightening the drama and creating an atmosphere of suspense. In such passages the narrator's presence is at a minimum, expository narration and authorial comment are practically absent and the narrator functions primarily as a stage director. In Dostoevsky's hands the direct representation of the characters' words becomes an ideal vehicle for creating a dialogic system because it enables him to turn all the great philosophical dialogues over to them. For *The Brothers Karamazov* enacts not only a criminal drama but a philosophical drama which is played out almost entirely in their speech. Effacing himself and setting his characters free from his speech zones, the narrator evinces his respect for their word, and maximally facilitates their full revelation of their ultimate life positions. In all these instances we orient our perception of the events internally, according to the characters' words. Consequently we become involved with them, with their experiences, and when they intensely discuss ultimate questions, for example, when Ivan and Alyosha meet at the tavern, we become drawn into their dramatised philosophical dialogues. Because the narrator does not 'intrude', this type of mimetic representation is felt to be more objective.

And so it is, but only up to the point where the narrator enters the reader's purview.

Whenever the narrator takes up his own narration, whenever he chronicles facts, reports the characters' actions and inner thoughts and conducts expository narration, he becomes what Stanzel calls the 'authorial narrator', that is, an independent 'teller–character' who is the agent of transmission of the story. He then represents the events indirectly, mediating them through his own word. In these passages the narrator's voice is always audible and consequently we orient our image of the events externally, according to the narrator's voice. These two types of third-person narration, the mimetic and the expository, promote a more objective representation of the characters and their world in order to 'make the fictional world appear as reality'.[3] Nevertheless, the objectivity of the authorial narrator is by no means absolute.

Any narrator, whether speaking himself or reporting the speech of others, inevitably represents his own speech and therefore his own views, beliefs and feelings, his own personality. The narrator of *The Brothers Karamazov* is hardly an exception for he too is a fiction created by Dostoevsky. Depending on the nature of the material he is narrating, and which character's words he is representing, he adopts various guises, styles, intonations, all of which carry his evaluative accents, his emotional emphases. When he speaks about Alyosha and Zosima, his speech becomes permeated with hagiographical accents of reverent affection. Describing Zosima's death, he says that the elder 'quietly and joyfully gave up his soul to God' (14,294). For Mitya's broad Russian nature he reserves sympathetic indulgence: 'for all his faults [he] was a very simple-hearted man' (14,332). When he turns to Rakitin, Fyodor and Miusov, 'double-voiced' phenomena such as parody and irony steal into his speech. We may take the chapter headings as typical; the one about Fyodor is headed 'The Old Buffoon' and the one on Rakitin, 'A Seminarian Careerist'. Uneasy ambiguity, subtle undermining and distanced respect mark his work whenever it touches on Ivan. For example, apropos Ivan's arrival he remarks: 'it was strange that a young man, so learned, so proud and apparently cautious should suddenly' come to visit 'such a father' (14,16). The narrator reveals his different attitudes towards the brothers by the names he uses for them. He always refers to Smerdyakov by his 'stinking' surname, derived from the verb *smerdet'*, 'to stink'. His Book on Ivan is headed with the formal respectful mode of address, 'The Brother Ivan Fyodorovich', whereas his Books on Aleksey and Dmitry are headed by their affectionate diminutives 'Alyosha' and 'Mitya'. When narrating facts he sometimes adopts the sober, documentary tone of a chronicler: 'He was married twice and he had three sons' (14,7). Just because he is talking about such varied characters, and not himself, he can adopt so many varied tonalities. And one need not even invoke Bakhtin's highly ideological view of language in order to reject claims to absolute objectivity for third-person narration. For the inescapable principle of selection reveals the author's evaluations of what he thinks is more or less significant, persuasive and aesthetically appropriate. Whenever the material passes through his word, it becomes reaccented and interpreted according to his thought, his beliefs. Thus the authorial narrator's objectivity is in fact inherently relative.

There is another critical factor which strongly limits the authorial narrator's objectivity apart from the nature of language. Where other authors might wish to assume a consistently impersonal and objective stance by relying exclusively on third-person narration, Dostoevsky turns his same authorial narrator into a personalised first-person narrator as both authorial source and spatio-temporal reference point for the entire novel. First-person narration is marked by a subjective perspective, it always introduces a particular mental, emotional accent into a work. In Jakobson's formulation, the first person 'is intimately linked with the emotive function' of language which 'aims at a direct expression of the speaker's attitude toward what he is speaking about'.[4] Clearly an unrelievedly dispassionate, distant and objective narrator did not suit Dostoevsky's artistic plan. The objectivity of the authorial narrator is reduced because it is, so to speak, contaminated by the presence of his personalised mode in the reader's mind, just as the latter gains an objective tinge and is restrained in his subjectivity by the preponderance given to his authorial mode. This means that whenever the narrator speaks in his personal mode, it is striking and important. The knowledge of a first-person narrator is necessarily limited by his restricted perceptual horizon. But precisely this limitation Dostoevsky uses to artistic advantage. Indeed, the first-person narrator is the central one for our topic.

The distinctive feature of the narration of *The Brothers Karamazov* is that it has been generated in its entirety by the memories of its first-person, author–narrator and his hero. With the opening words of the introduction, 'From the Author', Dostoevsky creates a first-person narrator who presents himself as the author of the novel.[5] Here, in the tone of an intimate conversation with the reader, he confides his worries about his readers' reception of his hero, explains the reasons impelling him to write his novel (and his introduction), discusses his future literary plans, attempts to forestall his critics, and takes an anxious sombre overview of a certain indefinable spiritual malaise pervading his time. This is not a narrator who appears to discover his story at the same time as he tells it. He calls himself the 'biographer' of his hero. Biography entails a retrospective view of its subject. It also lays a strong emphasis on a particular person's life, on his achievements, on his fate, on his significance for his own circle of intimates and associates, for his times and perhaps for history. It is significant that from a novel extraordinarily rich in major characters, the author singles out for special mention only one, Aleksey Karamazov, whom he affirms as his hero, a statement I mean to take seriously. It is equally significant that his hero is the author of a literary work based entirely on his memories which the narrator inserts *in toto*. We shall return to the hero's composition in a later chapter. For the present we shall focus on the narrator since his story forms the bulk of the novel. Let us outline the temporal scheme he establishes for the novel as a whole.

The 'author' says that his hero's 'life story' will require 'two novels'. The 'first novel' (*The Brothers Karamazov*), 'took place as far back as thirteen years ago'. The second was to have been the 'main novel' which would cover the 'activity of my hero already in our time, right in our present current moment' (14,6). These remarks, plus a few allusions to his future novel subsequently interpolated into the text, are the only statements which relate to the narrator's 'present current moment'. With important exceptions to be discussed shortly, all the narrator's other utterances refer either to the events of thirteen years ago, or to the deeper past; all the characters' words were uttered at least thirteen years ago. The temporal scheme then is as follows. Looking backwards from his present, the narrator marks out a gap of thirteen years separating him from his characters' story. The characters' present is in fact in the past. Their present is not the present of the narrator but is for him a Vorzeit of thirteen years ago. The story takes place in this Vorzeit over a period of just under two-and-a-half months. The narrator also juxtaposes the characters' present to a Vor-Vorzeit which forms most of Book One ('The History of a Certain Family') where he goes back to events of some twenty-five to thirty years before the 'catastrophe' and briefly brings his narrative up to the beginning of the story proper. He says he must first give the reader the 'most necessary information' without which he could 'not even begin the novel' (14,11).

In Book Three the narrator reverts to his biographical mode (he returns to the Vor-Vorzeit) where he devotes three chapters to Smerdyakov's antecedents. His delay in providing the essential background information about Smerdyakov has the initial effect of making his life story seem incidental. He disingenuously explains: 'but I am ashamed to distract my reader's attention for so long with such common menials' (14,93). Thus Smerdyakov is formally kept to the side as though he were a faintly embarrassing but nagging afterthought, just as he is Fyodor's embarrassing child 'on the side', his illegitimate son whom he has to take notice of but never acknowledges. In retrospect, this bringing in of Smerdyakov through the back door is not only symbolic of his origins, but conveys an impression of evil that has been lurking in the 'wing' of the Karamazov house for a long time.

Later the narrator furnishes us with some biographical material about Grushenka and Kolya, and various characters of secondary importance, but by the middle of Book Three all the 'most necessary information' about the main personages, the Karamazov brothers, is to hand.

These returns to an earlier time are essential for creating a set of parallels for the brothers' early lives which in their turn are juxtaposed to the present. These past and present parallels enable us to compare the brothers' fates in their present with their early lives, and to draw our own inferences about the connections between their lives in childhood and in the present of the criminal and philosophical dramas. Thus, the antecedents of the narrator's present story, which lie in the brothers' childhoods and the circumstances of their births, are clearly very important for the dramatic 'catastrophe' which is on the verge of erupting.

Thus, the narrator creates a temporal series of three chronologically ordered segments comprising two Vorzeits and a substantial gap which add up to approximately four decades. The longest temporal segment (the Vor-Vorzeit) is the most diegetically compressed; almost all the material it contains issues from the narrator's memory in the form of a summary. The shortest temporal segment (the Vorzeit) which is devoted to the drama and filled with the characters' dialogues, is enormously expanded to take in most of the novel. Clearly, the representation of the characters' words was paramount for Dostoevsky. But all the characters' experiences are retrospectively filtered through the narrator's memory as it is functioning in his 'present current moment'. Never is the gap between the narrator's 'current moment' and the 'here and now' of the characters explicitly bridged. Never does the narrator proceed progressively to bring his story up to his 'here and now'. There are a few vague hints and intriguing inferences which can be drawn apropos the future, that is, the relative future which in fact lies somewhere well after the Epilogue but before the narrator's present. But there are no narrated events, there is no further diegetic material after the Epilogue which was spoken 'thirteen years ago'. With this positioning of the first-person narrator well after the events he relates, Dostoevsky laid the narrative foundation for a poetics of memory in *The Brothers Karamazov*. His narrator's spatial position conduces to the same end.

We soon learn that the narrator lived in the same small town as the Karamazovs, that he was their neighbour as well as their compatriot and contemporary. Time and again he stresses their common provincial and national world in such phrases as 'our town', 'our local monastery', 'our court', 'our ladies', 'our social conditions', and many more. These inclusive first-person plurals convey the distinct feeling that this narrator identifies very much with his locale, with his people, with their traditions and socio–historical dilemmas. So while the narrator usually remains outside the novel's world physically, his strong feeling of solidarity with his native provincial Russia makes him very much a part of the fictional world mentally and emotionally. Such a personal attachment to a place, a country, a people, could only have been conveyed by a first-person narrator. However, while he shares the Karamazovs' geographical location, the realm he occupied then cannot be identified with their fictional world. This applies even to the trial where he keeps his distance, retaining his position of witness and observer. He vaguely implies that he was personally acquainted with the Karamazovs, in particular with Alyosha, though he never spells out how closely. He never divulges his name, nor recounts any incidents from his own life, with one minor exception. None of the events he relates impinge on his fate, nor was he a participant in the drama which forms his story. He was primarily an earwitness and an uncommonly absorbent, imaginative collector of hearsay. He treats mainly of matters that come within his personal knowledge, he depicts only the life of his provincial milieu. He gives the distinct impression of having always lived in this town, of never having left it while the events were in progress. He occupies that stable point which can insure a steady overall view. He is what Stanzel calls a 'peripheral first-person narrator' who is distinguished by his location 'at the periphery of the narrated events and his role is that of an observer, witness, biographer, chronicler'.[6] This is essentially the spatial position of Dostoevsky's narrator. Let us briefly trace his appearances through the novel.

Immediately after his introduction, the narrator partially switches to the authorial mode to narrate Book One, the biographical book of the novel. Throughout this Book, though, the reader is very much aware of him since this is his expository retrospect. Self-references of the following type abound: 'I repeat', 'it seems to me', 'as I've already explained'. Interestingly enough, the first direct dialogue of the novel, and the only dialogue represented in Book One, is that strange conversation between Fyodor and Alyosha on the topic of hell as the place of punishment for one's sins. With this timeless, placeless metaphysical exchange, the author momentarily lifts us out of the local context and takes us, through their words, straight away to where he most wants to go, to the eschatological questions of divine justice, of heaven and hell and the last judgment.

From Book Two the drama gets under way with the gathering of the Karamazovs at the monastery. From this point on the narrator's first-person voice further recedes, but never to vanishing point. Every so often he resurfaces and the points at which he chooses to do so prove very important for interpretation.

He finally enters the novel's world in person during Mitya's trial, the account of which comes solely from his memory: 'I shall transmit only what struck me personally and what I especially remembered' (15,89). Here he assumes the role of an eyewitness and stenographer of the proceedings: 'these two remarkable speeches [of the lawyers] I, at least in places, wrote down in full <...> as well as one extraordinary and quite unexpected episode' (Katya's second testimony) (15,95). He frequently appeals to the opinions of other witnesses: 'I'm sure and everyone else was too', 'Everyone said later', and so on. Several times he stresses that he does 'not remember all the details'. After Ivan's distressing exit from the courtroom, he remarks: 'I cannot remember everything in order. I myself was agitated' (15,118). When Katya gives her evidence the first time, 'sacrificing' her reputation for Mitya, the narrator has a chilling premonition: 'I turned cold and trembled listening [to her]' (15,112). He witnesses the novel's second 'catastrophe', Katya's hysterical revengeful revelation of Mitya's incriminating letter, an act which the narrator says 'undoubtedly influenced the sinister and fateful outcome of the trial' (15,95). His impressions, his psychological assessments and subjective evaluations regulate the reader's review of the whole Karamazov drama: 'All this tragedy as if anew appeared before everyone graphically, concentrated, illuminated by a fateful and inexorable light' (15,94). Why has he chosen only this moment to become embodied within the novel?

The trial scene is a recapitulation of the crime from many points of view, all of which we now know are in varying degrees mistaken or limited. The narrator's subjective view presides at the trial so that he can bear personal witness to the failure of earthly justice to reach the truth. He now assumes the spatio-temporal and psychological perspective he had then in order more effectively to recreate the suspenseful atmosphere of the courtroom and, more importantly, so that we may more keenly appreciate the discrepancy between the truth about Mitya and the objectifying (and hence falsifying) reconstructions put on his motives by the lawyers and witnesses. Speeches that might have seemed persuasive and convincing now seem superficial, misguided or even meretricious in the light of what we know about Mitya's inner revelations and the true roles of Ivan and Smerdyakov. The trial of Mitya for the murder of his father has become a national social event in which Russia herself is, so to say, on trial, her values, her social ills, her destiny. The calamitous troubles besetting the Karamazov family are seen as symptomatic of the moral and social ills plaguing Russian society. Indeed, the narrator's persistent references to this provincial family tragedy as a 'catastrophe' reflect his anxiety that such crimes are evidence of deep spiritual disorder and premonitory of destructive social upheaval. Here he vividly emerges as a thinking, feeling person in his own right, a moralist, a provincial intellectual keenly interested in the fate of his characters and intensely apprehensive for the fate of his country.

Thus, Dostoevsky creates the illusion of a personalised narrator in the reader's mind, then oversteps the limits of his point of view while retaining the overall impression of the novel being narrated by a first-person narrator. This allows him to go far away from the narrator's limited vision. Still, even when Dostoevsky leaves the first-person narrator behind, his presence is hovering in the back of the reader's mind; firstly, because there is a heavy emphasis on it in the beginning; secondly, because he occasionally intervenes throughout the novel to speak of his literary plans, address the reader and defend his hero; and finally, because he returns in full voice to narrate the trial scene. And even when he is not directly addressing the reader, he keeps in frequent contact with him through the novel's many open and hidden polemics which are often marked by his acute anticipation of his reader's response, for example: 'I foresee inevitable questions such as <...> why did you choose him [Alyosha] as your hero?' (14,5). His speech, his recollections form an all encompassing dialogic background for the whole novel. Once an individualised narrator has been created, the reader cannot completely forget him. This crucially affects the way we perceive time in *The Brothers Karamazov*.

Memory proceeds from a marked awareness of past time, but there is more than one way of viewing the past. Mendilow makes a nice distinction which bears directly on Dostoevsky's narrative technique in *The Brothers Karamazov*: 'There is a vital difference between writing a story forward from the past, as in the third person novel, and writing one backward from the present, as in the first person novel. Though both are equally written in the past, in the former the illusion is created that the action is taking place; in the latter, the action is felt as having taken place'.[7] Mendilow's idea approaches that of Hamburger who finds that the past tense of 'epic fiction' (her term for third-person narration) 'loses its grammatical function of designating what is past <...> it is felt as a depiction of a present situation'.[8] Following Mendilow's distinction, we have two different past perspectives for the narrator's memory since he tells the novel in both the first and third-person modes. The third-person past perspective comprises what the narrator says the characters remembered. This is memory *forward from the present* and it yields traditional past tense statements of the type 'he remembered'. In these instances we are hardly aware of the narrator and the illusion of the present is very strong. Thus, for third-person narration the past tense has the effect of keeping the characters' experiences in the foreground. Consequently the events capture the foreground so that we feel present at the scene of action.

The first-person perspective encompasses what the narrator says *he* remembers. This is personal memory *backward from the present* which conveys a strong illusion of the past. With this perspective we are always aware of the narrator. For first-person narration the past tense has the effect of foregrounding the narrator's subjective memory reactions. In short, one cannot build a memory generated novel exclusively through third-person narration because the illusion of the present is too strong owing to the withdrawal of the narrator and the consequent foregrounding of the events. On the other hand, only the remembering first-person narrator, who has an unrelenting consciousness of impending 'catastrophe', and the knowledge of its tragic aftermath, can provide the background of suspense and tragedy which runs through the novel; only he can make the present lie open to the past and to the future. Narrating from his authorial mode, he more effectively imparts the sense of the past entering the present. Since both narrative modes coexist, the reader continually senses the coexistence of the foreground and background, of the past, present and future. Bringing together these two narrative positions, Dostoevsky incorporated the three prime temporal perspectives in a way that greatly furthered his artistic aims. 'A truly authorial narrator', says Stanzel, 'is not subject to the passing of time', and hence cannot convey a sense of memory.[9] However, the use of the authorial mode, with its emphasis on the present and a minimum consciousness of time, enabled him to devote most of his novel to a dramatic representation of his characters' actions and ideas. Through his third-person narrator, Dostoevsky transfers almost all the moral, religious, epistemological questions to the characters and he transforms this material into art by making these questions part of the represented characters, by turning them into aspects of their views, feelings, problems and ideas. From the first-person perspective we receive the fullest consciousness of time past and future. Recalling Lotman and Uspensky's model, memory is mainly about the past and the future. Thus, Dostoevsky's first-person narrator provides the novel's dialogic system with the temporal perspectives essential for a poetics of memory. Moreover, the essence of a first-person novel is that it is retrospective. This is because a first-person narrator is an identifiable individual with a life of his own; only he can have a full consciousness of the pastness of time and can thus use the past tense in its true grammatical designation. He can take us backwards in time with him thereby transferring his deeper sense of the past to us. Only he can be a memoirist.

If we take a memoir as a record of events from a personal source, then *The Brothers Karamazov* can be seen as a fictional memoir of its author–narrator. Now the 'author' has plainly said that he is the 'biographer' of his hero. In fact he is not, at least not within the limits of this novel where he considerably abbreviates Alyosha's biography. He is not really contradicting himself since he says that his 'first novel' (*The Brothers Karamazov*) 'is almost not even a novel, but only one moment from the first youth of my hero' (14,6). This is a striking statement and very apropos to our thesis. Biography and autobiography trace a linear evolutionary course from the subject's birth to death, or to the present. A *memoir* concentrates on a part of a life which was particularly vivid for its subject such as childhood, or a dramatic turning point; it depicts unique events which decisively affected the subject's life and perhaps others as well. Dostoevsky's narrator has chosen two such dramatic events from the 'first youth' of his hero, the murder of his father, which proves a critical turning point for everyone in the novel's world, and the death of his spiritual father on the same day. In this view it becomes clear why Dostoevsky's narrator transmits only the 'most necessary information' about his protagonists since in a memoir much biographical material has either to be omitted or considerably foreshortened. Of course *The Brothers Karamazov* is a novel, not a memoir. But as a novel it is an expanded memoir which issues from the context of the narrator's memory. The memoir then takes generic precedence over biography for the narrator's broad organisation of the story.

Here an apparently awkward difficulty arises, namely, since the narrator is recollecting the experiences of others and not his own, how can he know so much about them? Of course, many things are narrated which he could and must have learned later, before his 'present moment'. Much of his information comes from others (hearsay, rumour), some from his own observations. However, some things are narrated which the narrator could not possibly have learned or witnessed, for example, Lise's whispering to herself 'I'm vile' after deliberately slamming the door on her finger. Nevertheless his omniscience calls for substantial qualification. Herein too, lies the importance of his present temporal distance. He has had a long time to ruminate over these past tragic events which have so occupied his own memory that he has decided to make a novel out of them. In fact the narrator owes much of his 'omniscience' to the benefit of informed hindsight and imaginative empathy. He relies on his memory for assembling the facts about them. Then, to the fragmentary testimonies and impressionistic memories of others, he joins his own intuitive, sympathetic and imaginative reconstructions, based on what he knows and remembers about them. He stitches their experiences together, makes the expository transitions and thereby creates a plexus of interconnections. But it is Dostoevsky's imagination which turns the material into an aesthetically coherent narrative and his fictional narrator is the instrument by which he achieves this. Indeed, the narrator is most significant aesthetically in his recreation of other peoples' memories. And right here, at the borderline between imagination and memory, is where we can mark a critical divide between the author and his narrator.

The narrator is not telling the story for its artistic value but is trying to get at the truth. The crime provokes the most acute questions of justice since it culminates in a 'judicial error', in the conviction of a man who did not in fact commit the crime. With this miscarriage of earthly justice, the author forces us to confront the problem of justice on the metaphysical level, to seek for manifestations of divine justice elsewhere in the novel's world. Moreover, parricide is a crime which puts the deepest social and moral values to an extreme test; socially it is a blow against the basis of the family and the stability of society, metaphysically it is shown in *The Brothers Karamazov* to issue ultimately from an annihilating attack against God the Father. The social theme turns out to be a reflection of the metaphysical theme. Indeed, the bringing together of parricide and deicide as two different aspects or levels of the same idea into a single artistic system is one of Dostoevsky's great achievements. Casting his thoughts back to that harrowing time, the narrator recollects these tragic events in the hope of reconstructing the truth so that he and his readers may extract some meaning from the suffering endured on all sides. In the process the provincial world of the Karamazovs steadily enlarges so that it becomes drawn into the wide world of history, Russian and universal. Similarly, the question of justice in the particular case of the Karamazovs gradually extends, by way of the characters' philosophical and eschatological dialogues, to eternal questions of human and divine justice.

With so much at stake it was essential to create a narrator who appears incontrovertibly reliable, truthful, both despite, and because, of his limited vision. The wish to tell the truth springs from a moral urge which in itself is an important aspect of the narrator's image as a moral truthful person. Vetlovskaia has comprehensively identified those traits of the narrator which served Dostoevsky's rhetorical aim of winning the reader's trust in his narrator's word; his open, good natured naivety, his bafflement, his confiding conversational tone, his respect for his reader as an intelligent interlocutor and confidant, his occasional lack of exact information, to name a few.[10] An unreliable narrator would have destroyed the very basis of the story. Dostoevsky's narrator, then, remembers in order to verify the story and bear witness for the truth. However, our impression of the narrator's reliability does not issue solely from his personality. It has also to do with the nature of memory work and the memoir genre. In a memoir based on personal recollections of historical persons and events, memory work aims at an authentic reconstruction of the past by bearing contemporary witness. In a fictitious memoir, memory is essentially a constructive function which pretends to be a reconstructive one. Still the authority adhering to an historical memoir can be assimilated to a fictional one thanks to their common form. Here we are reminded of the narrator's conscientious reporting, his occasional appeals to experts, witnesses and other external evidence in order to bolster his opinions and give credence to his facts.

The narrator's memory work also enhances the authority and truthfulness of his word because of the epistemological status of memory beliefs. Indeed, 'the essential fact about the narrator', observes Belknap, 'is his remembered knowledge'.[11] Malcolm points out that 'Two of the chief properties of memory are present knowledge and previous knowledge of what is remembered'.[12] Following Malcolm, let us consider the way the verb 'to remember' is used. There are two common locutions: (1) I remember and (2) As I remember. With (1) the speaker commits himself to what he remembers, he implies that he believes it is true. If we accept the narrator as reliable, then we also accept his memory statements as true. Now his memory may be partially incorrect, but if it is completely false, then the verb 'to remember' is incorrectly used. This would be what Malcolm calls a 'delusion of memory' which is no memory at all. He calls (1) a statement of 'factual memory' and concludes that even the 'incorrect memory of an occurrence presupposes some correct memory of it'. Locution (2), though, allows for incorrect memory. Of course all fiction is 'as if'; we do not demand the verification of fictitious facts, only that they form a consistent system within the fiction. Dostoevsky's narrator always uses (1) whether reporting his own memories or vouching for those of his characters. Now locution (1) is not, strictly speaking, logically identical to 'I know'. However, 'to know' in the sense of 'to be familiar with something, to have personal experience of something', applies directly to the sense in which Dostoevsky's narrator uses 'to remember'. And 'I remember' has the great advantage of sounding less dogmatic, less categorical and hence more open. This is one respect which makes this narrator so useful for Dostoevsky's publicistic and philosophical aims. Grounding his images of his contemporary reality on memory knowledge, the narrator can seem to have reasonably sound knowledge about his characters and the contemporary life in which they all move.

Two further points about memory are apropos in this respect. The narrator remembers a great deal *about* the characters and this too comes under factual memory, though in this case no images of them are necessary. However he has also seen them, talked with them, that is, he remembers *them*. This is perceptual and personal memory at first hand, which entails subjective impressions of living people. He can vouch for the facts he records with substantial authority while investing them with that vividness which only the remembered words of living experiencing persons can impart. Therefore the narrator has competence on three levels of memory, factual, perceptual and personal. His memory, then, can be seen to be grounded on a reasonably secure foundation of past and present knowledge despite his limited vision. Had *The Brothers Karamazov* been presented as the solely imagined tale of an omniscient narrator, then the Karamazov tragedy, so fraught for Dostoevsky with implications for the future of Russia, could more easily have been dismissed as fanciful, 'made up'. This certainly would have undermined Dostoevsky's publicistic concerns and rhetorical aims, but perhaps most of all his sense of truth and artistic realism. For there is a very close connection between the memory of actual concrete events and a sense of reality, of life as lived by real people. Fantasies and abstract ratiocination operate independently of reality, but the specific contents of personal memories are referentially bound to real persons and to events which have actually taken place. Since the events of *The Brothers Karamazov* are presented as remembered, the whole work takes on a quasi-factual basis. This also has the interesting effect of turning mimetic dialogue into quotation. All the characters' spoken dialogues, once set in the context of the narrator's memory, are subconsciously apprehended as words actually uttered and therefore the whole represented drama becomes a quotation. It may be imagined, but it still has the fundamental authoritativeness and vividness of a personal quasi-memoir recalled, written and quoted by a reliable narrator.

Important as the first-person narrator's memory is for generating and verifying the story, it is even more important for his personal way of apprehending the world. By making him the author of the novel. Dostoevsky encompasses the narrative with a subjective consciousness. His narrator inhabits the whole text as an identifiable person with his own memories, sympathies and antipathies, with his own ideas and beliefs about good and evil, God and immortality. And once we have a subjective consciousness we must have personal memory. A subjective narrator may cherish certain aspirations, hold strong beliefs, take sides, exhibit a lively interest in the fates of those who live in his milieu. He is bound to have his own personal opinions about them and their views, some he may dislike, others he may admire and warmly defend. Another person can be the subject of his intense feelings. Above all he can have a hero. If he has a hero, he has an ideal. He then becomes the intercessor for his hero, just as his hero is the mediator for his ideal. How then does the narrator conceive his hero, in which context of cultural memory does he place him?

With his very first words the narrator draws our attention to his hero and provides a critical signal for interpreting his image: 'In beginning the life story of my hero, Aleksey Fyodorovich Karamazov, I find myself in a certain perplexity' (14,5). As Vetlovskaia points out, the 'narrator's hagiographic orientation is definitely apparent' in the first sentence where the word he uses for 'life story' (*zhizneopisanie*) signifies here a saint's life.[13] The main personal attributes he evinces are directly related to his narrating task, his perplexity about how to tell his story, how to present his hero. At the same time, he reveals himself to be the sort of person who has a saint for a hero. This means the author will have to mediate his ideal, in part, through reviving the memory of the hagiographical genre. Hagiography is also a retrospective representation of a life but one based on prior models and therefore containing invariant features independent of the accidents of current events. Hagiographic narration evaluates all phenomena from a moral spiritual standpoint, it 'cannot be dispassionate', it is steeped in accents of love and veneration. Indeed, many of the first-person narrator's interventions are attempts to guide our sympathies in his hero's favour. During Alyosha's spiritual crisis he anxiously comes forward to defend his hero: 'I would only ask the reader not to hasten to laugh too much at the pure heart of my hero' (14,305). Now a hagiographical stance can only be convincingly maintained by a narrator who believes in God. And so he does: 'God did not give them children' he remarks of Fyodor's servants (14,88). In fact the narrator's most important belief for the author is his faith in God. Thus Dostoevsky fashioned this mode of mediation to form an associative bond between the narrator's memory, his faith in God and his hero-saint who is the subject of his commemorative memory work. The main reason he created the voice of his subjective truth telling narrator was so that he could mediate between the spiritual ideal which Alyosha represents and the earthly events of the criminal drama.

Of course this narrator is not a hagiographer pure and simple. No canonical hagiographer would adopt so many stylistic guises or betray such 'perplexity' about his subject. He only uses this voice when it suits his idealistic edificatory aims. Adopting a hagiographical tone only intermittently, the narrator can remind the reader at certain critical moments that the tragic events must be seen in their moral, spiritual aspects while as the authorial narrator he can keep a steady pragmatic eye on the dramatic earthly events.

Most of the events the narrator records lie within his living memory. Consequently he can and does personally vouch for their authenticity. If a reported event lies in the remote past, it can only be something the narrator has learned. Significantly this type of memory the first-person narrator exhibits primarily in his chapter 'Elders' where he appears as an amateur authority on the history of Orthodox and Russian monastic traditions who has a keen interest in miracles. This chapter is no mere antiquarian excursion but provides a vital historical context of cultural memory for establishing his hero's hagiographical image and for promoting the continuity of the Orthodox tradition. The elder/novice relationship afforded him an ideal model for creating a spiritual father/son relationship which he embodied in Alyosha and Zosima, and for providing an implied contrast to the deformed and fatally damaged relationship between Fyodor and his other sons.

It is also partly because of his hagiographical aims that Dostoevsky keeps his narrator strictly apart from any direct communication with his characters. Vetlovskaia argues that any direct familiarity with them 'would have inescapably lowered them as well as their whole catastrophe to the level of an ordinary criminal event and therefore would have interfered with his lofty authorial task, his striving to present in his main heroes a certain moral–philosophical synthesis of his contemporary Russia'.[14] But we may take it still further. The synthesis he seeks does not stop at 'his contemporary Russia'; his lofty task is at least equally devoted to creating a world wherein we may divine the transcendental universals in the particulars of his tale.

The fact that the story never overtakes or displaces the narrating allows the narrator complete control over his material from beginning to end. His few hints about developments in his characters' lives subsequent to the Epilogue refer to a future which is still in the past for him, it is a 'future' which he can still see. Bakhtin maintained that Dostoevsky retains no 'surplus' words about his characters, everything he knows about them they already know and could say themselves. But the narrator of *The Brothers Karamazov* does retain a substantial surplus of vision, for he speaks from a spatio-temporal perspective totally invisible and inaccessible to them just because he is narrating backwards from the present. This has important aesthetic consequences. The gap of thirteen years gives him an overall view, an unimpeded perception of the whole of his chosen temporal segment. Precisely because his memory work bridges the temporal gap, it enables him to give objective aesthetic form to his images of people and the world they live in. In Bakhtin's words:

> I have the *whole* life of another *outside* myself, and here begins the aestheticisation of his personality: its consolidation and completion in an aesthetically significant image <...> The *memory* of another and his life is radically different from meditation and reminiscence on one's own life: memory sees life and its content formally otherwise, and only it is aesthetically productive <...> The memory of a complete life of another (the anticipation of the end is also possible) possesses the golden key to the aesthetic completion of a person.[15]

If we assign Bakhtin's 'I' to the first-person narrator of *The Brothers Karamazov*, we have a succinct formulation of his perspective. He is the sole person who can now see everyone through his longer range focus of memory and can therefore project artistically complete in the sense of fully fledged images of their lives which in themselves become susceptible to extracting significance. Of course, we are unable to form completed images of the fates of some major characters because the narrator does not tell us what happened to them in the intervening thirteen years, though he promised a sequel. However, 'complete' need not mean that their lives are over, though several are, still less that they can now be evaluated, finished and closed off once and for all. For the images we receive of them emerge in large measure through their own words and the great ideological issues they variously embody are still open. But they, as vivid images of these ideologies, and even more, as symbolic representations of them, are so uniquely well defined that we recognise them at once, the proof being that the Karamazovs have by now entered the world as profound symbols of certain spiritual ideological positions.

Dostoevsky's use of the first-person narrator's memory for generating the novel has further important functions. Significantly, he never admits to incorrect memory but he does occasionally plead imperfect memory when accounting for lapses in his story. This particularly is important because in *The Brothers Karamazov* these lapses have often to be interpreted as metaphysical loopholes through which mystery, indeterminacy and transcendence enter the novel's world. This is why Dostoevsky is just as eager to avoid omniscience as he is to avoid error ridden unreliability. Indeed his narrator deliberately leaves much in obscurity, he refuses to externalise and explain everything. He affects astonishment at sudden, unexpected turns of events. Precisely these inherent imperfections in the narrator's memory – and consequently in the novel's memory system – play a great dynamic role in generating new and unexpected meanings. 'For the authorial narrator, the creative power of memory will never be operative to the same extent as it is for a first-person narrator who evokes his story in an act of recollection.'[16] The 'creative power' of the first-person narrator's memory, which is necessarily imperfect, is the crucial point. For if his memory were perfect, it would be static, and the novel would be little more than a container of old news rather than a dynamic generator of new meanings.

The first-person narrator is vital for conveying a sense of the future, both on the conventional level of creating suspense and on the philosophical level through his dialogic system. His surplus view over the characters' past uniquely places him to foreshadow events and it is one of his main functions.[17] He also extends a sense of anticipation to events beyond the novel. Thirteen years of the characters' future lie in the narrator's past. He hints at future developments which must have occurred in the intervening years (Mitya's escape, Ivan's recovery). He calls the novel before us his 'introductory novel' and at the outset speaks of a 'second novel' to come. Our anticipation is thus stimulated to look not only to the end of this novel but to its sequel. Later the narrator even interpolates his idea for another literary project when he will have finished the Karamazov story.[18] Thus we get a feeling of a mental life teeming with ideas, in a hurry to get them all down lest the future overtake him. Since Dostoevsky's narrator was a living witness, he can convey a personalised anticipatory excitement exceeding that of 'objective' third-person narration ('I'm running ahead', he repeats (14,331,345)). A narrator confined to retrospection would have been speaking about lives that were over, finished and now susceptible to a final evaluation. But Dostoevsky's narrator is impelled forward by a pressing sense of anticipation, a lively urgent concern for the future of his characters, his work and the time stretching beyond. Such a narrator was just what Dostoevsky needed for expressing his own intense preoccupation with the future. Hence the frequency of two of his most important locutions 'he remembered afterwards', and 'he remembered for his whole life'. In the first, 'afterwards' (*potom*) refers to the subject's (usually Mitya's) subsequent comprehension *within* the novel, but the second one is used only for Ivan and Alyosha. Meijer rightly remarks that the narrator uses this phrase to underline the importance of the 'thoughts, feelings and events that occasion these references'.[19] But it is most important for the novel's poetic memory system since it points to a future comprehension which links up with the novel's transcendental themes. With this phrase, the narrator brings Ivan and Alyosha to some vague point within the temporal gap, giving them alone a retrospective view of the novel's events. He thus projects the growth and continuity of their consciousnesses into the future beyond the novel. In this connection it is especially significant that the only passages which have not passed through the narrator's word are Ivan's delivery of the Legend of the Grand Inquisitor and Alyosha's Life of Father Zosima. These two philosophical religious compositions, so fraught with future implications, are presented entirely as extended unmediated quotations.

The narrator's memory opens on to still wider dimensions. Only a remembering narrator endowed with consciousness can learn from the past. An omniscient narrator has nothing to learn. Since the narrator is telling the story thirteen years later it is likely, even certain, that his own views have changed since he first heard and witnessed these dramatic events. Indeed the contrast between what he was then and what he is now becomes most marked if we compare his trial scene narration with his introduction which appears to have been written last; it sounds like the voice of a more mature, sadly wiser man.[20] This has several important effects, aesthetic as well as ideological. The word of hindsight carries a more authoritative accent because it permits us to assume that the narrator has learned something in the meantime, that he has gained some important insights into life, or perhaps even divined something. Within the story something happens whose significance is not and cannot be realised by either the characters or the narrator at the time it happens. But the narrator tells us now that he or they remembered this event, or thought, later. Indeed the narrator has to draw our attention to its significance, first because he is telling the story, and secondly because the 'later' is not represented owing to the short time span of the story. The remembering narrator is uniquely positioned 'now' to assess its significance, even though he seldom spells it out explicitly. But his subsequent understanding and evaluation now, after many years, permeates the whole novel, its organisation, its discourses, its ideas and its poetics.

And it is something very important. The transposition of recollections to writing tends towards commemoration which in turn imparts to the novel, despite its drama, an elegiac, tragic tonality. However the narrator's word of memory is not nostalgic, he does not turn on us the 'soft smile of reminiscence'. In fact he does not reminisce, he re-collects, that is, he is involved in a highly conscious process of selection and organisation. 'Selection is the very keel on which our mental ship is built', said William James, and 'in this case of memory its utility is obvious'. Since we cannot remember everything, he continues, 'All recollected times undergo accordingly foreshortening; and this foreshortening is due to the omission of an enormous number of the facts which filled them.'[21] The author, using his mediating narrator, orders the chaotic randomness of life through the selecting and preserving activities of memory. At the same time he leaves some chaos in in order to keep the memory system open, dynamic and creative. In fact, the art of the novel depends to a great extent on what is left out. Once we deliberately select certain elements from the past, we are necessarily entangled in an interpretation of the past. We may also be implying that these elements have some intimate connection with the present and, perhaps, with the future. Interpretation is a way of giving meaning to things. For

Dostoevsky it is the meanings that are decisive for which events are left in the memory and which are excluded.

In the final analysis, we receive the whole text through the Gestalten of what the narrator pretends to remember, and the memories he pretends to preserve. Recollecting he constructs anew a complex chain of past events. His memory is the node of consciousness selecting, mediating and re-presenting all the novel's discourses through two perspectives. But it is not enclosed by it. The narrator begins as if from a frame but he does not close the novel by rounding back on himself, by pointing us back to his narrating position. He 'disappears', leaving his hero to utter the last word of the novel, a word on memory, thus compounding our sense of the whole novel as an open system, structurally and thematically.

There is yet another aspect of narration from memory and it was probably the most important one for Dostoevsky. The temporal distance of the narrator permits the emergence of a particular pattern to the past. Only through the unifying tendencies of memory can we discern the shape of events past. The narrator never spells it out, he does not impose his own 'monological' interpretation. But his ordering of the story through his perspective of memory allows the pattern to emerge. From his standpoint, the characters are located 'then and there', from the reader's, 'here and now'. As we read the novel our focus gradually catches up with that of the narrator so that when we finish it, the characters' 'here and now' becomes for us too their 'then and there'. We then arrive at the narrator's unique temporal reference point, we too then gain his perspective of memory. Then we may in retrospect more easily see the pattern which Dostoevsky has so subtly embedded in the novel. And if the pattern takes its thematic, structural and symbolic features from an ideal prototype, then we may be able to identify the prototype through the selected features. A prototype is an open road to the enlargement of a theme from its particular instantiation to a universal one. Joyce, for example, took *The Odyssey* as his prototype for *Ulysses*. Our search then will centre on what prototypal pattern *The Brothers Karamazov* is meant to exemplify.

CHAPTER 3

Memory and the system of ascending plots

Reason discerns, memory keeps the conscience.

Various stories have long been circulating in the Western collective memory, some fictional (myths, folklore, imaginative literature), others having a basis in history (epics, biblical narratives, saints' lives). If an author believes that one of these stories has a pre-eminent claim to truth, and if it has long been the object of his searching meditations, he will usually attempt to incorporate this truth into his own work. All the more so if he is convinced that the old truths are relevant to his confused epoch and that his contemporaries need to be reminded of them. On the other hand, he knows he has to tell an absorbing new story that makes sense to his contemporaries, but which is sufficiently serious and problematic to carry the old truths, a story that is emblematic of his troubled times. Among the invariants which withstand the erosion over time of historically conditioned elements is the plot, that major structural pattern for unifying events, ordering meanings and mediating an ideal. One way of matching his modern story with an old one is to embed the old plot in his narrative. This is essentially the artistic task Dostoevsky set himself when he wrote his last novel.

Confronted with the scope and complexity of *The Brothers Karamazov*, most interpreters divide it into several 'plans' or 'levels', while some, finding the term 'novel' inadequate, annex another generic term to describe its dominant character.[1] While all these plans, levels and genres point to essential features of the novel's structure, I prefer to draw the novel's compositional organisation along three plots, first, because I take it as read that the Dostoevskian novel is multi-generic and multi-levelled, and secondly, because 'plan' with its rigid, static and finalising overtones does not do sufficient justice to the dynamism of Dostoevsky's art. A plot gives us the sense that a narrative is going somewhere. Something is always happening in a Dostoevskian novel, everyone is always mid-journey to somewhere, literally and metaphorically. Dostoevsky was always keenly aware that readers are interested in what happens to fictional characters in their fates or final conditions. This interest generally goes hand in hand with an urge to sort things out, to discover why things have turned out as they have. Given that the central event organising the novel's action pattern is a crime of parricide, Ivanov's term, 'tragedy–novel' is still perhaps the best. The story of the murder of Fyodor Karamazov conforms in many respects to Aristotle's prescriptions for composing the 'finest form' of tragedy. In particular, it has a complex plot in which discovery (recognition) coincides with peripety. Aristotle designates causality as the distinctive feature of a well made tragic plot. The discoveries and peripeties should be 'the consequence, necessary or probable, of the antecedents'. The hero must end in 'misery' and 'the cause of it must lie not in any depravity, but in some great error' of judgment 'on his part'.[2] Since the murder is a premeditated crime, the reader's interest is strongly focused on causality, on discovering and understanding the criminal's motives. The identification of the cause, or 'error', should offer us an explanation for Fyodor's murder.

Very early in the novel the narrator says that the 'catastrophe' he intends to relate forms the subject of his 'first introductory novel, or rather, its external side', thereby implying that it also has an internal side which is the most important (14,12). This further suggests that the 'external side' is but an effect of much deeper lying causes, or a manifest culmination of hidden forces which turn out to be the main subject of the novel. I take this differentiation between the 'external' and the internal to reflect a triadic plot system comprising two manifest plots over which reigns a unifying masterplot. Each plot is organised and superceded by an hierarchically higher genre and conception of the tragic which, taken in order, are the detective thriller, the classical tragedy and the Gospel narratives.

The 'external side' is the concrete story of the murder of Fyodor Pavlovich Karamazov, reprobate father of the brothers Dmitry (Mitya), Ivan, Alyosha and Smerdyakov. This story is worked into a scheme which tests the reader's intellectual and psychological skills in solving a highly original variation of a detective plot. It presents the familiar mechanisms of the genre combined with the characteristic elements of melodrama. It is a combination well known in the nineteenth-century sensational novel which Dostoevsky transposed into the register of his own novel. So we have the murder plan, its execution, numerous ingenious suspense devices, love and money intrigues, high psychological drama, the detection and exposure of the criminal, and finally a full blown trial scene which culminates in Mitya's conviction. This is essentially Mitya's story which revolves around passions of love and hate and forms the sensory, sensational base of the novel. Here causality operates on the level of highly plausible, immediately intelligible motives of sexual rivalry and financial gain. This 'external side' of the story, along with its complications and denouement, I call the 'pragmatic plot'. In the articulation of this plot, language is used to imitate the action pattern and memory has only a superficial and conventional role.

But Mitya's 'drama' need never have become a 'tragedy' since he did not kill his father. As it gradually becomes clear that the crime was committed because of certain ideas, the importance of the pragmatic plot recedes and we become drawn into the intricate plexus of what I call the novel's 'ideological plot', which also has its themes, development and denouement. The ideological plot is played out in all those representations of the characters' world views which run throughout the novel in continual counterpoint to the action, so that in the end it emerges that certain ideas have led to the tragic consequences portrayed in the novel.

It is here, where causality becomes fraught with ideological and historical significance, that the appeal to cultural memory begins. For this ideological plot bifurcates along an axis whose poles are two diametrically opposed religious, philosophical positions embodied in their fictional proponents and brought face to face into intense dialogic relationships. For Bakhtin, bifurcation of discourse along an axis of apologetics (*pro*) and polemics (*contra*) is typical of the dialogic genres. It is also typical of theological debate. Here we are reminded of the catechism on the existence of God Fyodor conducts between Alyosha and Ivan 'over the cognac'. Alyosha affirms that God and immortality exist, Ivan says categorically that they do not. In other words, Alyosha affirms the values transmitted by the Christian cultural memory, whereas Ivan negates the two cardinal ideas on which that whole system rests. Dostoevsky's (very dialogic) title for one of the 'culminating' books of the novel, *Pro and Contra*, succinctly encapsulates these antithetical positions. All the novel's hero–ideologists gravitate towards one or the other of these two poles, even in their doubts. These two beliefs, advanced as axiomatic alternatives, comprise the agenda for the novel's dialogic system, an agenda that was drawn up by the author. From his axiom that there is no God or immortality, Ivan concludes that 'there is no virtue' and consequently 'everything is permitted'; from his axiom that God and immortality exist, Alyosha (and Zosima) conclude that 'all are to blame for all'.[3] The axioms are not susceptible of proof. In Dostoevsky's fiction, the question of God's existence cannot be decided *in abstracto*, but can only be reached or approximated in a living dialogue and in life situations. Thus, Dostoevsky puts the brothers' corollaries to the test in life, in the world of his novel, by incorporating them into their dialogues and actions and making a plot out of them. Alyosha and Zosima's corollary, and the plot lines joining them to each other and others, are shaped according to different aesthetic principles than those of classical poetics. However, Dostoevsky turns the pragmatic plot into an ideological one by making Ivan's ideas serve as the catalyst for the crime. The protagonists of this plot are Ivan and Smerdyakov, and he constructed it along the lines of classical tragedy.

Dostoevsky binds Ivan and Smerdyakov to each other hand and foot both externally, by making their discoveries and denouements coincide, and internally, by their 'double-voiced' dialogues of half spoken thoughts and mutual understandings. This structural concurrence of their plot lines reinforces their roles as twin accomplices in murder. Their fateful turning points take place when Ivan departs leaving his father unprotected and Smerdyakov at once puts his plan in motion by faking a fit. Their discoveries occur during their last conversation when Ivan's uneasily suppressed knowledge gives way to sickening certitude, and Smerdyakov despairingly realises that everything is *not* permitted. The double-voiced dialogue on which their fatal relationship depended now comes to an end. And it is precisely to Ivan alone that Smerdyakov finally reveals the truth, laying the primary responsibility for the murder at Ivan's door: 'You murdered him, you are the main murderer, and I was only your accomplice, your loyal Licharda, and it was following your work I did it' (15,59). Shortly thereafter Smerdyakov identifies that 'word' of Ivan which led to parricide when he tells him that he killed 'most of all because "all is permitted". This you really taught me sir, for you talked a lot about that to me then: for if there is no everlasting God, then there isn't any virtue, and then there is no need of it at all' (15,67). This prompts us to review Ivan's function in the novel, to re-evaluate all that he has said, done or omitted to do. Now the philosophical discussions centering on his ideas, which initially seemed to be independent digressions, turn out to be inextricably connected to the crime. We then realise that the real evil seed was Ivan's idea and that it had fallen on the fertile ground of Smerdyakov's mind where it ripened into the fruit of cold-blooded murder.

Their denouements swiftly follow. Smerdyakov takes his life, Ivan, shattered by Smerdyakov's revelations, has his last nightmare which ends in his total mental breakdown. Ivan's theory is in ruins. The effects (murder, suicide, breakdown and Mitya's conviction) have utterly compromised the cause (Ivan's ideas), and compromised them maximally. We then realise that we have been following two plots, one misleading

(Mitya killed Fyodor), the other correct (Ivan and Smerdya-kov killed Fyodor), one directed to the empirical fates of the brothers and their father, the other to the fate of an idea. This path of realisation Vetlovskaia calls the 'regressive denouement' because it forces us to work back from manifest effects to the insidious cause.[4] Compromising Ivan's corollary (all is permitted), the author undermines his axiom (there is no God or immortality). Since there are only two axioms offered in this novel's artistic system, the refutation by consequences of the one tends to the affirmation of the other: conscience, virtue and morality exist and therefore God and immortality exist as well. This whole development forms the core of the ideological plot.

The 'catastrophe' is not restricted to Fyodor and his sons. Mitya's passions, and even more, Ivan's ideas are shown to have consequences not only for their lives, but for others in their world, some even unknown to them. This way they draw the non-ideologues and the innocents (Ilyusha) into the tragic drama as well, thus touching everyone in the novel's world. As Alyosha says to Lise before the murder: 'My brothers are destroying themselves < ... > my father too. And they are destroying others together with them' (14,201). Later, in his Life of Zosima, Alyosha quotes his elder's mystical formulation of this idea: 'for everything is like an ocean, everything flows and comes into contact with everything else, touch it in one place – at the other end of the world it reverberates' (14,290).

What is true for the world of the novel can be extended to the real world at large. For Dostoevsky wants us to believe that since atheism turns into a 'catastrophe' in the particular instance of the Karamazovs, it may turn into a 'catastrophe' in Russia, and in the world. This suggestion comes to the reader as a result of the nature of verbal art. In Aristotle's words:

the poet's function is to describe, not the thing that has happened, but a kind of thing that might happen, i.e. what is possible as being probable or necessary < ... > [The historian] describes the thing that has been, and the [poet] a kind of thing that might be. Hence poetry is something more philosophic and of graver import than history, since its statements are of the nature rather of universals, whereas those of history are singulars. By a universal statement I mean one as to what such or such a kind of man will probably or necessarily say or do – which is the aim of poetry, though it affixes proper names to the characters.[5]

In so far as Dostoevsky shows us what kinds of people will necessarily say or do given their particular ideas, and in so far as they suffer terrible fates from saying or doing those things, the novel has a strong didactic and cautionary trend, as Vetlovskaia emphasises.

According to Bakhtin, the pragmatic plot in a Dostoevskian novel is just a 'service function' for provoking voices to enter a dialogue.[6] Without the pragmatic plot, though, the novel would lose its moorings in reality, in those sequential concrete events of which this plot is the shaping outline. Moreover, without this connection between ideas and empirical 'fates', there would be no proofs that the murder of Fyodor Karamazov followed from Ivan's way of viewing the world. The ideas would be left stranded, interesting in themselves, but in an abstract way, in a way not inextricably related to life. In Bakhtin's view, the idea in Dostoevsky's fiction 'is a *live event*, played out at the point of dialogue meeting between two or several consciousnesses' (88). But an idea becomes a 'live event' because of the way it affects peoples' lives. This is what stories and plots are for. Apropos Ivan's idea that 'all is permitted', Bakhtin comments 'what an intense dialogic life that idea leads throughout the whole of *The Brothers Karamazov*' (89). But it receives its dialogic intensity from being continually forced to interact with its counter idea 'all are to blame for all'. Moreover, the 'life' of Ivan's idea ends in death, in murder, suicide and the living death of mental breakdown. These fates are exemplary and final except possibly that of Ivan, and they are in complete agreement with the Aristotelian tragic denouement. Thus, the pragmatic plot serves as a necessary empirical refutation of the ideas. The two combined plots resolve into a major empirical refutation of the ideas. The two combined plots resolve into a major ideological theme which Vetlovskaia pinpoints: 'Lack of faith turns into a "catastrophe". The associations called forth by the character of the retrospective denouement strive to emphasise precisely this idea first of all.'[7]

Here a leading question arises: where does this leave Bakhtin's central thesis that the Dostoevskian novel is 'polyphonic'? By this he means that Dostoevsky never imposes his own 'monologic' views on his characters but creates them as completely free, autonomous personalities who are subjects of their own fully signifying discourses. (7) However, plots have to do with the genesis of an artistic narrative, they are part of its process of production, of its 'deep structure'.[8] Just because of this, some of the author's deepest views and judgments are implicit in the very way he has arranged his characters' fates. And what, too, of Bakhtin's insistence that the Dostoevskian novel is devoted to representing a 'plurality of equally valid consciousnesses < ... > within several fields of vision, each full and of equal worth', if this novel presents only two fundamentally opposed views? (16) For any given character, his views will seem of equal or greater worth to himself, but are they 'equally valid' within the context of the whole novel? In fact, the poles of *pro* and *contra* cannot be 'of equal worth' given the way Dostoevsky has represented them (we need only think of Rakitin, Smerdyakov and the devil). Indeed, so opposite are the *pro* and *contra* that it is impossible to entertain them both simultaneously. Therefore the reader feels compelled to choose, and therefore the novel must be read as *pro* or *contra*. As Vetlovskaia says 'there is no third way in the novel between good and evil, God and the devil < ... > all are compelled and free < ... > to choose only between these two possibilities'.[9] But precisely this *pro* versus *contra* is a very dialogic situation, and a very biblical predicament. Speaking of the Gospel of St Mark, Auerbach remarks: 'And the story speaks to everybody; everybody is urged and indeed required to take sides for or against it.'[10] Into an approximately similar situation did Dostoevsky place his characters and readers. Indeed, it is the juxtaposition and the struggle between *pro* and *contra* which makes the novel what it is.[11]

In short, Dostoevsky initially arranges his material in order to tempt the reader into believing that what has occurred is a *crime passionnel*. This would mean that Mitya killed his father. However, as soon as we learn, or suspect, that Smerdyakov is the murderer, we simultaneously realise that he could not kill for such a motive, and that consequently a totally different kind of causality is involved. This inevitably leads us to Ivan, the intellectual brother who is Smerdyakov's mentor and chief interlocutor. Once our concentration is focused on Ivan, we are as inevitably led to Ivan's ideas and hence to an ideologically motivated crime. This means that the crime turns out to be something far more momentous than a local *crime passionnel*, because ideas spread, generalise and consequently enter the Zeitgeist only to emerge from history (memory) and determine peoples' lives. Ivan, the original theorist, loses control over the fate of his ideas. Launched into the world, they float in the air where the Smerdyakovs can appropriate them. Thus, ideologically motivated crimes can multiply, influencing not only the fates of individuals, but the destinies of nations. Specifically, atheism generates nihilistic immoral ideas which, once propagated, must lead to immoral, destructive acts in reality, to murder and universal mayhem. It was these connections between life and ideas which exercised Dostoevsky and which he aimed to prove were 'necessary and probable' through the interrelated operation of the pragmatic and ideological plots. In all these respects, then, Bakhtin's assertion that 'there is no causality in Dostoevsky's novels' has to be qualified (29). As regards the working out of pragmatic and ideological plots, the classical principle of causality prevails. Though they alternate in prominence, they simultaneously intersect and reinforce each other. Together they lay the groundwork for a coherent and gripping narrative.

This seems a fair summary of the two interrelated plots, but we are bound to feel that something rather large and important has been left out of our scheme. Together these two plots fall well within the artistic conventions of modern realism with its neo-classical assumptions about cause and effect. As Bakhtin points out, the realistic novel (biographical, family, social, psychological) is built on 'a deep and organic unity' between the hero and the plot (101). The hero and his objective world 'must be made of one piece' (101). His links with others are 'not as one person to another person' but are defined by his social relationships (father, husband, merchant, landowner) (104). The characters in a realistic novel cannot establish any connections 'exterior to the plot', they are 'born of the plot itself' and 'finalised' within it (104). Causes (and motives) grow out of character, out of desires (Mitya), ideas (Ivan) and volition (Smerdyakov), and out of society, defective family relationships (Fyodor and his sons), class resentments (Smerdyakov, the 'lackey'), current intellectual trends (Ivan, Rakitin, Kolya) and various plausible contingencies (Grigory's unshakeable conviction that the door was open). The realistic novel depends almost entirely on convincing the reader that everything that happens is either probable or necessary (pure chance is also possible). It is guided by the conviction that things happen for reasons which can ultimately be made intelligible to rational human beings. However, Smerdyakov's motives cannot be totally reduced to his having fallen under the influence of Ivan's ideas. Nor can the complex inner life of Ivan be entirely accommodated within the sphere of his ideas. Mitya does not end in total 'misery'. Moveover, as Vetlovskaia has shown, the theory that the environment (*sreda*) causes crime, a favourite idea of sociological determinists, is overturned by Mitya's story. All the circumstantial and psychological evidence is against Mitya. True, had he seen Grushenka with his father, he could have done it. Yet he is innocent. This warns the reader against ascribing the ultimate causes of human behaviour to the laws of social determinism. Causes which can be traced solely to other inaccessible agencies such as fate, pure contingency or totally unconscious psychological processes have no place in this novel. Even ideas *per se* are not the exclusive causes. In fact, the Aristotelian notion of combining all events according to a logical sequence of what is 'necessary and probable' has only a limited, albeit essential role in *The Brothers Karamazov*. 'The real connections begin where the ordinary plot ends < ... > The unity of the whole in Dostoevsky < ... > is a unity above plot and above idea' (277,298). Bakhtin evidently did not elaborate this important insight, but I think we can indicate where the higher unity has to lie and how these 'real connections' may form a higher plot. For this, we need other ways of viewing a plot and realism, ways that place memory at the very centre. In classical tragedy a peripety describes a sudden descent from prosperity to irreversible ruin. The most important of the novels' many discoveries and peripeties turn out to be the type that depicts a sudden reversal from a fall to a spiritual elevation. None arises as a 'necessary and probable' development from either the pragmatic or ideological plot. These plots are the surface systems, directly evident to the reader, from which deeper spiritual movements gradually emerge in the contours of a divine plot pattern.

Dostoevsky singled out four passages as the most essential 'culminating points' in his novel, namely, Books Five (*Pro and Contra*) and Six (*The Russian Monk*), 'Cana of Galilee' and the last chapter, 'The Burial of Ilyusha. Alyosha's speech by the stone'.[12] What John Jones calls the 'real novel' is organised around them. Only the first passage, where Ivan sets forth his ideas, forms a link with the criminal plot. None is contained by the ideological plot, none displays an Aristotelian plot sequence. All place the novel's main 'voices' in settings 'exterior to the plot'. Two portray four reverse peripeties, from a fall to spiritual renewal (Markel, Zosima, the Mysterious Visitor and Alyosha). In every passage Alyosha is present and they are all profoundly involved with memory, cultural and individual.

The regulation between the novel's events also presents us with a mystery, what Forster calls 'a pocket in time'. A plot 'with a mystery in it', he remarks, is a 'form capable of high development. It suspends the time-sequence, it moves as far away from the story as its limitations will allow'.[13] Temporal suspensions point to another way of viewing time than as an evolving linear sequence. Pockets in time are bridged by memory. Forster assigns a leading role to the reader's creative memory work in apprehending the aesthetic and semantic function of the plot:

And over it [the plot], as it unfolds, will hover the memory of the reader (that dull glow of the mind of which intelligence is the bright advancing edge) and will constantly rearrange and reconsider, seeing new clues, new chains of cause and effect, and the final sense (if the plot has been a fine one) will not be of clues or chains, but of something aesthetically compact, something which might have been shown by the novelist straight away, only if he had shown it straight away it would never have become beautiful.[14]

Forster's idea that the aesthetic patterns organised by memory yield meanings which override ordinary causality is most apropos to *The Brothers Karamazov*. In traditional stories such as those found in myths, folklore and biblical narratives, the meanings inhering in their underlying parallel patterns and symbolic systems prevail over the logical 'clues and chains' of causality. Ordinary notions of causality can be applied to understanding the pragmatic and ideological plots, but *The Brothers Karamazov* is not primarily concerned with ordinary causality. Dostoevsky set his sights by a conception of reality that comes from the memory of a spiritual tradition and is not bound by common notions of causality. *The Brothers Karamazov* is not only, or perhaps not even, primarily a realistic novel. The writer who called himself a 'realist in the higher sense' only uses the concrete events of empirical life in order to reach a higher reality. He does not break the rational chains of causality in order to assert the absurdity or meaninglessness of the universe – this he leaves to his evil characters – but in order to seek and affirm a higher meaning. He assimilated his tale of parricide to a sequential pattern which comes from a different 'genre memory' altogether.

The classical theme of tragedy is that there exists a limit, a divine moral law, which must not be transgressed. The tragic hero meets his downfall because he oversteps the limit, through passion or blindness. Mitya's passions bring him to the verge of overstepping the moral law, but he never doubts its absolute authority. In Ivan's intellectual rebellion against the moral law, we meet a modern ideological version of the classical 'error of judgment'. Ivan does not simply transgress the moral law (this Smerdyakov does), but with his theory of 'everything is permitted', he tries to destroy the very idea of a moral limit, arrogating to the 'clever people', among whom he includes himself, the right to violate all limits. He thus goes to the extreme of nihilism. At the same time, Dostoevsky provides Ivan with a very persuasive justification for his revolt (*bunt*) against the divine order ('God's world'), namely, the suffering of children. For without such justification we would not have a tragedy but a case of psychopathology. Nevertheless, Dostoevsky implicitly structured his classical plot in order to uphold the idea that the law must not be broken and cannot be abolished. Where then does Dostoevsky locate the moral law, and how is it defined in his artistic system? For what is important for Dostoevsky is not only the transgression, but the exposition and affirmation of the divine law that has been violated. The moral law, said Kant, must be 'enunciated' and presented in its 'supreme purity and holiness', because 'it must be a model, a pattern, a standard' to which man can look for divine aid.[15] The enunciation of this pivotal law he gave to Zosima, his ideal image of a saintly contemporary man who could present the moral law in all its 'purity and holiness'. This is the point where Dostoevsky reaches for the higher realism by going back to the sacred texts of cultural memory for a model for moral and spiritual guidance.

A crime of parricide poses the questions of conscience and punishment in a particularly acute form. Zosima interprets them in the sense of Christian redemption. Defining true punishment, Zosima uses the old Russian word *kara* which forms the initial root of the Karamazov surname and which, significantly, means both 'punishment' and 'retribution':

real *kara*, the only effective, the only deterring and reconciling one consists in the consciousness of one's own conscience < ... > If anything does preserve society even in our time, and even reforms the criminal himself and brings about his regeneration it is again solely and only Christ's law which reveals itself speaking in the consciousness of one's own conscience. Only by acknowledging his own guilt as a son of Christ's society < ... > will he acknowledge his guilt towards society itself. (14,59–60)

Given this, Dostoevsky was faced with the artistic task of bringing his protagonists' voices into a dialogic relation with the voice of Christ, of making them aware of this voice within themselves. The awakening and growth of conscience is conceived as an internal dialogic process between the human and divine voices within a single consciousness. Instead of God as a transcendent being, Dostoevsky's God is the incarnate Son of God with Whom one can talk. Brought into contact with this divine collective memory, the subject then reflects on his memories of his wrongdoings at a higher level and from this contact, he receives its true meaning. The internalisation of 'Christ's law' leads to an open confession and spiritual renewal. Every one of the wrongdoers in this novel hears this voice of conscience sooner or later, or too late. Moreover, Zosima assigns to individual conscience the function of preserving society. His conception of society reflects Dostoevsky's ideal of the communal *sobornost'*, the union of all in brotherhood under Christ's law. Since Christ no longer exists incarnate in the world, He can only be pre-existent in the memory, cultural, collective and individual. The continuity of the Christian memory is held in texts, canonical, folkloric, apocryphal, and in communal traditions and rituals. The characters' recognition of the highest law will have to come through their memories (direct, intuitive, subliminal) of these texts. Our aim, then, is to discover how Dostoevsky uses various modes of memory to bring the words, images and symbols of these texts into the consciousness (memory) of his characters so that they may achieve redemption.

Speaking of the influence of the Bible in his life, Zosima exclaims: 'What a book the Holy Scripture is, what a miracle and what strength is given with it to man! Just like a mould cast of the world of man and of human characters, and everything is named and shown forever and ever. And how many mysteries solved and revealed' (14,265). Fictitious lives created to match a pre-existent, eternally given 'mould of the world' do not conform to a unifying sequence of cause and effect prescribed by classical poetics, but are based on similarities (and differences) to the mould (the Bible), on the aesthetic principle of the Urbild/Abbild relationship. This suggests that with his last novel Dostoevsky aimed to create an analogy with Scripture where every story has two senses, the earthly and the spiritual, the earthly being subordinate to the spiritual of which it is an imperfect reflection. Events in the realistic novel are reflections of themselves, or concrete earthly conditions. Any connections they establish with other phenomena are of a chronological, causal or evolutionary nature. But there is another view of reality which reaches far back into the collective memory. Here is where Auerbach's ideas on figural interpretation apply so strikingly to Dostoevsky's artistic vision. Figural interpretation, or what Auerbach also calls 'figural realism', depends on discerning in all historical events a double level of signification. The persons and events in *The Brothers Karamazov* simultaneously signify themselves and certain persons and events in the Bible so that the former fulfil and confirm the Word said for eternity. The biblical events are located in historical time, the fictional, as a representation of reality, pretend to be in historical time. Because the temporal gaps between them are so great, the 'connection between occurrences is not regarded as primarily a chronological or causal development but as a oneness with the divine plan, of which all occurrences are parts and reflections'.[16]

Discussing the suffering of Job, Zosima rhetorically quotes the 'mockers and revilers, the words of the proud' who tauntingly accuse God of having allowed His most beloved saint to suffer unjustly 'for the amusement' of the devil. To this Zosima gives an 'indirect answer' to Ivan, to all the suffering and injustice so powerfully depicted in the novel, an answer which at the same time expresses the essence of that hidden force shaping the novel's events:

But the greatness of it lies in the fact that here is the mystery – that the passing earthly show and eternal verity have here been brought together. In the face of earthly justice the action of eternal justice is accomplished. (14,265)

Zosima clearly distinguished two critical words which English translations blur. *Pravda* means both 'justice' (righteousness, veracity, integrity) and 'truth' in the ordinary empirical sense. *Istina* means 'verity', 'truth' in the highest philosophical or religious sense. It is the absolute opposite to a 'lie'. The difference between them is illustrated in the saying 'Justice is verity in action' (*Pravda – istina na dele*). In the English Bible the word is preserved only in Christ's 'verily, verily' sayings. In the Russian Bible and Orthodox liturgy, *istina* occurs as a synonym for Christ: 'I am the way and the truth (*istina*) and the life' (John 14:6). In other words, true justice springs from *istina* whose incarnation was Christ. Dostoevsky sought to embed the action of 'eternal verity' in the 'passing earthly show' he created for the novel. The intermingling of 'eternal verity' with earthly events for the purpose of accomplishing 'eternal justice' on earth is equivalent to the idea that divine truth ultimately decides human fates, that it will have the last Word, just as it had the first Word, whether on earth, or in 'other worlds'. As is well known, the highest repository of 'eternal verity' for Dostoevsky was the New Testament, and he chose from that text one utterance of the incarnate Word as the mould for his novel's world.

The very first words of *The Brothers Karamazov* are a quotation from Christ: 'Verily, verily, I say unto you, Except a grain of wheat fall into the earth and die, it abideth alone; but if it die, it bringeth forth much fruit' (John 12:24). With his choice of Epigraph Dostoevsky gave us a leading clue for interpreting his last novel and for immediately recognising the system of cultural memory which forms its all encompassing context. Following Picchio we may call this Epigraph a 'biblical thematic clue'; which he defines as any quotation from the Bible (or other sacred text) occurring near the beginning of a work in a 'structurally marked position' and bridging 'the semantic gap between its literal and spiritual sense'.[17] The biblical thematic clue announces the 'main theme, that is, the "higher theme" which explains the hidden meaning of any earthly event related in the narration'. It is the 'leit-motif which governs the semantic system of the work'. The interpreter's task is to 'grasp the spiritual senses that lie behind' the narrative. In *The Brothers Karamazov*, these senses form themselves into a divine master pattern.

The biblical context of the Epigraph is one in which Christ invokes this parable to prophesy His Passion and Resurrection. Christ sets before us two possibilities for human fates: either a seed will not fall to earth and die, and thus will remain alone, barren, or it will fall to earth where it will die but in so doing will be fruitful. The main meaning of Christ's parable is that new life comes only through death, in itself a logically paradoxical idea, but one that is fundamental to Christianity, and to Dostoevsky's art. To 'die' here means to germinate, to become regenerated and transformed. The old person must die (be spiritually cleansed) so the new one can be reborn.

These two possibilities are enacted in *The Brothers Karamazov*. Indeed one could say that Dostoevsky wrote his novel as an elaborated realisation of Christ's parable, as two sets of systematic variations on this paradigmatic bifurcation, on redemption achieved and redemption frustrated. Christ's parable is built on a *pro* or *contra* opposition which, in Dostoevsky's novel, resolves into a division between those who are redeemed and those 'contemporary dead men' who, in Bakhtin's words, 'are as sterile seed, cast on the ground, but capable neither of dying (that is, of being cleansed of themselves, or rising above themselves), nor of being renewed (that is, of bearing new fruit)' (147). The 'figurative idea' here, notes Bakhtin, goes back to 'Eleusinian mysteries', to archaic regeneration myths and rituals. To these, Christianity brought a radically new interpretation with the idea of personal salvation and immortality. The individual life thereby acquires a moral dimension lacking in the mythical, archaic variant. In a nineteenth-century novel, the redemptive pattern has to be a memory structure (a memory of a memory). It is the memory of this parable which provides the plot for the *pro* and *contra* and which guides *The Brothers Karamazov* from beginning to end. It is the memory of the prototypal drama of Christ's Passion and Resurrection which lies at the basis of the Dostoevskian conception of tragedy and which ultimately shapes the protagonists' fates.

Dostoevsky's assimilation of his characters' fates to Christ's parable transforms the whole conception of tragedy guiding the novel. For Christ's tragedy is at the same time a triumph, an overcoming of death in the Resurrection, a paradigm of the promise of universal salvation and immortality. This means that no tragedy, however terrible, is absolute or final. As Auerbach points out, 'the Christian figural view of human life was opposed to a development of the tragic < ... > high above the events of earthly existence stood the towering and all-embracing dignity of a single event, the appearance of Christ, and everything tragic was but a figure or reflection of a single complex of events, into which it necessarily flowed at last'.[18] This is why Dostoevsky's tragedy does not culminate in a bleak denouement of classical tragedy, but is both hopeful and sorrowful. And this is one reason why *The Brothers Karamazov* is an open, dialogic novel. The circle of causality is not perfectly closed, it breaks down because all denouements on earth are only partial, provisional. There can be no absolute denouements in his fictional worlds because the final denouement is yet to come. In this connection, it is particularly significant that Alyosha's spiritual crisis over Zosima's death, says the narrator, 'formed a turning point which shook but also fortified his mind now once and for all, for his whole life, and for a certain aim' (14,297). And he describes his hero's denouement in terms of a triumph: 'He had fallen on the earth a weak youth, but he rose a steadfast fighter for his whole life' (14,328).

A novel which plots its most essential events on a Christian pattern of fall, redemption and rebirth cannot be a literal imitation or reflection of reality, nor can it be governed by a classical plot. Only on the negative side, where there is a denial of 'eternal verity', does the plot follow Aristotelian descent. In the classical sequence, the hero's discovery is usually of some terrible external fact hitherto unknown to him (Oedipus is a prime example). His peripety describes a sudden descent to permanent ruin. His fate is final, closed off, no further development is possible and the tragedy comes to an end. Aristotle took human fate out of the ritualised mythological sequence and modernised it by focusing on the isolated fate of an individual and representing human greatness in the face of misfortune. The hero realises the terrible thing he has done, suffers and thus is worthy of pity. But the redemptive factor is absent. The Christian redemptive pattern is a complete inversion of the classical plot, structurally and semantically. It begins from a fallen state (sin, pride, wrongdoing). The keystone of its structure rests on its definition of discovery as a recognition (a memory) of 'eternal verity', and peripety as a spiritual renewal upon acceptance of that truth. It culminates in a fundamental spiritual change in one's life, in the way one lives in the world. The Christian pattern is reversible, or is always potentially so, in that while a tragedy cannot be undone, it can be atoned. The classical tragedy is irreversible. In the Christian view, suffering is redemptive, in the classical, it is irreducible. To restore the fallen human being is, as Grossman long ago pointed out, Dostoevsky's major subject and profoundly shapes his plot patterns. Thus, Dostoevsky dialogically combined two opposed plot structures for connecting the novel's events, each governed by different aesthetic principles. He used the rational classical structure for the ideological plot, that is, he used reason (causality) to defeat reason (Ivan's logical theory). On this plot he gradually superimposed the Christian memory structure, giving his characters a symbolic pattern by which they could transcend themselves and the limitations of reason. The memory structure of the redemptive plot steadily acquires a primary motivating function in the novel, as a plot structure which moves the other plots forwards in order to leave open the possibility of redemptive change. We have thus to see the relationship between the plot and the memory structure in terms of the characters' redemptive memories.

This gives us another perspective on Bakhtin's metaphor of polyphony which he uses to express the *differentia specifica* of Dostoevsky's art. Bakhtin did not conceive of polyphony as relativism. He clearly acknowledged the authoritative primacy of Christ in Dostoevsky's art when he said that the 'image of Christ represents for him the resolution of all ideological quests. This image or this highest voice must crown the world of voices, must organise and subdue it' (97). If we understand polyphony as that type of multi-voiced musical composition based on a liturgical *cantus firmus*, and if, following Børtnes's insight, we identify the voice of Christ as the *cantus firmus* of *The Brothers Karamazov*, we may be able to reconcile Bakhtin's thesis with the exemplary fates represented in the novel.[19] A *cantus firmus* is a pre-existent melody 'which remains firm to its original shape while the parts around it are varying with the counterpoint'. It is the sole, completely autonomous voice in an imitation. All the other parts are only relatively independent since, while interacting with each other, they are all variously imitating that voice. This gives us two voice levels, the *cantus firmus* and all the others, radically differentiated by oppositions such as independent/dependent, invariant/variants, singular/plural, heavenly/earthly, and divine/human, among others. The narrator, characters and author are located on the latter level. Their words and images are all variations on this unique voice, whether they are accepting it in the form, of various imitations, or denying it through a range of inversions and perversions, they are all responding to Him. Each voice is independent in that it retains its distinctive identity, its own melodic line which never completely merges with any other. At the same time, all the parts are equal not relative to each other, but in their subordination to the voice of 'eternal verity'. Thus, for Dostoevsky, truth is not something he has got, though he knows the direction in which it lies. Truth is something Other, something he tries to find by listening with the utmost acuity to others, from the basest scoundrel to the righteous saint. Amongst all the discordant and harmonious voices, he is seeking the one voice which is ultimately the voice of Christ. Only by letting all the earthly voices sound together with the utmost freedom can he hope to divine this one voice. And if he can then demonstrate the presence of this voice in everyone without exception, he will have achieved his great goal of demonstrating its omnipresence in the world. Thus, truth for Dostoevsky is not relative but dialogic in this special sense of seeking. Once we know what this kind of polyphony is, we can hear it.

Dostoevsky also seeks that 'highest image' in the world of images he created for his novel. From the most debased (Smerdyakov), grotesque (Fyodor) to the most beautiful

(Alyosha, his mother Sophia) he aims to discern and represent various aspects, even the faintest reflections, of that highest image in their acts and gestures. If the memory of His Word can be shown to exist in the individual memories of the novel's protagonists, then we would expect that the shape of their voices becomes subject to various subtle interferences from the *cantus firmus*. Thus, the realisation of Dostoevsky's polyphonically attuned artistic vision depends on representing the *cantus firmus* and its image in everybody's memory, in each individual consciousness. The extent to which the characters remember and heed this voice, and act according to that image, will bear in the most decisive way on their fates. These pressure points where the *cantus firmus* breaks in are just what Dostoevsky is listening for, those moments when the highest image becomes perceptible are what he attempts to represent. They are the real turning points of the novel.

When viewed from the divine pattern, then, Bakhtin is basically right in relegating plot and ideas to the functional or secondary aspects of Dostoevsky's novel. Dostoevsky represents in his novel what he sees as the working of the divine, of the trans-real or trans-rational in the world. The 'higher reality' as a reflection of the divine is a poetic reality which transcends the prosaic world of causality towards a world of correspondences and equivalences. As Roman Jakobson has shown in his analyses of the most diverse verbal material, the creation of equivalences, similarities and differences is a primary feature of the poetic function of language. The world Dostoevsky created in *The Brothers Karamazov* is held together by these poetic principles and not by the principle of causation. He aimed to transcend the mundane world of cause and effect into a world of art where the divine can be poetically represented. It is when the pragmatic and ideological plots move from the level of causality to the level of 'imputed equivalences' to the Christian pattern, that they acquire a genuinely poetic function. In the creation of this plot we encounter Dostoevsky as a Christian poet. It is here that his art becomes an expression of a 'higher realism'.

Initially Christ's words present us with an enigma which

may linger in our memory as we read. Only in retrospect, only after we have followed the individual fates of the characters and analysed their memories can we know that the Epigraph is a genuine anticipation.

CHAPTER 4

The memories of the characters: forms of affirmative memory

Their memorie Shall as a Patterne, or a Measure, live.

Henry IV Part II

ALYOSHA: ICONOGRAPHY AND HAGIOGRAPHY

When analysing the characters' memories, we soon find that we have to divide them into two main categories, those that affirm the system of Christian memory and those that negate it. To the affirmative category belong above all the memories of the hero. Alyosha is the only brother whom the narrator introduces into his expository retrospect of Book One with a specific memory from childhood.

After briefly recounting the tragic life of Alyosha's mother, the narrator brings his hero into the family history with the following remark: 'When she died Alyosha was going on four and although it is strange, I know that he remembered his mother afterwards for all his life, – like through a dream, to be sure' (14,13). There is already discernible in his utterance about Alyosha a more intimate, partial accent, absent from his chronicling of the other characters' lives. This has to do with the way the narrator's memory meets that of his hero. Significant for poetic memory is the narrator's implicit positioning of himself at a point where he has a perspective on Alyosha's whole life. In fact, he is now, for the sake of narration, remembering that his hero remembered his mother for 'all his life'. He personally vouches ('I know') for the truth of his hero's memory. Logically this can only mean that he knows because he remembers Alyosha's having told him. But so far he is cautious and, as if anticipating objections from his reader, he acknowledges that his assertion is 'strange' and adds a concessionary qualification 'like through a dream, to be sure'. The terms 'strange', 'remembered', 'mother' and 'dream', he attaches to his hero's semantic sphere at the outset. He thus presents the reader from the very beginning with the idea that there is something 'strange' about Alyosha who first enters the story with his personal support and in conjunction with his dream-like memory of his dead mother. And indeed it is a dream-like vision of Alyosha, subtly prefigured here, which will later constitute the transcendental heart of the novel, and which he will also remember 'for all his life'.

In the chapter devoted to Alyosha's childhood, the narrator brings in a new variation on the same theme, beginning in a seemingly casual manner but now with more far-reaching implications: 'By the way, I already mentioned about him that, though he lost his mother when only going on four, he remembered her afterwards for all his life, her face, her caresses, "just as though she is standing before me alive"' (14,18). Repetitions in Dostoevsky's fiction are used to extend and intensify the semantic range of an idea by passing it through another's voice, another context. The idea that Alyosha remembered his mother for his whole life is now given in his direct speech as opposed to the reported speech in the narrator's first version of the theme. The vaguely embodied image of Alyosha's mother is that seen (and remembered) from the viewpoint of a small child for whom the mother's face and caresses (a metonymy for his mother's love) are all important. Alyosha's first words in the novel are a direct quotation about his memory of his mother: 'just as though she is standing before me alive'. Coming at the emphatic end position of the sentence, Alyosha's direct present-tense speech seems to burst from the embrace of the narrator's indirect past-tense context. This sudden shift from the narrator's past tense to the hero's present harmonises with the content of the message. Through this figure of grammar, the narrator breaches the rigid boundary separating Alyosha from his mother, the past from the present, the dead from the living, before launching into a general discourse on childhood memory: 'Such memories may be remembered (and this everyone knows) from an even earlier age, even from two years old, but only standing out all one's life like points of light from the dark, like a little corner torn out from an enormous picture which had all been extinguished and disappeared only except for that tiny little corner' (14,18). The narrator draws us in with a rhetorical parenthetical appeal to our childhood memories. Mid sentence he shifts into the poetic register with two graphic similes for memory (light and picture) which become vital constituents of Alyosha's image. Though very small in scale, they may, like seeds, become large and powerful in their long-range effects. Points of light may burst into radiant effulgence, a little corner may expand into a full fledged image.

The narrator's general discourse on childhood memory serves as a metaphorical transition to the third, most elaborate and most important variation on the theme of Alyosha's early memory:

That was just how it was with him: he remembered one still summer evening, an open window, the slanting rays of the setting sun (it was the slanting rays he remembered most of all), in the room, in the corner, an icon, before it a lighted icon lamp, and before the icon on her knees, sobbing in hysteria, with shrieking and wailing, his mother, seizing him with both hands, embracing him hard, till it hurt, and praying for him to the Mother of God, holding him from her embrace with both hands up to the icon as though to put him under the protection of the Mother of God ... and suddenly in runs the nurse and snatches him from her in fright. There's the picture! (14,18)

Two voices, two similar emotional cadences merge in this key passage. Alyosha is not reporting his memory himself in the 'here and now' of the story. Nor does the narrator reproduce his hero's memory in his own indirect speech. Rather he perceives Alyosha in the act of remembering and mimics that act by representing Alyosha's memory in Alyosha's language, trying to preserve his hero's diction, visual imagery and intonations. This is Alyosha's memory but it is formally delivered by the narrator as though it were his own. This 'talking in another's stead' is what Bakhtin–Voloshinov call 'substituted direct discourse' which is characterised by a 'parallelism of intonations', a complete interchange of tones between the narrator's voice and that of the character.[1] Such discourse serves to express a 'complete solidarity' between author and hero, 'no interference takes place' in their merged languages. The narrator's emotive exclamation, 'There's the picture!', is symptomatic of this discourse which 'all the more underscores the author's identification with his hero'. Only for Alyosha does the narrator adopt this type of discourse. In other words, the narrator fully shares his hero's veneration of his memory, he is remembering with his hero, alongside him. To do so, he abolishes his own context, he again relinquishes his control. In imitating his hero in the act of remembering, the narrator at one stroke verifies his hero's memory, demonstrates his solidarity with him, and attempts to make Alyosha's mother stand before the reader as though she were 'alive'.

The dominant participial structure of the passage (in the Russian text) and the enframing deployment of finite verbs furnish us with an example in prose of the 'poetry of grammar and grammar of poetry'. The perfective verb 'remembered' which introduces Alyosha's memory underscores its singularity. From the end of 'he remembered' to the suspension points, there is no finite verb except the one contained in the narrator's parenthetical remark which is not a representation of the memory *per se* but his comment on it. All the actions within the memory-image featuring Alyosha with his mother are conveyed through participles which are by definition weakly marked temporally. Two past passive participles used adjectivally qualify two 'passive' inanimate objects: the 'open[ed] window' and the 'lighted icon lamp'. These participles, because they denote actions which entailed the purposeful touch of human hands, tend, by contiguity, to animate the objects, one devotional, the other opening out to the world. The mother's screams are transmitted by two temporally indeterminate verbal nouns 'shrieking and wailing' which, as Terras notes, suggest 'prolonged wails and screams', and hence prolonged suffering.[2] Her manner of holding her son is conveyed by past active participles, '[was] seizing and embracing', a desperate grip of the maternal hands which Alyosha vividly experienced. Significantly, his mother's suffering ('sobbing'), her ritual devotional acts ('praying, raising her son up to the icon') and the symbolic image of the 'setting sun' are cast in present active participles which are the least marked temporally. In this verbless, and therefore timeless space, the sacralised memory image is mounted.

The sudden entry of the frightened nurse who grabs the child away from his mother, breaks the spell. Her hasty actions, conveyed by present tense verbs, come as a rude eruption into the picture. This switch to finite present tense verbs keeps the sacralised image strictly separate from the reality of domestic life represented by the nurse. Again the poetry of grammar reinforces the author's most important message. Since the narrator designates this scene as a memory, it is by definition a past event. But he also wishes to convey the atemporality of sacred memory and the sense that this memory remained alive in Alyosha 'for all his life'. This he achieves most effectively by casting the memory-image in participles and framing it in finite verbs. Whatever is atemporal partakes of the permanent, the eternal.

The reader is pulled back to the narrator's present by his exclamation: 'There's the picture!' which literally emphasises the imaged nature of this scene. The representation is narrated in the same terms one might use to describe a picture before which one was 'standing'.[3] This image, distanced by memory and veneration, is animated by an extraordinary surface agitation, and at the same time, is held in suspension like a painting. It is precisely the participles which simultaneously restrain the action from moving along a linear temporal plane and keep the scene from congealing into the stasis of a still-life. But to which genre does this 'picture' belong?

I believe it belongs to iconography. The image of Alyosha and his mother is reminiscent of iconographic images of the divine Mother and Child. Whenever events or images cease to stand only for themselves, whenever something lies behind or beyond them, then the text calls out for completion, interpretation. This scene is both generic and highly individualised because there are two other figures here besides Sophia and Alyosha (before the nurse's frightened entry). Sophia is praying to an icon of the Mother of God (*Bogoroditsa*) to protect her child. The very appellation 'Mother of God' evokes the image of her Child. By this juxtaposition the creative imagination of the reader is activated: since Sophia is portrayed with her mortal child, we supply the *Bogoroditsa* with her divine Child in order to complete the similarity relation between the two. This is the poetic function of the parallel. Two mother-child images face each other, the one serenely divine, merciful and elevated, the other mortal, innocently suffering and supplicating. The two sets of figures are brought together in a crucial configuration in Alyosha's memory. Their proximity creates an idea of similarity between the sacred historical figures on the icon and the earthly fictional characters. At the same time, there are a number of intrinsic differences between them, the first hierarchical.

By juxtaposing a holy image to an earthly one, the author establishes a relationship between them which has both analogous and antonymous features. Lotman distinguishes between parallel members wherein both members are equally analogous to each other and parallels wherein one member is subordinate to a second one, taking analogous features from it as a model.[4] The parallel between the two sets of figures here can only be of the latter kind, Christ and the *Bogoroditsa* being the divine prototype. We have here a relationship based on the Urbild–Abbild–Aesthetik which governs the composition of *vitae* and icon-painting in the Eastern Church.[5] The sacred Urbild is used as a model for the earthly Abbild in order to endow the hero with certain traits vital for the author's largest aims. However, although Dostoevsky has configured Alyosha and his mother into an imitation of the *Bogoroditsa* and Christ-child, it is an imitation with jarring dissonances owing to other crucial differences between the parallel sets of figures.

Alyosha and his mother are not divine beings but earthly mortals destined to suffer and to know death. Dostoevsky's attempt to give human suffering a meaning begins here, with

Alyosha's memory, where he is juxtaposed to the Child foreordained to become the 'Man of Sorrows', the prototype of redemptive suffering. Later, when Zosima prophesies to Alyosha that he will know 'much sorrow' in his life, the reader may recall that the future hero's path of sorrow was prefigured here. Alyosha's treasured memory of his mother is one of turbulent fright and suffering. The mother of Alyosha's memory is a *mater dolorosa* with the object of her agony inverted – a living child rather than a dead adult divine Son. (A representation of the archetypal *Mater Dolorosa* finds a habitation in Zosima's cell among his varied holy images.) This dissonance reflects a very traditional Orthodox idea. Alyosha's iconic memory-image is an inversion in this world of a heavenly harmony, an adumbration of heavenly bliss by its opposite, earthly suffering. In Alyosha's memory, his innocent mother's screams tear across the image leaving it just barely intact. His mother is depicted in an unrelieved sobbing and shrieking fit which prevents her from realising that her tight grip on her son is hurting him. Such an experience could only be extremely frightening and bewildering to a small child. And yet this scene becomes a venerated image for Alyosha which, it soon emerges, determines his path in life. Why should this frightening episode become a precious memory for him, and why is his mother praying so desperately for him? Merely to say that she was a 'shrieker' will not do. To answer these questions we have to combine our knowledge of subsequent developments with the symbolic motifs embedded in this passage.

The narrator's parenthetical 'it was the slanting rays he remembered most of all' – is outside the memory-image proper, but for that very reason attracts attention. Normally what a child would remember 'most of all' would be his mother and his fright over her inexplicable suffering. But Alyosha remembered 'most of all' 'the slanting rays of the setting sun'. This implies that the sun is no mere scenic adjunct but has a symbolic meaning transcending fear, suffering, maternal love and death. It is one of the most important memory statements in the novel.

Interpreting a symbol, one has to take into account its traditional meaning as well as the particular meaning it acquires within a given artistic system. The setting sun, which traditionally symbolises the 'death' of the day, is also a symbol of the approaching death of a human being. The first appearance of the symbol here hints at the imminent death of Alyosha's mother who died less than two years after this episode. Given the context of the narrator's references to Sophia's early death, it is as though this transfigured moment is Alyosha's last memory of his mother alive. Indeed, the depiction of Sophia here is a mimesis of a person *in extremis*. Now the reader already knows what sort of a 'father' Fyodor Karamazov is. Thus, at the moment represented in the memory, Sophia may have sensed her approaching end and, given Fyodor's abandonment of his first son, she would be desperately fearing for her beloved son's fate. Last memories, final gestures, project this scene into a threshold situation, a critical turning point condensed into a graphic image. And at the threshold between life and death the vespertine sun rays, standing out against the darkening room, fall on mother and child like a benediction. This image of the setting sun is very likely a reminiscence of an old Orthodox evensong hymn, *Vespertine Light*, which would have been familiar to Dostoevsky, where the image stands as a symbol of Christ.[6]

The ritual aspect of this scene is also important. Sophia's gesture of lifting Alyosha towards the icon in the rays of the setting sun is an imitation of a consecration. She, a suffering mother, appeals to a serene image of the merciful Mother who, because she also once suffered for her Son's sake, will be moved by her plight and answer her prayer. Sophia's plea to the Mother of God to put Alyosha 'under protection', to take over her role, acquires for him a sacred authority, implants in him a sense of mission and a trusting feeling that he lives under divine protection. The word for protection, *pokrov*, is biblical; it also denotes an Orthodox holiday devoted to the *Bogoroditsa*, and is often invoked as an attribute of Christ in the phraseological formula 'Lord, my protection' (*Gospod'*, *pokrov moi*). So, early in life Alyosha gained the spiritual

Mother, just as later he is meant to find a spiritual father in Zosima.

The slanting rays of the setting sun are a visible symbol of the presence of divine Grace. With this symbolic motif the author establishes the first connection between the mortal and the divine, between heaven and earth. But so far the connection is suggested solely by an image. A two-year-old cannot tell what he is experiencing. He experiences images before he can name things. Altogether, Dostoevsky favours the use of image over verbal memory for representing the early stages of his hero's life. Indeed, not a word is spoken in this scene, its gestural aspect being underscored by the narrator's further arresting comment: 'Alyosha remembered at that moment the face of his mother too: he used to say that it was frenzied, but beautiful, judging by what he could remember. But he rarely liked to entrust this memory to anyone' (14,18). Alyosha's reticence underlines the sacred nature of this memory and establishes the narrator as a trustworthy person. More importantly, it poetically aligns Sophia with the divine prototype. This image of Alyosha's mother is an extreme variation on the trace of sorrow traditionally depicted on the Mother of God's face who foresees the suffering of her Son.[7]

This memory has become an icon *for* Alyosha, a venerated image which can be evoked through repeated recollection. It is also an icon *of* Alyosha, for by way of symbolic parallelism, the author transposes his hero's memory-image onto the transcendental plane, and marks him as a singular mortal, chosen to fulfil some divine purpose. Alyosha's memory of his consecration to the Mother of God is the founding hagiographic episode of his 'life story'.

The final meaning of this epiphanous passage will always elude logical analysis. This is because the hero's iconic memory is meant to suggest three main ideas which do not lend themselves to rational determination: the omnipresence of the divine, resurrection and the efficacy of prayer. The first idea is suggested by the sun which, divinised as an image of Grace, sheds its ever recurring light over the world. As for resurrection, the memory itself is a mimetic representation of this idea.

Together the rememberers, Alyosha and the narrator, resurrect a vivid image of a person long dead so that she seems to be 'alive' before us. The author, in 'painting' his new 'picture' of mother and child, 'resurrects' the tradition of the icon. The perpetuation of culture proceeds by intermittent re-creations and re-interpretations of past models. The literal resurrection of human beings in the Christian sense is an idea the author also attempts to broach through memory motifs expressed in figures of grammar which break down the oppositions between past and present, the eternal and transient, the living and the dead. The third idea, the answering of prayers, is a promise which the narrative has yet to fulfil as events unfold.

The hero's iconic memory image is set within the chapter devoted to an exposition of his childhood, 'The Third Son Alyosha'. As Børtnes and Vetlovskaia have shown, Dostoevsky used a collection of hagiographical topoi, modified for incorporation into a novel of contemporary life, in his depiction of Alyosha.[8] Typical for this genre is the emphasis on saintly traits which are innate (since they are divine gifts) and which manifest themselves in childhood. Thus the narrator tells us that Alyosha 'even then was already very strange, beginning even from the cradle' (14,18). He places particular emphasis on two traits. The first, and most important is Alyosha's 'gift for arousing a special love for himself' which 'he contained within himself, so to speak, in his very nature, unaffectedly and directly <...> Yes, and everyone loved this youth, wherever he appeared, and this was so even from his childhood years' (14,19). A second innate quality of Alyosha, subsequently repeated, sets the divine action plan in motion: 'and if he struck out on the monastic road that was only because at that time it seemed to him, so to say, an ideal end for his soul longing to burst out of the darkness of worldly malice to the light of love' (14,17). It is not so surprising, then, that the seeker after 'the light of love' should remember the slanting sun rays 'most of all'.

Further saintly traits the narrator emphasises are Alyosha's deep inner absorption, his phenomenal chastity, his indifference to material riches, his refusal to judge others and an inviolable core of his personality which took it as an 'axiom' that no one could offend him. All events revealing these traits stand for repetition; they issue from the narrator's memory. The iconic memory issues from the hero's memory and depicts an event that occurred only once. The very singularity of the memory event highlights the uniqueness of both image and hero. Thus, in creating the image of his hero Dostoevsky is simultaneously resurrecting the memory of two ancient genres, iconography and hagiography, which share a common purpose and meaning. All icons and hagiographies are variations on and interpretations of the paradigmatic biblical narratives. In the Orthodox Church a hagiography is a verbal, and an icon a graphic, representation of an eternal truth. Through them one reaches closer to that truth. The author's aim was to establish a similarity between his selected elements from the traditional set of hagiographical and iconographic topoi, and his new set of Alyosha's inherent characteristics in order to transform his hero into an image of the divine prototype. The memory-image establishes a contiguity relation between the fictitious hero and the historical Christ; the childhood narrative is based on a metaphorical relation to hagiographical models. Thus, Alyosha not only represents a particular, psychologically unique individual living in a particular time and place, but is meant to remind the contemporary reader (and those in the novel's world) of those prototypes, of those ideal truths. He thus comes into the novel saturated with memory, with the long background of the Christian tradition. This is why the reporting of Alyosha's sacred memory and the narrative of his childhood can have no causal connection with the criminal ideological plot. Nevertheless, the reader has been encouraged to expect that they will play a vital role in the hero's 'life story', a story which finds its primary significance on the providential level of the divine masterplot.

Dostoevsky's narratives begin to expand when the evolutionary tempo of his protagonists' lives is suddenly interrupted by some dramatic event catapulting them from a status quo to a critical turning point. Thus we would expect that Alyosha's 'sudden' urge in early youth to visit his native town will lead to a dramatic change in his life, as indeed it does:

After arriving in our town, to the first queries of his father: 'just why have you come without finishing your course?' he made no direct answer but was, as they say, thoughtful as usual. It soon emerged that he was seeking his mother's grave. He himself was even on the point of acknowledging that that was the only reason why he came. But that hardly exhausted the whole reason for his arrival. It is most probable of all, that he himself did not know then and could not have explained for anything: just what had suddenly as if risen from his soul and drawn him irresistibly on some sort of new, unknown but already inevitable path. (14,20–1)

The reticence, the vagueness of both hero and narrator are one with the content and the author's aims. The narrator subsumes Alyosha's purpose under the vague 'It soon emerged', rather than a causal construction or conventional explanation. 'Then' Alyosha 'was on the point of acknowledging' implies that later he came to see his arrival in a different light. Although the narrator is speaking long after the event, he does not take advantage of his hindsight by even attempting to provide an omniscient explanation, beyond asserting that his hero's ostensible motive 'hardly exhausted the whole reason'. Indeed the search for his mother's grave cannot be the 'whole reason', for it is only a pointer on the way to a larger goal. And right here we see the contours of the divine masterplot emerging. Silences, fragmentarily expressed thoughts and feelings impart a sense of mysterious background which call for interpretation. Cautiously hedged with a cluster of indefinite words, quietly slipped into the phrase – 'already inevitable road', is the first intimation of the obscure, delayed but 'inevitable' workings of Providence. Alyosha is driven by an unknown, invisible force, but it is a force with an aim, irresistibly drawing the hero to a 'new road'. The sudden upspringing of this force masks the designs of Providence with an appearance of fortuity. For if this road is 'already inevitable', that can only mean that Alyosha was predestined to take it, that Providence has chosen this moment to intervene in determining his path. Because he has been marked as a potential saint, Alyosha is not autonomous in the usual sense. Like all saints, he is guided by a higher power in order to fulfil a destiny already prefigured in his early memories.

The old loyal servant, Grigory, takes Alyosha to his mother's grave which he himself has erected and funded. The modest grave of the 'shrieker', the devotion of Grigory and the unbroken silence of Alyosha form a mute scene of restrained and humble pathos. This is the first of two graveside scenes in the novel, both presided over by Alyosha. Here he is speechless. In the last scene of the novel by Ilyusha's stone, he is eloquent. His change from silence to commemorative speech will then be a measure of his spiritual growth in the course of the novel.

The consequences of Alyosha's visit to his mother's grave quickly follow when he 'suddenly' announces to Fyodor that he 'wants to enter the monastery' and asks his 'solemn permission, as his father' (14,22). Another hagiographical topos emerges here; the imperative to leave the father's house in order to enter the spiritual path.

Shortly thereafter the narrator locates that force which drew his hero to Zosima and the monastic path in Alyosha's childhood memories:

From the memories of his childhood, perhaps something was preserved about our local monastery where his mother may have taken him to early evening mass. Perhaps the slanting rays of the setting sun before which his shrieker-mother held him up affected him too. Thoughtful he came to us then perhaps only to take a look: is everything here or are there only two roubles here, and – in the monastery he met this elder ... (14,25–6)

Each of the three reasons the narrator offers to explain what brought Alyosha to the local monastery is prefaced by a qualificatory 'perhaps'. He intends all three to be taken seriously, but in cultivating an air of uncertainty about it he aims to indicate that there is a zone of reality here beyond ordinary experience and understanding. Alyosha is configured as one who both seeks, and is led, by 'something' preserved in his memories of early evening prayer services (*obednia*), the time of sunset, impelling him back to the monastery after an absence of many years. The 'something' obliquely emerges in the next sentence where the narrator invokes his hero's iconic memory, selecting its kernel image – the shrieker mother holding up Alyosha before 'the slanting rays of the setting sun'. This first recurrence of the solar symbol in the context of the hero's choice of path in life confirms that he moves under divine direction, that the memory of the slanting rays of the sun is drawing him to the crucial meeting of his young life. Alyosha's 'everything, or only two roubles' is a variation on a favourite Dostoevskian theme of 'all or nothing', which reflects the largest 'all or nothing' of the novel, faith or atheism. The concluding phrase highlights the role of Zosima in settling Alyosha's decision. It is set off with a dash and comes to a halt on three suspension points. These graphic retarders force a pause. It is as though the narrator cannot find words adequate to express this extraordinary elder, this extraordinary meeting. His inability to continue typifies the hagiographic tones of the inexpressibility topos which Curtius defines as an 'emphasis upon inability to cope with the subject'.[9]

Vetlovskaia says the initial meeting between Alyosha and Zosima 'is fortuitous'.[10] However, combining these passages together with subsequent developments compels the conclusion that what Vetlovskaia ascribes to fortuity is more apparent than real. Fortuity is a veil masking a balder statement which the author's artistic tact prevented him from spelling out literally. Both childhood memories, the iconic memory and the memory of monastery services, are memories featuring prayers. Years later Alyosha is 'suddenly' seized by a wish to honour his mother's memory by visiting her grave in his native town. Just as she took Alyosha to the monastery in childhood, so years later the memory of her, still alive in him, leads him back to that same monastery where he finds his spiritual father Zosima, his 'light' out of 'darkness'. We have come one full circle. When the criminal story begins, Alyosha has already chosen the spiritual path and been under Zosima's guidance for a year. Something 'suddenly' urged Alyosha to find his mother's grave, bringing him to his native town; 'something' stirred Alyosha's latent memories of childhood visits to

Zosima's monastery subconsciously drawing him back there. What is the agency and function of this impulsive subliminal calling? Auerbach says, 'God is always <...> represented in the Bible' as having background, 'for he is not comprehensible in his presence <...> it is always only "something" of him that appears, he always extends into the depths'.[11] The audible voice of God calling to the biblical heroes and the great Christian saints was a voice that could no longer be used directly in the nineteenth century. As a replacement, Dostoevsky used the common phenomenon of sudden, involuntary memory as a way of naturalising those impulses he believed were of supernatural origin, while retaining a sense of their mysterious origins.

At the time of the story Alyosha is not conscious of this process, nor does the narrator impose his own explanations. For the author knew that investing either Alyosha with full consciousness, or the narrator with omniscience, would have destroyed his hero's hagiographical image and turned him into a psychologically comprehensible human character in a realistic novel. Using sudden sequential memories, along with hints from the narrator, to move the narrative over many years, the author leaves it to the reader to make a connection which he wishes to be unavoidable, namely, that the prayers of the faithful raised up from suffering to the Mother of God are not lost or futile. She hears them, remembers them and intercedes with God who eventually answers them. The introduction of Alyosha in a novice's cassock is evidence that his dead mother's prayers have been answered, so far.

This is the last explicit reference to Alyosha's iconographic memory. But its symbolic power is not extinguished, for it continues to ramify in diverse ways throughout the novel, silently exerting an influence on the hero's life and on all those close to him. The workings of memory, both in the life plot of Alyosha and in its circulations through the text, continue to take on transcendental functions and meanings. The workings of providential Grace are revealed along a route mapped out by memory, in the subtle embeddings of this idea throughout the novel. The 'something' acting at a temporal distance on the unconscious or preconscious of the heroes, may account for Rosen's identification of the 'real hero' of *The Brothers Karamazov* as 'the spirit of God acting through all the Karamazovs'.[12] While agreeing with Rosen, I would extend the action of God to everyone in the novel's world, and would make a slightly different emphasis in identifying the real hero as God in His Incarnation as Christ. To find Christ is the ideal end of all journeys in this novel and the route goes through memory, cultural and individual.

ALYOSHA AND ZOSIMA

Dostoevsky saw his society as one in which there was 'little poetry, little spiritual nourishment'.[13] He believed that Russia was under mortal danger from the forces of nihilism, materialism and atheistic socialism. Should these menacing forces gain the upper hand, moral anarchy and apocalypse would universally ensue. At the same time he was convinced that the highest truth and moral beauty lay in the Bible, and secondarily in those sacred texts derived from it, especially hagiography. He was equally convinced that these truths had to be conveyed to his compatriots, and the world, if they were to be saved from catastrophe. Because of the contemporary demand for realism, he knew that mere quotation from these sacred ancient sources would not suffice to bring them fully to life in a persuasive, moving way. He could not simply copy the protagonists of the Bible and hagiography. Nor was it enough to have his narrator discuss 'ancient legends', the history of elderdom and the theological concept of the bond of obedience between elder and novice. He also created an 'artistic picture' of a contemporary elder, Zosima, and his novice, Alyosha. This picture he constructed almost entirely on the principle of poetic memory, cultural, personal and narrational. Memory, not fantasy, is a way to give an impression of reality to events, and to link that reality with the great paradigmatic memorials of the past. Reality should not be confused with history or factography. Dostoevsky never aimed to convince only by a rhetoric of realism, a rhetoric under whose sway we still make our aesthetic evaluations. He was himself greatly stirred by the unique poetics of the biblical and hagiographical genres and he created his two ideal protagonists mainly from them.

First and foremost Alyosha and Zosima are closely bound together by the memory of the two genres they impersonate, hagiography and the Bible. However, they are not mere schematic, allegorical figures such as these genres may be expected to produce. On the contrary, many convergent personal memories conjoin their life paths, bringing them together into a spiritual father–son relationship. Both the genre reminiscences, and their personal memories, form a poetic system of synonymous parallels where the memories, thoughts and experiences of the one reinforce those of the other through repetition, similarity and supplementation. For example, Zosima's discourse in the *Life* on the importance of precious childhood memories reinforces and supplements Alyosha's iconic memory, just as it semantically prefigures Alyosha's speech in the Epilogue.

Sometimes the narrator plays a part in this parallel process as when he introduces a motif that harks back to Alyosha's memory of his mother. Alyosha, he says, was especially moved when, accompanying Zosima on his rounds, he would see the simple people flocking to his elder for his blessings. Twice the narrator says: 'the peasant women held up their children to him' (14,28,29). This pluralised repetition of the gesture of Alyosha's mother in his memory sets her individual gesture in a social context that reinforces its ritual meaning. Coincidentally, it links her faith with that of the people just as it affirms Zosima as a holy person with compassion for their suffering. Discussing the phenomenon of 'shriekers', the narrator inserts a rare autobiographical remark: 'in my childhood I often happened to see and hear these shriekers in the villages and monasteries' (14,44). The narrator's insight into the plight of the shriekers who represent not only an individual phenomenon (Alyosha's mother) but a social one emphasises the social character of memory.

The next memory motif occurs when Zosima interrupts the Karamazov family gathering, leaving his cell in the company of Alyosha to minister to a waiting crowd of peasant pilgrims. The narrator's focus shifts over several confessing pilgrims, pausing longest to highlight one of the novel's most important episodic figures, the grieving mother who has just lost her last child, having buried three before him. The representation of the mother's grief is an example of controlled pathos which depends on the direct transmission of her memories of her dead son.

The mother relates how she lays out all her dead son's articles of clothing, his 'little shirt' and 'little boots', looks at them and 'wails'. Interesting here is the way Zosima uses his memory of sacred texts, biblical and hagiographical, to comfort the mother. He first relates an episode from the Russian Orthodox *Prologue* where St Julian succeeds in consoling a bereaved mother with his assurance that her children have gone to heaven.[14] However, Zosima's pilgrim remains unconsoled. In one of the most powerful auditory images in Dostoevsky's fiction, the mother imitates the child's voice and footsteps so that he can almost be heard running towards her in the silence of our reading. As she expresses her unassuageable longing to see him 'just for a minute', to hear his footsteps, and his call 'Mama, where are you?', the dead child seems to come to life. Violently sobbing, she shows Zosima the child's 'little belt'. Zosima responds with a direct biblical quotation: 'It is Rachel weeping for her children and would not be comforted because they are not' (Matthew 2:18, Jeremiah 31:15). In fact, the 'ancient Rachel' was not weeping over her dead children, but over her barrenness (Genesis 30:1,22). Striking here is Zosima's superimposition of the biblical image on the grieving woman kneeling before him ('It is Rachel'). Zosima has so internalised the Word that he sees the whole world in which he lives as an image of that text, of that Word. Linking the pilgrim's grief with the weeping of the biblical 'ancient Rachel', Zosima sanctifies the woman's suffering and universalises her image. In Zosima's vision of the world, the archetypal biblical events are being repeated now, everywhere in his contemporary Russia. Finally, Zosima encourages her to weep and prophesies that in the end her weeping 'will turn into a quiet joy' (14,46). Embedded in his last phrase is a hidden quotation of the words Christ uttered to comfort his disciples by prophesying His Resurrection: 'Ye shall be sorrowful but your sorrow shall be turned into joy' (John 16:20). Zosima's memory of sacred texts describes an ascending order of authority and inspiration, from Orthodox hagiography, to the Old Testament and the Evangelist and finally culminates in a quotation from Christ, the prototypal comforter and prophet of the greatest consolation of all, the promise of immortality. Thus, Dostoevsky makes an Old Testament episode serve the central New Testament prophecy in a context of grief and loss of a child precisely at the first direct affirmation of immortality in the novel, and after a powerful evocation of memories of maternal love.

Zosima promises to remember the child in his prayers and asks her his name: 'Aleksey, batyushka. – A sweet name. After Aleksey Man of God? – Of God, batyushka, of God, Aleksey Man of God' (14,47). As other commentators have remarked, the silent presence here of Alyosha, the saint's living namesake, serves to associate him to this popular saint and the people's faith. This scene also parallels that of Alyosha's visit to his mother's grave, only there is a complementary inversion; here a mother grieves for her dead three-year-old Alyosha, in the earlier scene the young man Alyosha silently mourns his long dead mother. This mother's suffering love for her Alyosha inevitably reminds the reader of Alyosha's mother's love for him. The pilgrim lost her Alyosha who was about the same age as Alyosha when he lost his mother. There are two little child Alyoshas in the novel, the one, the hero, now a young man, the other a dead child momentarily summoned to life by his mother's memory. In one of those metamorphoses which art can effect, Alyosha the hero becomes a fleeting 'resurrection' of the dead child Alyosha, just as the 'shriekers' and this mother are momentary 'resurrections' of his own mother. These parallels are underlined by synonymous memory motifs and syntactic parallels, almost word for word. Remembering her child, the pilgrim mother intones: 'I can't forget him. It's just as if he is standing right here in front of me, he doesn't go away'

(14,45). Her phrase almost exactly mirrors Alyosha's utterance about his memory of his mother: 'just as though she is standing before me alive'. Once again, an abiding memory expressed in the present tense 'resurrects' a beloved dead person, thus bridging the chasm between the dead and the living.

The theme of neglect, of forgetting, is also part of this scene. Absorbed in her grief, the woman has abandoned her husband: 'He's begun drinking without me <...> he's weak. But now I don't think about him <...> I've forgotten about everything and I don't want to remember <...> I've finished with him, finished, I've finished with everyone' (14,45). Zosima rebukes her: 'Only it's a sin for you to leave him', and urges: 'Go to your husband and take care of him.' Zosima concludes with the first impassioned affirmation of immortality (the last will be uttered by Alyosha): 'He's alive, alive, for the soul is alive forever <...> Go to your husband.' The truth of this suddenly seizes her. She at once vows to return home, and seems almost to be already there as she leaves the novel calling to her husband: 'Nikitushka mine own, Nikitushka, you're waiting for me, my dear, you're waiting!' (14,46–7) Once addressed, he is evoked, he exists and perhaps nothing could conjure up his absent image, his heavy lonely waiting, more than this cry.

There are two further echoes of the pilgrim mother's memory of her dead son in the novel's last chapter where a dead child's 'little boots' appear as a pathos-laden image of absence and stilled mobility. After returning home from Ilyusha's burial, Snegirov notices his son's 'little boots standing side by side', falls on his knees, snatches one up, and 'greedily' kissing it, cries: 'Ilyushechka, dear batyushka, where are your little feet?' (15,194) Minutes later, Alyosha includes this motif in his last speech in which he tries to impart the image of Ilyusha as an eternal memory: 'Let us remember his face, and his clothes and his poor little boots' (15,197). All these memory scenes are graphic instances of mutual love and trust between 'living' adults in the 'here and now' who cherish their (or others') children. These facts have often been forgotten by readers who become gripped by Ivan's horrific 'collection' of 'little facts', but they must be set against his imminent dossier of adults who maltreat children.

HAGIOGRAPHY AND THE BIBLE: ALYOSHA'S LIFE OF ZOSIMA

Hours before his death, Zosima for the first time divulges to his assembled followers his memories of his brother Markel with whom he mystically links his beloved novice Alyosha:

> never to this day have I said, not even to him, why the visage of this youth is so dear to my soul. Now only shall I tell: his visage was for me, as it were, a remembrance and a prophecy. At the dawn of my days, while still a small child, I had an elder brother who died while a youth <...> And then afterwards in the course of my life, I became gradually convinced that this brother of mine was, as it were, a guidance and a sign from on high, for had he not appeared in my life, had he not existed at all, perhaps, so I think, I would never have taken the monk's habit and entered upon this precious path. That first appearance was still in my childhood, but here at the end of my path there appeared before my eyes as though a repetition of him. It is miraculous, fathers and teachers, that Alyosha, who does not resemble him so much in his face, but only a little, seems to me so like him spiritually that many times I have taken him for that youth, my brother, who has mysteriously come to me at the end of my path as a certain remembrance and an inspiration, so that I even wondered myself at such a strange waking-dream (*mechta*) of mine. (14,259)

Looking back over many years, Zosima can now discern God's providential pattern to his life which moves in symbolic harmony with the sun. Markel at dawn, that time metaphorically associated with childhood, passed on to Zosima that light which accompanied him through his life's long day. Alyosha at sunset, that solar time symbolically associated to him, accompanies his elder to the end of his life which for them is the beginning of the eternal one. If Alyosha is a 'repetition' of Markel, mysteriously come back to him, then symbolically Markel has not died since the sun that rises and sets is the same. Here Zosima turns the spiritual similarity relation between Markel and Alyosha into a contiguity relation of coincidence (repetition), thus transforming them into twin brothers in spirit. Thus, Alyosha is at once a remembrance of Markel (a resurrection) and a prophetic figure of Markel's reappearance (his resurrection). The beginning is in the end and the end is in the beginning: the boundary between the past and present, the dead and the living, has been bridged by a circle of remembrance. Alyosha, then, represents for Zosima the miracle of resurrection, 'a sign from on high' of immortality who is thus at once an 'inspiration' and a 'prophecy'. This is the miracle, mystery and authority which Dostoevsky sought to affirm over those of the Grand Inquisitor.

In his last words uttered in the 'here and now' of the story, Zosima says: 'My heart has filled with tenderness, and I contemplate my whole life at this minute as if I were living all of it anew ... ' (14,259) From such a comprehensive vision, reminiscence and interpretation can begin their mutual process. These words are immediately followed by the narrator's brief introduction to Alyosha's *vita* of Zosima, the largest inserted genre in the novel. The *Life* has particular importance for a poetics of memory since it is entirely a personal memoir.

Introducing Zosima's *Life*, the narrator informs us that the 'long conversation' which took place on the 'last evening' of Zosima's life 'was a kind of last expression of tender emotion (*umilienie*)'. He also forewarns us that Zosima will die 'suddenly', 'on this very night'. All Zosima's following words, then, will be apprehended as confessional 'last words', and thus will carry particularly authority and dramatic intensity. Balanced on the border between life and death, Zosima now occupies the unique position for viewing all that lies behind, and for glimpsing what lies ahead.

In his prefatory and appended remarks to the *Life*, the narrator says that Alyosha wrote down part of Zosima's last conversation, including excerpts from previous ones, 'some time after the elder's death, from memory' (14,260,294). Alyosha's *vita* of Zosima contains the great bulk of the elder's memories and teachings. Thus, almost everything we know about Zosima has been mediated through Alyosha's memories of him. The very fact that he has retained them in his memory

and committed them to writing attests to their importance for
the hero and consequently for the whole novel. The narrator
stresses that Alyosha's account is not a verbatim record of
everything said on that last evening, that 'only an idea of the
spirit and character' of Zosima's utterances in his last conversation is given. Twice he calls Alyosha's manuscript 'a story'
and adds that the whole speech of the elder is carried on 'as
though he were expounding his life in the form of a tale'
(14,260).[15] Alyosha, then, has represented Zosima's discourses
as a literary artist, omitting all repartees which would have
detracted from his 'artistic picture' of his elder. Thus, it is not
correct to say that Alyosha is just an amanuensis, the dutiful
mouthpiece of Zosima. The *Life* is Alyosha's own artistic
composition which contains his selected words of Zosima and
it is he who has shaped his notes into a *vita*, complete with
hagiographical headings.[16]

This calls for a few general reflections on reported speech.
Reported speech is the word of another and, at the same time, a
word about another's words. Speech refers to things, but when
speech quotes someone else, it refers to words. The things still
retain their referential status, but in reported speech the
immediate referent is to another's words. Moreover, one
cannot represent another's word without conveying one's own
evaluation of it. Alyosha's exposition of his teacher's life
inevitably reflects his evaluation of that life. In choosing the
genre of the *vita*, he exhibits his elder's word as a paragon of
truth and righteousness. Thus, although Zosima has the word,
we constantly sense Alyosha supporting that word, or rather,
his memory of that word. Here two words, two languages, meet
in one work, and consequently the *Life* represents a dialogue
between Alyosha and Zosima. Apart from 'Cana of Galilee'
this is the only sustained harmonious dialogue of the novel.
These are all words Alyosha heard from a beloved person, they
were all spoken to him with love, they are all inspired by love
for God and His whole creation. Dostoevsky said that he wrote
'The Russian Monk' with 'great love'.[17] Thus, the entire *Life* is
Alyosha's re-creation of Zosima's verbal image, and his interpretation of the meaning of his elder's life and teachings.

The *Life* is also a word set within, and apart from, the narrator's word. Zosima's personal reminiscences and discourses on memory come after the narrator's earlier passages on memory. In the new context of 'The Russian Monk' Alyosha's memories reverberate anew. Such echoing cross-correspondences poetically integrate the text and render it multi-layered, compositionally and semantically. The narrator directly transmits Alyosha's memories of his elder intact as he found them in Alyosha's manuscript, stressing that he preferred to limit himself 'only to the elder's story from Aleksey's manuscript' (14,260). He does not translate Alyosha's memory of Zosima through the prism of his own memory as he did with Alyosha's memory of his mother. Since Alyosha's memories of Zosima are not mediated yet again by the narrator, they are not further refined and interpreted by him either. Clearly, Dostoevsky wanted to reserve one place in his novel where the hagiographical word could ring pure and whole, without 'perhaps', without tentative circumlocutions, without a narrator who, for rhetorical and narrational reasons, is restricted to occasional hagiographical tones. Here we are given an integral hagiography *per se* where the existence of God is assumed and glorified, but which has also been renewed and modernised in various interesting ways.

In the first place, there are no supernatural events: Zosima does not perform or witness any miracles, or struggle with the devil or demons (unlike Father Ferapont). Nor does he have any visions. This means that his word alone, its style, themes and eloquence, will have to carry the hagiographical weight. It is a word more saturated with memory than any other in the novel, personal and cultural. There are also innovatory narrative manoeuvres. The conventional hagiographical heading is followed by an unconventional subheading, the factual 'Biographical Information'. Yet the whole *Life* is told by Zosima in the first-person autobiographical mode, an unusual manoeuvre for a hagiographer. This combination of three genres is a subtle narrative arrangement which answers the author's aims. In an autobiography the hero is his own narrator. In a hagiography the hero–saint is usually presented in the third-person by the narrator–hagiographer. Auto-biography is an attempt at self understanding. Like hagiography it is not so much an account of factual truth, but the truth of inner development. In a hagiography, though, the most important realities are spiritual realities. Conventional wisdom has it that no one can really speak the truth about himself, no matter how sincere their motives. Dostoevsky then, was faced with the problem of presenting the spokesman for his most cherished ideas as an irreproachably righteous, wise and truthful man and, at the same time, as a persuasive, moving and believable bearer of those ideas. This problem he solved beautifully by having Alyosha transmit as a direct unbroken quotation the words he has remembered Zosima saying to his small circle of beloved intimates. Therefore, unlike auto-biography, Zosima's personal memories enter the dialogic context of a free, unselfconscious and intimate conversation. In this way Zosima's message is maximally uncontaminated by vanity, solipsism and direct didacticism. He can freely sound forth in all his urgent subjectivity. Essentially the same narrative device governed the Evangelists' representations of Christ.

A similar principle applies to Alyosha, the narrator having somehow obtained the *Life* in manuscript form. It has not been made public by Alyosha, unlike the 'careerist seminarian' Rakitin's hagiographical composition, *The Life in God of the Deceased Elder Father Zosima*, a work, says the lawyer for the defence, 'full of deep and religious thoughts', published as a 'brochure' (15,100). Not a single line of Rakitin's *vita* of Zosima is reproduced in the novel.

The author placed Zosima's *Life* in the dramatic context of those three days during which a murder was brewing and just before it was committed. Alyosha heard Zosima's reminiscences of Markel, and possibly those of the Mysterious Visitor, only during that 'last conversation'. All Zosima's other reminiscences and teachings are an amalgam of words drawn from the last year of his life. In their written form, Zosima's discourses are the words of a man who, for the narrator, has been dead for some thirteen years. But their compositional arrangement gives the dramatic impression that they are all being said in the story's 'here and now', just before Zosima's death. Consequently, Zosima's word enters the dialogue of the novel's present in order to give us a higher perspective from which to assess Ivan's Legend and the novel's tragic events.

This temporal gap has another important function. At the time of the main narrative, Alyosha does not possess the maturity to compose such a work although the onset of his growing spiritual stature is already apparent at the very end of the novel in his speech by Ilyusha's stone. What is important is that the *Life* was written *after* the events, that Alyosha is looking back, that the *Life* is a memory of a spiritual maturation. The discrepancy between our image of the reticent young novice and the eloquence of the *Life* is itself evidence of Alyosha's own spiritual growth over the intervening years, of his retrospective comprehension of the truth of his elder's word.

Alyosha divided Zosima's *Life* into two parts. The first part is devoted to Zosima's personal memories, to representing him reminiscing over his spiritual development from childhood and early manhood up to the turning point of his life when he decides to become a monk. It also includes Zosima's personal reminiscences of the critical spiritual turning points in the lives of his brother and his Mysterious Visitor, as well as his memory of the role of Holy Writ in his life. The second part of the *Life* consists of excerpts from Zosima's 'conversations and teachings' organised under five topical headings which Alyosha heard in the last year of his elder's life. The large chronological gap between the two parts is not filled in except for a few references to Zosima's years of wandering on pilgrimages. In Dostoevsky's poetics, what matter are the turning points, the role played by sacred memories in their spiritual transformations and the way Zosima contextualises and retrospectively interprets them.

Zosima begins where he left off in the story, with his childhood memory of his older brother Markel, the atheist who became a believer in the last weeks of his life. Zosima represents Markel's conversion almost entirely through his viewpoint as an eight-year-old child. We are never given any

access to Markel's inner life. But Dostoevsky left an essential
canonical clue by setting Markel's conversion within the most
important period of the Orthodox spiritual year, from Lent to
Easter. Lent is the period of fasting and penitence in commemoration of Christ's fasting in the wilderness which culmi-
nated in His triumph over the three temptations, an episode
which plays a central role in Ivan's Legend. Like Alyosha's
older brother Ivan, Markel was a clever boy who kept to
himself and who came under the influence of a remarkable
teacher, a 'learned' professor exiled for being a 'freethinker'.
By the onset of Lent, Markel mocked religious faith, refused to
fast and denied the existence of God: 'it's all raving nonsense,
he would say, and there is no God either' (14,261). The crucial
turning point occurs when Markel, realising that he will soon
die, suddenly decides at the beginning of Passion Week to
receive communion and confess. Zosima remembers the
change which came over his brother in his last days:

That's how I remember him: sitting, quiet, gentle, smiling, he himself
is ill, but his countenance is cheerful, joyous. He had completely
altered spiritually – such a marvelous change had suddenly begun in
him! The old nurse would come into his room: 'Let me light your icon
lamp before the image, dear' <...> I remember, once I went into his
room by myself, when no one else was there. It was the evening hour,
clear, the sun was setting and it illumined the whole room with a
slanting ray. Seeing me, he beckoned me, I went up to him, he took
me by the shoulders with both hands, looks me in the face tenderly,
lovingly; he said nothing, only looked at me like that for about a
minute: 'well, he says, go now and play, live for me!' <...> And later
in my life I remembered with tears how he told me to live for him.
(14,261,263)

The contextual and semantic resemblances between Alyosha's
memory of his mother and Zosima's memories of his dying
brother are too close to be accidental. The symbolic meanings
are equivalent thanks to the recurrence of the symbol of the
setting sun on a 'quiet evening' in a threshold situation of a
beloved person's suffering and imminent death. In both scenes
the image of the sun's setting rays remains impressed on their
memories, only Alyosha remembered them 'most of all'. But

important new elements have been added in this variation. Giving, so to speak, his life to his young brother ('live for me!'), Markel metaphorically performs an act analogous to Christ Who gave His life so that everyone could attain eternal life. Accepting the sacraments in Easter week, Markel's memory of Christ's redemptive suffering and Resurrection has been stirred, enabling him to find meaning in his own suffering and impending death and thus to be spiritually reborn and fulfil the redemptive pattern.

Zosima closes his reminiscences of Markel with: 'I was young, a child, but on my heart everything indelibly remained, a hidden feeling remained. In its time it all had to rise up and respond. And so it happened' (14,263). Clearly, the memory of Markel is not revived so that Zosima may nostalgically revisit his childhood. Memory in this novel takes transcendental journeys which powerfully affect the future. In Zosima's view, memories are retained for a higher purpose, everything has its time, memories of loved persons long dead can arise and affect the living according to some destiny configured by an unseen power. And he can now verify it.

Zosima recounts his memories of the critical early morning hours before his duel. Watching the sunrise and contemplating the awakening of nature in his garden, Zosima recalls with 'shame and torment' how he had beaten his defenceless servant the night before with 'bestial cruelty' and weeps. At this low spiritual moment he remembers suddenly recalling his brother's last words to his servants: 'My dear ones <...> am I worthy that you should serve me?' Zosima turns this question on himself: 'Really, what am I worth that another man, just like me, the image and likeness of God, should serve me?' Hereupon he also recalls Markel's words which express the two central ideas of his subsequent teaching: 'Mother, my little heart, in truth each is blameworthy before all for all, it's only that people don't know this, but if they would realise it – it would be paradise at once' (14,270). Then and there Zosima begs his servant to forgive him and resolves not to shoot his opponent at the duel. That very day he announces his decision to take up the monk's calling. The memory of Markel, speaking to him over the years, has saved Zosima from the potential crime of killing his innocent opponent. Thus, it is at the point when Zosima sees in his servant the 'image and likeness of God', when his servant ceases to be just a servant but a reminder and carrier of the sacred Urbild, that Zosima's conversion is achieved. He then realises that beating his defenceless servant was not only base, but a desecration, an offence against God's world spread out before him in the paradisiacal garden awakening to the 'little sun', the symbolic objective correlate of his own spiritual awakening.

Zosima's acts of public contrition soon bear fruit. The Mysterious Visitor seeks him out and thence begins his redemption. The Visitor's conversion is achieved only after an intense inner struggle. On the eve of his public confession, the Visitor demands of Zosima that he decide his fate. Zosima answers by quoting the novel's Epigraph. The Visitor leaves, whereupon Zosima, in yet another echo of Alyosha's key memory, exclaims: 'I threw myself on my knees before the icon and wept over him to the Most Holy Mother of God, the intercessor and helper' (14,281). The Visitor unexpectedly returns but after a few minutes kisses Zosima and leaves. On his deathbed he reveals to Zosima how close he was to murdering him. Yet again the author allows the reader to draw the transcendental inferences about the salvational and providential intercessions of the Mother of God. But for Zosima's living example, the Visitor could not have accomplished his 'great deed' (*podvig*) and finally died with a clear conscience.

Zosima's personal reminiscences appropriately end with his entry into the monastery: 'after five months I was deemed worthy by the Lord God to set out on that firm and blessed path, blessing the unseen finger which had so clearly guided me to this path' (14,283). Here, then, at the end of his life, Zosima clearly spells out that irresistible force which directed his 'blessed path', the same one which guided Alyosha's 'inevitable road'.

The *Life* is generated *from* memory, and it is also very much *about* memory, above all the memory of the World. Every saint's life is a panegyric which glorifies the Christian faith just

as much as its subject whose saintly life exemplifies it. A whole
chapter is devoted to Zosima's discourse on the role of Holy
Scripture in his life. As Perlina has noted, the total absence in
Zosima's words of any allusions to great secular literature
'indicates the primacy of religious morality over aesthetics in
Dostoevsky'.[18] This chapter, which Dostoevsky called 'ecstatic
and poetic', is replete with Zosima's inspirational comments
on sacred texts and his teachings on the salvational efficacy of
precious childhood memories.[19] These teachings he illustrates
by relating his memory of his first conscious religious experience during a reading of the Book of Job:

I remember how for the first time a certain deep spiritual feeling
visited me, while still in my eighth year. My mother had taken me
<...> during Passion Week to mass. The day was clear and,
remembering now, I as if see anew how the incense rose from the
censer and softly floated upwards, and from above in the cupola,
through a narrow little window, God's rays of sun streamed down on
us in the church, and the incense, rising up to it in waves, as if melted
in them. I watched tenderly moved and then for the first time in my
life I consciously took into my soul the seed of God's Word. (14,264)

This second pair of memory motifs highlights Zosima's and
Alyosha's shared remembrances of being taken to mass by
their mothers and of the falling rays of sunlight. Only now
Zosima identifies them as 'God's rays' and combines them
with the insemination of the Word. If memory revives the
image of the sun's rays, the sun revives the cherished memories. In this way the sacred merges with the earthly:

I bless the daily rising of the sun, and my heart as before sings to it,
but now I love even more its setting, its long slanting rays, and with
them the soft, gentle, tender memories, the dear images from all my
long and blessed life, and over all God's justice, touching, reconciling, all-forgiving! My life is ending, I know and sense it, but I feel
on my every remaining day how my earthly life is already coming into
contact with a new, infinite, unknown but closely approaching future
life. (14,265)

The setting sun has now become a symbol of resurrection. As
Zosima approaches the threshold of eternal life, its rays
become peopled with all those who have gone before. The

heavenly world, so to speak, comes to meet the departing saint. Analysing this solar symbol, Børtnes concludes that 'the Christian idea of resurrection in death to a new form of existence, is the fundamental meaning of the symbol of the setting sun in *The Brothers Karamazov*'.[20]

The way Zosima remembers his life, the quality of his remembering and his attitude to his memories are particularly revealing. He remembers his past experiences not as so many unrelated, discrete incidents, but all together, as a continuous whole. The life he has lived is always present to him, every new experience is significant, is incorporated into that pattern of memory which gives him the sense and faith that his life has a purpose. Everything in his past life, all his experiences which have made him who he is, have taken on significance for him. Nothing is ridiculed or rejected, though some things are morally condemned (the duel, the blow). This feeling of piety towards what has happened to him is, in Otto Weininger's view, 'akin to filial piety' and accounts in part for what he calls 'the extraordinary piety of memoirs'. Weininger thought that the very attempt to compose a truthful autobiographical account indicates an exceptional personality: 'For in the really *faithful* memory the root of *piety* lies'.[21] And if this is so, then Alyosha's preservation of his elder's memories creates a double level of 'filial piety'. Of all the author–characters, only Alyosha's composition is preserved and transmitted as a full-fledged literary work. A written word is, in every sense, a committed word. His work is the sole 'memorial' devoted to a 'living' person. Transmitting all Zosima's words as though he were speaking in the present, Alyosha creates the impression that Zosima is, as it were, among us now. This way he too erases the boundary between past and present, the living and the dead. Preserving Zosima's word and image in written form, Alyosha turns the whole *Life* into a loving resurrection of his elder and thus performs an act of filial piety in the highest sense.

And Zosima not only aims to discover the truth about himself, but he sets that truth within the context of the Word and he tests it against that Word. Things which enter our memories become fuller for us, become our own. Zosima makes the whole world his own ('love every blade of grass') because it all arouses the memory of the Word which he took into his consciousness as a child. Zosima lives in continuous conversation with the Word and he reads the world by It. Everything partakes of a double level of signification, the sacred and earthly. His whole consciousness is so filled by his memory of the Word, that for him, memory, the Word and consciousness have completely merged and become one and the same.

In his sermon on our 'contact with other worlds', Zosima introduces a metaphor which, as other interpreters have noted, gives us a spiritual and structural key to the whole novel. It is a mataphor rooted in Zosima's memory of his spiritual turning point when he beheld the garden wakening to the sunrise, bringing Markel's words back to him:

Much on earth is hidden from us, but to make up for that, we have been granted a secret, innermost sense of our living bond with another world, with a heavenly, higher world, and the roots of our thoughts and feelings are not here, but in other worlds. This is why philosophers say that we cannot comprehend the essence of things on earth. God took seeds from other worlds and sowed them on this earth and His garden grew up, and everything came up that could come up, but what has grown lives and is alive only by the feeling of its contact with mysterious other worlds; if this feeling grows weak or is destroyed in you, then what has grown in you dies. Then you will become indifferent to life and will even come to hate it. (14,290–91)

This is Zosima's implicit memory, implicit when we read the novel poetically, and his interpretation of the Epigraph and Christ's parable of the sower (Matthew, 13:1–8); it is another symbolic expression of that memory organising the structure of the whole novel. If our roots are in God's 'other worlds', then everything that grows on earth partakes of the divine, of the roots of piety. Contact with our otherworldly origins is achieved not through logic or reason, but through a secret sense, a 'feeling' anchored in memory as intuitive knowledge. All the protagonists' lives are generated by this idea, and are formed by varying degrees or gradations of contact with God, from continuous communion (Zosima) to moribund separation and loss of contact (Smerdyakov, Ivan). Alyosha has quoted these words of Zosima from memory, and his life will be the fullest fulfilment of this memory structure. The final representation of this idea will be his closing speech to the boys.

Alyosha's manuscript abruptly breaks off on Zosima's sermon on hell. At this point the narrator returns and, in another intriguing departure from traditional hagiography, it is he, and not Alyosha, Zosima's hagiographer, who gives an account of the elder's death, thus leaving us with a completed aesthetic image and completing the hagiographical pattern. All saints' lives include accounts of their deaths, for it is only after death that their apotheosis and canonisation can occur. Zosima's apotheosis is fulfilled in Alyosha's dream-vision of 'Cana of Galilee' where his elder appears to him as having transcended his earthly life and joined 'our Sun' in 'other worlds'. Without this experiential confirmation, it is unlikely that Alyosha would have written the *Life*.

The narrator, then, is not the sole memoirist–biographer. Alyosha has written his memoir of Zosima from a position similar to his. He too, writing 'some time later', can see Zosima's life as a whole, his beginning and end. This is the privilege of the rememberer, and the artist. No other character is given such a large retrospective and integrated view of the past, of another's life. Three characters are united by this hagiographical memory parallel; Zosima is Alyosha's hero just as Alyosha is the narrator's hero, but only Alyosha is a hagiographer pure and simple. The retrospective deciphering of the true import of things is one of the chief functions of memory. Dostoevsky cast this function in the form of a hagiographical word. He wrote his last novel for the sake of Zosima's discourses and these, in turn, he wrote 'for the few'.[22] Apart from the biblical quotations, they occupy the highest position in the novel's hierarchy of poetic utterances. This means that of all the words Dostoevsky composed for his characters, Alyosha's word is hierarchically the highest in the novel, on a par with the author's, if not above it.

ALYOSHA AND LISE

The theme of good childhood memories runs intermittently through the lives of other characters. The bond between Lise and Alyosha is anchored in their childhood and is mentioned several times.[23] Lise makes her first appearance with allusions to her childhood memories of Alyosha. At the end of her mother's conversation with Zosima, she bursts out: 'And why has he forgotten everything? He used to carry me about in his arms when I was little, we used to play together <...> he said that he would never forget me, that we are eternal friends, eternal, eternal! <...> Why doesn't he want to come and see us?' (14,55) Thereupon Zosima takes a fateful decision for Alyosha, mentally noting to himself: 'I shall certainly send him.' What appears to have decided Zosima, in addition to the pathos of Lise's childhood memories of Alyosha, is her manifest illness, physical, emotional and spiritual. Shortly thereafter Zosima tells Alyosha he must marry. Though he does not name his future wife, the subsequent engagement of the young couple is both consequence and fulfilment of Zosima's decision. Concurrently with this announcement, Lise composes her letter to Alyosha declaring her love for him 'since childhood', and her choice of him as husband. Just at this point, Dostoevsky brings Lise into the novel's system of sacred memory motifs when she writes that 'before I took up my pen, I prayed to the icon of the Mother of God, yes and now I'm praying, and almost crying' (14,146). Much later Zosima's prescient insight into Lise's precarious spiritual condition is vindicated in the chapter 'The Little Demon' where Lise, in the grip of demonic possession, appeals to Alyosha to 'save' her. Whether he will or not remains an open question for this novel. The same is true for Ivan. Given Alyosha's function, it is clear that only he can 'save' her. And the novel implies that this will be possible because of their shared childhood memories and because she remembered the Mother of God in her prayer when she turned to Alyosha.

THE MEMORY OF RELIGIOUS FOLKLORE AND LEGENDS: GRUSHENKA

It is well known that folklore played an important role in Dostoevsky's creative work.[24] Folk tales are traditional stories passed on by word of mouth and deeply rooted in the national life in which they circulate. Preserved through the generations, they form part of a people's collective memory. Unlike literary works, the folk tale depends for its creation and survival on its collective acceptance by the community. In Jakobson's words, the folk tale is 'a typical collective property' which 'represents a typical interpersonal, social value'.[25] Thus, a moral or religious value contained in folklore is a value which has been long and widely sanctioned by the people. In this consisted much of its importance for Dostoevsky. Folklore, and particularly religious folklore, were for him living evidence of the moral, spiritual treasure preserved in the hearts of the Russian people.

Dostoevsky incorporated a fable from Russian religious folklore into one of the key turning points of *The Brothers Karamazov*. 'A Little Onion' is a folk variation on the theme of Christian salvation through good deeds. Significantly, the fable arises as a spontaneous childhood memory of Grushenka who tells it to Alyosha. In order to bring out the poetic significance of Grushenka's fable, we have to see it in the context of the novel's memory system.

The meeting between Alyosha and Grushenka begins from a mutual spiritual nadir: Alyosha has fallen into near despair over the events at the monastery while Grushenka is revengefully contemplating taking a knife to her impending reunion with her Pole. The critical turning point is initiated by Grushenka who, upon learning that Zosima has died, 'devoutly' crosses herself and jumps away from Alyosha's lap ('Lord, what am I doing, sitting on his knees now!' (14,318)). Her spontaneous reverence for the deceased elder and her instinctive sympathy for Alyosha's sorrow restore his faith in human beings, in God's world. His beloved elder, reviled at the monastery, is revered in an unlikely quarter, good is found where it was not expected: 'I came here to find an evil soul because I was base and wicked, but I found a sincere sister, I've found a treasure – a loving soul <...> You've just restored my soul' (14,318). Grushenka too has found good where she least expected it: 'He called me his sister and I shall never forget it from now on.' Moved, her first response is to confess: 'Now I'll tell everything!', whereupon a tale she heard in childhood from her old servant suddenly wells up in her memory.

Just before Grushenka relates the fable, the narrator draws our attention to the fact that this exchange between Grushenka and Alyosha constituted a spiritual peripety: 'everything that could shake their souls exactly coincided as happens not often in a lifetime' (14,318). James Joyce describes an epiphany as 'the gropings of a spiritual eye which seeks to adjust its vision to an exact focus. The moment the focus is reached, the object is epiphanised.'[26] The difference between Joyce and Dostoevsky is that in Dostoevsky's art the epiphany has retained its meaning of 'a manifestation of a divine being'. For the 'object' here is a dialogic relationship between two people whose uttered words and inner feelings come into a rare harmonious focus on the basis of shared, subliminal recognitions. For Dostoevsky a divine being always has his word, his image and his response. The dialogue between Alyosha and Grushenka is ultimately based on the memory of an ideal dialogue which has penetrated and shaken their souls. It is the coincidence and interaction between the two dialogues, earthly and divine, which transforms their meeting into a crucial event in their lives, into an epiphany. Memory again, individual and cultural, opens a way to interpretation.

The fable momentarily transports Grushenka (and the reader) from the fraught atmosphere of the present, to universal story-time of childhood when the most fantastic tales seem real and when, in the author's view, the soul is still uncorrupted. Certain apparently simple, childlike ideas, which in ordinary discourse would sound banal, can be poetically expressed in folk tales so that they win our acceptance, or at least our indulgence. And this is largely because of their association with childhood. The fable hangs by one remembered good deed. A 'mean evil old woman' is suffering in the 'burning lake' of hell because she left no good deeds behind her in life. Her Guardian Angel, taking pity on her, recalls that she once gave an onion to a passing beggar woman. He holds out the onion to her in order to pull her up to paradise. The other sinners grab onto the woman hoping to be lifted out with her, but she kicks them away saying 'It's my onion.' With that the onion snaps and she falls back into the lake where she 'is burning to this day' (14,319). But her Angel's response is telling: 'And the Angel wept and moved away.' The Angel's withdrawal is denoted not with *ushel* ('went away', out of sight, beyond calling) but *otoshel* ('moved away', still within sight). Thus, through a small verbal prefix a compassionate loophole slips into the fable, and this is true for every evil case in the novel.

Since Grushenka identifies herself with the evil old woman – 'I am that very malicious old woman' – the reader can simultaneously associate Alyosha with the divine Guardian Angel of the tale, and metaphorically identify him as Grushenka's guardian angel on earth.[27] And these substitutions will come all the more easily to the reader since 'angel' is Alyosha's epithet and Grushenka herself calls him her 'cherub'. However, in order for this identification to be established on a more persuasive basis than association by epithets or allegorical tales, the salvational function of the novel's 'angel' will have to be assimilated to that of the fable's Angel. In other words, we should expect this encounter to have salvational consequences in their lives. In Dostoevsky's fiction salvation begins with confession. Grushenka immediately follows her narration of the fable with a confessional outpouring ('And now, Alyosha, I'll tell you alone the whole pure truth!'), with a release of long pentup feelings of rage and revenge, accompanied by tears and hysterics.

The confessional dialogue, as Bakhtin points out, has enormous significance in Dostoevsky's art. Bakhtin defines it as 'a *free* self-revelation *from within* <...> an encounter of the deepest I with another and with others (the folk) <...> on the highest level or ultimate instance'.[28] A confessing person is driven by an overwhelming need to be judged and forgiven by another. The addressee of a confessional word is usually underpinned by an image of an ideal understanding judge (higher voice). Grushenka's memory of the fable has reunited her with her childhood, with the sources of goodness in her life, with the time when her conscience was pure and she was not just 'evil'.[29] In this novel, the voice of conscience has been defined as the voice of 'Christ's law', the highest voice of all. Since Grushenka sees Alyosha as her 'conscience' ('sometimes I look on you, Alyosha, as my conscience'), she sees him as a representative of 'the Other', the highest voice (14,317). Her urge to confess to him simultaneously reflects her wish to be forgiven by that highest voice and transforms Alyosha into a living embodiment of that voice.

The culminating word of Grushenka's confession is, I believe, the key passage:

> 'I don't know, I don't know, I don't know anything, what it was he said to me, it went straight to my heart. He wrenched my heart <...> He was the first, the only one to take pity on me, that's what it is! Why didn't you come before, you cherub', she suddenly fell before him on her knees as if in a frenzy. 'All my life I've been waiting for someone like you, I knew that someone like you would come and forgive me. I believed that someone would love me too, vile as I am, not only for a shameful love!' (14,323)

Grushenka's spiritual reversal is graphically represented by a dramatic gestural reversal, from seductively sitting on Alyosha's knees to falling on her knees before him. This image of Grushenka, falling 'on her knees' as if in 'a frenzy' forms a distinct parallel to that of Alyosha's mother, weeping 'on her knees', holding Alyosha up with a 'frenzied face'. And when Alyosha sees the 'treasure' in her soul, does he not obscurely 'remember' the image of his mother in Grushenka who, five years earlier, was also a 'shy, meek, pitiful' girl, also an orphan (*sirotochka*), also 'rescued' by a much older lecherous avaricious man at approximately the same age and also the daughter of a provincial 'deacon'? Or, does he not see Grushenka as an incarnation of his mother, the novel's archetype of abused innocence?[31] And to whom is Grushenka responding here? Not just to Alyosha, the twenty-year-old youth, but to Alyosha her 'cherub', an Abbild of the sacred Urbild. Christ's infinite compassion is the Urbild subliminally shaping Grushenka's perception of Alyosha at this moment. Christ is pre-eminently the One waited for, the One Who came to forgive and redeem the world. Grushenka's deepest longings, then, are focused on that highest voice and image. Thus, the mutual peripety between Alyosha and Grushenka is an epiphany in its primary (not Joycean) sense: for Grushenka, a subconscious manifestation of Christ's love and compassion, for Alyosha, a proof of His presence in the world. The long awaited emotional and spiritual catharsis has been accomplished.

Here Dostoevsky goes further than usual in assimilating the two series, fictional and divine, to each other. But he just avoids stepping over into sentimentality by playing on the negative invariants, on the negative Urbild/Abbild. Throughout this chapter the sneering cynical voice of Rakitin has been interrupting and counterpointing the exalted harmonious exchange between Grushenka and Alyosha. The dissonances of Rakitin's mocking voice have the effect of enhancing their dialogue, rhetorically and poetically. Towards the end of this chapter Dostoevsky aligns the protagonists of this scene directly with their canonical prototypes by introducing through Rakitin's voice two biblical reminiscences which enable us to make more far-reaching metaphorical substitutions.

Just after Rakitin and Alyosha leave Grushenka's, the seminarian sneers: 'Well, you've turned the sinner? – he spitefully laughed at Alyosha. – You've turned the fallen woman onto the path of truth? You've driven out the seven devils, eh? Here's where the miracles we've been expecting so recently have been performed!' (14,324). Now we can have no doubt which ideal dialogue, which memory code, is informing that between Alyosha and Grushenka. Those readers familiar with the Bible will associate Grushenka, even if only for a moment, to Mary Magdalene, the 'fallen woman' and heroine of the *New Testament* who was freed of her devils and spiritually transformed by Christ, who was the first to see Him resurrected and to whom was vouchsafed the announcement of His resurrection (John 20:11–18). The biblical miracle to which Rakitin refers comes from Luke 8:2, a chapter devoted to the healing of demonic possession and one which played an exceptionally important role in Dostoevsky's fiction, giving him the Epigraph for *The Devils*. In this view, Grushenka's falling on her knees before Alyosha can be seen as a fugitive reminiscence of the cured demoniac 'sitting at the feet of Christ'. On the same metaphorical principle, Rakitin enters the company of the 'mockers and revilers' of Christ and the Christian miracles. Rakitin's cynical mockery of the biblical likeness inclines the reader to take them seriously. Here Dostoevsky uses what we may call a negated biblical reminiscence. It depends on placing an idea which the author wishes to be taken positively in the utterance of a compromised, unsympathetic person who negates it. When Zosima, a righteous man, quotes the Bible, the quotation reinforces his saintly image and creatively renews the Word. When the shallow careerist Rakitin quotes the Bible it serves to dissociate him from its positive message and to associate his addressee to it. When a compromised person mocks the beliefs of the truthful, the reader tends to affirm them, and when he sneers at the suffering and joy of the good, those he denigrates will tend to win the reader's sympathy. We do not even have to wait until the trial when Rakitin becomes absolutely compromised by his lie about his family relationship to Grushenka. Another biblical reminiscence immediately following from his lips achieves the author's aim here, one equally compromising, the betrayal of a friend. After accepting the 25 roubles from Grushenka as his payment for bringing Alyosha to her, Rakitin, says the narrator, was 'really ashamed'. But shame leads to spite and now Rakitin turns on Alyosha: 'You despise me now for those 25 roubles? He sold, you say, a true friend. But you aren't Christ and I'm not Judas' (14,325). Rakitin's very negation of the identities establishes them as an affirmation in the reader's mind. And since Rakitin's association is backed up by a fact, he did 'sell' his true friend, he becomes assimilated to Judas and Alyosha to Christ. At the same time, Rakitin's open allusion to the biblical episode shows that the sacred texts are very active in his memory too. He remembers the example, negatively, with spite, but also with 'shame', the painful consciousness that he acted basely. Thus, the fact that Rakitin is capable of feeling shame over his 'Judas' role indicates that he too is governed by the highest voice. In all these instances, the biblical reminiscences transform the individual fictional incidents into variations on collective memory themes.

In Grushenka's fable, the passage from hell to paradise is abruptly broken off. The old woman's selfish greed prevails; she cannot return the divine compassion received to others. In the novel's story, though, there is a mutual exchange of confessions and a very different outcome. As the chapter closes, the seed of compassion Alyosha has sown, the subliminal memory of the Urbild of infinite compassion, begins to grow, affecting Grushenka's life, and then spreading to others throughout the novel's world. At the beginning of this scene, Grushenka, waiting for her 'officer's summons', said she did not want Mitya now 'at all'. Her confession, though, has apparently awakened some tender memory of Mitya for she leaves this chapter shouting to Alyosha from her window: 'oh, tell him <...> that his Grushenka loved him for one little hour of time <...> so that he should remember this little hour all his life from now on' (14,324). She flies off to Mokroe knowing that she has given and received an 'onion', that she is not just 'evil'. After receiving a true word of brotherly love, Grushenka can now distinguish a genuine love (Mitya) from a counterfeit one (the Pole). Forgiven herself, she can now forgive her 'offender' and ask for forgiveness from Mitya for tormenting him. Her 'little hour' of loving Mitya turns into a love for life. During their revels, the memory of the fable and her encounter with Alyosha is very much on her mind: 'Today Alyosha said words to me for my whole life <...> I gave an onion' (14,397). And forgiven, she now, unlike the 'evil old woman', wishes forgiveness for everyone: 'If I were God I'd forgive all people.' Her encounter with Alyosha changes her vision of the world: 'All people are good <...> it's good in the world <...> we're all vile and good, vile and good.' And before the police take

Mitya off, Grushenka declares her resolve to share his fate, to follow him to Siberia, and hence sustains Mitya through his ordeals (*mystarstva*) ahead. Thus, in this indirect way, Alyosha has also given 'an onion' to his brother. The 'acquisitive' buyer of bad debts now takes pity on her Pole, sending him and his companion money, and she takes in the homeless old buffoon Maximov. Over his protestations that he is not worthy of her benefactions, Grushenka returns: 'Ech, everyone is needed. Who's to say who's more useful?' (15,8). Grushenka's belief in the absolute worth of every human being is, so to speak, her answer to Ivan and his Inquisitor. The 'onion' Alyosha gave Grushenka has pulled her out of her 'burning lake of hell' of revenge and misery. A potential crime of vengeance has been transformed into a willingness to forgive.

And Alyosha understands the significance of what has been averted. The knife she threatens to use seems never to have accompanied her to Mokroe. For these events receive their highest meaning subsequently when Dostoevsky transfers the essential elements of this episode into Alyosha's vision of paradise. Praying by Zosima's coffin on the threshold of his great dream vision, Alyosha repeats to himself: 'she went to the banquet . . . No, she did not take the knife, she did not take the knife' (14,326). The 'onion' Grushenka gave Alyosha takes him to the 'gates of paradise' and enters his dream vision when Zosima appears to him saying 'I gave an onion, and that's why I'm here too. And many here have given only an onion <. . .> Today you knew how to give an onion to a famished woman <. . .> Begin, dear boy, begin, my gentle one, your work!' (14,327). The encounter with Grushenka is a first manifestation of Alyosha's spiritual gifts, his saving of her, his casting out of her demons, is his first miracle. In this lies its greatest significance for the author, and for the novel's poetic system of sacred memory. The death of Zosima has brought forth its fruits and thus fulfilled the redemptive pattern of the Epigraph.

The larger moral of the fable belongs to Alyosha's and Zosima's world vision, which is that one good deed may save not only the performer, but many. For had the evil old woman allowed the others to join her, perhaps all hell would have been emptied. It did not happen in the fable because the fable has a cautionary didactic function, it shows what might have been and what could be. If only 'all would feel to blame for all', perhaps earth would become paradise and hell would vanish, as Markel taught Zosima. 'A Little Onion' illustrates the idea that a single good deed, no matter how modest, is a seed with potential for infinite growth. This is a folk variation on the expansional motif, condensed in the Epigraph, which lies at the heart of the whole novel.

The fable of 'A Little Onion' is symbolic of the salvational power of remembered good deeds, both on the plane of the fable and the events of the novel. Its pictorial brevity converts it into a kind of folk icon invested with protectional and salvational powers. Grushenka's fable, just as Alyosha's memory of his mother, has functioned as a seed planted early in her soul, dormant until a moment of spiritual crisis when it suddenly springs to life and requires a redemptive function. In retrospect, its sudden revival in her memory, thanks to Alyosha's word and presence, transforms Alyosha into an agent of salvation. Thus, the images of Grushenka and Alyosha become doubly compounded with spiritual significance, folk-loric and biblical. The religious folklore reminiscence serves to associate them to the peoples' faith, the biblical reminiscences, to activate in contemporary life the divine prototypes.

IVAN

Grushenka's fable is not the only eschatological tale about a merciful divine intercession. Ivan begins his 'confession' with a résumé of a Russian medieval religious legend, 'The Mother of God's Journey Through the Torments' in which she descends to hell and sees the sinners submerged in a 'burning lake'. In all the editions of this medieval legend the sinners writhe in agony in a 'burning river'.[31] However, 'lake' is the canonical term (Revelation 14:15, 19:20, 20:10). Dostoevsky most likely replaced 'river' with 'lake' in order to assimilate the apocryphal legend to Grushenka's fable because of their thematic similarity, and most importantly, to connect Ivan with the canonical images of hell. By presenting Grushenka's fable as a spontaneous recollection from early life, the author creates a link between her childhood memory and Russian religious folk memory, between the present earthly events and timeless heavenly intercessions. But for Ivan this link is absent, or broken. His allusion to the apocrypha is not a personal remembrance which stimulates a full confession (a release of negative memories), but a literary reminiscence forming a prologue to his temptational sermon of the Legend. This is why his telling of it has no cathartic, not to speak of salvational, effect on him. Moreover, the eschatological image associated to Ivan does not feature a potentially salvational good deed, but centers on a merciful release from the agony of eternal punishment. Nevertheless, he too relates it to the novel's 'angel', and in his memory too the Mother of God has found a place even if only at second remove to his own experience.

MITYA

Mitya's redemptive turning point is also stimulated by the folk memory of a merciful visit to hell (Christ's harrowing of hell) which we take up in our last chapter. But he also retains a sacred memory from childhood. During his trial, Dr Herzenstube, in the midst of giving evidence 'highly interesting for the prosecution', unexpectedly testifies in favour of Mitya's 'good heart'. He 'suddenly' remembers Mitya as a neglected child, and recalls that he once bought him a pound of nuts 'for no one had ever bought the little boy a pound of nuts'. Then and there he taught him to say: 'Gott der Vater, Gott der Sohn, Gott der heilige Geist' (15,106). The significance of this childhood episode for the theme of memory is revealed in its sequel. Herzenstube also recollects that Mitya, whom he had not seen since, recently called on him, greeting him with the German phrase and saying: 'I've just arrived and come to thank you for the pound of nuts because no one ever bought me a pound of nuts, you alone bought me a pound of nuts.' Recalls Herzenstube, 'And I wept. He laughed but he wept too <...> I saw it.' Responding, Mitya booms out from the dock one of his

inimitable utterances which pierces through the many objectifying, falsifying words encircling him: 'And now I'm weeping,
German, and now I'm weeping, you man of God!' (15,107)
The bag of nuts has long disappeared, but the permanent
bridge between the widely spaced times are the holy words
which have lodged in Mitya's soul. The idea of the mutual
sanctity of fatherhood and sonhood has remained in Mitya's
memory. Terras says: 'Herzenstube, by assuming fatherhood
of the neglected boy, albeit only for a moment, plants the seeds
of goodness, of "the Holy Ghost", in his heart.'[32] Both Mitya
and Alyosha, then, have a spiritual father, Ivan dreams up his
(the Grand Inquisitor and the devil).

Now Mitya's visit to Herzenstube must have taken place not
long before his father's murder. When Mitya learns during the
preliminary investigation that Grigory is alive, he exclaims:
'Lord, I thank Thee for the greatest miracle, it's because of my
prayer! <...> how you've resurrected me. That old man, he
carried me in his arms <...> when everyone abandoned me, a
three-year-old child, he was a real father!' (14,414) Subsequently, Mitya tries to explain what held him back from
killing his father at that critical moment under the window 'in
the dark'. There is nothing 'necessary or probable' about it.
Indeed, it is most improbable: 'whether it was someone's tears,
or my mother entreated God, or a bright spirit kissed me at the
moment – I don't know, but the devil was conquered'
(14,425–6). Mitya's utterance – 'my mother entreated God' –
unexpectedly casts a new light on her. The narrator never gave
us the slightest indication that she was either a devout believer
or a loving mother. On the contrary her 'emancipation' was
the object of his irony. It seems that Dostoevsky radically
changed her image just here, clearly assimilating it to Sophia's,
in order to introduce what was probably his most cherished
idea. Mitya's mother has also long been dead. How could she
have known of Mitya's earthly predicament, how could she
have entreated God just at that very moment Mitya was
tempted to kill his father? Where is she now? Vetlovskaia is
surely right when she remarks that Dostoevsky wanted to
suggest 'the thought that not a single person, neither the living

nor the dead, is separate from another'.[33] And again the idea of resurrection is introduced through a dead, or not dead mother's answered prayer, 'the devil was conquered'. Here, as Terras observes, the word 'devil' is used in its canonical sense.[34] Shortly thereafter Mitya attributes his salvation to a mediator of the opposite canonical power: 'But, you see, I didn't kill him, you see, my guardian-angel saved me – that's just what you haven't taken into account' (14,428). Clearly, this is exactly what Dostoevsky wished the reader to 'take into account'. The 'bright spirit' of 'der heilige Geist' preserved in Mitya's memory since childhood, 'someone's tears' (perhaps his guardian angel's) and his dead (or not dead) mother's prayers saved him from the crime of parricide. All Mitya's reasons for not killing his father come from memory.

The remembrances of Grushenka and Mitya have been assimilated to the novel's central code of affirmative memory. Both Grushenka and Mitya have been saved from a potential criminal act by latent childhood memories which acquired a salvational function at a moment of extreme crisis. The two who will be joined in 'real' life, share childhood memories joined by the motif of a guardian angel and two ordinary foods which become transformed into symbols of spiritual nourishment. These memories in turn form part of a still larger artistic project. If the memories of certain fantastic elements of a fable, the biblical narratives, the prayers of dead mothers and a holy phrase beneficently influence persons and events in the 'real' world, then perhaps these fables, narratives, prayers and words are not so fantastic, or, perhaps the real world is more fantastic and miraculous than we think. In *The Brothers Karamazov*, 'fantastic realism' is realised mainly through memory.

One of the great artistic quests which dominated Dostoevsky's later work was to find a way to represent a dialogue between human words and the divine Logos. One readily available way was to incorporate biblical reminiscences, hidden and overt, into his heroes' words. Another was to assimilate his protagonists' images to the biblical and hagiographical images of speaking, acting people. Yet another major mode was prayer whereby the protagonists themselves remember God and initiate a dialogue. But Dostoevsky also aimed to pass the Holy Spirit through his characters' words and acts. This presents the literary artist with a far more difficult task since the Holy Spirit is 'Incomprehensible, Indescribable, Unknowable, Unspeakable and Invisible and it acts, watches and shields everywhere and touches invisibly', rather like a guardian angel.[35] One way he attempted to solve this task was by an appeal to childhood memory, an appeal based on his belief that the Spirit is immanent and exists in its purest form in childhood. In 1877 Dostoevsky made a very characteristic entry in his notebook which may illustrate our point. It is one of those strange, incomparable mini-dialogues which lay bare the essence of his dialogic art, an art in which Bakhtin finds every word, 'every gesture, every mimic movement on the hero's face' is penetrated by dialogue. Two interlocutors discuss the Holy Spirit. The first, a believer, is acutely aware of the conflict between the human and divine voices in the other:

– Say Christ my God, say it!
– Well, alright, Christ my God.
– And even though you don't believe, even though you speak with a smile (but with a kind one), Christ will forgive you – both you and me. He Himself said: blasphemy (*xula*) against Me I shall forgive, only blasphemy against the Spirit shall not be forgiven.
– And what is the Spirit?
– The Spirit is what is now between us and is why your face has become kinder, why you felt like weeping, because your lips trembled – you lie, don't be proud, they were trembling, I saw it, and the Spirit is what brought you from America to remember on this day the Christmas tree in your parents' home. That's what the Spirit is.[36]

An approximately similar dialogic configuration will take place between Ivan and Alyosha.

The last chapter of the novel, Dostoevsky said, is a 'completely separate scene: the burial of Ilyusha and the graveside speech of Aleksey Karamazov to the boys in which in part is expressed the meaning of the whole novel'.[37] The impulse for Alyosha's speech comes from a sudden memory while on his way to the funeral supper with the boys. Passing Ilyusha's stone, the 'whole picture' of Ilyusha's suffering for his father rises up in Alyosha's memory and becomes epiphanised: 'Something seemed to shake in his soul' (15,194). Alyosha's last words are a personal reminiscence and a discourse on memory which recapitulate the meaning of all the novel's important memory passages. Speaking to the *twelve* boys gathered around Ilyusha's stone, Alyosha tells them that they will soon part for he is shortly leaving, 'perhaps for a very long time'. He then creates a memory motif which parallels the key affirmative memories of the novel. Alyosha's commemoration of Ilyusha takes place in a context of loss, death and impending dispersal, which he tries to compensate by leaving the boys (and the reader) with a lasting memory of Ilyusha. Recalling Ilyusha's bravery, goodness and loyalty, Alyosha asks the boys always to remember Ilyusha and this moment of their unison in love and brotherhood. In the way Alyosha re-creates Ilyusha in his memory for the benefit of his young audience, there emerges an analogy between the pairs: the narrator/ Alyosha, Zosima/Markel and Alyosha/Ilyusha. He presents Ilyusha to the boys as a spiritual model in order to give a permanent future meaning to Ilyusha's suffering and death, to insure that Ilyusha did not live, suffer and die in vain. There is not a single canonical reference in Alyosha's last speech, but in the way he apotheosises Ilyusha's suffering for his father, his standing up alone for 'honour', there is an implied variation on the Urbild of Christ's suffering for His Father. His purpose is contained in his following words: 'Know that there is nothing higher, more powerful, more wholesome and more beneficial for life ahead than some good memory and especially one carried from childhood <...> If a person gathers many such memories with him in life, then he is saved for his whole life <...> What's more, maybe just this memory alone will keep him from a great evil' (15,195). Just as Alyosha knows that the memory of Markel saved Zosima, he believes that the memory of Ilyusha's life and death may be the redeeming seed of their future spiritual rebirth. This is one way new life comes from death.

But there is another way which goes infinitely beyond the commonplace idea that beloved people who have died continue to live in our memories, thereby influencing our lives for the better. Towards the very end, Kolya asks Alyosha the question to which the whole novel seeks to supply an affirmative answer:

'Karamazov!' cried Kolya, 'is it really true what religion tells us, that we shall all rise from the dead and shall return to life and see each other again, everyone, and Ilyusha too?'

'Certainly we shall rise, certainly we shall see each other, and shall tell each other gladly, joyfully everything that has happened', answered Alyosha, half laughing, half enraptured. (15,197)

As Zosima took Alyosha's hand in his dream, so Alyosha, the young Pater Seraphicus, joins hands with the boys and leaves the novel to the accompaniment of 'eternal memory' and Kolya's joyous, exultant shouts of 'Hurrah for Karamazov!', a secular 'Hosanna' to Alyosha.

This scene also invites the reader to 'resurrect' in his or her own memories redeeming words or images, or, perhaps to take the whole fiction as such. By creating these memory parallels, these invocations to salvational memories, Dostoevsky emphasises their importance for this ending where all memory motifs converge in the synthesis of Alyosha's speech, where 'in part is expressed the meaning of the whole novel'.

From this exposition of affirmative memory motifs several fundamental ideas can be discerned. First, good memories in *The Brothers Karamazov* grounded on love and faith in themselves retain salvational powers. They are not simply objects of fond, sentimental rumination, but are potential instruments of salvation, guarding against evil and temptation. Hence Alyosha's (and Zosima's) emphasis on the salvational and redemptive function of even one good memory. The romantic idea of memory as nostalgic reminiscence, as a longing for lost loves, personal happiness, vanished youth or hopes has no place in the novel. Nor do we find Proust's longing to recapture the past, to bewitch time itself so as to fix the past into permanent images of aesthetic contemplation. Rather memory in *The Brothers Karamazov* is used to inform and direct the characters' lives in the future towards the ultimate goals of personal and national salvation. Every good memory receives

a sacralised accent by virtue of either a similarity or a contiguity relation with sacred sources. They thus function as
reminders of the novel's paradigmatic memory, taking us back
to the memory of that 'eternal mould' of the world. These
memories always arise suddenly to coincide with a critical
turning point and serve to remind the protagonists of their
higher nature, of the divine 'image and likeness' in which,
according to Dostoevsky, they were created. Every biblical
reminiscence serves to join the earthly 'passing show' with
'eternal verity'. Every instance of spiritual catharsis and
renewal takes place on the basis of remembrances of living
spiritual models. Thus, we have the following pairs: Markel/
Zosima, Sophia–Zosima/Alyosha, Zosima/the Mysterious
Visitor, Dr Herzenstube–Grigory/Mitya, Alyosha/Grushenka
and, potentially, Alyosha/Lise, Ilyusha–Alyosha/Kolya and
the boys. The characters' memories of these living models
summon up, in turn, numinous presences of positive divine
prototypes (the Mother of God, Guardian Angels, God the
Father, Mary Magdalene and Christ).

This structure enabled Dostoevsky to bring the action of
divine mercy into his characters' lives, his novel's world and
thus to affirm the second idea, namely that providential Grace
works through memory. Sacred memories are a vital medium
through which Grace works to accomplish the sanctification
and regeneration of human beings. All those who can freely
and wholeheartedly respond to Grace achieve renewal and
salvation. Others, such as Ivan, cannot give a willing response
because they lack or have yet to find a persuasive, redeeming
spiritual model.

The third, most important idea concerns the relationship
between memory and resurrection. Good salvation memories
never die but remain latent. Alyosha gives expression to this
idea in the Life where he quotes his elder's belief that 'the
righteous man departs, but his light remains <...> People are
always saved after the death of the one who saves' (14,292).
Alyosha and Zosima treasure memories of beloved people long
dead, who come to life by virtue of their remembrances. On
earth the dead live only in the memories of the living. In this

novel, the author repeatedly breaks down the absolute sense of the past, by bringing the dead into the memories of the living in such a way as to suggest that the dead are affecting their lives now. By combining sudden memories of the dead who themselves exemplified the highest spiritual models with critical turning points, Dostoevsky aimed to put across the idea that they are involved now in a redemptive resolution of a crisis. This way we receive a sense of the simultaneous coexistence of all people which in turn is a reflection of paradise when 'time shall be no more'. A memory act can be an earthly mimesis of divine resurrection. And the reality of divine resurrection is what *The Brothers Karamazov* wishes most to affirm.

All the protagonists' crucial redeeming memories originate in episodes in childhood, before they can rationalise their experiences. This lends them psychological credence, but also imparts to them poetic significance. Children are symbolic of birth and rebirth, of new beginnings and new eras. The paradigmatic model of the Resurrection is expressed in numerous rebirth motifs throughout the novel, from seeds to spiritual renewals, from Zosima's great metaphor of the world as a garden planted with the seeds God has taken from 'other worlds', to Alyosha's vision of Zosima resurrected in heaven.

These main attributes of memory in *The Brothers Karamazov*, salvational, providential and resurrectional, can be related to the Epigraph. Speaking metaphorically, good or sacred memories are like seeds which can save, guide and resurrect souls. The following admittedly simplified and schematic parallel pattern emerges. Zosima and Alyosha were drawn to the religious life by their childhood memories of two beloved persons, then long dead, Markel and Sophia. Both are remembered illumined in the declining rays of sunlight, symbol of a sheer act of compassionate Grace. Markel, accepting faith before death (falling to earth), sowed the first seed of a sacred memory which later led to Zosima's spiritual rebirth and his choice of the monastic path, bringing him eventually to the monastery in the Karamazovs' town. Sophia's religious faith, distilled in Alyosha's iconic memory and diffused in his vague recollections of being taken to the monastery in childhood, informed those barely conscious impulses causing his path to converge with Zosima. For Alyosha the memories became obscurely activated when he decided to visit his mother's grave; for Zosima the sacred memory of Markel was vividly revived after he beat his servant. Zosima, in living for his brother, multiplied the seed and bequeathed it to others. Just before his death, he sends Alyosha into the world to spread seeds of faith sown in the soil of sacred memories, first among his family, then to others near to him, then to the new generation represented by the local schoolboys. Ilyusha, in dying, may increase it twelve-fold thanks, in part, to Alyosha's funeral eulogy which strives to guarantee the boys' future memories of Ilyusha. By the end of the novel, Alyosha, Markel's spiritual brother, is poised for departure to spread the sacred seeds amongst the larger family of mankind in that unknown but hopeful future which takes leave of the novel. Thus, within the novel we observe a branching out effect which illustrates the redemptive path Christ marks out in the Epigraph; the corn of wheat that falls into the earth (dies) and 'bringeth forth much fruit'.

This brings us back to the narrator's function. Only a temporally distanced, reminiscing narrator could represent the past so as to reveal such a pattern, for life patterns emerge only retrospectively. If there is a coherent pattern in life, then life has meaning, and then so do suffering and death. More, in *The Brothers Karamazov* they are given a transcendental meaning, contrary to Ivan's Inquisitor and devil. Good ramifies, and this may be what Dostoevsky meant when he remarked that to the arguments of Ivan and the Inquisitor, 'the whole novel serves as an answer'.[38]

CHAPTER 5

The memories of the characters: forms of negative memory

And nothing in all nature,
Did he want to bless.

The Demon, A. S. Pushkin

Dostoevsky's artistic imagination always moved along oppositions embodied in characters brought together in the most intense and varied dialogic relations. Thus, memory in *The Brothers Karamazov* sometimes assumes painful, subversive and destructive forms which cause suffering and 'catastrophe'. This category of memories we may label negative memory. Such memories form a system of negative responses to the system of affirmative memory, integrated into the novel's encompassing context of cultural memory through various modes of mockery, denial, hatred or subversion of the values contained in the sacred memory. Thus, forgiveness, veneration, faith, remembrances of good deeds, being the keeper of one's brother, love of God and humanity meet their opposites and struggle with revenge, sacrilege, cynicism, mockery of good deeds, fatal abandonments, hatred of God and contempt for humanity. If the timely arousal of a sacred memory illustrates the action of providential Grace, then the unrelenting painful memories of evil acts describe a moral drama of divine Retribution. And if there is the good seed of the Word inscribed in the characters' memories and the novel's cultural context bringing joy and compassion into their lives, there is also the evil seed of various anti-Words which settles in the recesses of their minds and spreads misery and destruction throughout the novel's world.

Negative memory about the characters has to be distinguished from the characters' negative memories. A very broad spectrum of painful memories is represented, some through the narrator's biographical material, others through the characters' flash-backs or confessional revelations. In the first case, the narrator's ambiguous memories about some of his protagonists are to the forefront as he shapes his representations of their words and images. In the second case, the characters' negative memories occupy the foreground as they play their harmful roles in the novel's dialogues and events.

Several main types of negative memory can be distinguished. First are those corrosive personal memories of hurts and betrayals which turn into rankling hatreds and desires for revenge. Grushenka vows to get even with her former lover who betrayed her when she was only seventeen. By teasing Fyodor and Mitya she tries to take revenge on men for her past hurt. Hence, she also plays a role in the 'catastrophe'. Katerina harbours lacerating memories of real and imagined humiliations. She seethes with a deeply rooted desire for vengeance to which she disastrously succumbs at the trial in a desperate attempt to save Ivan. Mitya wronged her, but she too contributed to the 'catastrophe' by tempting him with her ruse of asking him to post three thousand roubles to her half-sister. A distinctive feature of these memories is that they are exacerbated, nurtured. As Grushenka says: 'You see, Alyosha, I've grown terribly fond of my tears in these five years. Perhaps I only love my resentment and not him at all!' (14,322).

A different function, both morally and poetically, is represented by Ilyusha. In the novel's typology of negative memory, he serves as a living example of Zosima's teaching 'cast a bad seed' in a child's soul and 'it will grow' (14,289). Ilyusha suffers keenly from the burning memory of Mitya's public humiliation of his father, who, in his turn, will 'never forget' what his son's 'little face' was like at that moment when Mitya pulled him by his beard into the square. Father and son suffer for each other in contrast to Fyodor and his sons.

Another type in the negative series comprises those involuntary memories of base or evil acts which haunt the perpetrators. The novel presents a number of variations on the theme of an unrelenting bad conscience. Mitya suffers from the nagging memory of having stolen Katerina's money to win Grushenka. During the trial he shouts: 'of course it was a disgrace, a disgrace which I don't deny, the most disgraceful act of my whole life <...> I could've returned it, but I didn't return it! I preferred to remain a thief in her eyes <...> but the main disgrace was that I knew beforehand that I wouldn't give it back!' (15,110). The Mysterious Visitor's story is, as Peace says, 'a parable about the terrible power of conscience'.[1] For fourteen years, he confesses to Zosima, he has been haunted by the memory of the murder he committed, now with increasing torment. He cannot accept love anymore, the faces of his children have become a torture to him. Although he decides at last to make a public confession, the thought that agonises him most of all is 'the memory, what a memory of me I shall leave in their hearts!' (14,279) Zosima still remembers 'with shame and anguish' his 'bestial cruelty' of forty years ago when he violently bloodied his servant's face with blows in a fit of rage. These protagonists, though, are able to join their own memories with the paradigm of redemptive memory, to heed and accept the voice of 'Christ's law'. This brings them to an internal recognition and condemnation of the wrongs they have done others and, through a free open confession, they pass through the process of spiritual cleansing and thus realise the redemptive plot. Others do not. This brings us to the most destructive type of negative memory.

Because the moral law must be an irreproachable standard for judgment and guidance, 'it is the height of transgression', wrote Kant, 'to detract a whit from its purity'.[2] In *The Brothers Karamazov*, all those who deliberately attempt to detract from the purity of the moral law, from the memory of Christ's voice, are the prime agents of suffering and catastrophe. Thus, while almost everyone shares some blame for the suffering depicted in the novel, the main actors in the drama of sin, conscience and Retribution are Fyodor, Smerdyakov and Ivan, that unholy trinity who occupy the same premises. These three protagonists are 'structured as equivalent elements'.[3] The metaphorical principles of similarity, equivalence and parallel patterning are fundamental for understanding their moral and poetic function in the novel. Their story and plot lines occupy the same 'contextual field' because it is they who play the decisive roles in the crime of parricide. Finally, and most important for the novel's poetic memory, their images are saturated with similar symbolic motifs, that is, they are parts of the same negative symbolic system. And this is directly related to their most crucial equivalence, they all engage in varying gradations of mockery, desecration and wilful, malevolent subversions of the whole system of the collective sacred memory. As a result, the consciousness of conscience (redemptive memory) has become suppressed, attenuated or detached in them. The unnatural, bedevilled interrelationships between these sons and their father cause their paths to converge in parricide, paths laid down by their father.

FYODOR

The primary antecedents of the crime are Fyodor Karamazov's unexpiated sins. Sacrilege is defined as a profound outrage committed on consecrated persons or things. Fyodor literally sowed the seeds of his own destruction by grossly violating two holy innocents, fathering within the same year his two murderers. First he raped Lizaveta Smerdyashchaya when he had just gone into 'mourning' ('with crepe on his hat') for his first wife, thus compounding the sin of violation of a holy fool in God with his desecration of the memory of the dead. If the mute 'idiot' Lizaveta cannot leave any words of accusation behind her, she does leave her eloquent act of giving birth to Smerdyakov in the bathhouse situated in Fyodor's garden. Discussing how the diminutive Lizaveta managed to climb the high fence in her condition, the narrator mingles a natural explanation with a mysterious one: 'Some were convinced that "they lifted her over", others that "it lifted her over"' (14,92). Appending the eerie 'it lifted her over', the author suggests through the back door of rumour that transcendental forces helped Lizaveta bear powerful witness against Fyodor Karamazov by leaving behind an embodied memory, a constant living reminder of his violation. For on 'that same day' Fyodor's servants, Grigory and Marfa, buried their 'little deceased one'. Marfa is awakened by the newborn Smerdyakov's cry which she fearfully takes to be the cry of her dead infant calling her. Lizaveta's dying groans lead Grigory to Smerdyakov who is immediately adopted as a substitute for their dead infant. After many years Lizaveta's act literally brings destruction on Fyodor Karamazov's head, thus retrospectively transforming her into an instrument of Retribution. Two separate instances of spontaneous memory arousal on the fatal night of the murder establish this important connection. Mitya gains his fateful access to his father's garden by knowingly choosing exactly the same place to jump over the high fence as Lizaveta did: 'If she could climb over it', God knows why flashed through his mind 'surely I can too', whereupon he jumps over with ease (14,353). Nearby, notes the narrator, stood the bathhouse. And just after the murder, Marfa, wakened by Smerdyakov's 'terrifying epileptic scream', hears groans coming from the garden: 'Lord, just like Lizaveta Smerdyashchaya then!' (14,409). The holy fool's dying groans are answered by the murderer's scream across twenty-four years in these powerful auditory images of cries for vengeance and vengeance accomplished.

Shortly after raping Lizaveta, Fyodor violated another orphaned holy innocent, Sophia Ivanovna, mother of Ivan and Alyosha, an 'orphan', a 'very young person', 'gentle, mild and meek'. Suffering and pathos dominate the narrator's brief representation of her short life, her early orphanhood, her misery in the home of her tyrannical 'benefactress', her attempted suicide, her desperately rash elopement with Fyodor. Most important are her obscure religious origins, her 'phenomenal humility' and devout religiosity, all gathered into her name, the eponym of Holy Wisdom, the Hagia Sophia of Eastern Orthodoxy. Fyodor, a man well into middle age, married this sixteen-year-old 'little girl' (*devochka*) barely out of childhood, because he 'was attracted only by the remarkable beauty of the innocent little girl, above all by her innocent appearance, which so struck him, the sensualist <...> "Those innocent eyes slashed through my soul like a razor then", he would say afterwards, vilely sniggering in his own way' (14,13). Before her 'innocent eyes' Fyodor 'carried on orgies of debauchery' in the marital home. These repeated outrages against one who symbolises the prototype of holy innocence are a sacrilege exceeding the rape of Lizaveta. From some hints of the narrator we can deduce that Fyodor's conjugal life with Sophia amounted to legalised rape which led to her nervous shrieking illness. In effect, if not with intent, he drove two holy innocents to their early deaths.

Fyodor is also a profaner of sacred rites and texts, and a desecrator of holy images (the latter instance we take up in our next chapter). At the monastery, he performs the role of blasphemous buffoon in which he mocks and travesties the sacred memory at every turn, in word and gesture. He parodies the sacrament of baptism with his absurd false anecdote about Diderot; and he cynically misascribes a miracle performed by St Denis, patron saint of France, to the Orthodox *Lives of the Saints*. With a parodically theatrical gesture of falling to his knees before Zosima, Fyodor asks: 'Master, what shall I do to inherit eternal life?' Fyodor is mocking salvation and tempting Zosima; his is a verbatim quotation of the query the lawyer put to Christ 'to tempt Him' (Luke 10:25). Ludicrously quoting the woman who called out to Christ: 'Blessed is the womb that bare Thee, and the paps that gave Thee suck', Fyodor lecherously adds 'especially the paps', but omits Christ's answer: 'Rather blessed are they that hear the Word of God and keep it' (Luke 11:27–28). Jumping up to kiss Zosima's hand with an inflated exclamation of 'Blessed man', Fyodor asserts: 'Verily, I am a lie and the father of a lie. Though, perhaps not the father of a lie, I'm getting mixed up in my texts, well, at least the son of a lie, and that will be enough' (14,41). This is a mocking quotation of Christ's characterisation of the devil as 'a liar and the father of a lie' (John 8:44), and a parodic appropriation of Christ's language. Christ uses the 'verily' locutions to enunciate a truth, the 'I Am's' to express in similes the mystery of His synthetic divine and human nature. Fyodor also debases the novel's central affirmative idea of resurrection when he repeatedly dubs Maximov 'von Sohn', a man murdered in a brothel ('It is the real von Sohn, risen from the dead!') (14,84). Zosima sees a reflection of the divine archetypes in the world ('It is the ancient Rachel, weeping for her children'), Fyodor takes for his model of resurrection a man lured to death by his sensuality who turns out to be an ironic prefiguration of his own fate.

And yet, the 'consciousness of conscience' is not totally absent in Fyodor. The theme of divine Retribution is introduced by him in that only dialogue represented in Book One, a dialogue between him and Alyosha which is entirely given over to his preoccupation with hell: 'I keep thinking, I keep thinking, from time to time, of course, not all the while. It's impossible, I think, that the devils will forget to drag me down with their hooks to their place when I die' (14,23). Fyodor continues with some grotesque speculations about whether the hooks are made of 'iron' and whether there are 'ceilings' in hell. The *PSS* editors note that 'iron hooks' are an allusion to verses from Russian spiritual folklore on the theme of the biblical parable about the rich man and poor Lazarus (Luke 16:20–31), (15,525–6). The image of devils dragging the souls of sinners down to hell with hooks appears on accompaniments to the liturgy, on icons depicting the Last Judgment. Such an icon, evoking the memory of hell and Retribution, is the one the author associates to Fyodor Karamazov. And does not Fyodor dimly hear through his irony 'the voice of Christ's law' when, continuing, he says to Alyosha, 'if they [the devils] don't drag me down <...> where is there justice in the world? *Il faudrait les inventer*, those hooks, for me on purpose, for me alone, because if you only knew, Alyosha, what a shameless person I am!' (14,23).

Fyodor may be mocking biblical and folk beliefs about hell, but it is a mockery mingled with genuine fear. During his sleepless nights, when all alone in his large empty house with only rats for company, Fyodor, says the narrator, 'would suddenly sense in himself sometimes, in his drunken moments, a spiritual terror and moral trembling'. At these moments he would especially feel the need to have a loyal person close by, someone who would not judge him, reproach him or threaten him, the need 'for someone who would defend him - from whom? From someone unknown, but terrifying and dangerous' (14,86–7). Later the reader can make the correct substitution for that 'terrifying and dangerous someone'. And this 'someone' is metaphorically equivalent to that equally anonymous third person whom the Grand Inquisitor invokes when he says 'We are with *him*!', and from whom Alyosha flees when, after listening to Ivan's Legend, he rushes back to Zosima to save him 'from *him* forever!' (14,234,241).

Since childhood is the locus of salvational memory, it should be revealing to turn to the narrator's representation of the childhood of Ivan, the major ideological adversary of Zosima and Alyosha, and then to that of Smerdyakov, Ivan's disciple and Fyodor's *de facto* murderer.

IVAN

The narrator introduces Ivan as follows:

However, of the elder brother Ivan, I shall merely report that he grew into a kind of morose and withdrawn boy, far from timid, but already from his tenth year he had become aware that they were nevertheless growing up in someone else's family and on other people's charity and that their father was the sort of man of whom it was shameful even to speak, and so on, and so on. (14,15)

The narrator is keeping his distance from Ivan. Although he speaks about Ivan in the first person, the formal chronicling verb, 'report', renders his tone more dry, noncommittal. Mid-sentence (from 'nevertheless') Ivan's intonations of wounded pride penetrate the narrator's speech. Ivan's rankling resentment at having to live on 'other people's charity', and his shame at the very thought of his disreputable father evidently occupied a disproportionate share of his young mental life. The narrator's appended 'and so on, and so on' suggests that Ivan's inner complaints were repeated *ad infinitum*. The first sound of Alyosha's voice enters the novel in a direct quotation with his loving memory of his mother; Ivan's slips into the narrator's word in the quasi-direct mode with his resentful memory of his father.

The narrator gives his own testimonial to one of those 'other people' on whose 'charity' Ivan and Alyosha depended, their guardian Yefim Petrovich: 'And if the young people were indebted to anyone for their upbringing and education, for their whole lives, then it was to that very Yefim Petrovich, a most noble and humane man, the likes of whom one rarely meets' (14,14). Ivan makes quite a different evaluation of his guardian: 'Ivan himself used to relate afterwards that everything happened, so to say, because of the "ardour for good deeds" of Yefim Petrovich, who had got carried away by the idea that a boy with the abilities of a genius should be educated by a teacher of genius' (14,15). Again Ivan's voice, in both quotation and indirect discourse, permeates the narrator's word. Ivan introduces Yefim's 'idea' along with Yefim's idealistic tones only to twist them with his sarcasm. He also inserts the important idea that his education can be causally linked to 'everything' that happened. Ivan, in mocking Yefim's 'ardour for good deeds', can only see Yefim as having been 'carried away' with his 'idea'. This is an ironic projection to the future when, in a similar way, the devil will mock Ivan's belated intention to perform a noble act, to tell the truth at the trial. Ivan's mockery of Yefim, when compared to the narrator's testimonial to Yefim's nobility and humanity, points to a serious flaw in him. Alert to ideas of noble deeds performed far away and long ago, Ivan is evidently blind to the generosity and good intentions of real people in his own life. Ivan's resentment of his natural father so pervades his mental life that it prevents him from seeing any goodness in his 'humane and noble' surrogate father, in marked contrast to Mitya who gratefully remembers the kindness of Grigory and Herzenstube. Ivan's denial from childhood of goodness in others prepares the ground for his susceptibility to ideas which are based on sweeping denials of human goodness, worth and dignity.

The narrator stresses the hardships Ivan endured in his first years at university, adding:

It must be noted that he did not want to make even an attempt then to correspond with his father – maybe out of pride, out of contempt, and maybe on account of a cold commonsensical reasoning which prompted him that he would not receive any even slightly serious support from his papa. (14,15)

Ivan's total rejection of his natural father bespeaks an accumulation of negative memory over many years. His reasons for avoiding all contact with him, 'pride', 'contempt' and 'cold commonsensical reasoning', reveal traits which developed as a response to his father's rejection and shamefulness, and which tend to guarantee his self-contained isolation in the world altogether.

Important also are Ivan's literary activities thanks to which the author can open up the novel's central ideological themes. While still at university Ivan wrote successful, *piquant* (a word from his father's vocabulary) 'little articles' about 'street events', and so began his 'collection' of 'little facts', an activity which he subsequently exploits for a malignant purpose. Ivan's journalistic *nom de plume*, 'Eyewitness', is particularly characteristic; it is an anonymous mask allowing him to conceal his identity while assuming the role of the detached observer, a role he will carry over into his relations with his family. However, Ivan's literary career eventually blossoms under his own name and he 'suddenly' became 'noticed' and 'remembered'. The occasion for this is a 'strange article' he wrote on the topical issues of the 'ecclesiastical court' which takes everyone by surprise 'because he graduated in natural science'. His article is so ambiguous that people of totally opposite persuasions, believers and atheists, see in him a champion of their views. Summing up, the narrator supplies the interpretative clue: 'In the end, some shrewd people decided that the whole article was only an insolent farce and a mockery' (14,16). And so the main ideological split in the novel, that between faith and atheism, first issues from Ivan on a note of mockery of 'Christ's society'. Winding up his initial representation of Ivan, the narrator returns to the theme of Ivan's resentment, and now pointedly opposes him to Alyosha, who 'never cared on whose means he was living. In this respect

he was a complete contrast to his elder brother Ivan Fyodorovich, who <...> from his very childhood bitterly felt that he
was living at the expense of his benefactor' (14,20).

Thus negative memory has two facets as regards Ivan. First
there is the narrator's subjective memory work which takes on
a decidedly uneasy, not to say ominous tone whenever it
touches on Ivan, creating a sense of nameless anxiety about his
intentions. Secondly, there is Ivan's attitude of all-pervasive
resentment extending over his childhood which allows us to
infer either an absence or a burial of good memories and
consequently a negative memory of childhood altogether. No
specific bad memory is given, and this is poetically right. For
even a single painful memory of a concrete incident would have
allowed the reader to construct an easy psychological, and
therefore reductive, explanation for Ivan's massive negation of
'God's world'. The author is aiming to expose a much larger
negation, one which though rooted in Ivan's resentment
towards his father, will later go far beyond it to harden into an
ideological position of nihilism. Feelings of resentment and
injured pride permeate his entire life so far represented. Such
deep resentments of long standing turn out to be the most
destructive form of negative memory.

SMERDYAKOV

It is a pertinent fact that only Alyosha and Smerdyakov are
accorded eponymous chapters detailing their childhoods. The
pair Alyosha/Smerdyakov forms the most absolute opposition
among the brothers. This can be demonstrated from the
narrative of Smerdyakov's childhood where it emerges that
Alyosha's inborn saintly nature forms an absolute contrast to
Smerdyakov's genetic demonic traits.

Demonic motifs make up the essence of Smerdyakov's image
from the very beginning of his life. The deceased infant whom
he replaced was born with six fingered hands which struck
such 'sorrow and terror' in Grigory's heart that he objected to
having it christened because 'it's a dragon', one of the canonical
names for Satan (Revelation 12:13) (14,88). Here Dostoevsky

uses folk memories of the devil in order to suggest the idea that Smerdyakov is a diabolic changeling. Handing over the infant Smerdyakov to his wife, Grigory says: 'A child of God – an orphan is everyone's kin <...> Our little lost one has sent us this, and this one comes from the devil's son and a holy innocent' (14,92–3). Grigory speaks more truly than he knows. The editors of the *PSS* take Fyodor's 'mistake' in styling himself as the 'father of a lie' to refer indirectly to Ivan (15,530). But it just as equally, if not more so, refers to Smerdyakov. Grigory and Marfa name the infant Pavel; soon he acquires the patronymic Fyodorovich. Fyodor's patronymic is Pavlovich, the son of Pavel. If Fyodor is the son of the devil, then Pavel Fyodorovich Smerdyakov is at once the *de facto* son of Fyodor and metaphorically the devil. And if Fyodor is the 'father of a lie', then he is metaphorically the devil whose offspring is a lie, Ivan. Poetically, then, Fyodor is not so 'mixed up'. Through Fyodor's memory, he and his sons Ivan and Smerdyakov are brought together in this canonical definition of the devil. Finally, Fyodor himself gives Smerdyakov his surname thus unconsciously insuring that the 'stink' of his sin remains in his ears.

Smerdyakov is apparently deficient in good memories but he does betray a talent for corrupting the collective sacred memory from early childhood on. And he harbours some profound resentments. 'In childhood he was very fond of hanging cats and then burying them with ceremony. He used to dress up for this in a sheet which formed a kind of surplice, and chant and swing something over the dead cat as though it were a censer. All this on the sly, in the greatest secrecy' (14,114). Rituals are expressions of the collective memory; religious rituals symbolise those values the community holds sacrosanct. Sacrilege is also defined as the 'sin of stealing or misappropriating what is consecrated to God's service'. The mock religious 'ceremony' Smerdyakov morbidly performs over the corpses of cats he has hung is a sacrilegious perversion of one of the primary commemorative rites of the Church, the funeral service which memorialises the departed and enacts the hopeful faith in life eternal (eternal memory). In the

Orthodox service, censing is a physical means of venerating the image and likeness of God in the deceased who is not viewed as a corpse. Smerdyakov retains the outward forms of the ceremony but he corrupts its meaning by putting it to a debased use. He steals the priestly function and substitutes cats for human beings as the object of the ceremony. Smerdyakov thus usurps divinely ordained prerogatives, debases the human being and denies the immortality of the soul. When Grigory catches the boy at his 'ceremony', he gives him a thrashing and turns on him: 'Are you a human being? <...> You're not a human being, you grew from the mildew in the bathhouse, that's who you are.' Denying Smerdyakov the status of a human being, Grigory too makes his contribution to the 'catastrophe'. The narrator adds in an utterance heavy with foreshadowing: 'Smerdyakov, as it turned out afterwards, could never forgive him those words' (14,114). With this sole entry into Smerdyakov's inner life, the narrator gives us a humanly comprehensible motive for his baleful resentment, a resentment which finally surfaces in Smerdyakov's own words when, during his last meeting with Ivan and on the verge of suicide, he accuses his mentor: 'You always considered me a midge – not a man' (15,67). Smerdyakov ends by hanging himself, thus performing the ultimate perversion on himself, his final denial of his human and divine nature. He himself prefigured his suicide and retribution in the diabolic 'ceremony' he performed in childhood.

Smerdyakov also perverts the holy texts. His obsession with his illegitimate origins first appears as a negation of divine cosmic origins.[4] Grigory's attempt to teach Smerdyakov 'sacred history' quickly 'came to nothing'. Smerdyakov is immune to the sublime power of the Word. Convinced he has discovered a logical inconsistency in the first verses of Genesis, he says with sarcastic triumph: 'The Lord God created the light on the first day, and the sun, moon and stars on the fourth day. Where was the light shining from on the first day?' (14,114) (Smerdyakov is unacquainted with the doctrine of God as the uncreated Light.) Grigory responds to Smerdyakov's insolent mockery by 'furiously' striking the boy on the face. Within days Smerdyakov suffers his first attack of epilepsy. But he stores up his casuistic perversion of Genesis and, many years later, he uses it to impress Ivan, the man who 'taught' him 'how to talk', and who at first found him 'original' (14,242–3).

There are other diabolic traits. Smerdyakov grew up, says the narrator 'looking at the world from the corner' (14,114), his habitual place of retreat from where he glowers after Grigory's beatings. Here we are reminded of Lise's and Alyosha's shared dreams which feature devils advancing towards their beds from the 'corners' of the room.

But Smerdyakov does not kill Grigory. Oddly enough, he never voices any personal hatred of Fyodor, though he has ample cause to resent him for treating him like a contemptible lackey. However, Smerdyakov fails to see a good natured element in Fyodor's belated attempts to assume fatherhood. Fyodor, says the narrator, 'not only was sure of his honesty, but for some reason even loved him' (14,116). This information makes Smerdyakov a parricide in spirit as well as in fact. There is a decidedly impersonal aspect to Smerdyakov's murder of Fyodor, as though he were acting like an automaton in obedience not only to orders heard from Ivan, but from another's only dimly heard, from some obscure evil memory driving him along a road just as inevitable as Alyosha's.

As the criminal story gathers momentum, the narrator's representation of Smerdyakov's image is progressively permeated with symbolic signs of evil coming to fruition. Smerdyakov has the traditional 'evil eye' which, when conspiring with Ivan, takes on a life of its own by acquiring a voice: 'His left, slightly screwed up little eye was winking and grinning as if it were saying: "why are you going, you won't pass by, you see that both of us clever people have something to talk over" '. And again the sinister eye 'speaks' the most sinister phrase in the novel: 'And what I smiled at, you yourself must understand, if you're a clever man, his screwed up, left little eye seemed to say' (14,243,244). The winking left eye of Smerdyakov symbolically complements the slightly elongated left leg of Ivan which Vetlovskaia interprets as a demonic symbol.[5]

Smerdyakov has also grown up to become an adept profaner of sacred texts. He perverts the idea of faith with his casuistic distortion of Christ's parable of the mustard seed. Like Fyodor, he is a desecrator of icons (he 'taught' Fyodor to hide the 3,000 roubles behind the icon in his bedroom). During his last talk with Ivan, he covers the blood money on the table with St Isaac of Niniveh's Sermons. Finally, and perhaps most damningly, Smerdyakov is a corrupter of children; Ilyusha's last days are overshadowed by his remorse over the cruel trick Smerdyakov taught him to play on the dog Zhuchka.

Smerdyakov perverts Fyodor and his half brothers in the primary sense of the word, that is, he causes them to turn the wrong way at critical moments. First, he gives Mitya a false time for the meeting at the monastery, thereby undermining this sole attempt at a reconciliation between Fyodor and Mitya. For Mitya was in a conciliatory mood when he agreed to the meeting, 'since he secretly reproached himself for many especially sharp outbursts in his arguments with his father' (14,30). Had he not arrived one hour late, the meeting might have taken a more favourable turn. Second, when Alyosha asks about Mitya's whereabouts, Smerdyakov sends Alyosha to the tavern, knowing that Mitya never received the oral message Ivan asked him to deliver, thereby deflecting Alyosha from finding Mitya. On the morning of the murder, Smerdyakov tells Fyodor that Grushenka will definitely come that night. Finally, and fatally, he succeeds in sending Ivan out of town. Whether Smerdyakov was consciously lying or not in all these cases is relatively unimportant. Important are the misdirections which emanate from him, the loyal servant of malevolent forces. There is a distant parallel here to his distortions of collective memory, ritual and biblical, and these perversions from the right paths.

Smerdyakov suffers from a deep, unassuageable resentment over his lowly origins. By the time of the narrator's story, his rankling grievance over having been deprived of his rightful place and status in life has reached murderous levels, towards others and himself: 'I'd have killed a man in a duel if he'd have called me a lowborn scoundrel (*podlets*) because I came from the Stinking Woman without a father' (14,204). Here again the Russian text continues a telling nuance lost in English translations. No human being can be born 'without a father', only demons (and angels) whose origins are usually vague. He also deeply resents the 'peasant' turns of speech people use when speaking about his mother: 'From my childhood up, whenever I hear "a wee bit", I could dash myself against a wall' (14,205). It now emerges that Smerdyakov has never forgotten another rebuke of Grigory who branded him a murderer right from his birth: 'Grigory Vasilyevish reproaches me for rebelling against my birth: "You", he says, "rent her belly".' Smerdyakov adds, in a statement which expresses the depth of his self hatred and despair: 'Well, I don't know about the belly, but I'd have let them kill me while I was still in the womb so that I wouldn't have come into the world at all' (14,204). Thus, Smerdyakov's suicidal urge was deeply ingrained long before he ever met Ivan. This, too, compels us to qualify the notion that Smerdyakov, in murdering Fyodor and killing himself, was acting solely under the influence of Ivan's ideas.

Much later, Alyosha replies to Ivan's question 'who was the murderer' with 'You yourself know who.' And when Ivan sarcastically invokes 'that fable' that it was Smerdyakov, Alyosha only repeats 'You yourself know who.' And when Ivan 'furiously' insists on a definite answer, Alyosha just as insistently repeats seven times over the space of a page, 'it *wasn't you*' who killed father. Alyosha is not only empirically right. Ivan himself indirectly identifies the ultimate murderer when he suddenly whispers: 'You've been at my place! <...> you've seen him [the devil] <...> You know ... otherwise how could you ...' (15,39–40). In order to reinforce the idea that the devil is the ultimate cause of the catastrophe, Dostoevsky passes it through a variety of voices. 'Oh, the devil did it, the devil killed father', says Mitya (14,431); 'Well ... well, that means the devil himself was helping you!' exclaims Ivan (15,66) and finally the *vox populi* at the end of the trial: 'Aye, the devil, just the devil, without the devil it wouldn't have happened' (15,177). Once we discern the diabolical forces playing into the novel's pattern of sin, sacrilege and Retribution, we may agree that Ivan is not altogether wrong when he tells Smerdyakov just after he has learned the truth: 'maybe I was guilty too, maybe I really had a secret wish that ... father would die, but I swear to you, I wasn't as guilty as you think, and maybe I didn't incite you at all. No, no I didn't incite you!' (15,66–7) If so, then Ivan was just as much incited as inciting.

This series symbolically represents the slow but inexorable procession of divine Retribution. For the chain of circumstances surrounding Smerdyakov's birth is the critical factor leading to his murderous resentment which proves fertile ground for parricide. Had Lizaveta not given birth in Fyodor's garden, Grigory and his wife would not have adopted Smerdyakov who grows up to murder his father. Thus Smerdyakov must be viewed as both an agent of demonic forces and an instrument of divine Retribution. But is he, like Judas, a mere helpless unconscious agent of divine justice? Is he not damned from the very beginning as the infant 'sent' by a 'dragon' and the offspring of a 'devil's son'? Does this not clash with Dostoevsky's well known aversion to determinism? Attempting to resolve this problem, Vetlovskaia argues that the novel shows that the responsibility for evil rests solely with people.[6] Evil is not inherent, and if people act badly it is only because they are ill and have forgotten their higher natures. God is not involved in their evil thoughts, words and deeds. Evil and suffering originate from, and belong to, the devil's realm. Of course God did not force Fyodor to rape Lizaveta or Ivan to abandon his father. But this explanation cannot adequately account for the sources of illness, for Smerdyakov's congenital evil traits, and it overlooks the fact that in Christian theology the devil has a function in the divine economy.

There are no clearcut answers to these questions. What the novel does say is that evil deeds have long memories, they remain over generations in the memories of people, of the community and history and thus cast long shadows over the future. Only when confessed and expiated can forgiveness heal, freedom be regained and harmony restored. Fyodor could have desisted from raping Lizaveta, but once he committed this sin a pattern was formed which in retrospect looks predestined. If a good deed can shape the future, so can an evil one. Good seeds bring forth much good fruit, evil seeds beget catastrophes. Devils are abroad, as Zosima warns Alyosha after the family gathering in his cell. Evil in *The Brothers Karamazov* exists potentially and actually.

Still, Smerdyakov did not act alone. Without Ivan he would never have killed Fyodor. The planter of the seed of parricide is Ivan, for he is the one who harbours the deepest hatred of his father, and who suffers the deepest resentment of all, the constant bitter sense of wounded pride. The humiliating, unrelenting awareness that his father was too shameful a person even to mention, that he and Alyosha had to live off the 'charity' of others are, as we have seen, facts carefully recorded by the narrator in his exposition of Ivan's childhood.

The strange symbiosis between Ivan and Smerdyakov is founded above all on resentment, on prolonged, strong feelings of impotent anger and profound ill will against those who have wronged them. Smerdyakov's feelings of aggression are frustrated by his keen sense of helplessness in childhood and his inferior position in adulthood (the lackey). Ivan's conscience will not allow him to express his resentful aggression against Fyodor in direct action. A distinctive feature of their resentments is that they do not recede into the past, they are ever present, they are all-consuming and poison from within. They cannot forget the injuries done them because they cannot forgive them, and they cannot forgive because they have no internally persuasive model of forgiveness to aid them. By the time Ivan has graduated from university his resentments from childhood have been converted into theories of atheism and nihilism which catastrophically combine with Smerdyakov's diabolic traits, his resentment over his inferior status, and his need for a hero who can provide him with a rationalisation for that obscure force driving him to avenge the violation, humiliation and death of his mother.

The images of Ivan and Smerdyakov form some striking parallels where Smerdyakov always represents a deeper degree of negation than Ivan. Both were lonely, unsociable boys: Ivan, 'proud', 'morose, withdrawn', Smerdyakov, 'taciturn', 'arrogant and seemed to despise everyone' (14,114). Ivan's mockery of his guardian's good intentions to help him develop his abilities is exceeded by Smerdyakov's total blindness to Fyodor's flawed but sincere attempts to help him. Fyodor's insight that Ivan 'loves no one', while not absolutely true, parallels Grigory's comment that Smerdyakov 'loves no one'. People who 'love no one', can only have a mental, emotional and spiritual life permeated by negative memories, or lost good ones. Smerdyakov and Ivan both engage in spying. Fyodor accuses Ivan: 'You want to keep an eye on me here, that's what you want, malicious soul', and later he tells Alyosha shortly before he is murdered: 'He wants to spy' (14,125,159). And they both converge in their refusals to be their brother's keeper. When Alyosha queries Smerdyakov about Mitya's whereabouts he receives the reply: 'How could I know about Dmitry Fyodorovich. It isn't as if I was his keeper, is it?' (14,206) Within the hour Alyosha hears the same sentiment from Ivan who, in response to Alyosha's concern about Mitya irritably returns: ' "Am I the keeper of my brother Dmitry?" <...> but then he suddenly smiled as if bitterly, "Cain's answer to God about his murdered brother eh?" ' (14,211). Ivan 'suddenly' remembers the canonical source (Genesis 4:9) and 'bitterly' makes the important connection between it and himself. Bitterness is a symptom of inner pain and grieving. But for Smerdyakov this biblical memory is absent, in his speech it is a hidden quotation which the reader can recognise. This idea has become so internalised in him that he has become its incarnation.

When Ivan returns to his father's house as a young man he is all at once confronted with the memory of his childhood, of having been excluded and abandoned. As these childhood memories come back to him he simultaneously realises that he hates his father. This process is not depicted, but its result is amply demonstrated. We recall Alyosha's distress when Ivan refuses to restrain their father's buffoonery in Zosima's cell:

What seemed strangest of all to him was that his brother Ivan Fyodorovich, the only one on whom he placed his hope and who alone had such an influence on their father that he could have stopped him, was now sitting quite immobile on his chair, his eyes lowered and, evidently, with some kind of inquisitive curiosity was waiting to see how it would all turn out, as if he himself were completely a stranger [*postoronnyi*] here. (14,40)

Ivan's curiosity and withdrawal are extremely hostile. From letting the old man make a fool of himself, he is only a few steps away from letting him be murdered. This is a prefiguration of the lowest, most fateful moment of his life when Ivan's curious eye-witnessing degenerates into outright spying and when, hours later, he withdraws from his father's house, abandoning him to his fate. He has also recently become acquainted with Dmitry for whom he feels 'great contempt, almost loathing' and 'indignation' that Katerina could prefer his elder brother, whom he considers his inferior (15,42). His hatred of his father and brother reaches a pathological intensity which is not at all unconscious: 'our little papa was a pig but his thinking was correct'; and: 'I hate the scoundrel [Mitya], I hate the scoundrel! I don't want to save the scoundrel, let him rot in prison!' (15,32,88) But his most fateful words are uttered shortly before the murder, just after Mitya has violently beaten Fyodor. Turning to Alyosha, Ivan says 'in a whisper', 'maliciously grimacing': 'One reptile [Mitya] will devour another reptile [Fyodor] and serve them both right!' (14,129) This is precisely the scheme Smerdyakov puts into action.

Shortly thereafter Alyosha finds Ivan sitting on a bench outside, noting 'something in his notebook'. Replying to Alyosha's anxious query whether anyone has the right to decide who is worthy to live, Ivan declares that everyone has the right to wish 'even for another's death'. He then promises 'always' to defend his father but in the same breath, he claims the 'right' to wish for his death: 'But in my wishes I retain for myself in this case full latitude' (14,132). Ivan's wish soon fathers the deed. We are never told what entry Ivan was making in his 'notebook' when Alyosha came across him. What we do know is that Ivan has amassed a 'collection' of 'little facts' and 'anecdotes' detailing human bestialities. What we can be sure of is that if Ivan was just entering the two 'reptiles' into his 'collection', he left himself out of the entry, just as he leaves himself out of his memories. This may be the most sinister image of Ivan in the novel.

Ivan's estrangement is a key point for our topic. Ivan is a man 'to the side' (*postoronnyi*), the one who belongs to no group, not to his family, his country, the monastic brethren or 'God's world' to which he 'returns his ticket'. And he has 'no friends' (14,213). The image of the outsider was positively conceived in the history of European Romanticism. However, in the history of Russian literature and ideas, it came to have ambiguous or negative connotations (Pushkin, Lermontov, Gogol). For Dostoevsky, the romantic is someone who sets himself apart from the *sobornost'*, from the Russian communal life. All Dostoevsky's problematic characters isolate themselves from their surrounding world and recede into a world of reading, ideas and dreams. They thus lose their living links with their fellow men. Ivan cuts himself off from the memory of the collective to which he belongs. It becomes alien to him because he has become absorbed by a cultural heritage (West European) that is alien to Russia, from Dostoevsky's point of view. This heritage is not isomorphic with the novel's positive memory because it is a different kind of memory, one that is asymmetric to the Russian tradition. This results in a moral and aesthetic conflict of world views, a different set of moral values which is set out allegorically in the Grand Inquisitor's discourse.

When Ivan and Alyosha next meet, in their famous dialogue at the tavern, the reader learns the contents of several items in Ivan's collection. Significantly, their meeting takes place solely because of Ivan's hatred of his father. As Ivan, no frequenter of taverns, tells Alyosha: 'Would you believe it, I dined here today only to avoid dining with the old man, that's how loathsome he's become to me' (14,212). Ivan has been endowed with the largest and most varied store of cultural memories, but these are impersonal, distanced. They intermingle with his life only in indirect, profoundly doubled-voiced ways. And they are used negatively. He seldom personally refers them to himself, unlike Mitya who relates the poetry he has memorised to his own life, his own predicament. The differences between Ivan's confessional word and Mitya's can be readily seen by comparing the role memory plays in their respective confessions. The author first gives us Mitya's word in the three chapters headed with the phrase 'The Confessions of an Ardent Heart'. Here we hear the genuine confessional word, a word addressed to a higher listener and which springs from the need for that listener's judgment and forgiveness: 'You're an angel on earth. You'll listen, you'll judge and you'll forgive ... And that's just what I need, that someone higher should forgive me' (14,97). Mitya's word bears the chief hallmarks of a confession, a word full of remorse, of his own painful memories of his own past failings and misdeeds, without attempt at concealment and guided by an overpowering wish to unburden the heart. In the three chapters devoted to Ivan's discourse (culminating in 'The Grand Inquisitor'), Ivan calls his word a 'confession'. But he rarely makes autobiographical statements, whereas Mitya's confession is replete with his personal reminiscences and feelings. The self need not be involved in communicating ideas, but it is necessarily involved in reporting one's own memories, especially one's confessional memories.

William James finds that personal memories are invested with feelings of 'warmth and intimacy'. Such feelings characterise 'all experiences "appropriated" by the thinker as his own'.[7] This is because they belong to the self, are an inseparable part of the self, whereas the thoughts or memories of others are 'merely conceived, in a cold and foreign fashion, and not appearing as blood-relatives, bringing their greetings to us from out of the past'. Ivan's mental life is marked by a heavy preponderance of conceived experience (ideas, history, facts, science, etc.). He represses any warmth within himself as soon as it arises, and he wards off intimacy on all sides. Only once in the chapter ambiguously titled 'The Brothers Get Acquainted', does a shared memory from childhood flicker up when Ivan recalls Alyosha's love of cherry jam (good memories again gravitate to Alyosha). 'I remember everything, Alyosha', he adds. But at once he oddly contradicts this in a remark which betrays a massive repression of memory: 'When

I went away to Moscow, for the first years I didn't even remember you at all' (14,208). This sole attempt to unite his life with Alyosha's on the basis of shared memories rapidly gives way to an avalanche of general accusations against the evils in the world.

Ivan says he wants only to stick by the facts, that is, by his 'collection' of 'little facts' and 'little anecdotes' he has gleaned from hearsay, newspaper cuttings and 'from wherever they turned up'. Horrible as these 'little facts' are, they do not fall within the orbit of his own experience but are at second or third remove to him. They are substitutes which testify to Ivan's failure ever to join his own personal memories with any native system of collective memory, with his family, his native culture, community or religion, from which he feels excluded and alienated in any case. Ivan suppresses his own personal memories, replacing them by anonymous incidents he reads about which seem to confirm his own reading and experiences in the social, historical context. These, in turn, he projects into an ideology of atheistic socialism and nihilism. Furthermore, however noble and sincere Ivan's indignation over the injustices he reads about, he does not have to involve himself personally in them because they all happened someplace else and, in some cases, long ago. However passionate and genuine his protest against the suffering of innocent children, it is not a call to remedy injustices against children now, as are Zosima's exhortations, and as is Mitya's urgent wish to do something 'now' for the 'babe'. Nor does he involve himself in the suffering of children going on before his eyes, as Alyosha does. Restricting his examples to events beyond his own purview, Ivan does not have to take responsibility for his word, he can 'play' with nihilism. The voice of conscience in Ivan is satisfied with substitutes. This is an outcome of his substitute negative memories which have blinded and detached him from the full consciousness of his own conscience, leading him to commit murder by proxy. His personal memories have disintegrated and been displaced by a variegated 'collection' of 'little facts and anecdotes'. As Vetlovskaia has shown, Ivan fits them into a rhetorical discourse in support of ideological arguments whose purpose is to undermine Alyosha's faith. His memories have also been displaced by fantasies and obsessive ideas. Significantly, Ivan's 'little poem' on the Grand Inquisitor is not a personal reminiscence, as is Alyosha's 'Life' of his elder Zosima, but a philosophical, theological fantasy, a tirade from which personal reminiscences have been all but expunged. Ideas, like fantasies, may not only be very abstract, but irresponsible because they are free of attachments to others, including oneself. Ivan's Grand Inquisitor poem is an enraged expression of obsessive negations, distortions and corruptions of the Gospels, an attack on the very foundations of Christian memory.[8] The Grand Inquisitor sequence depicts the endpoint of a process whereby Ivan's negative memories have been transformed into a universal resentment against the whole world. All these 'little facts' and fantasies he substitutes for his own personal negative memories, except one.

The narrator describes Ivan's inner thoughts on the last night he spent in his father's house, hours before he abandoned him to his fate:

he suddenly felt persistently and unbearably like <...> beating up Smerdyakov <...> he also felt as though he had lost all his physical strength. His head ached and was spinning round. Something hateful was rankling his soul, as though he meant to avenge himself on someone. He even hated Alyosha remembering the conversation he had just had with him, and at moments he intensely hated himself too. Of Katerina Ivanovna he almost forgot to think and wondered greatly at this afterwards. (14,251)

In that 'conversation' (at the tavern) Ivan took the devil's side and Alyosha has made him obscurely aware of it. Since Alyosha reminds Ivan of his higher self, it follows that 'even' hating Alyosha 'while remembering the conversation', Ivan hates himself totally and his own dialectic. Rejecting his brother's love at the end of that conversation, and banishing Katerina, the woman he is in love with from his memory, Ivan has, at this critical moment, excluded himself from all the sources of good and sacred memory in his own life. This is why he felt 'that he had lost all his ends', which leaves Ivan with nothing but his evil, Smerdyakovian self. He is then thrown back on his negative memory, on his hatred, violence, and urges 'to avenge himself on someone', which so overwhelm him, that he suffers a paralysis of will. He is now at the mercy of evil powers:

Remembering that night afterwards, a long time later, Ivan Fyodorovich recalled with particular loathing how he would suddenly get up from the divan and stealthily, as though he were terribly afraid of being watched, would open the doors, go out on the staircase and listen below to Fyodor Pavlovich stirring and pacing about there below, in the ground floor rooms, he would listen – for a long time, for about five minutes with a kind of strange curiosity, holding his breath with a thumping heart, and why he was doing all this, why he was listening, of course he himself did not know. This 'act' all his life afterwards he called 'vile' and all his life he considered it, deep inside him, in the inmost recesses of his soul, the basest act of all his life. (14,251)

This whole passage is informed by the 'benefit of hindsight' and shaped by a subtle intersection between memory past and future. Ivan's subsequent evaluation has been superimposed on the narrator's description of his past actions. This account of what Ivan did does not coincide with what he experienced on that night. For had Ivan actually thought on that night that he was committing the 'basest act of all his life', he almost certainly would not have left his father's house. Awareness came only 'a long time later', well after the events of the novel, and so did Ivan's judgment on himself. And just here we can appreciate the significance of the narrator's surplus perspective of memory. The narrator, and not Ivan, is 'remembering the future', he is projecting Ivan's future insights back into the past. The author wants us to know beyond any doubt that Ivan eventually came to this judgment because his whole worldview, and his artistic system which gives it expression, fundamentally depends on the existence of conscience, of Christ's law speaking in the human consciousness. Only that law, in Dostoevsky's view, gives us the pure, absolute standard for judging an action or word as 'base'. For the very fact that Ivan could subsequently judge his actions on that night as 'vile' and 'base' testifies to the presence in his soul of a higher conscience.

Kant identified conscience as 'the representative of the *forum divinum* within us', because 'it is only *per conscientiam* that our actions can be assessed before the *forum* of God'.[9] Conscience exists within us as 'an instinct, an involuntary and irresistible impulse in our nature, which compels us <...> to judge and pass sentence on our actions, visiting us with an inner pain when we do evil'. It is just this involuntary attribute of conscience which Dostoevsky poetically transposed into his characters' painful involuntary memories of their past evil actions. For Ivan, this process of bringing himself before the *forum divinum* has already begun within the present of the story.

After the murder we learn that Ivan's memory of that night has been preying on his mind. Returning from his second visit to Smerdyakov, Ivan's tortured memory is at last illuminated by a piercing moment of insight: 'And again he remembered for the hundredth time how on that last night in his father's house he eavesdropped on him from the staircase, but with such agony he now remembered it that he even stopped on the spot as though pierced: "Yes, I was expecting it then, it's true! I wanted it, I wanted the murder!"' (15,54) The work of *kara* is taking hold in Ivan's consciousness independently of his will. However Ivan quickly represses his insight when he straightway calls on Katerina, who produces the 'document' proving Mitya's 'guilt'. But the agonising doubts remain, driving him to seek his last meeting with Smerdyakov when the truth he suspects (and subconsciously knows) is fully confirmed beyond any doubt. It is from then on that he has to condemn his act that night as the 'basest act of all his life'. The narrator's perspective of memory provides just that sense of long duration which the author needs at this juncture. For what he wishes to convey is that this memory continued to haunt Ivan for his whole life. This tormenting memory is, and has to be, Ivan's punishment, because Dostoevsky has so arranged Ivan's situation that there can never be a case for judicial punishment, a punishment in which he clearly had little faith in any case. The truth about Ivan, just as the truth about Fyodor, Mitya and Smerdyakov, cannot be revealed and expiated at a public trial. In this novel's artistic system, only the 'voice of Christ's law speaking' in the consciousness of their consciences can bring them to redemptive atonement. Mitya's memory of his 'most disgraceful act' pales beside that of Ivan. There could hardly be a greater contrast between Ivan's lifelong harrowing memory of his 'basest act', and Alyosha's lifelong memory of his mother.

This use of the narrator's memory for projecting subsequent understanding and re-evaluations into the present dramatic events points up another important feature of memory which Dostoevsky used to powerful artistic effect. Memory work not only reproduces an image of a significant past event along with its emotive and ideational content, but re-interprets it, generating new insights, meanings and enhanced understanding. The overlaying of varied psychic strata is one of the ways in which Dostoevsky renders his text multi-dimensional, semantically multi-layered. It is also one of the chief ways of representing consciousness wherein memories, impressions, ideas, feelings, all coexist. Memory and consciousness are inseparable. They are contained simultaneously in the space of one mind. This concurrent play with memory past and future supports Bakhtin's idea that simultaneity as a principle of artistic composition predominates over that of evolution in Dostoevsky's representation of consciousness. It also allies his prose with poetry where, as Pomorska reminds us, 'simultaneity prevails over successivity'.

Smerdyakov's self-judgment and self-punishment come quickly. His crime has also been preying on his mind. As others have noted, each of the three Karamazov brothers is an author. So is Smerdyakov. We never see the crime *in actu*, only its reconstruction through Smerdyakov's memory. This is Smerdyakov's artistic composition, like Ivan's Legend, it is an oral narrative, but one based on a real negative memory, an horrifically compelling autobiographical account of the murder of his carnal father forming an absolute contrast to Alyosha's resurrection of his spiritual father in the *Life*.

In sharp contrast to this series of negative memories, there are no tormenting memories of hurts or wrongdoings recorded for Alyosha, only his bewilderment that he forgot to find

Mitya. In fact, the narrator annuls the very possibility of Alyosha harbouring hatreds or resentments when he says that his hero 'never remembered an insult', and, later: 'Alyosha was convinced that no one in the whole world would ever wish to hurt him, and not only would not wish to, but could not. This for him was an axiom given once and for all' (14,19,93). This extraordinary inner inviolability is one of the most important hagiographical, or rather, Christological components defining Alyosha's image and function in the novel.

In Dostoevsky's poetics, punishment and Retribution go through memory. He invested his representations of the characters' wrongdoings, and their consequent sufferings, with those traditional symbolic motifs taken from the dark side of Christianity where sin, hell and the devil find their place. The desecration of sacrosanct people, texts, images and rites bodes evil in this novel and brings down Retribution. The negative memory series is characterised by perversions, distortions and violations of the sacred collective memory, its words, rituals, values and embodied representatives. Denigrations of Russia go hand in hand with a contempt for the Russian people, and a mockery or perversion of the Russian religious tradition (Fyodor, Ivan, Smerdyakov). Fyodor performs some memorable carnivalised variations on the subversion of sacred memory marked by various types of reduced laughter, mockery, cynical wit, blasphemy, parody, salacious anecdotes, buffoonery. Fyodor is associated to the 'stupid devil' who incites him to mock the institution of confession. In the case of Smerdyakov, the element of carnival or ironic laughter is lacking. If, as Alyosha tells the boys, a sacred memory is something one 'will not dare to laugh at inwardly, in one's heart', then a malevolently serious perversion of a sacred memory is also something one can never inwardly laugh at (15,195–6). The many diabolic motifs Dostoevsky combined in Smerdyakov's image served his purpose of bringing into the novel's world an embodied emanation of the devil. Smerdyakov's corruption of the collective sacred memory defines his prime evil function in the novel. He is the affirmation of Ivan's 'spirit of negation' and is thus unambiguously diabolic, the absolute negation of Alyosha. Together, the images of Alyosha and Smerdyakov mark the poetic extremes between the angel and the devil so crucial to the novel's poetic system.

In the Orthodox tradition, the activation of memory proceeds by an internalisation of the sacred texts (Zosima takes the Word into his consciousness in childhood). One's experiences in the world are then interpreted by this standard. This way they grow in the conscience and are resurrected at critical moments as a realisation of what the higher reality is. Smerdyakov's immunity to the Word left him without this crucial internal formation and thus he cannot ascend through memory to a vision of the higher reality, to redemption. Ivan engages in the most serious intellectual distortions of Scripture in the novel, using the most subtle rhetorical weapons of irony and ambiguity to destroy the original intentions of the sacred texts. As Sandoz has shown, Ivan's key idea 'all is permitted' is a verbatim quotation from the First Epistle to the Corinthians (6:12, 10:23) where St Paul uses it polemically to reprove those who have falsely interpreted the true nature of Christian freedom.[10] Detaching it from its true context, Ivan heretically perverts it to mean unlimited self-will and egoism. It is the most fatal corruption of the Bible in the novel because Ivan builds his whole theory on his wilful distortion of this passage which, as we have seen, provides Smerdyakov with the ideological justification for parricide. The Legend is not just a rhetorical composition but an artistic one. Setting forth his negation of the sacred memory in an artistically compelling 'poem', Ivan engages in the most subtle subversion of all because of the power of art to fascinate, and thus to mislead. And he makes the Russian collective memory (Christ's society) the butt of an 'insolent farce and mockery' (the church article). Distorting these vital texts and contexts of sacred memory, Ivan ends up by falsifying the picture of the world with his 'little facts' and, as Vetlovskaia has demonstrated, is disabled from noticing the positive facts amply present in his own world. True, Ivan's negations of Christian memory are deeply ambivalent, but his hatred of his father and brother is not. But it is just his undermining doubts about the basis of morality, combined with his hatred, which are so dangerous since they cause Smerdyakov to misread him. Belief and unbelief are stable whereas doubt is wavering. This is why James designates the 'true opposite' of belief as 'doubt' and not unbelief.[11] Not surprisingly, it is Ivan who warns, 'But the devil does not doze', when speaking of heresy and doubt in the biblical miracles and the Second Coming (14,226). Doubt, not negation, makes Ivan unable to join his memory with the memory that he needs for his regeneration.

Dostoevsky's artistic vision was dominated by antonymous words and images. Every important thought or image gives rise to its opposite. He consistently chose motifs which, applying Jakobson's terms, 'fluctuate between the equivalence of synonyms and the common core of antonyms'. In *The Brothers Karamazov*, all the characters' important memories form a complementary system of variations on the 'great code' of biblical cultural memory. Dostoevsky modelled many of their most essential qualities on negative and positive biblical paradigms, and their hagiographical, patristic and folkloric derivatives. The novel's poetic memory system resolves into two sets of elements all derived from one 'common core', the biblical prototypes. The members of each set are constructed as poetic equivalents to the prototypes, differing in degrees or gradations of saintly or demonic topoi and symbolic motifs. All those who parody, corrupt and pervert the sacred memory emanate reminiscences of hell and the devil, the ultimate negative cultural memory. Whereas those who affirm the sacred memory are saturated with reminiscences of positive biblical models and ideas (immortality). Smerdyakov is a variation on the devil and two other negative biblical paradigms; with Rakitin he shares the Judas prototype of betrayal, and with Ivan, the image of Cain, the brother murderer. Ivan typically partakes of both negative and positive paradigms, first Cain and then the Good Samaritan. Opposed to them are variations on the positive divine prototypes giving us three correlated pairs each of which features Alyosha: Rakitin–Alyosha/Judas–Christ, Mother–Child/Sophia–Alyosha and

Mary Magdalene–Christ/Grushenka–Alyosha, thus promoting the most important similarity relation of the novel, Christ–Alyosha.

All the redemptive peripeties in *The Brothers Karamazov* are coincident with the arousal of sacred memories, whereas the negative peripeties are made to coincide with memory arousal retrospectively. In this view memories are divine signals which may either be providential or retributional. In the latter case, these signals become insistent, a torment. Every important crisis in this novel occurs in conjunction with a symbolic transfiguration, diabolic or divine. Every instance of redemption (forgiveness, renewal, the arousal of conscience leading to spiritual change) takes place on the basis of remembrances of ideal, spiritual models for it is through these models, and only through them, that one overcomes one's negative memories. Those who travesty, parody or pervert the highest voice and image, those who subvert its meaning with irony, have so deformed the purity and holiness of the moral law, that it has become barely recognisable to them. Their conscience then becomes detached from their consciousnesses with destructive, tragic results. In this connection it is significant that Ivan's Legend is a self quotation. He has too many diabolic others (the Inquisitor, Smerdyakov, the devil) and no stabilised, good 'other'. The lack of a higher spiritual model leads to a loss of faith in good, moral actions, to a onesided focus on people's failings, sins and weaknesses (the Inquisitor and Ivan). Those who see only the beast, cannot be redeemed, but lapse into cynicism and nihilism. The essential meaning of negative memory in this novel, then, is that when one distorts, corrupts or subverts the highest spiritual models, one no longer has a pure standard by which one can be redeemed, and no guide to save one from evil. One cannot redeem or transcend oneself through an Inquisitor (Ivan), or Sodom (Fyodor) or sacrificial cats (Smerdyakov). Thus, when these protagonists take these debased persons, objects or ideas as their models, the end result can only be their own spiritual debasement which ineluctably leads them to catastrophe.

Here it seems well to say a word about Dostoevsky's

conception of suffering, often misunderstood. That suffering which leads to a purging of debasing or corrupting elements in the soul has a positive goal and meaning in Dostoevsky's fictional worlds. People should suffer pangs of conscience when they do wrong; a person without conscience is a horror, and hardly even a human being. The voice of conscience is the voice of Grace ('Christ's law') which strives to bring wrong-doers to atonement through a stage of temporary suffering (purgatory) in order to clear the soul of sin and guilt and prepare it for heaven.

In creating this complementary system of interacting affirmative and negative memories Dostoevsky established an unbroken link between earthly life and 'other worlds', and found a powerful way to express aesthetically his belief that God and the devil are involved in human events. After the mid-nineteenth century such beliefs came into conflict with the increasing demand for facts, scientific proofs and logical explanations. By using the common psychological phenomenon of involuntary memory, sudden and persistent, Dostoevsky could naturalise messages or promptings which he believed to be of divine supernatural origin, while retaining that universal sense of mystification often accompanying their arousal. Memory is a medium which mysteriously bridges the gap between past and present experience within one consciousness. The existence of this gap provides, as Malcolm says, 'one metaphysical aspect to the topic of memory' since the mechanism by which memory acts at a distance-in-time is not understood.[12] The essential poetic function of memory in *The Brothers Karamazov* is to take the characters (and the reader) back to the Bible, the repository of divine prototypes, affirmative and negative. This interplay and struggle between positive and negative memories, individual and cultural, results in an intricate and dynamic poetic system based on a binary symmetry of light and dark motifs. Indeed one could argue that the 'points of light' shine all the brighter for being juxtaposed to motifs of darkness in a continuous fugal movement throughout the novel.

CHAPTER 6

Forgetting

Memory [is] Exemption from Oblivion.

Dr Johnson's Dictionary

Not everything in heaven have I hated,
Not everything on earth have I disdained.

The Angel, H. S. Pushkin

Remembering implies forgetting, for they are both complementary aspects of the same process of selection. Both are related to the past, only in radically opposite ways. Remembering is essentially a reconstructive activity, whereas forgetting is a destructive one which obliterates the traces of past experience either temporarily or permanently. Attached to memory are notions of fullness and presence. Thoughts, feelings and images of persons and events, along with their contexts, coexist in that individual and collective storehouse we call memory. Amnesia, though, denotes the contrary notions of occlusion, absence or emptiness. Amnesia is a condition, whereas forgetting is a mental activity whose end result is depletion or disappearance of remembrances. With the loss of remembrances comes the loss of whole contexts, personal, social and cultural. Certain elements either exist but are temporarily obscured, or they have vanished; whole regions of the storehouse are bare, uninhabited. What is obscured may have to be revealed, and what has vanished may have to be recovered, before a spiritually whole human being, or culture, can emerge. What has been destroyed may be beyond recovery.

In practical life forgetting has positive uses; forgetting the trivial is necessary in order that the essential be preserved and the new accommodated. Our concern is with the poetic function of forgetting in *The Brothers Karamazov*, with the ways in which Dostoevsky selects and dialogically combines the varieties of amnesia with the forms of memory, so that they become significant components of his artistic system. As in any great artistic work, instances of forgetting, including the narrator's omissions, reflect the author's deliberate aesthetic and ideological choices.

Remembering lends itself naturally to verbal art. Since it is a mental process during which particular events are recounted, it builds up a narrative, creating images of speaking persons. Forgetting creates nothing, forgetting overlooks, subtracts or erases texts, narratives and people. Instances of forgetting, just as remembering, are represented in images of persons who have forgotten something. Thus forgetting equally provokes questions of who forgets whom, or what, and under which circumstances. One cannot easily represent a person in the process of forgetting. Forgetting in the novel has to be reported after the fact, whether by a narrator, or by a character who now realises that he has forgotten something, who now remembers. The reporting of forgetting is almost entirely in the hands of the narrator and it is among his most important narrative and poetic tasks. Thus we must consider what the narrator specifies as having been forgotten, thereby drawing our attention to it and marking it as significant. Some forgetting is volitional, involving conscious acts of suppression; a person forgets because he wants to forget, or does not want to know something. In these instances the narrator represents a character as remembering something for a moment and then deliberately pushing it out of his mind. Involuntary forgetting functions similarly to sudden memory arousal, only it signals the movements of negative forces at work in the novel's world. Then there are lacunae in the memory which point to pathological or sinister processes. These are conveyed with the aid of symbolic devices or coded equivalents to depict the inarticulate, involuntary and mysterious. Our present aim is to consider what is forgotten and subsequently remembered, or remembered too late, or never remembered. In all these respects forgetting, just as remembering, brings into greater relief salient aspects of a person's consciousness, of his mental, emotional profile.

But Dostoevsky was never exclusively concerned with psychology. In his fiction the emergence of personality goes hand in hand with the revelation of a person's worldview, of his conscious ideology which reflects his choices amongst the ideas at large. All forgetting is set within the novel's encompassing context of the collective Christian memories. These are the reference points of remembrance within the text from which amnesia proceeds. In *The Brothers Karamazov* the conscious rejection of these memories becomes involved with ideological questions of cultural, historical amnesia. In this respect forgetting, like remembering, reveals a systematic character, only in a negative, destructive sense. Certain memories stored within the collective tradition are to be liquidated. Thus, since *The Brothers Karamazov* offers us a system whereby sacred memories are preserved and renewed, we may expect to find that amnesia presents an inverse system whereby not only these memories, but their very elements, are to be destroyed so as to prevent permanently their reconstitution. Significantly, the narrator leaves the discourses on ideological forgetting to those characters who are its proponents.

This leads to a further problem for interpretation. No important ideas enter Dostoevsky's fiction without being tested and challenged by their opposites. We shall also attempt to ascertain how, and to what extent, denials or rejections (forgetting) of the affirmative memories undergo modification in the dialogic process. Analysing the various forms of amnesia in *The Brothers Karamazov* we find that they form an inverted hierarchical typology descending from the relatively innocent to the sinister, from baffling involuntary memory lapses to social moral neglect, from wilful repression and spiritual lacunae to the extreme destructiveness of total oblivion. Let us begin where the author does, in childhood, in the Karamazov 'no-home'.

NEGLECT

Home is that small social world where the child's first experiences form the basis of his lasting memories, and where he receives the moral, spiritual values deriving from the larger cultural tradition. If this world is fragmented, corrupted or broken by neglect, the child will usually bear the painful effects for life, sometimes with tragic consequences. The disintegration of the family spells the disintegration of the social fabric whose cohesion depends on the shared basis of collective memory.

At the centre of the novel is one of those broken, 'accidental families', the Karamazovs, whose increasing incidence in Russia was a matter of deep concern for Dostoevsky, a concern he transposed into his last novel on a large scale. Almost everyone is an orphan or semi-orphan, whether through neglect or early loss (all the brothers Karamazov, Sophia, Kolya, Lise, Katerina, Zosima), or through having been cast out, disowned or unacknowledged ('Stinking' Lizaveta, Grushenka, Smerdyakov). Others are homeless (Maximov) or rootless by choice (Fyodor, Mitya's mother, Miusov, Rakitin). Almost all the households have an improvisatory, provisional character.

The themes of neglect and orphanhood begin in Book One where the narrator goes back to the protagonists' childhoods. Mitya's life from infancy to young manhood is briefly sketched in the chapter headed 'He Gets Rid of His First Son', a phrase which does not bode well for Fyodor's paternal image. Indeed, after three-year-old Mitya is deserted by his mother, who shortly thereafter dies, the narrator remarks of Fyodor: 'he totally and completely abandoned his child < ... > not from malice towards him, not because of any outraged conjugal feelings, but simply because he had completely forgotten about him' (14,10). Excluding conventional 'malice' and 'outraged conjugal feelings', the narrator gives a more disturbing reason for Fyodor's abandonment of his motherless child, total amnesia.

The reader is bound to wonder what became of the child, why his father 'had completely forgotten' him, and at once learns:

While he [Fyodor] was plaguing everyone with his tears and complaints and had turned his house into a den of debauchery, a faithful servant of this house, Grigory, took the three-year-old Mitya into his care, and if he hadn't looked after him then, perhaps there would have been no one to change the child's little shirt.(14,10)

The reader may judge the scale of Fyodor's debaucheries and maudlin complaints by his total neglect of his child. At the same time, the narrator quietly contrasts and counter-balances the father's neglect with the humane, responsible care of his loyal servant. His sympathy for the forgotten child, and his implicit approval of Grigory's care, sound in his last clause which is permeated with pathos, one of Dostoevsky's great affective modes. With the homely detail of the 'little shirt', and 'there would have been no one', he conjures up the terrible fate Mitya barely escaped, that of an abandoned three-year-old child in a dirty 'little shirt' continually subjected to the corrupting spectacles in his father's home become 'den of debauchery'. Variations on this image of Mitya as a neglected child will be repeatedly evoked much later in tragic circumstances.

Mitya is virtually an orphan, all his relatives being ill, dead or having 'forgot about him at first'. His father however is very much alive and fit for energetic orgies and is keenly attentive to his flourishing 'little business deals', facts which make his neglect of his child all the more stark. But more is to come: 'However, if his papa had remembered him (or could not, indeed, have not known of his existence), then he himself would have sent him back to the cottage, since the child would have got in the way of his debaucheries' (14,10). Employing the unreal conditional mood, the narrator excludes any paternal remembrances and simultaneously predicts with certainty paternal rejection. His parenthetical acknowledgement of the common-sense objection rules out any excuse of ignorance and this, along with Fyodor's shady financial activities, casts his behaviour in the most damaging light. And Fyodor has not the excuse of poverty. At the outset we learn that at the time of his death, Fyodor had amassed a fortune of 100,000 roubles as a ruthless moneylender and 'founder' of numerous taverns in his district, in other words, as an exploiter and corrupter of his neighbours.

Next, Miusov, the rich cousin of Mitya' mother, appears on the scene. The narrator introduces, the wealthy, middle-aged landowner with qualities which at first seem commendatory: Miusov is 'special', 'enlightened'. But these are at once admixed with more ambiguous epithets: Miusov is also 'urbane', 'well travelled', a 'European' who is ending his days as a 'liberal of the forties and fifties'. Among the acquaintances he has made 'in the course of his career' are Proudhon and Bakunin, historical persons whose names were bound to arouse approbatory associations in the author's radical, pro-gressive readers. But then the narrator provocatively overdoes it when he characterises Miusov's acquaintances as 'the most liberal people' and thus implies that liberalism is a kind of 'career'. In assembling these associations, the narrator with one stroke parodies Miusov, 'the most liberal people', and all those who are impressed by them. The narrator goes on to undermine Miusov's liberal views with the information that Miusov had an estate with 'about one thousand souls', that he kept a sharp eye on the monies from his property, and was engaged in an interminable legal battle with the 'clericals' over their rights to a modest fishing access on his land. In short, Miusov is a representative of Russia's alienated Westernised intelligentsia and an exemplar of a well known social type, the absentee landlord whose land and serfs are for him no more than sources of income to spend abroad. Into this biographical sketch the narrator introduces one of Miusov's memories: 'already nearing the end of his wanderings, [he] especially loved to reminisce and talk about the three days of the Paris revolution of forty-eight, hinting that he himself had almost taken part in it on the barricades. This was one of the most gratifying memories of his youth' (14,10). As Terras remarks, 'almost' carries 'the poison', and so does 'hinting'.[1] The 'most gratifying memories' of 'youth' are usually those of experiences we have shared with others, of events in which we have actively participated. Here the author invests Miusov with a hollow memory based on inflated self-deception in order to expose the falsity and hollowness of his revolutionary ideals.

Still, the young Miusov attempts a good deed. Seeing the plight of his cousin's child, he overcame his 'indignation' with Fyodor and insisted on undertaking Mitya's upbringing. '[Fyodor] for some time looked as though he completely did not understand what child he was talking about, and even as though he were surprised that somewhere in his house he had a little son' (14,11). Mitya does go to Miusov, but not for long:

since he [Miusov] had no family of his own, and since he himself, after securing the revenues from his estates, at once hastened back again to Paris for a long time, he left the child in charge of one of his aunts < ... > It so happened that, settling permanently in Paris, he too forgot about the child, especially when that February revolution broke out which so staggered his imagination and which he could never forget all his life. (14,11)

One well aimed stone kills two images. Fyodor shunts Mitya off like a piece of goods, while Miusov rushes off to Paris where, in due course, 'three days' as a spectator at the barricades blot out all memory of Mitya. Fyodor 'completely forgot' what he should have remembered, Miusov 'could never forget all his life' what is not worth remembering. These passages are revealing examples of Dostoevsky's use of the interplay between memory and amnesia as a technique of parody and irony. His immediate aim is to travesty Miusov's revolutionary 'heroism'. His real target is the ideas of Ivan's generation, the radicals of the 60s and 70s, which he traces to the imported ideals of their father, the liberals of the 40s and 50s. The reader is left to infer the guiding principles of Miusov's life: sojourns in Paris and a foreign revolution take precedence over events at home, abstract ideals overweigh the needs of the heart and are worth forgetting one's responsibilities to a child, to one's country, home and peasants. Miusov is without family, without national roots, without deep, continuous human ties. He only has 'meetings' with famous revolutionaries. His most treasured memories are of faraway events in a foreign land. Miusov's conscience, like Ivan's, is also satisfied with noncommital watching at a safe distance, with secondhand experiences and substitute memories. Miusov's views and Fyodor's behaviour are compromised by their neglect of their most pressing duties at home. Miusov abandons his country, Fyodor his family. Miusov is shown as unable steadfastly to sustain his humane aim of looking after his cousin's abandoned child. His impulsive indignation quickly fizzles out, his good deed was performed 'as though on a stage'.

Fyodor and Miusov embody two kinds of abdication and exploitation, two variations on the negation of one of the novel's implied central morals: charity begins at home. The narrator's irony towards Fyodor occupies the moral plane; his parody of Miusov lies on the ideological political plane. What should be remembered, children, neighbours, family, serfs who have legitimate claims on the attention of those responsible for their welfare, have been ignored, neglected, obliterated from memory. Actions as well as inactions are often made to speak louder than the characters' words in this novel where certain ideas are continually being compromised and repudiated not by intellectual discourses, but by repeated failures to take responsibility. Forgetting, here in the form of social and parental neglect, functions as a critical index of morality, personal, familial, societal and national.

Nor is this the end of the matter. Given that Mitya changed his 'nest' four or five times, it is hardly surprising, nor is it meant to be, that his 'adolescence and youth passed in disorder; he did not finish his studies < ... > led a wild life and ran through a good deal of money' (14,11). Mitya comes to his father's town in the expectation of getting the remainder of his inheritance. However he learns that, according to his father, he has no money left from his mother's estate. By the time the narrator's story begins, Mitya is in a desperate frame of mind: 'the young man was thunderstruck, suspected a lie, deception, almost flew into a rage and as if lost his mind. And just this circumstance led to the catastrophe' (14,12). Integrating the course of events so far, we discover an implied causal chain deployed by the author. Mitya's present desperate state follows the narration of his deprived precarious childhood, of the total breakdown in the natural relations between father and son. The sequence begins to acquire the force of a logical outcome: child neglect eventually leads to rage, near insanity and 'catastrophe'.

And so it does. The image of Mitya as a neglected child is re-evoked on three fateful occasions featuring a shirt or soiled and unmended clothes. The night before the murder, Mitya despairingly contemplates suicide: 'why go on suffering any more < ... > Here's the willow tree, I have a handkerchief, I have a shirt, I can twist them into a rope right now < ... > and – no longer burden the earth, no longer dishonour it with my vile presence!' (14,142) Under interrogation, Mitya is ordered to undress, to his acute embarassment. As an officer, he feels dishonoured, as a man, humiliated. He delays taking off his shirt:

'What, do I really have to take off my shirt?' he asked sharply. 'I ask you for the second time: do I have to take off my shirt or not?' he said, still more sharply and irritably. < ... > 'You must take off your shirt too, that's very important' < ... > Mitya flushed red and flew into a rage. 'What, am I to stand naked?' he shouted < ... > He felt unbearably embarrassed. 'It's like a dream, I've sometimes dreamed of such degrading things happening to me.' It was even tormenting for him to take off his socks: they were very dirty, and so was his underwear and now everyone would see it < ... > He pulled off his shirt himself. (14,434,435)

The child's potential dirty 'little shirt' is now the real shirt which the grown man must remove in a situation which insults his dignity. This fulfilment of Mitya's repeated prophetic dreams of 'such degrading things' proceeds from a deeply embedded notion of Retribution which underlies the whole text. The sins of Fyodor are still accomplishing their nemesis for his sons who have compounded them by their own words and acts. This passage extends the causal chain by association. The last evocations of Mitya's neglected childhood more explicitly establish its conclusion. Giving evidence at Mitya's trial, Grigory concedes that without him, three-year-old Mitya 'would have been eaten up by lice' (15,96). On the witness stand, Dr Herzenstube remembers:

the poor young man might have an incomparably better lot, for he had a good heart in his childhood, and after childhood, for this I know. < ... > Oh, I remember him very well when he was still such a little chap so high, abandoned by his father to the back yard, where he ran about in the dirt without boots and with his little breeches hanging on one button. < ... > And now, alas! (15,105–6)

The image of the child Mitya who, but for Grigory, would have had 'no one to change' his 'little shirt', turns out to be a symbolic anticipation whose fulfilment, validated by the spontaneous recollections of two truthful men, seals the causal Aristotelian sequence. All Mitya's intervening misdeeds, his misuse of Katerina's money, his violence towards his father, and his humiliation of Snegiryov before Ilyusha's eyes have to be set beside this image of parental neglect and deprivation. The first cause of Mitya's tragedy lies in childhood when he, innocent, 'good hearted' and vulnerable, was 'completely forgotten', sacrificed to his mother's 'full emancipation', his father's 'debaucheries' and his cousin's removal to Paris and barricade tourism.

The pattern of neglect and orphanhood, which lies at the basis of the Karamazov 'little family', is further augmented when, after the premature death of Sophia, Ivan and Alyosha 'were completely forgotten and abandoned by their father and fell to the care of the same Grigory'. (14,13) And it is 'the same Grigory' who erects a tombstone over their mother's grave, at his own expense 'after Fyodor Pavlovich, whom he had many times annoyed with reminders about this grave, went away, to Odessa, after waving his hand not only at the grave, but at all his memories too' (14,22). When, many years later and a scant year before the murder, Alyosha arrives seeking his mother's grave: 'Fyodor Pavlovich could not show him where he had buried his second wife because he never visited her grave after her coffin had been covered over with earth, and after so many years he had entirely forgotten where she was buried then' (14,21). The commemorative tending of graves is one of the main expressions of memory, collective and individual. It is the responsibility of those left behind to preserve the memory of those who have gone before. Neither the living nor the dead have any lasting place in Fyodor's memory, so far. Fyodor's debaucheries and pursuit of money have totally obscured and almost destroyed any remembrances of others, and consequently any sense of responsibility towards them. His life exemplifies a negation of Zosima's teaching on responsibility and an affirmation of Ivan's theory of unrestrained egoism. Employing devices from classical rhetoric, Dostoevsky presents Fyodor in the worst possible light in order to bring across the enormity of his forgetting, to caution the reader not to accept him as just an amusing old bastard, a fascinating blasphemer. Too much is at stake. Mulling over the problem of nihilism in 1880, Dostoevsky noted 'we *are all nihilists* < ... > all to the last man are Fyodor Pavlovichs'.[2] Fyodor's annihilation from memory of his whole family is in effect a kind of murder. His nihilism began at home and home is largely where it remains. Ivan, the son most like him, will attempt to extend unrestrained egoism to a universal principle. The reader may conclude from this family history that it is small wonder that Ivan preaches the idea of 'all is permitted', that he builds his case against God's world on child abuse and that he abandons his father to be murdered.

But Dostoevsky does not leave the theme of neglect to be tied up by a neat Aristotelian sequence of socio-psychological cause and effect. The final stroke of damnation falls on the 'fathers' near the end, during Ivan's nightmare, when the narrator describes the devil as a man 'nearing fifty', once a gentleman of fashion, now a 'wandering sponger'. He belongs to that general type of 'solitary men, either bachelors or widowers', whose children, 'are always brought up somewhere far away, by some kind of aunts whom the gentleman almost never mentions in decent society < ... > Little by little he becomes totally estranged from his children, every now and then receiving from them birthday or Christmas letters and sometimes even answering them' (15,71). The reader can recognise in Ivan's devil a composite of the 'bachelor', Miusov, and the 'widower' and 'sponger', Fyodor Karamazov. The reader may also recall

that Ivan never 'even wanted to make an attempt to correspond with his father'. Every important idea in this novel (here
paternal neglect) Dostoevsky sooner or later raises to transcendental significance. This is the point where Dostoevsky
abandons the causal chain of prose and juxtaposes the set of
realistic characters to the devil in an equivalence relation of
poetry.

The diabolic is only one side. What Ivan fails to see, the
narrator supplies. Almost buried in his accounts of neglect are
the rescuing actions of various people who took responsibility
for Fyodor's family. Assuming parenthood for Fyodor's sons,
defending and commemorating his 'shrieker', they quietly
restore as best they can the threads of collective memory. Their
good deeds slip in almost unnoticed amidst many sentences
narrating Fyodor's noisy wrongdoings. Without them the
children could not have survived. Some are lightly sketched in,
others remain faceless and anonymous. Some are active in the
present story, like the 'kind person' who 'out of compassion'
placed a pillow under Mitya's head while he was dreaming his
great revelatory dream of the 'babe'.

But Dostoevsky was also a poet who aimed to transcend
conventional, prosaic images of humanitarian compassion by
uniting them with invariant archetypes through symbolic and
metaphoric relationships of similarity and contrast. To Fyodor
and his sons, he opposes the love between Ilyusha and
Snegiryov, father of the only intact family in the novel. Despite
all the objective environmental factors militating against their
cohesion, they hold together. One brief episode in their drama,
which highlights the complementary meaning of remembering
and forgetting in *The Brothers Karamazov*, suggests why this is
so. Just after Snegiryov has learned that Ilyusha will soon die:
'"I don't want a good boy! I don't want another boy!" he
whispered in a wild whisper, grinding his teeth, "if I forget thee,
Jerusalem, may my tongue ..." He broke off, and sank < ... >
to his knees' (14,507). After leaving the Snegiryov house,
Kolya asks Alyosha:

What was that he said about Jerusalem? ... What did he mean by
that? It's from the Bible: 'if I forget thee Jerusalem', that is, if I forget

all that is most precious to me, if I let anything take its place, then may my ... I understand, that's enough! (14,508)

Alyosha's interpretation contains the key message. Jerusalem occupies a unique place in Western collective memory. It is the historical locale of all that is most sacred in the Judaeo-Christian tradition, the geographical focus of a dispersed people in the Old Testament and the scene of Christ's Passion in the Gospels. Psalm 137, to which Snegirov alludes, is a lament of the Jews held in the Babylonian captivity, a lament for lost Jerusalem, an expression of longing for home, to return to the native holy land. The psalm affirms the constancy of Jewish memory in the face of calamity, slavery, exile and tragedy. It is also a warning that if one forgets Jerusalem, 'all that is most precious', then justified Retribution will ensue: 'may my tongue cleave to the roof of my mouth, if I prefer not Jerusalem above my chief joy'. Jerusalem is also the spiritual destination of the Christian future and a reminiscence of the promise of resurrection. The New Testament culminates in the sublime image of the new Jerusalem, in a figure of the heavenly future fulfilled. These ideas also find expression in *The Brothers Karamazov*; the banquet scene in Alyosha's great dream vision of Cana of Galilee is the most sublime variation on this image in Dostoevsky's *œuvre*. It is a common feature of all the negative characters in the novel that they cut themselves off from their native soil, forget their 'Jerusalem', their children, family, neighbours, compatriots and holy Russia. Miusov has abandoned his homeland, Fyodor despises it ('Russia is swinishness'), Smerdyakov is a potential traitor ('I hate all Russia', the 'clever' French should have 'conquered' and 'annexed' us in 1812) and Ivan is eager to get away from it and wander about Europe. Their destination, actual and ideological, is the same, to Western Europe, the land of liberalism, socialism, catholicism, the land, in the author's view, of modern Babylon, spawning ideas that would be harbingers of an apocalyptic catastrophe. They are all homeless, alienated, estranged from their native land, they are all spiritually, and actually, living in a Babylonian exile. Indeed the idea that the forgetting of

'Jerusalem' leads to tragic consequences is one of the organising ideas of the novel.

Thanks to Snegiryov's invocation of this sanctifying image,
the two father 'buffoons' now stand in sharpest contrast to each
other. Snegiryov's buffoonery has taken on a sacralised tinge of
yurodstvo, whereas Fyodor's, lacking the sublime element, is a
degraded version. Snegiryov is a living refutation of Ivan's
thesis that all grown-ups are 'disgusting and unworthy of love',
a living counter example to his dossier on child abuse, just as
his loyalty to all that is 'most precious' is an implicit reproach
to Fyodor's negligence.

REPRESSION

Two main ways of banishing memories from consciousness are
suppression and repression. Suppression entails a deliberate,
conscious rejection or stifling of something from consciousness.
Repression, though, is an unconscious mechanism for keeping
certain unacceptable thoughts, wishes or intentions from ever
reaching consciousness. The danger here is that one can lose
control over a situation when one represses awareness of it.

ALYOSHA AND FYODOR

One of the most remarkable instances in Dostoevsky's fiction of
memory recovered after years of blank repression occurs in
Fyodor Karamazov. Belknap notes that 'Book One < ... >
sets up a careful opposition between the way old Fedor forgets
and the way Aleša remembers.'[3] Indeed, Dostoevsky uses this
opposition throughout the novel in building his poetic world. It
has never been sufficiently remarked that Fyodor changes,
slightly but significantly. This change is registered in several
passages highlighting Fyodor's growing love for his youngest
son and culminates in a dramatic scene which combines a
sudden vivid memory of Alyosha's mother with a striking
instance of amnesia. Fyodor's deep seated amnesia promises to
become permanent when Alyosha's visit to his mother's grave
produces a 'very original' effect on his father. He donates 1,000

roubles to the monastery in 'memory of the soul' of his first wife (Mitya's mother), having never in his life placed a 'five kopeck candle before an icon', an extraordinarily lavish benefaction for such a tightfisted father. The seed of conscience, symbolised by this belated atonement, is coming to life under the influence of Alyosha's quiet commemoration. Fyodor, who had forgotten his family for many years, is no longer totally devoid of memory, nor of respect for the dead, no matter how paradoxically he expresses it.

Within just two weeks of meeting his son Alyosha, Fyodor, says the narrator: 'began terribly often to embrace and kiss him < ... > true, with drunken tears, with sottish sentimentality, but it was clear that he'd come to love him sincerely and deeply, and as one like him had never, of course, succeeded in loving anyone' (14,18–19). This passage is about Fyodor, but its most important message concerns the hero. Alyosha's 'gift for arousing a special love' is so uniquely powerful that it can inspire a uniquely 'sincere and deep' love even in a Fyodor Karamazov, a love which, so it gradually emerges, goes beyond their literal kinship.

After charting Fyodor's moral and physical deterioration during the three years preceding Alyosha's arrival, the narrator recalls:

Alyosha's arrival seemed to affect him even on the moral side, as though something had awakened in this prematurely old man which had long been smothered in his soul. 'Do you know – he often began to say to Alyosha, looking intently at him – that you resemble her, the shrieker, I mean?' < ... > 'Alyosha, would you believe it, I've truly come to love you.' (14,21–2)

Several ideas of cardinal importance for the novel emerge through the narrator's memory. Alyosha, and uniquely Alyosha, awakened his father's 'moral side', a side that 'had long been smothered' in his soul, but never totally extinguished. Fyodor's vestigial moral awakening coincides with his dawning awareness of Alyosha's resemblance to his mother, bringing memories of her back to mind. His recognition of the resemblance between Alyosha and his mother and the contrast between Alyosha and himself explains the new relationship between him and his son. Language gives us a clue to the author's highest aim: the 'truly' Fyodor uses when declaring his love to Alyosha is *voistinu*. Many Russian readers will immediately recall the congregation's response in the Orthodox liturgy to the phrase 'Christ has risen!', 'In truth He has risen!' ('On *voistinu* voskres'). For once, Fyodor's biblical diction is not parodic.

The 'something' that stirred the 'moral side' in Fyodor's soul is not defined, but later the narrator says:

Alyosha 'pierced his heart' in that he lived, saw everything and condemned nothing. Moreover, he brought with him an unprecedented thing: a complete lack of contempt for him, the old man. On the contrary, [he brought] an invariable affection and a completely natural straightforward devotion to him who so little deserved it. All this was a complete surprise for the old profligate who had dropped all family ties, it was completely unexpected for him who hitherto had loved only 'nastiness'. After Alyosha's departure he confessed to himself that he had understood something which hitherto he had not wanted to understand. (14,87)

Filial affection, a love which 'judges not', despises not and pierces the heart, a love which is something radically other than 'nastiness' – these are all attributes of divine love (agape). What Fyodor had hitherto loved were things similar to 'nastiness'. He now begins to love the dissimilar, which he did long ago when he married Alyosha's mother to whom he was attracted precisely by her dissimilarity to himself, 'above all by her innocent appearance'. Alyosha, her son, is now the living carrier and messenger of that image of love and inviolable innocence. And since it has found a response in the 'old profligate's' heart, his new stirrings of long dormant emotions evince a dim recognition of the divine prototype in Fyodor's soul, which had so 'long been smothered'.

Later, in conversation with Ivan and Alyosha, Fyodor spontaneously reminisces about their mother. Among his memories of her, one is particularly striking:

She prayed a great deal then, she especially kept the feasts of the Mother of God and she would drive me out of her room then. I thought, just let me knock this mysticism out of her. 'You see, I say, you see, here's your icon, here it is, here I'll take it down. Look, you take it for a miracle working icon and I'm going to spit on it right now in front of you and nothing is going to happen to me for doing it!' ... As soon as she saw, Lord, I think: she'll beat me now, but she only jumped up, wringing her hands, then suddenly covered her face with her hands, began to tremble all over and fell to the floor ... that's the way she sank down. (14,126)

In Orthodox theology, the icon is a visible sign of a divine presence, the image of what is represented is felt to be present. Thus, Fyodor's act of spitting at a holy face is one of extreme desecration. By his act of desecration, the pair of divine images on the icon is poetically transferred to Alyosha's mother, who, covering her face with her hands in a gesture of vicarious instinctive protection, trembling and falling, suffers for the Mother of God and her Child. Vicarious suffering was always highly characteristic of Dostoevsky's mode of thought and he would have found its paradigm in the suffering of Christ. The Russian text does not allow us to decide unambiguously whether Fyodor actually spat on the icon or not.[4] However, in this Christian context, Fyodor's very threat constitutes a desecration, and his boast, a temptation. What we do know is that something does 'happen' to Fyodor many years later. And what we can say is that Dostoevsky created an ambiguity just where we learn that Sophia believed her revered icon to be a 'miracle working' one, doubtless the same one before which she held Alyosha, as his 'sudden' reaction to Fyodor's reminiscence confirms:

Alyosha, Alyosha; what's the matter with you! What's the matter with you! The old man jumped up in fright. From the very time that he began to speak about his mother, Alyosha little by little began to change in his face. He blushed, his eyes blazed up, his lips quivered ... The drunken old fellow spluttered on and did not notice anything until that very minute when something very strange happened to Alyosha, namely, exactly the same thing was repeated with him that he had only just told about the 'shrieker'. Alyosha suddenly jumped up from the table, exactly as his mother was said to have done, wrung his hands, then covered his face with them, sank back on his chair and suddenly trembled all over from a hysterical paroxysm of sudden shaking silent tears. The extraordinary resemblance to his mother especially struck the old man. (14,126–7)

Alyosha's uncontrollable mimesis of his mother's fit of helpless anguish dramatically identifies him totally with her, with her suffering, her emotional complexion and her faith, turning him into an involuntary vessel for her momentary 'resurrection', into the bearer of a graphic image whose message is directed to Fyodor. On a relationship of contiguity (mother/son), Dostoevsky, through Fyodor's memory, superimposes a relationship of similarity between mother and son as incarnations of the divine prototypes. This series describes an increasingly closer movement of presence, from resemblance to identity to resurrection. And does not Fyodor's 'fright' on witnessing his son's 'extraordinary resemblance to his mother' register his dim comprehension of a divine message? This last appearance of Alyosha's mother comes through Fyodor's memory in conjunction with her fits, her suffering and her devotion to her icon of the Mother of God, the same features, among others, which remain in Alyosha's memory. The author juxtaposes a memory image of desecration to an earlier one of veneration.

There is another brother here, Ivan, also the son of Sophia. Alarmed, Fyodor orders Ivan:

Ivan, Ivan! Quickly give him water. It's like her, the exact copy of her, like his mother then! Sprinkle him with water from your mouth, that's what I used to do to her. It's because of his mother, because of his mother ... he muttered to Ivan.
But she was my mother too, I think his mother, wasn't she? – Ivan suddenly burst out with irrepressible angry contempt. The old man shuddered before his glittering gaze. But at this moment something very strange happened, true, only for a second: it seems that the notion that Alyosha's mother was also Ivan's mother really went clean out of the old man's mind ...
How do you mean, your mother? he muttered, not understanding. – Why do you say that? Whose mother are you taking about? ... Was she really ... Ah, the devil! Yes, she was really your mother too! Ah, the devil! Well, brother, that was an eclipse (*zatmeniie*) like never happened to me before, excuse me, why, I was thinking, Ivan ... he-he-he! – He stopped. A long, drunken half-senseless grin extended his face. (14,127)

Fyodor's thought, halted in mid-sentence, remains for posterity to speculate on. The identity of a father can be in doubt, but never that of a mother. It is not so surprising that a man who 'completely forgot' his children should momentarily forget which of his sons belongs to which mother. But Fyodor's memory eclipse is more important for what it tells us about the two brothers than about himself: it disconnects Ivan from his mother in the very context which most stresses Alyosha's virtual identity to her. Alyosha is so like his mother, and Ivan apparently so unlike her, that Fyodor cannot imagine that she could also have produced Ivan. And indeed it is an enigma almost to the end of the novel. Fyodor breaks the most vital and intimate of all contiguity relationships (mother/child) on the implied basis of Ivan's extreme dissimilarity to his mother. This imputed dissimilarity arouses such fury in him ('his glittering gaze') that it causes Fyodor to 'shudder' in fear. The brothers' responses to their father's memory of his maltreatment of their mother, are also markedly contrasted; Alyosha suffers for his mother and the Mother of God, Ivan hates his father, not without reason. Fyodor's amnesia about Ivan's maternal origins not only blots out Ivan's vital connection with his mother, in effect leaving him motherless, but it also betrays his deep rejection of his son. This is the only time Ivan mentions his mother. But in place of a personal memory of her, we have only a blank and a consciousness flooded by 'angry contempt' for his father.

There are also symbolic clues for interpreting this episode. The spit motif is particularly interesting. The image of Fyodor 'sprinkling' Sophia with water from his mouth in an effort to bring her out of her shrieking fit is a faint, debased reminiscence of Christ's healing of the mute with His spit (Mark 7:33). The two spit motifs in these passages (spitting on the icon, spitting on Sophia) form a negative/positive pair of sacrilege/healing, which, combined in Fyodor's image, create that impression of moral ambivalence so typical of Dostoevsky's sinners. The negative component though predominates. Time and again Fyodor's greedy sensuality is evoked by one of the most repellent traits of his image: the spittle that frequently drools from his slack, fleshy lips, a sight that could only be intensely revolting to the fastidious Ivan.

There are other symbolic motifs. Clearly a mischievous thought has stopped Fyodor in his tracks and provoked his malignant giggle, the 'he-he-he' signature tune of evil thoughts voiced by other 'devils' in the novel. Twice Fyodor exclaims 'Ah, the devil!' a figure he, like Ivan, often invokes. Fyodor calls his lapse an 'eclipse' (*zatmeniie*), a natural phenomenon traditionally associated with evil omens.[5] Solar eclipses stealthily blot out the life giving sun, the central mystical symbol of the divinity in Dostoevsky's fiction. Here he uses the concept of an eclipse metaphorically when referring to Fyodor's amnesia and thus links the forgetting of what is most precious with darkness and dark forces, just as the memory of what is most sacred is associated to sunlight and Grace. Ivan's origins were momentarily shrouded in darkness and oblivion by Fyodor. In a poetic text, this causes a shadow to steal across Ivan's image. And just at this point Mitya erupts into the house in a murderous rage, cutting short this scene which ends on Fyodor's cry: 'He'll kill me!', and he grips Ivan for protection, precisely the son who will not protect him at his critical hour.

This is not the end of Sophia's icon. After Mitya has beaten Fyodor, Alyosha tends his father who tells him: 'That icon, the one of the Mother of God I was just talking about, take it for yourself, take it with you. And I allow you to return to the monastery ... I was just joking, don't be angry < ... > Good-bye, angel, you stood up for me just now, I shall never forget it' (14,130–1). Fyodor's 'good-bye' (*proshchai*) means both 'farewell' and 'forgive'. From a desecration long ago, Fyodor now offers the icon as an instrument of atonement. The icon returns to Alyosha, to him who bears the image of the icon. Now image and icon are united, as they were in Alyosha's sacred memory. The final stage in the lifting of Fyodor's amnesia is the reuniting of the image with its prototype. The 'miracle working' icon has become ultimately a thing of forgiveness.

Fyodor's slow moral awakening is rounded off by one further

little episode the very next day when Fyodor tells Alyosha: 'Only with you alone have I had good moments.' After Alyosha leaves, having seen his father for what neither knows to be the last time, Fyodor drinks a 'half glass', but then adds, 'I won't have any more!' and closes the liquor cabinet (14,158,160).

Shortly before his death, Fyodor, who had forgotten his family for many years, is confronted at once with all its scattered members, living and dead, who now converge on him in the manner of a tragic nemesis. Though he has now 'understood something', it is too late to alter his earthly fate. This does not mean that Fyodor is reformed, but he does have redemptive potential. The changes occurring in him were effected by Alyosha's loving presence and the surfacing of repressed memories which he arouses. Thus, it is not true to say that Alyosha's goodness is ineffectual, that he has no positive influence on people or events. We have had one example with Grushenka and will have another with Kolya. He has already made a profound impression in Ivan. The devil flees at his appearance. Only Smerdyakov remains impermeable to his influence. If the seed of new spiritual growth can reside in a Fyodor Karamazov, then perhaps it exists in everyone, even in Smerdyakov. These changes, unlikely from the viewpoint of conventional psychology, are perfectly in line with Dostoevsky's dynamic, Christian conception of human beings. People, even the most corrupt, retain some memory, however smothered, of that highest voice and image. Consequently they are not just what they are now, fixed once and for all. They change, or they always retain the potential for redemptive change. 'With us, once a thing has fallen, so it must lie forever. That's not as it should be! I want to get up', exclaims Fyodor in the great carnivalised 'scandal' scene at the Father Superior's dinner (14,82). Fyodor may be playing the 'last act' of his 'performance' at the monastery, but through his buffoonish mockery still rings his wish 'to get up'. In Dostoevsky's poetic world all are striving for regeneration. Without this belief, the whole Christian foundation of the novel would collapse.

IVAN

If memory grows in social contexts of shared experience, amnesia sets in with isolation from others. According to Halbwachs, when one is long separated from a social group, one can no longer construct memories of its members. This general socio-psychological phenomenon Dostoevsky uses to powerful poetic effect in his last novel where forgetting what should be remembered owing to prolonged isolation and repression turns out to have more sinister meanings and tragic consequences.

Ivan is both detached and unattached. He arrives from 'a university', and his future destinations are equally vague, he would like to roam about Western Europe. His discourses are screens warding off, seducing or puzzling others. Ivan's lack of good personal memories encloses his image in self-sufficient isolation, emphasising his emotional distance from his childhood and his estrangement from his fellow man. As he tells Alyosha, one can love one's neighbour 'in the abstract and even sometimes from a distance, but up close almost never'. Ivan finally chooses to 'get acquainted' with his brother only when he is poised for departure: 'I think it's best of all to get to know people just before parting with them' (14,209). Acquaintance before departure entails no involvement, no commitment, a kind of relationship which may suit a rootless person, or an idealist. Ivan's proud, self imposed isolation is extreme: 'I want to take up with you, Alyosha, because I have no friends, I want to give it a try.' (14,213) This is not a genuine call to friendship, but an experiment Ivan is performing on the eve of his planned departure. And yet he does say it to Alyosha, and although he laughs, he is 'not entirely joking'.

What memories does Ivan cherish? The following passage is often quoted as evidence of Ivan's love of life:

Though I don't believe in the order of things, yet dear to me are the sticky little leaves that come out in the spring, dear is the blue sky, dear is some person whom sometimes, would you believe it, you love and you don't know what for, dear is some great human deed in which, perhaps, you have already long ceased to believe, but all the same for old memory's sake you revere it with you heart. (14,209–10)

Here we have another example of Dostoevsky's subtle use of the semantic potentials of grammar in the service of poetic memory. The only phrase with a first-person is the initial one, Ivan's truest remark. Those who do not believe in the order of things easily become sowers and reapers of disorder. The four 'dear to me' locutions are in the impersonal form in Russian. In English versions they are translated as 'I love', thus weakening the connection between Zosima's definition of hell – 'the inability any longer to love' – and Ivan, to whom the words particularly apply. The 'yous' belong to another type of impersonal form (the second person singular used for general statements) and can be rendered by 'one'. The sensuous image of the 'sticky little leaves' is a hidden quotation from a lyric poem by Pushkin which could be easily passed over by many readers as a traditional, even if striking, symbol of spring. Ivan's featureless 'blue sky' is far above man and is a cliché. This is not Alyosha's sky, populated with God's 'other worlds' and manifesting the glory of His creation. Nor is Ivan's love of nature the same as Mitya's, even though the images they invoke are markedly similar. Mitya begins his confession to Alyosha with: 'Let us praise nature; you see how much sun there is, how clear the sky is, the leaves all green, it's still summer' (14,97). Mitya invites Alyosha to join him in his celebration of nature; he expresses it in a garden in full summer and in the context of a genuine, open confession of love, for his brother Alyosha and Grushenka. And he draws Alyosha's attention to the effulgent sun, the novel's central sacred symbol which is never once associated to Ivan. In fact, Ivan never exhibits any love of nature, only this distanced literary reminiscence recalled in a 'stinking tavern'. 'Some person' whom 'you/one' love 'sometimes' not knowing 'what for' is so vague and abstract as to be virtually equivalent to loving no one anytime for any reason. Ivan does not mention a single real living person who is 'dear' to him. 'Some great human "deed"' in which 'you/one' have, maybe, 'long ceased to believe', but which 'you/one reveres with your/one's heart' because of an 'old memory' is so indefinite and generalised as to be almost meaningless, or evasive. Which memory, which great deed?

Thus, at first glance, Ivan's love of life proceeds from a negation – 'I don't believe in the order of things' – and is at the same time based on abstract, impersonal and literary reminiscences.

Still, it is not wholly impersonal but ambiguous. The words 'perhaps' and 'heart' are loopholes pointing to potentially opposite resolutions. Nature, with its regular seasonal cycles, is pre-eminently a manifestation of 'the order of things'. The 'sticky little leaves that come out in the spring' do speak of eternal rebirth. Some readers will recall the opening line of Pushkin's lyric, *Chill winds still blow*, where the image appears in the form of a question about the rebirth of nature: 'Will the sticky little leaves soon come out on the leafy birch tree?'[6] The poet's question is really *the* question which the whole novel poses for Ivan himself. The poet's title line is where we metaphorically encounter Ivan in whose head 'chill winds still blow'. Thus, Ivan's reminiscence from Pushkin's poem can be seen within the fiction as a distanced but genuine expression of his love of nature as a symbol of rebirth. It is a variation on the rebirth theme, so central to the novel. And that 'old memory' of a great human deed (*podvig*) may be seen as a fleeting prelude to Ivan's quasi-humanist Christ of the Legend where the Inquisitor repeatedly speaks of Christ's work as a *podvig*, noble and miraculous, but futile, over and done with. These veiled, literary reminiscences of memories, however faint, hidden and distanced are still alive and revered in Ivan's heart. 'Maybe' his heart can still love, remember and believe in the 'old memory'.

But Ivan immediately attempts to banish these memories still further from his life:

I want to travel to Europe, Alyosha, from here I shall set off; and yet I know very well that I am going only to a graveyard, but to the very, very dearest graveyard, that's what it is! Precious are the dead that lie there, every stone above them speaks of such a burning past life, of such a passionate faith in their great deed, in their truth, in their struggle and in their learning, that I, I know beforehand, shall fall on the ground and shall kiss those stones and weep over them – at the same time convinced with all my heart, that all that has long been a graveyard and nothing more. (14,210)

Inanimate objects, images of death and burned out faith dominate this description. Three times Ivan calls Europe a 'graveyard' whose 'stones' speak of the past faith and struggles of the 'dear deceased'. Twice he refers to stones, but these are not the stones which led Alyosha to befriend the boys, nor the stone which Alyosha loved. Nor does the graveyard of Europe preserve the tombstone over the grave of that long deceased, saintly Russian monk on which Father Paisy found Alyosha sitting alone, 'bitterly weeping' and 'convulsively sobbing' for his deceased elder (14,297). Nor are they the graves of people Ivan has known such as Alyosha visits. They are inert, dead, far-away, without living human associations to his own life. They belong to an alien cultural heritage, for Ivan they are lost or rather repressed memories. Ivan imagines that he will fall down and weep and kiss the cold stones of Europe, not the warm Russian earth on which Alyosha really prostrates himself, kissing and watering it with his tears in his ecstasy. 'I want to weep', he says, but he cannot. In fact, Ivan never weeps once in the novel. Instead, he concludes this passage with a laugh. Still it is a 'double voiced' laugh through whose self mockery the strains of despair can just be heard, despair that the age of heroic faith is over, dead and buried forever, so he thinks. Still, Ivan's attitude to European culture is very ambiguous. On the one hand, he turns it into dead memories, on the other, he laments its death. Underlying Ivan's words is a profound nostalgia caused by his prolonged emotional, spiritual absence from his native sources. Ivan's imagined tears, the graveyard, the stones and the 'precious' dead are images of deep mourning and melancholy. All this suggests that Ivan's feelings, his sensibility, will save him in the end.

And Alyosha knows it. In one of the most intriguing utterances in the novel he says to his older brother:

Half your work is done, Ivan, and achieved: you love to live. Now you've only to try to do your second half, and you're saved.
– You're already saving me, but I'm not lost, perhaps! And in what does it consist, your second half?
– In this, that you have to raise your dead who, perhaps, have never even died. (14,120)

Terras remarks apropos this passage that the denial of death and belief in resurrection are leitmotifs embodied in Alyosha and Zosima. But Alyosha's words have also to be related to Ivan, to his spiritual life. These perhaps non-dead are not just anybody's non-dead, but Ivan's non-dead, 'your dead' says Alyosha. And if they 'have never even died' but are 'dead' to Ivan, then he must have, so to speak, killed them. Ivan has then to search back within himself to find them, to remember them and hence to 'raise' them in order to resurrect himself in this life and perhaps for eternal life. Given the novel's affirmation of eternal memory, it matters little whether these 'dead' are literally dead or dead within Ivan's soul. Dostoevsky's art again and again comes to the fatality of solipsism. In his world there is a fateful bond between all people, a communality (*sobornost'*) which precludes any possibility of becoming whole alone, totally on one's own. In this view, Ivan cannot raise himself unless he raises his 'dead'. The word 'saved', coming from Alyosha, can only mean saving one's soul for this life and eternity. And the task is urgent. Ivan says he will dash the cup of life at thirty. Earlier Zosima concluded his words to Ivan with the hope: 'May God grant you that the decision of your heart reaches you while still on earth, and may God bless your paths!' Zosima's phrase 'still on earth' emphasises Ivan's responsibility in the present life. Now is the time for him to be raising his dead because after death he will no longer be in control. Speaking on the topic of childhood memories, Zosima says, in words that can be applied to Ivan: 'And even from the very worst family precious memories can be preserved, if only your soul is capable of seeking what is precious' (14,264). Zosima believes that Ivan does have such a soul: 'Thank the Creator that He gave you a higher heart'.

But what does Ivan do? At the most critical moment in his life, he allows Smerdyakov to extract from him his fateful decision to leave his father unprotected. According to Bakhtin, in Dostoevsky's art 'consciousness is much more terrifying than any unconscious complexes'.[7] Sometimes it is, but not always. Ivan's hatred of his father, and his wish for his death are fully conscious. Such wishes are in fact quite common

('Who does not wish for his father's death?' exclaims Ivan at the trial (15,17)). What is uncommon and truly horrifying is to act on the wish. Whether one does so on one's own or by proxy makes little difference morally. This Ivan can only do by repressing his awareness that he is becoming an accomplice to a murder that will really take place.

Returning home from his meeting with Alyosha, Ivan sees Smerdyakov waiting for him at the gate. The sight of the lackey fills him with loathing, and his instinctive impulse is to shake him off with the words 'Be off with you, villain < ... >!' But to Ivan's 'greatest surprise, something quite different flew off from his tongue: "Is the old man asleep?"' (14,244). Ivan's initial impulse to drive Smerdyakov away is a fugitive reminiscence of the prototypal rejection of temptation, of Christ's command to Satan in the desert, 'Get thee hence, Satan!' (Luke 4:8, Matthew 4:8), a biblical episode which so grips Ivan's imagination. The similarity relation Smerdyakov/Satan and Ivan/Christ lasts but a second. Ivan suppresses the way of Christ, but the impulse to follow it was and is in his 'higher heart'. Thus, what is really 'much more terrifying' is Ivan's irresistible attraction to Smerdyakov, his loss of will and autonomy to Smerdyakov. Unable to sleep on the night before his departure, Ivan 'felt that he had lost all his ends < ... > he was tormented by the unbearable desire < ... > to beat Smerdyakov, but were he asked why, he himself would not at all have been able to give a single reason < ... > his soul was overcome by an inexplicable, humiliating timidity from which he < ... > suddenly seemed to lose his physical strength' (14,251). It is the way Ivan is unconsciously driven which is more terrifying than the conscious contents of his mind. Where psychologists see only Oedipal conflicts, Dostoevsky sees them in conjunction with the action of diabolic forces. Alyosha says of his brother early in the novel: 'His mind is in captivity' (14,76). In this novel the captor is not unconscious complexes, but the devil.

The very next day Ivan's nocturnal paralysis of will is followed by a deliberate act of self induced amnesia. Riding in the carriage which is taking him to the Volovya station, his literal and spiritual crossroads, the narrator reports Ivan's inner thoughts: 'The images of Alyosha and Katerina Iva- novna flashed momentarily through his mind; but he softly grinned and softly blew at the dear apparitions and they flew away: "their time will come", he thought' (14,254–5). Like his father who 'waved away all his memories' of his family, Ivan 'blows away' the fleeting images of the only two people he loves. Now only 'the lackey sits in his soul'. When Ivan says 'their time will come', he unconsciously (and ironically) pre- figures 'their time' which comes at the end of the novel when they tend him in his mental illness. Minutes later Ivan, unaccountably to himself, decides to go not to Chermashnya, but even further away, to Moscow. At first the prospect of the distant journey puts him in the euphoric mood which often initially attends a complete break with the past, with the ties that bind us to others: 'Away with all the past, I've done with my past world forever, and may I have neither news nor echo from it; to a new world, to new places, and no looking back!' But one cannot away with the past in this novel's world. Ivan will soon have evil 'news' and 'echoes' from his 'past world' that will last a lifetime. The haunting begins at once. Immediately following comes the narrator's beautifully judged 'but', heralding a complete reversal of mood:

But instead of delight, there suddenly descended on his soul such gloom and in his heart took hold such an anguish he had never felt before in his whole life. He lay awake thinking the whole night through; the carriage flew on, and only at daybreak, while entering Moscow, did he suddenly seem to come to: – I'm a scoundrel! – he whispered to himself. (14,255).

The descent of 'gloom' on his soul symbolically seals and foreshadows the imminent evil act. That very night Fyodor is murdered. Ivan's 'anguish' betokens a submerged sympathy for his father, an obscure recognition of his complicity which brings him to his whispered self-judgment. His *kara* has begun. And then the narrator, leaving Ivan hurtling in the train towards Moscow, describes the 'strange' screams of Smerdya- kov's 'fit' as he falls down the stairs in the dark cellar, in a mimesis of a demon's hellbound plunge.

When Ivan 'blows away' the 'dear apparitions', evil phantoms take their place. His desperate attempts at repression finally fail. However, repression at least leaves open the possibility of recovery from his emotional and spiritual amnesia.

OBLIVION

Oblivion is the absolute limit of amnesia; it denotes complete emptiness, the total non-existence in the mind of anything to be remembered. In this case, something is not just put aside, retaining a potential for recovery, but it is obliterated, it ceases to exist and hence is permanently irrecoverable. Augustine clearly distinguishes ordinary forgetting from oblivion: 'if we even remember that we have forgotten [something], then we have not completely forgotten < ... > But if [something] is wiped out of mind, then we do not remember even when reminded.'[8] And if there is no one or nothing left to remind us, then we have reached a state of universal collective oblivion. This variant of forgetting Ivan, the intellectual brother, works into an ideological system.

Ivan arrives from an intellectual milieu (the university and journalism) where the cultural paradigm of remember/forget is undergoing change. Christianity is under attack from atheism in alliance with the rapid rise of science and the new ideas of socialism and positivism, facts and ideas which cannot be incorporated into the system of Christian cultural memory because they contradict or negate its very foundation. This leaves two choices: either the Christian memory can be left to wither away, to be stored and transferred to a potential, or deliberately destroyed, 'wiped out of mind' by a regime of compulsory collective amnesia.

The theme of idological amnesia moves through several important passages, describing a pattern typical of Dostoevsky's art. It first sounds with a leitmotif composed of a few essential notes, gradually gains in depth, intensity and semantic resonance and finally reaches a crescendo towards the novel's end. The dominant and increasingly isolated actor in all passages is Ivan.

Miusov introduces the theme at the gathering in Zosima's cell with his résumé of Ivan's theory that there is no virtue if there is no God and immortality. Ivan offers no objections or emendations. Next Ivan comes forward as a participant in the carnivalised catechism which Fyodor conducts between him and Alyosha on the subject of God and immortality. Fyodor importunes Ivan:

Speak: does God exist or not? Only be serious! I want you now to be serious.
No, there is no God.
Alyoshka, does God exist?
God exists.
Ivan, is there immortality, well, of some sort there, well at least a little, a little tiny bit?
There is no immortality either.
None?
None.
That is, a completely absolute zero or something. Maybe there is some sort of something. Not just nothing!
An absolute zero. (14,123)

In order to achieve the goal of final annihilation one begins with absolute denial which can serve as its philosophical foundation. Here Ivan, in clear assured accents, voices the atheist position, for the first and last time. Indeed, the very next day, just before he recites his Legend, Ivan 'confesses' to Alyosha that he 'was teasing' him 'on purpose'. But Smerdyakov, who for some three months has been listening intently to Ivan's ideas, is not just 'teasing'.

Nor is Ivan just 'teasing'. In their ensuing eschatological dialogue he moves over to the offensive. Vetlovskaia rightly says that Ivan is not really interested in Alyosha for himself. But he *is* interested in his younger brother as an interlocutor and the reasons are telling.

I've learned to respect you; the little man stands firm, I thought. Notice, although I'm laughing now, I'm speaking seriously. You do stand firm, don't you? I like such firm men like you, no matter what they stand for, even if they are such little fellows like you < ... > I see you're in a kind of inspiration. I'm terribly fond of such *professions de foi* from such ... novices. You're a firm man, Alexey. Is it true that you mean to leave the monastery? (14,209)

The reader can hardly miss Ivan's condescending irony towards his younger brother which pervades his patronising language here. Most important is his subtly undermining repetition of 'stand firmly', first as statement, then as insinuating question, and finally, with his closing query, as an oblique innuendo that Alyosha is abandoning his faith. Even so, Ivan's probing is deeply ambiguous. For what emerges most strongly here is Ivan's fascination with Alyosha's steadfast faith and his envy of a faith that is 'firm' (four times repeated). Thus, through his condescension we can just perceive a kind of respect for his younger brother, a sense of a lack in himself and his own wish that he too could 'stand firm'. Later, the narrator gives a firm answer to Ivan's querying innuendoes when he reports that Alyosha rose up from his crisis a 'firm fighters for his whole life' (14,328).

The significance of Ivan's scientific education in the novel's poetic and ideological system of forgetting now comes to the fore. After declaring to Alyosha that 'really, man has invented God', Ivan suddenly performs a *volte face* saying that he accepts God 'directly and simply'. He next asserts that he will 'avoid all hypotheses', and yet he enframes the question of God's existence within the standard hypothetical construction of 'if ..., then ...': 'if God exists and if He really created the earth, then, as we know perfectly well, He created it according to Euclidean geometry, and the human mind with a conception of only three dimensions of space' (14,214). Here Ivan assumes that God exists only in order to point out the absurdities to which this assumption must lead. He also says he wishes to eschew axioms, but seconds later he takes it as axiomatic that the earth and the human mind are modelled on three-dimensional Euclidean geometry. There are, Ivan continues, 'geometers' and 'philosophers':

and even some of the most outstanding, who doubt that the whole universe, or to put it more widely, all existence, was created only according to Euclidean geometry, who dare even to dream that two parallel lines, which according to Euclid can never meet on earth, may meet somewhere in infinity. (14,214)

If Ivan believes these 'most remarkable' geometers and philosophers (and he gives no sign of disbelieving them) then he has already contradicted himself. But there is another logical slippage here. Ivan overlooks the fact that it was precisely human beings with earthly 'Euclidean minds' who had these insights into non-Euclidean planes, and thus demonstrated that people are capable of conceptualising more than three dimensions. Ivan's reasoning leads him to a *non-sequitur*, and to another 'if-then' construction: 'I, my dear fellow, have decided that if I cannot even understand this, then how can I understand about God. I humbly acknowledge, that I have no faculties for solving such questions. I have a Euclidean mind, an earthly one, and therefore how can we understand what is not of this world' (14,214). Ivan pleads his own limited Euclidean mind, including Alyosha's, in order to assert that these problems are insoluble. Thus, Ivan unconsciously contradicts himself because he is bent on using his inability to understand non-Euclidean geometry in order to mount his accusation against God's world.

But all this is because geometry is not the main point. Geometry proves nothing one way or the other about the existence of God. What Ivan is really aiming at is the idea that God is not of this world. What really troubles Ivan is not geometry, but God's remoteness. God is infinitely far away. He is at that place where two parallel lines meet. God has forgotten mankind, and him. This means that God has, in effect, abandoned humanity, that God is 'not of *this world*'. This is the source of his nihilism and aching despair. Non-Euclidean geometry, then, is for Ivan a symbol for God's absence from this world, for the *Deus absconditus*.

Nor are Ivan's hypothetical constructions just a matter of logic. In this context of what Vetlovskaia calls Ivan's 'temptational sermon', Ivan's 'ifs' are variations on the theologically defined 'Satanic if' which challenged Christ's divinity at the Temptation (the episode on which Ivan's Legend is based): 'If

Thou be the Son of God, ...', and at the Cross where the mocking crowd challenged Him to perform a miracle: 'If Thou be the Son of God, come down from the cross' (Matthew 4:3, 4:6). Fyodor's boast that if he spits on the icon, 'nothing will happen' to him is a variation on these canonical challenges of the mockers and revilers.

Finally, why does Ivan seek to prove to Alyosha that God is infinitely remote, incomprehensible and therefore, for the purposes of this world, non-existent? He says: 'And I advise you never to think about this, my dear Alyosha, and most of all about God, does He exist or not? All these questions are utterly inappropriate for a mind created with a conception of only three dimensions' (14,214). Here too the reader can hardly miss the air of patronising condescension which hovers around Ivan's attitude towards Alyosha during this meeting. The reader, though, is justified in suspecting that it is not a tender solicitude for Alyosha's sanity that prompts Ivan to offer his unsought advice, but his malicious wish to undermine Alyosha's faith. In a final ironic twist, it is Ivan who, listening to the devil within him, has jeopardised his sanity by thinking about 'questions not suitable to a mind created with a conception of only three dimensions'.

Nevertheless, Ivan is not motivated by pure malice. His despair and feeling of cosmic loneliness are genuine and so are the problems he raises. Ivan, as is well known, suffers from an inner conflict between faith and atheism which he cannot resolve. This leads to a constant nagging internal dialogue which gradually splits his personality. Although Ivan does almost all the talking, the tone of his 'tirade' is unmistakably dialogic. His inappropriate laughter when recounting serious things evidences Zosima's insight that he is 'amusing' himself 'with despair'. Ivan acutely suffers from his awareness of his lack of wholeness. He is also aware that Alyosha's 'heart' is 'whole' and this enormously attracts Ivan to him. Thus, he needs his younger brother as a listener for the only way to acquire an integrated self is to establish a relationship with another. One cannot expunge this need which informs the note of seriousness in Ivan's voice when he tells Alyosha: 'My dear little brother, it's not you I want to corrupt and budge from your foundation, maybe I'd like to heal myself with you, – Ivan suddenly smiled quite like a little meek boy. Never had Alyosha seen such a smile on his face' (14,215). Ivan's 'maybe', however tentative, stands and so does his sudden childlike smile, inwardly noted by Alyosha. This is why it is wrong to hear only the evil voice in Ivan's discourses and to isolate it rhetorically from the poetic content of the novel. The sinister half of Ivan, now in the ascendant, does want to 'corrupt' Alyosha by undermining that whole tradition for which his brother 'stands firm'. But Ivan's wish to be 'healed', to be made whole by his brother, is at bottom another reminiscence of Christ's healing of the demoniac in Luke 8:26–36. Indeed, Ivan uses the same verb for 'heal', to 'make whole' (*istselit'*) we find in Luke 8:36. The biblical demoniac, who 'had devils a long time', who 'abode < ... > in the tombs' and ends at the feet of Jesus 'in his right mind' forms a poetic similarity to Ivan whose 'mind is in captivity', whom Mitya calls a 'tomb', who wants to roam about the 'graveyard' of Europe. Thus Ivan, in another hidden biblical reminiscence, expresses his wish to be healed by Christ of Whom his brother reminds him. His submerged memory of the divine healer prompts his rare childlike smile, a visible sign of the Spirit. This longing remains, subtly refracting his every word, shaping all his intonations. He does not hear them yet, but Alyosha and Zosima do, and so can the reader. They emerge more clearly in the next variation where Ivan passes from modern mathematics to medieval religious literature.

Ivan introduces his Legend of the Grand Inquisitor with a summary of a medieval Russian 'little monastery poem', *The Mother of God's Journey through the Torments*, in which the Mother of God descends to hell and is shown the various torments of the sinners. She comes to the burning lake where the worst sinners 'have sunk so deeply into the lake that they can no longer come to the surface: these God forgets', quotes Ivan, and appends his own appreciation of the phrase: 'an expression of extreme depth and power' (14,225). For no one else in the novel could this idea resonate with such force. The Mother of

God, moved by the sinners' suffering, falls before God's throne, 'and begs for mercy for everyone in hell'. She wins for 'everyone without discrimination' an annual respite from their agonies. The sinners thank the Lord and sing to Him 'Thou art just, Oh Lord' (14,225). Now just before this Ivan told Alyosha that he did not want to join in the chorus of 'Thou art just, Oh Lord' because the evil done to children is forever unforgive-able, irredeemable. But in this tale, as Terras points out, the Mother of God forgives all her Son's tormentors. Thus Ivan answers his own rebellion with his remembrance of the apocry-phal poem, though ironically he remains unconscious of this contradiction. For one so clever and skilled in argumentation, why should this be so?

Ivan's remembrance of this tale reveals an intricate fusion of his various psychological, ideological and spiritual layers of repression. Ivan's mother prayed to the Mother of God to protect Alyosha, but as far as we know she never evinced such ardent solicitude for him. Orphaned in childhood by maternal death and paternal abandonment, Ivan subsequently never acquires any other mother, or a good father, earthly or spiritual. In adulthood he becomes an uneasy atheist, convert-ing his lifelong experience of unhappy isolation into destruc-tive ideological propositions. Alyosha, rich in mothers and fathers (Sophia, the Mother of God, Fyodor, his guardian, Zosima, God) takes the opposite path. Unlike Alyosha, Ivan apparently aroused no 'special love' in anyone in his child-hood. He was not his guardian's favourite. His father hates and fears him; he complains to Alyosha: 'And I don't recognise Ivan at all. I don't know him at all. Where did such as he spring from! He's not one of us in soul at all < ... > Ivan loves nobody, Ivan isn't one of us, these people like Ivan, they, my boy, are not our people, they're rising dust ... When the wind blows up, the dust will be gone' (14,159). The striking sym-bolic image of 'rising dust' evokes ancient biblical associations with death, human mortality and the devil ('and dust shall be the serpent's meat', Isaiah 65:25). Fyodor's abandonment of Ivan, his forgetting of his maternal origin now recede before this total rejection of his son as a human being, as mere inanimate 'rising dust'. And Ivan is aware of it. Describing what proves to be the last farewell between father and son, the narrator reports that Fyodor: 'was not at all moved by their parting. He even seemed at a loss for something to say; Ivan Fyodorovich particularly noticed this. "He's sick of me though", he thought to himself' (14,254). Ivan's unspoken observation practically seals Fyodor's fate. Minutes later he announces to Smerdyakov that he is going to Chermashnya. Thus, Ivan's accusation against the absconding God who had abandoned His children to senseless suffering is a veiled accusation against his natural father who 'completely abandoned' him in childhood. His cultural allusions are shrouded remembrances of his lonely, loveless childhood and youth when he was 'completely forgotten'. Ivan's interest in this apocrypha reveals that he has retained in memory the image of the merciful compassionate Mother of God who does not forget those whom the Father forgets. Thus, his literary reminiscence expresses his own hidden wish for merciful, loving recognition, his own wish to be remembered, wishes which his pride will not allow him to acknowledge directly. Ivan's memory of the Mother of God is a literary reminiscence from an apocryphal legend which is a prelude to his impersonation of a heretical apostate. For Alyosha, Dostoevsky created a contiguity relationship with the Mother of God through his hero's personal iconic memory. Ivan remembers the Mother of God in hell, Alyosha, as a venerable image above the icon lamp in the 'slanting rays of the setting sun'.

Ivan's allusion to the apocrypha is also a prefiguration, for he himself will soon be in dire need of mercy. Mercy for 'all' means just what it says, for all, including atheists and murderers. The sinners in the burning lake of hell turn out to be symbolic of Ivan's predicament, the proclaimed atheist and inciter of his father's murder who lives in 'hell' on earth. As Alyosha exclaims near the end of their meeting: 'How will you live < ... > with such a hell in your heart and head?' (14,239) Those whom 'God forgets' are for Ivan reminders of his own spiritual condition, and frightening prophetic figures of his own destiny. But the loophole of God's merciful respite means that He is not after all totally oblivious of them. Even the worst sinners are not totally forgotten, even in hell God is not totally absent, for no one in the Inferno has lost the knowledge, the memory, of God's existence. Nor has Ivan.

In the next gradation of amnesia Ivan is the ventriloquist of his fantasy spokesman, the Grand Inquisitor, who takes the idea of God and immortality a great deal further along the way to extinction. The totalitarians' age-old method is to deprive memory of autonomy, to twist or deny past and present evidence, to rewrite history in order to pre-empt the future and shape it to their own image. The Inquisitor and his coterie set themselves up as the sole correct interpreters of the Christian message. Christ was wrong. They have revised His ideas in order to bring them into line with their will to power which they disguise with their ostensible concern for humanity's happiness. The Inquisitor's reading of three temptations forms the kernel of his atheistic argument. As Sandoz and Malcolm Jones have convincingly argued, this passage incorporates a suppression of God in that the Inquisitor suppresses those replies of Christ to Satan which emphasise His personal relationship to God, specifically, a relationship based upon His obedience to 'God's authoritative word'.[9] Rejecting the temptations by an appeal to the Word ('it is written'), Jesus proved Himself the true Son of God because he lived by the Word of God. Moreover, Jones argues, the Inquisitor's response to Jesus, 'is the result of a *double suppression*'; he rewrites the Gospels to suppress God, and he speciously accuses Jesus of imposing too great a burden of freedom on man for him to bear without God. The Inquisitor appropriates the Word he has corrupted with his elimination of God in order to establish a universal totalitarian state. His systematic deletions, revisions and specious additions to the biblical texts (of the sacred memory) constitute a programme of compulsory, universally enforced amnesia. What Christ really stood for – the authoritative Word made internally persuasive through Him – must be expunged from human consciousness, from human memory. When Christ comes to restore the memory of its real meaning, He has to be liquidated.

After Christ kisses him, the Grand Inquisitor relents on his resolve to have Him burned to death, but he sends Christ away ordering Him never to return again: 'Go, and come no more ... come not at all, never, never!' (14,239) Nevertheless, the Inquisitor's scheme is a perversion of memory, but not a total destruction of it. Even in this case some fragments of the 'sacred testament' remain, retaining a potential for discovery and renewal if only because the elite of the Inquisitor's 'utopia' rule in Christ's name ('in Thy name').

Ivan's hellish vision of a totalitarian world from which Christ has been banished is both context and stimulus for one of the most important and frequently misunderstood instances of individual forgetting in the novel.

ALYOSHA'S MEMORY LAPSE

Alyosha's forgetting to find his brother Mitya during the critical hours before the murder is often cited as evidence of his repressed wish for the murder of his father and therefore of his shared 'guilt' in the crime. Mochul'sky argues that 'all' the brothers 'consciously or half consciously wished for [Fyodor's] death'. Alyosha was 'guilty passively. He knew and allowed it, he could have saved his father and did not'.[10] A careful consideration of the text together with that hagiographical context of cultural memory in which the hero is placed do not support such interpretations. There is not the slightest evidence that Alyosha ever secretly wished for his father's murder, much less connived in it. On the contrary, as we have seen, Alyosha never 'condemned' his father, but treated him with an 'invariable affection and a completely natural, straightforward devotion'. Alyosha's premonitions of catastrophe can no more be equated with his certain foreknowledge, than Zosima's clairvoyant intimations of imminent tragedy can be construed as evidence of his complicity. Still, Dostoevsky let Alyosha forget Mitya. We shall attempt to find the motivation.

Belknap comes closer when he says that the 'association of memory with the good things and forgetting with evil ones prevails when Aleša mysteriously forgets his brother Dmitry after the legend'.[11] 'After the legend' is a key point. Alyosha's forgetting is proactive and involuntary, that is, something intervenes, causing him unwittingly to forget. Involuntary forgetting often occurs when something we intend to remember is driven out of mind by a sudden turn of events which arouses overpowering sensations of fear, grief or shock. What, then, were those mysterious evil forces which momentarily prevailed, deeply disturbing Alyosha's consciousness and causing him to forget Mitya?

Setting out to find Mitya, Alyosha, 'with his whole being',

> was longing to get back to the monastery, to his 'great' dying elder, but the necessity of seeing his brother Dmitry overpowered everything: in Alyosha's mind with every hour the conviction was growing that an inevitable, terrible catastrophe was about to happen. Just what the catastrophe was and what he meant to say to his brother at this moment he himself, perhaps, could not have said definitely. 'Let my benefactor die without me, but at least I won't reproach myself all my life that maybe I could have saved something but didn't, that I passed by, and hastened home.' Alyosha resolved [to find Mitya] even if it meant not getting back to the monastery that day. (14,202–3)

Alyosha's good intentions could not be plainer, his sense of urgency and impending, unspecified 'catastrophe' more emphatic. Hoping to catch Mitya 'unawares', Alyosha goes to the garden where they met the previous day. But then, while waiting for Mitya, signs premonitory of evil accumulate: Alyosha wonders why he chose exactly the same place to sit as when he listened to Mitya's confession; he begins to feel 'very depressed, depressed from anxious uncertainty'; 'suddenly' hearing the strains of a guitar, he recalls having seen a bench 'on the left' by the garden fence. An unwitting eavesdropper on Smerdyakov's conversation with Mar'ya Kondrat'evna, Alyosha 'suddenly' gives his presence away by sneezing, an involuntary expiration which folk superstition ascribes to the devil's presence. Alyosha, true to his honest nature, at once approaches Smerdyakov and asks where Mitya is. This is the only time they enter into a direct conversation, one which proves fateful when Smerdyakov misdirects him to the tavern, knowing that he failed to deliver Ivan's message to Mitya. Alyosha runs off to the tavern where he finds Ivan alone.

From this meeting to his turning point at Grushenka's, Alyosha undergoes a time of testing and temptation. Ivan detains Alyosha for a long time with his 'tirade'. Alyosha willingly, though anxiously listens because he wants to draw closer to his brother. But Ivan has other intentions than intimacy. As Vetlovskaia has shown, 'Ivan's sermon is directed against God, [thus] it becomes not simply a sermon but a temptation', a temptation of Alyosha to join with him in his rebellion against 'God's world'.[12] Ivan's temptational aim is laid bare when, after Alyosha 'sorrowfully' asks his brother why he is 'tormenting' him with his appalling cases of suffering, Ivan replies: 'Of course I'll tell you, that's just what I've been leading up to. You are dear to me, I don't want to let you go, and I won't let you go to your Zosima' (14,222). But Alyosha finally rejects Ivan's ideas. He has seen the 'hell' that reigns in Ivan's 'head and heart' which so frightens him that his first thought on parting from Ivan is to run to Zosima to save him 'forever from *him*'. In a Christian context there can be no fear more intense than the fear of the devil. The only salvation 'forever from *him*' is turning to God, or man of God. The narrator remembers the future:

Afterwards he remembered with great bewilderment several times in his life how, *after parting with Ivan*, he could suddenly so completely have forgotten about his brother Dmitry whom only several hours ago < ... > he had so firmly resolved to find and not to go away without doing so, even should he not be able to return to the monastery that night. (14,241) [my italics]

The straight arrow of Alyosha's intention was broken by Smerdyakov and Ivan who, though unbeknownst to each other, are at this critical moment working in tandem. If, 'tempting his brother, Ivan fulfills the devil's mission', then it was the devil's disciple who sent Alyosha to his master in the first place, and the devil's advocate who detained him.[13]

Alyosha receives one further warning after he arrives at the monastery. Learning that Alyosha has failed to find Mitya,

Zosima urges: 'Make haste to find him, go again tomorrow and make haste, leave everything and make haste. You may still be in time to prevent something terrible' (14,258). But 'tomorrow' (the day of the murder) the drama of Zosima's last words and death comes on the heels of his exhortation. Grief and the scandal at the monastery overwhelm Alyosha, plunging him into momentary rebellion. But this lapse the narrator extenuates in the most partial intercession by the narrator on behalf of a character in Dostoevsky's fiction. Entering a dialogue with the reader, the narrator devotes half a chapter ('Such a Moment') to his personal defence of his hero centering on the theme of love and the pathos of inexperienced youth:

It would be hard for me myself to convey clearly the exact meaning of this strange and indefinite moment in the life of the hero of my story, so beloved by me and still so young < ... > I would only ask the reader not to hurry unduly to laugh at the pure heart of my youth < ... > I firmly problaim that I feel a sincere respect for the nature of his heart. (14,305–06)

He then employs a rhetoric of contrast between two types of loving. He presents a hypothetical, average youth who loves 'lukewarmly and therefore calculatingly'. Such a youth would have avoided Alyosha's suffering, but his 'value is cheap. That's my opinion!' To this youth, the narrator opposes his hero who 'gives himself up' to sorrow over an irrational event from 'great love'. He then comes to the heart of the matter. He stresses that it was not his hero's faith which was shaken, nor the failure of the expected miracle to manifest itself, but the apparent absence of the 'higher justice' which allowed his beloved elder, 'the most righteous of the righteous', to be exposed to communal shame and ridicule, to the jeering and spiteful mockery of the crowd 'so frivolous and so inferior to him'. Another deftly embedded biblical reminiscence emerges: the handing over of Christ, the archetypal 'most righteous' One to the malicious mockery of the crowds during His Passion. Alyosha has forgotten the example of Christ's Passion. If He was not spared derision, why should Zosima be? Perhaps, then, this is the meaning of the narrator's comment that 'all Alyosha's love' had 'at times entirely concentrated, and perhaps even wrongly on only one person exclusively < ... > at moments even to the forgetting of "everyone and everything"' (14,306).

At just 'such a moment', Alyosha suffers his version of *Deus absconditus*: 'Where is Providence and Its finger? Why did It hide Its finger? < ... > as though It had wanted to submit Itself to the blind, dumb, pitiless laws of nature?' The laws of nature (death, decay and corruption) seem to Alyosha to have triumphed over immortality, over the Resurrection. Just at this point, the narrator makes the critical link with Ivan:

> I do not want to remain silent about < ... > a certain strange phenomenon < ... > which surfaced in Alyosha's mind. This new *something* which appeared and flashed across his mind consisted in a certain agonising impression of yesterday's conversation with his brother Ivan which was persistently being remembered now by Alyosha. Just now < ... > not that his faith had been shaken < ... > Yet, all the same, a kind of vague, but tormenting and evil impression from the recollection of yesterday's conversation with his brother Ivan suddenly stirred again now in his soul and kept demanding more and more to come to its surface. (14,307)

Precisely at this moment when Alyosha is deeply troubled by his memory of Ivan's conversation 'it began to get very dark' and Rakitin, the petty demon, appears to tempt Alyosha with a visit to Grushenka. Then, the 'higher justice' momentarily absent, that phrase of Ivan's which sums up his rebellion, enters Alyosha's speech almost verbatim: 'I just "don't accept His world"'. If, as Vetlovskaia puts it, 'Alyosha (and the reader), listening to Ivan, is listening to the devil himself', then Alyosha is speaking the devil's thoughts.[14] And the moment Rakitin imparts the fateful information that Ivan has gone to Moscow, the narrator steps in to draw our attention once again to Alyosha's forgetting of Mitya. 'The image of Mitya flashed through his memory, but did not reach his heart [it] flew out of his memory and was forgotten. But for a long time afterwards Alyosha remembered this' (14,309). Alyosha's 'great bewilderment' that he forgot Mitya continues into the future, but the reader may interpret the darkening of Alyosha's memory as the distracting effect of evil forces at work in the novel's world, and that Smerdyakov, Ivan and Rakitin are its subconscious agents in the hero's spiritual drama. Ivan has sown doubt in Alyosha's soul, doubt which the events at the monastery seemed to have confirmed. Once he doubts divine Providence, he forgets his brother. As soon as he fails to accept the 'higher justice' and doubts immortality, Mitya's image fails to 'reach his heart'. Succumbing to the temptation of doubt has fatal consequences. And the prime sower of doubt is Ivan. However, Alyosha overcomes his temptations. After Jesus proved His divinity by rejecting Satan's temptations, Satan was bound and Jesus was gifted with the power to cast out devils. After Grushenka restores Alyosha's faith by reuniting him with the highest image, he casts out her 'devils' and then goes on to have a vision of Zosima raised incorruptible. Later, Alyosha will remember Zosima's words – 'do not doubt in the power of the heavenly light' – and he will know and preserve their truth in the Life (14,292). The temptation of Alyosha is a modernised variation on the temptation of Christ, an essential element of his hagiographical image. In this view, Alyosha's forgetting is necessary for establishing the memory of the genre, the hagiographical and canonical pattern.

Intense fear, grief over the loss of a most beloved person, a heart 'cruelly wounded' by 'injustice' and, most of all, demonic influences, these events form the cause and context of Alyosha's memory lapse. Alyosha's blame is clear since 'all are to blame for all'. However 'guilt', in its primary sense, is the 'state of having wilfully committed a crime or heinous moral offense'. The hero is not guilty. If he were, his Christological function in the novel would have been irreparably damaged, and we would have had a totally different novel.

OBLIVION: THE DEVIL

The most radical form of nihilism is the consignment of something to permanent oblivion. In classical mythology, oblivion is associated with death and a phantom existence in the netherworld. The dead who dwell in Hades are phantoms who have drunk from the underworld river Lethe in order to

obtain complete forgetfulness of living. In *The Brothers Karamazov* these ancient motifs are associated with Smerdyakov,
Ivan and the devil.

Death envelops Smerdyakov's image. His very name *smerd*
('stink') is bound to echo the noun *smert'* ('death'). He was born
in the short interval between a communal memory of the dead
(the 'dragon') and the dying (Lizaveta). He is the son of a mute
idiot who died giving birth to him, and the replacement for a
dead child rejected by his father as a 'dragon' and buried on
the 'same day' he was born. Smerdyakov wishes he had never
even known living ('I'd have let myself be killed in the womb
rather than come into the world at all'). The unwitting
murderer of his mother at birth, the sadistic murderer of
animals in childhood, he grows up to become the wilful
murderer of his father and himself. Fyodor never openly
acknowledges him. Thus, any possibility of Smerdyakov's
having memories of his parents is annulled. Whether he ever is
aware that Fyodor is his father is not indicated, though he
could hardly have been ignorant of the rumours. Smerdyakov
suffers from epilepsy, the disease that intermittently induces
temporary oblivion, and is a metonymic symbol for Smerdyakov himself. After his culinary course in Moscow he returns
home having 'suddenly somehow remarkably aged, he had
even, quite disproportionately with his age, grown wrinkled,
sallow [and] began to resemble a eunuch' (14,115). Thus
barred from having progeny, Smerdyakov cannot perpetuate
his own memory, he will die with himself. His premature aging
and emasculation suggest that once he avenges his mother, his
role, and his life, are over. On his first visit to Smerdyakov after
the murder, Ivan finds him lying next to a dying man. Smerdyakov has no loving bonds with others either in his past, present
or non-future. He never was a son or brother, he will never be a
father. His tragic role is to be the unconscious avenger of his
mother. He is the most lonely, solitary and isolated of all the
living persons in the novel. In his sterile isolation, Smerdyakov
presents the closest analogue to Ivan's phantom devil. Smerdyakov's suicide encloses him in a final oblivion. While Ivan has
his nocturnal meeting with the Devil, Smerdyakov, the man

who would have murdered himself before beginning life, is sending himself to oblivion, his death unlamented. Unlike his three legitimate brothers who still have a future before them, his personal story is over, his earthly fate closed, and while his meaning is still open, his death does impart some sense of an ending to the narrator's account of a 'catastrophe'.

In the dialogue between Ivan and the devil, oblivion is taken to its logical and poetic limits. During his nightmare Ivan is the soloist of the two sides of his divided self. The frequent use in Dostoevsky criticism of the term 'double' to describe any subordinate character who has traits in common with a dominant character is not strictly accurate. Plato's concept of the *eikon* may clarify our present point.[15] An *eikon* is an image having only some features of an original thing, but always enough so that we can recognise its resemblance to the original. A double is a perfect copy, an image where there exists a one-to-one correspondence between all its features and those of an original. The devil is not really Ivan's double because he represents only one half of Ivan, the evil side, which Ivan now wants to expunge. Nor are there any true doubles in this novel. There are only characters who are ideologically and spiritually similar to each other. By designating as Ivan's doubles all those who in one degree or another share his ideas, we lose sight of those nuances of difference on which many of Dostoevsky's most ingenious poetic effects depend.

The devil releases Ivan's repressed knowledge about himself. But the devil's word is still his word and not Ivan's. Their divergences can be seen from Ivan's copious inaccurate quotations of the devil in the chapter following the nightmare, 'It Was He Who Said That'. It was not 'he who said that' but Ivan who says it now to Alyosha.[16] If the devil is no more than Ivan's hallucination, then what are we to make of Alyosha's, Zosima's and Mitya's frequent references to the devil as the source and cause of evil? Ivan may be hallucinating in his illness, but evil does exist in this novel's world. For Dostoevsky evil was no figment of the imagination, but an active force in the universe to be continually reckoned with, until the Second Coming and the Kingdom.

The differences between Ivan's devil and the biblical Satan
emerge through the devil's defective or distorting memories of
the canonical text. The original Satan was the arch representative of evil and the tempter of Christ. Upon the outcome
of their unique struggle depended the future of the world.
Ivan's devil is a devil for our times, a degraded version of the
biblical Satan, a trivialised figure of the tempter of the
Gospels. He is not the grandiose, theatrical devil Ivan invented for his Inquisitor, the 'great spirit', the 'terrible and clever
spirit, the spirit of self destruction and non-being'. For Ivan's
interlocutor, Dostoevsky created a petty minion, shorn of all
romantic glamour, a seedy 'gentleman', a shabby poseur who
is not sure that he is *the* Satan. The biblical Satan spoke with
God (in Job) and with Christ in the desert. Ivan's devil is a
garrulous 'sponger' who is only too eager to be accommo-
dating to his social betters. The biblical Satan knows and
remembers his past, his titanic struggle and revolt against
God. But Ivan's devil, speaking of his origins, tells him: 'in
society it is usually accepted as an axiom that I am a fallen
angel. I swear to God, I can't conceive how I ever could have
been an angel. If I was once, then it was so long ago that it's no
sin to forget' (15,73). The devil's amnesia about his pre-
existent angelic state is a subtle denial of the biblical account
which deprives him of canonical status, and of a model of his
angelic self. His reliance on 'society' rumour for his identity is
another parodic variation on the canonical invariant, created
in order to degrade and parody Ivan's ideas. He is a humanised devil and that is why he has to be presented in part as a
psychological product of hallucination. Dostoevsky has pulled
away the canonical ground from under Ivan's devil, leaving
only a few essential fragments for establishing the most important similarity relation, the one that associates Ivan and his
ideas to the diabolic.

The devil's indeterminate location in the vast empty spaces
of the universe is another subtle component of memory loss, of
oblivion. Halbwachs finds that without a concrete spatial
context in which to locate our memories, we cannot hold on to
our past feelings, thoughts, images or experiences. As soon as

we are unable to represent places to ourselves, 'we have arrived at the regions of our past experience inaccessible to memory'.[17] Only the familiar spatial image, 'by reason of its stability, gives us an illusion < ... > of retrieving the past in the present'. The devil's indeterminate space, then, is a symbol for the erasure of memory. In this consists much of the universal horror of infinite space. Memory loss means the dissolution and loss of the self. Indeed, the devil offers further non-self definitions: 'I'm the X in an indeterminate equation. I'm some sort of phantom who has lost all ends and beginnings, and even I myself have forgotten, finally, my own name' (15,77). X is the symbol used when a person's name is unknown, or is to be left undetermined, and this perfectly accords with the devil's having 'forgotten' his own name. But here the devil takes the metaphor much further: he is that critical element which converts determinacy into indeterminacy. 'I am the X', where 'X' is the universal symbol of the unknown factor, is a metaphor of the type 'A is B'. This is an inversion on Christ's self defining metaphors of 'A is B', (I am the light of the world', 'I am the door') and thus it complements the image of the devil as Antichrist, the total inversion of all Christ's qualities, of His two natures. The devil's amnesia about his 'ends and beginnings' conveys a sense of metaphysical horror because there is no closure, no shape, form or sense to his existence, and no end, no renewal, no transition to being, let alone to a higher mode of being represented in the resurrected Zosima. Perlina points out that the devil's phrase 'ends and beginnings' is a quotation of the title of Herzen's book and thus is another facet of Dostoevsky's travesty of Ivan's ideas and his 'polemic with radical and nihilistic concepts'.[18] There is another subtext. The devil's loss of 'ends and beginnings' is an inverted reminiscence of God's self-definition in Revelation (21:6, 22:13): 'I am Alpha and Omega, the beginning and the end, the first and the last', and thus can be understood as another covert denial of the divine plan.

Another non-self definition involving a mathematical symbol gives us the metaphor 'I am the necessary minus' (15,82). Now 'minus' is not equivalent to non-existence but to a negative quantity or quality. In other words, if we have −x, we still have a notion of x. Even the devil is not equal to that 'absolute zero' Ivan teasingly gave in reply to Fyodor's catechism on the existence of God and immortality. His role in the universe is to be the agent of disorder, the 'necessary minus'. The devil's mathematical figure is a perfect analogue to Ivan's 'absolute zero', another paired motif which joins the two figuratively and ideologically. Mathematics in Ivan's speech is a metaphor in the service of his *Deus absconditus* thesis with respect to this world. In his devil's speech it is a metaphor to express the emptiness of the universe. These reflections, among many others, steadily arouse Ivan's rage, indignation and horror.

Finally, it is the devil who quotes back to Ivan his most recent composition, his 'poem' on *The Geological Cataclysm*, where he argued that in order to build a new utopia only one thing is necessary:

'There are new people', you decided only last spring when you were getting ready to come here, 'they propose to destroy everything and to begin with cannibalism. Stupid fellows, they didn't ask my advice! In my opinion one does not have to destroy anything, one has only to destroy in humanity the idea of God, that's what we have to begin our work with!' (15,83)

Thus while Ivan was 'getting ready to come' to his father's house, he was professing nihilism. The way we receive it in the poetic representation, Ivan has moved from denial to annihilation, performing an inversion on his ideas about God and immortality. Instead of God 'forgetting' some people most of the time, all people will totally forget God all of the time. The very idea of God and immortality will be blasted from their minds and hearts forever. The consignment of anyone or anything to permanent oblivion is the ultimate murder. By now this proves too much for Ivan. Precisely while the devil is provocatively drawing out his exposition of Ivan's utopian fantasy, Ivan hurls the glass at him. Seconds later his brother Alyosha, the 'pure cherub' urgently knocks at Ivan's window, whereupon the devil vanishes. What we witness in the novel is a concomitant crumbling of these ideas and of the man. Let us reconstruct the acutal chronology of Ivan's four compositions.

It may serve as our most revealing guide to Ivan's intellectual and spiritual development towards the annihilation of the collective sacred memory.

Ivan gives ample evidence by way of copious allusions, direct and indirect, of having known the Bible from childhood. His earliest work, the 'legend' about the philosopher's glimpse of paradise, he composed while still a schoolboy at the gymnasium. Barely out of childhood when, in the author's view, one is purer, more innocent, Ivan's 'higher heart' can still imagine the possibility of the heavenly paradise. At the same time, doubts are creeping in since Ivan's 'philosopher', an atheist 'on principle', is clearly derived from the French *philosophes* of the Enlightenment. A year or so later Ivan enters university where he encounters a whole host of new (or popular) ideas, socialism, positivism, materialism, utilitarianism, rational egoism, which were rapidly eroding and superceding the Christian worldview, and whose common denominator is a denial of any transcendental first principle. Ivan elects the new path and eventually graduates in natural sciences. Then, while close to completing his university course ('about a year ago'), Ivan composed the Legend. By this time he no longer believes in the Bible. His Inquisitor invokes it only in order to destroy its meaning. Ivan intended the Legend to be a damning indictment of humanity and a proof of Christ's failure, but at this point he was not yet able to end his poem on a note of absolute denial. With his next composition, his article on the church courts, Ivan launches his attack on Christianity closer to home, singling out the Russian Orthodox Church for 'mockery'. Ivan's negation is becoming firmer and is addressed to a wider audience; this article he had published a few months before his arrival. His last composition, *The Geological Cataclysm*, his humanist Golden Age fantasy, Ivan wrote just as he was preparing to come to his native town, in late spring. Here, finally, Ivan has moved to absolute negation not only of Christianity but of the very principle of transcendence; the very 'idea of God' is to be expunged forever. We may add the catechism because it brings into the clearest relief Ivan's nihilism expressed as the 'absolute nil', though by now Ivan is 'teasing', and hence is beginning to have doubts. This he says on the first day of the story. Such is the actual chronology of Ivan's ideological development.

In the order in which Dostoevsky represents this sequence, we have first the ambiguous article, then the catechism in which the reader can pick up the basic leitmotifs and then the Legend. In these instances, Ivan narrates his ideas. When Ivan finally comes 'home' he sees his brother Alyosha again after an absence of many years. For three months he has been observing his younger brother, aware of his eyes upon him. He comes to love Alyosha, and just here begins the crumbling of his theory. After the murder, the devil is the main narrator. It is he who narrates Ivan's 'legend' about the philosopher and his last work, *The Geological Cataclysm*. By this time Ivan is on the retreat. As Smerdyakov taunts him at their last meeting: 'You were always so bold then sir, < ... > but now how frightened you are!' (15,61) Thus, according to proper sequential chronology, Ivan has moved from the attack to the defensive. In terms of his representation, though, we arrive at both his initial and his final position only at the end when that final position has become thoroughly compromised by his guilt and illness and the initial 'glimpse of paradise' seems infinitely remote. The revelation of Ivan's absolute nihilism occurs just at the moment when this idea most fully emerges in all its true destructive colours, with all its worst consequences accomplished. In the Christian system, when God is absent, only His opponent remains; when He is banished, the devil moves in. This is why it is Ivan alone, who wants (and does not want) to kill the very idea of God, who sees the devil. Dostoevsky originally had Ivan reveal his wish to destroy the 'idea of God' much earlier. In his Notes for 'Rebellion' (the chapter immediately preceding the Legend) we find Ivan telling Alyosha: 'I would wish completely to destroy the idea of God' (15,228). How much more effective poetically that the most destructive idea of the novel should finally emerge at the culmination of Ivan's breakdown, and that it should be spoken by the devil, who in turn is quoting Ivan.[19]

Ivan's physical image progressively becomes a graphic

reflection of his demonic ideas. It is a striking fact that Ivan is the only major character in Dostoevsky's fiction who is not given a physical description. We have no idea of his face, of what he looks like. Significantly, the only physical features mentioned are his symptoms of illness (Smerdyakov remarks on his 'yellow face') and his demonic trait (his crooked gait). This effacement is another part of the unsettling ambiguity Dostoevsky creates around Ivan. When Ivan arrives for their last conversation, Smerdyakov comments 'You don't look like yourself', a phrase that is much more revealing in Russian (*lica na vas net!*), literally, 'there is no face on you!' The absence of the face is a demonic topos which the narrator explicitly connects with death. As Ivan slowly approaches the witness stand, the narrator recalls his 'painful impression' of Ivan's face: 'there was something in his face as if touched by decay [the earth], something resembling the face of a dying man' (15,115). Illness, demonic gait, effacement, and finally the moribund face form an absolute contrast to the radiant iconic face of Alyosha.

And as Ivan deteriorates, he sees the world populated with phantoms. During his last visit to Smerdyakov, he says: 'I'm afraid that you're a dream, that you're a phantom sitting before me' (15,60). And Smerdyakov, on the verge of suicide, seems to dissolve and metamorphose into that other 'phantom', that other 'lackey' sitting before him at home, the devil. To him Ivan expresses the same idea, 'You're a lie, you're my illness, you're a phantom' (15,72). And finally the devil calls himself 'some kind of phantom'. Still, Ivan's maladies of memory, his repressions, leave open the possibility of recovery.

But no recovery is depicted in this novel. Ivan has still a long walk ahead of him before he will be able to 'raise' his 'dead'. Indeed at the trial the Moscow doctor gives very curious evidence which the narrator quotes verbatim: 'He was certainly not in a healthy state of mind, he confessed to me himself that he was seeing visions when awake, that he was meeting on the street various people who had already died, and that every evening Satan came to visit him' (15,122). Terras remarks that 'every evening' is an 'overstatement', but the reader may remember that Alyosha's exhortation to Ivan to raise his dead is addressed to a chronic condition of Ivan's soul. Now the situation is dire for Ivan's 'dead' have broken free from his unconscious and are palpably haunting him. Fyodor sees in a living man (Maximov) a resurrected embodiment of a man murdered in a brothel (von Sohn). His son 'sees' ghosts. Instead of remembering these dead alive, he is 'seeing' them as animated phantoms in an ordinary setting ('on the street'). This is memory in its grotesque nightmarish variant, reminiscent of Hoffmann. Ghosts are debased, diabolic inversions of resurrected people. Appearing concurrently with 'Satan's' nocturnal visitations turns them into diabolic emanations. And yet, in a grotesque way, these phantoms attest to Ivan's yearning to believe in resurrection. Lest we forget Ivan's strange visions, the prosecutor reports: 'He himself [Ivan] had admitted to the doctor and his intimate friends, that he was seeing visions, that he was meeting people who were already dead' (15,142). Ivan does not identify these 'dead people'. We can only say that they are people whom he knows to be dead, hallucinatory fragments of his disintegrated memories. Perhaps they include his mother, his old guardian, his father, or those 'precious deceased' from the graveyard of Europe. What is important for the interpretation of the novel is not so much who they are, but that they are. To remember them would be to resurrect them, and himself. For this novel, the author appropriately chose to leave them anonymous, and neither dead nor alive, as he leaves Ivan.

The Brothers Karamazov is a story about a double parricide, and the main murderer in each case is Ivan. The novel is designed so that the killing of Fyodor Karamazov follows Ivan's theoretical call for killing the idea of God as effect follows cause. In so far as Ivan wishes for his father's death and subconsciously incites Smerdyakov to murder him, Smerdyakov becomes Ivan's 'loyal Licharda'. And, conversely, in so far as Ivan loses his will to Smerdyakov and allows the lackey to 'sit in his soul', he becomes Smerdyakov's instrument. Seduced by diabolic ideas, they have both become the devil's instruments. In these diabolic entanglements lies one of the main joins between the pragmatic, ideological and spiritual plots.

Amnesia negates memory. Combining motifs of memory and amnesia, Dostoevsky created a larger poetic system of binary oppositions in which the positive elements of the memory system are denied, suppressed, repressed or obliterated in the amnesia system. Together they form a contrastive, symmetrical system of contrapuntally interweaving pluses and minuses, memory and its absence becoming attached to opposing moral and transcendental values. The amnesia system presents a destruction of the sacred memory system by degrees, describing a descent from the mockery and fragmentation of those spiritual sources by which, according to Zosima, all life has its vital principle, to Ivan's scheme for inducing permanent amnesia of them. The failure to accept moral responsibility (Fyodor) literally fathers the wish to destroy the very foundations of morality (Ivan) which for the author reside in Christ and His teachings. Ivan constructs a new paradigm of nihilism in order to subvert and liquidate the old paradigm of sacred memory. To Zosima's and Alyosha's belief that God is everywhere, Ivan opposes the *Deus absconditus*. The three leading ideas of the memory system are subverted: salvation is twisted into perdition, Providence is reduced to diabolical absurdity, the universe is devoid of Grace and resurrection is sent to oblivion. Ivan's programme of forgetting calls for the silencing of the voice of 'eternal verity'. In the Orthodox tradition, the knowledge (memory) of God is imparted by its incarnated Logos Who is the model for the divinisation (theosis) of human beings, for transforming them after the divine image. Those who deform the Logos (negative memory) go astray and become images of their own perverted deformations, more or less diabolic depending on the degree of distortion. If the memory of the incarnate Logos is 'smothered', suppressed or obliterated, then transformation, and hence rebirth in redemption becomes unlikely or impossible and the universe becomes, in the devil's words, an 'absurd comedy', in the image and likeness of the devil. The decay or loss of his highest memory through egoism, repression, suppression and annihilation leads to catastrophe. Memory is presence and speech, and presence and speech are life. Amnesia is a deaf-mute, forgetting is absence and silence, and absence and silence are death. This is the essence of Ivan's nihilism. His call for eternal amnesia is an inversion on the novel's parting refrain of 'eternal memory' voiced in chorus by the boys and Alyosha. In Dostoevsky's universe, remarks Bakhtin, 'Absolute death (non-being) is the state of being unheard, unrecognised, unremembered', the state of oblivion.[20] In *The Brothers Karamazov* all those who aim to efface the memory of Christ are consistently associated with the novel's darkest, most evil motifs. Attempts to consign God and His promise of immortality to oblivion lie at the metaphysical nadir of *The Brothers Karamazov*, just as faith and resurrection, that ultimate act of remembrance, occupy the ideal zenith of its poetic memory system.

CHAPTER 7

Foretelling

All the Scripture is called a prophesie.

John Daus

Oh, memory of the heart! thou art more powerful than the memory of sad reason.

Batyushkov

Of all Russia's great writers of the nineteenth century, Dostoevsky is the one who seems most modern, who speaks most to our century. He was by far the one who was most intensely preoccupied with discerning the future. Uppermost for him were the questions 'Whither strives the world, what is its aim'? as Müller puts it, and, we should add, what is the ultimate fate of every soul?[1] To these questions Dostoevsky brought his extraordinary gift for hearing his epoch as a great 'Russian and world wide dialogue', in which he heard not only the 'voice-ideas' of past and present, but also 'latent ideas heard as yet by no one but himself, ideas that were just beginning to ripen, embryos of future worldviews'.[2] He brought these 'voices' into his novels by giving them a dialogic form in which past, present and future could 'meet and quarrel on the plane of the present'. Dostoevsky's striving to divine and overtake the future finds its fullest, most varied and urgent expression in his last novel where the 'plane of the present' covers those hectic months of 'thirteen years ago' in which the dialogues about the future take place. Both past and future impinge on this dense temporal node into which Dostoevsky compressed those tragic events and dramatic dialogues which reverberate backwards

212

and forwards beyond the story into history and eschatology. All the participants in the novel's great ideological dialogues attempt to answer these questions about the direction of the world and individual fates by giving utterance to a word which can serve as the foundation for the creation of a new world and the emergence of a new man. This at once provokes the question of whether one can move into the future with a mental slate wiped clean of those collective memories in which people and societies have their life. Recalling the ideas of Lotman and Uspensky, every distinctive system of cultural memory is at once a mechanism for preserving the past and a programme for directing the future. When we speak about the creation of a new culture, of a 'reconstructed future', we are inevitably looking ahead to 'what will' or should 'become a memory'. Thus, whenever important new ideas, values, texts arise, demanding a place in the individual and collective consciousness, we are faced with having to select which of the older memories of culture are to be carried over into the future.[3] In the process, a rearrangement in the hierarchy of values takes place. As we have seen, the dramas enacted in *The Brothers Karamazov* are played out within the context of Christianity, a system of cultural memory which rests above all on prophecy and promise. The position the ideological protagonists take with regard to this collective memory turns out to be an all-important determinant of their visions of a future world.

I use the term 'foretelling' to denote the general category of all those words in *The Brothers Karamazov* which relate to the future, as well as those poetic structures which evoke the things to come. Three main future times can be distinguished: the immediate future which covers several months and takes in the events of the story; the long range future which is projected by the word of prophecy and concerns the ultimate fate of ideas; and time-transcending eternity which encompasses past, present and future. Each approximately corresponds to the novel's three plots, to those large narrative structures which give the story a strong impulse forward towards a denouement.[4] Each future is told and evoked in different ways.

We may borrow a formulation of Genette to define narrative

foreshadowing as 'any narrative manoeuvre that consists of narrating or evoking in advance an event that will take place later'.[5] Here belong all the narrator's and the characters' allusions to imminent events which are explicit, what Genette calls 'advance notices'. On the level of the criminal plot, many advance notices assume the forms of clues, snares, dark hints and similar ominous premonitory devices. The characters are all caught up in the immediate future of the story, in the drama of current and impending events. The whole atmosphere of the novel is agitated with their acute expectations (predictions, anxieties, warnings, hopes, forebodings) concerning an extra-ordinary variety of anticipated events (the crime, the verdict, a miracle, the finding of a lost dog, the deaths of Zosima and Ilyusha, and so on). Some events turn out as they expect, others do not. Rakitin, for example, cynically sizing up the Karamazovs, tells Alyosha early in the novel that a murder is brewing in his family. Fyodor is a shrewd psychologist whose judgments and predictions about others are often right. Two are fatally wrong: his delusive hope that Grushenka will choose him, and his misplaced trust in Smerdyakov. His suspicion of Ivan proves tragically correct: 'I'm afraid of Ivan, I'm more afraid of Ivan than that one [Mitya]' (14,130). Ivan's malicious prediction is dead wrong: 'one reptile' (Mitya) does *not* 'eat up the other' (Fyodor). Smerdyakov turns out to be a psychologist of unexpected but 'monologic' acuity who reads Ivan's evil wishes with deadly accuracy. His fatal error is his inability to detect Ivan's ambivalence, to perceive that Ivan is just talking, or just 'playing with his despair'. When Ivan threatens to tell the truth at the trial, Smerdyakov accurately predicts: 'No one will believe you there' (15,68). These examples may stand for many. All such highly charged anticipations about the immediate future are vital for creating a gripping story of suspense and for grounding the novel in the real world of concrete, human events.

Many words are devoted to evoking a future which extends far beyond the narrator's (and author's) lifespan, and knowledge. Some express their anxieties about the afterlife (Fyodor, Ivan and Lise are preoccupied with hell, Khokhlakova fears there will be 'nothing'). Then, there are the dialogues voiced primarily by the novel's prophet–ideologists concerning the ultimate fate of ideas, of the world and the soul. This future the author threw open almost entirely to the intentional prophetic utterances of his characters.

Finally, there is the future contained within and without the novel, the future which comes from the past (from memory), lives in the present and points to all possible futures. This future is evoked by prefigurations which require an analysis based on figural interpretation. In the representation of this future we are most aware of the author as the producer of the text. All these 'forms of a future' share a future orientation, but each serves different aims and gives a different aesthetic impression.

Various poetic and narrative devices also cast a shadow of things to come, not only within the novel but beyond it. Most prominent among them are symbolic motifs embedded in the narrator's and characters' language. There is a strong proleptic trend in the very way in which Dostoevsky organised the text so that certain portions of it prefigure subsequent events through symbols, gestures, dreams, visions, poetic tropes and parallel patterning. Those motifs and narrative manoeuvres which evoke future events, or point to delayed significance, without the narrator or characters *explicitly* drawing our attention either to the first element as a prophecy or to its complementary sequent as its fulfilment are prefigurations. Prefiguration applies to any motif which imperfectly figures beforehand, whether by act, image or an unintentional prophetic utterance, a subsequent motif which rounds out its meaning. Prefiguration is not mere repetition but the reappearance of an element semantically enriched and transformed for having passed through various contexts. In other words, a motif appears first in reduced form, or as a variation on another for which it has an affinity. When subsequently another element occurs which rounds out its meaning, we experience the satisfaction of completion which is a main source of the aesthetic pleasure we derive from literary art. Prefiguration is the most indirect, attenuated form of a future since the prefiguring motif is always spatially and temporally separate from the fulfilling one. The links between them are not primarily causal or logical. A character may be unaware, and the narrator may pretend to be unaware, or barely conscious of the future implications of an idea or event. But the author has established the links through his textual ordering of similar and contrasting symbolic and semantic motifs. Prefiguration is a pattern of meaning which the reader has to decipher. Here belong all 'dress rehearsals' of major events, unconsciously prophetic words and gestures as well as those verbal seeds which later come to fruition on the transcendental level of the divine plot.

The opening sentence of the story is an excellent example of the way Dostoevsky uses his narrator to deliver an advance notice which combines narrative with ominous symbolic foreshadowing: 'Alexey Fyodorovich Karamazov was the third son of the landowner of our district Fyodor Pavlovich Karamazov, so well known in his time (and even now still remembered among us) because of his tragic and dark end which occurred exactly thirteen years ago and which I shall relate in its proper place' (14,7). Belknap observes that the 'theme of memory emerges in the *first* sentence <...> with the statement that Fyodor Karamazov's death was still recollected after thirteen years'.[6] What dominates this sentence, though, is the ominous foreshadowing of Fyodor Karamazov's 'tragic and dark end'. Fyodor is 'so well known' and 'still remembered' precisely because of the nature of his death. But the narrator forestalls the reader's curiosity about the manner of Fyodor's death and says not a word about parricide. His immediate artistic aim is to create a feeling of suspense, but the fact that he and many others are still remembering Fyodor's tragedy implies that it has a broader, mysterious significance which has still not been exhausted.

With his intrusion in the first person ('I shall report'), the narrator sheds his personal accent over his recollected and anticipated material, bringing to bear on it his own worldview. This emerges most vividly in those elements of symbolic foreshadowing which fill his speech. 'Dark' is a metonymic figure for evil in *The Brothers Karamazov*. Noteworthy too is the play with symbolic and ominously loaded numbers. The hero was the 'third son' and his father's death occurred 'exactly thirteen years ago'. The folk-tale motif of the third son, which has been traced by Vetlovskaia, sets in train not only fairy tale but religious associations, and Catteau has demonstrated the importance of three for structuring the whole novel.[7] The old, deeply rooted superstition that 'thirteen' is an unlucky number is another dark subtextual instrument orchestrating the narrator's ominous foreshadowing. These elements, combined with the deferred information, suggest an unnatural, dramatic and mysterious death. The adjectives 'dark' and 'tragic' come from the narrator's language and reflect his own evaluation of Fyodor's end, an evaluation which is stamped on all the material that follows. When first remembered, then, Fyodor is associated with darkness and tragedy rather than with his characteristic traits of buffoonery, lying, cunning, sensuality and blasphemy. Evil tragedy overshadows Fyodor's image and foreshadows the novel's subject.

We have been led to anticipate a story concentrated on an end rather than on the evolutionary unfolding of a life. The narrator is talking about a man who is already dead. Thus, no matter how buffoonish, degenerate and reprehensible Fyodor appears, we have a different attitude towards him when we know, and he does not, that he will soon die tragically. Our foreknowledge, then, tends to cast a tinge of pathos over his image, and the scenes in which he subsequently appears, 'resurrected' by art, become in advance his memorials.

The grammatical subject of the opening sentence is the hero, Alexey Fyodorovich Karamazov; his father heads the long dependent clause, syntactically and semantically overwhelming his son. The father/son theme is ushered in on a predominant note of tragedy. The hero enters the story genetically branded by the 'black smear' (*kara, maz*) and 'punishment/retribution' (*kara*) of his surname, and burdened by the tragic background of his father's dark end.

If the death of the hero's natural father is still remembered, so is the death of his spiritual father, both of whom he loses on the same day. Zosima's death is also attended by unusual and disturbing circumstances. In words and intonations similar to those of his opening sentence, the narrator simultaneously remembers and foreshadows: 'something happened so unexpected for everyone and, from the impression it made in the monastery and in the town, so somehow strange, disturbing and bewildering, that even till now, after so many years, that day, so upsetting to so many people is still vividly remembered in our town ...' (14,294). This is not the memory of a tragic end, but of an all too natural mortal end: Zosima's corpse emits a premature odour of corruption, precipitating Alyosha into a severe spiritual crisis. Two fathers, two memorable deaths and two public scandals. But the first memory foreshadows a sensational crime which ends in the image of Fyodor in his 'new striped silk dressing gown with silk cord and tassles round the waist', bludgeoned to death, 'skull broken', lying 'on his back, face upwards, all covered with blood' (15,65). The second death will culminate in Alyosha's vision which prefigures Zosima's glorification in the world to come, in which he sees his elder rising up from the 'great table' of the wedding feast at Cana, 'in the same clothes' he wore in life, coming up to Alyosha, 'joyful and softly laughing', the black funeral gauze gone from his 'face all uncovered, eyes shining' (14,327). On the chaos of dramatic events, Dostoevsky imposes the aesthetic principle of symmetries which always fall on one side or the other of the major division, *pro* or *contra*. In Dostoevsky's poetics, every important motif of prefiguration/fulfilment interacts with its opposite. In the dissonant clash between antonymous images, the violent death of the carnal father and the serene passing of the spiritual father, emerges the dynamism of Dostoevsky's art.

After connecting Dmitry with the imminent 'catastrophe' in his expository retrospect on the Karamazovs, the narrator remembers his reaction to Ivan's arrival in his father's house several months before the murder: 'Just why Ivan Fyodorovich came to our town then – I remember even then asking myself this question with a certain almost anxiety. This so fateful arrival, which served as the foundation for so many consequences – for me long afterwards, almost always remained unclear' (14,16). The narrator recalls a 'request' and some 'affair' of Dmitry which 'in part' brought Ivan to his father's town, but this additional information fails to clear up the enigma: 'Nevertheless, even then, when I already knew about this particular circumstance, Ivan Fyodorovich still seemed to me enigmatic and his arrival in our town seemed all the same inexplicable' (14,17). Again, the narrator's memory work makes a dominant impression of ominous foreshadowing. This is because the narrator is superimposing his present knowledge over the past and simultaneously withholding it from the reader, just as he did with Fyodor. At the time Ivan arrived, the narrator could not have known that it was a 'so fateful arrival', nor could he have known the 'consequences' of which it was the basis. Now he does, but only up to a point. The author uses his narrator's nameless anxiety about Ivan's arrival in order to plant the first seed of ominous mystery which will culminate in the most sinister arrival of the novel, the appearance of Ivan's devil. Thus, the narrator's bafflement about Ivan is also a bafflement in the face of obscure, evil forces, forces which cannot be satisfactorily accounted for by empirical reasons but which seem to come on a 'gust of wind'. This is why Ivan is still an enigma, his significance cannot and never will be fully explained or finalised.

In contrast to Ivan, there is no mystery about Mitya's motives. He came for a clear, open purpose, to get the money he honestly believed his father owed him. The narrator's advance warnings of impending catastrophe occur in connection with Dmitry and Ivan; the first we know is a false snare, the other the earliest clue which might lead the attentive reader to implicate Ivan and to exclude Mitya as the murderer well before his innocence is confirmed. These initial allusions to a 'tragic and dark end', a 'catastrophe' and a 'fateful arrival' cause a load of predestination to hang over the whole story.

The narrator never links Alyosha's arrival to the 'catastrophe' or 'fateful consequences'. On the contrary, Alyosha, he tells us, 'had been living in the local monastery for a year' before his brothers arrived. He thus effectively detaches

Alyosha from any worldly motives or criminal entanglements. For his hero he has a very different and far more important role. The commemorative impulses which sent Alyosha to his native town, and determined his decision to remain with Zosima are but the outward manifestations of a prior, innate and larger quest. Twice the narrator says that Alyosha chose the monastic path 'because it seemed to him the ideal escape for his soul struggling to break out of the darkness of worldly malice to the light of love' (14,17,25). This quest sets Alyosha off from his brothers absolutely and assimilates his image to the hagiographical topos of life as a spiritual journey to find God. Alyosha's longing to break out from the sphere of 'worldly malice' into the 'light of love' is the ideal paradigm for all quests and future destinations in the novel. It is conceived dynamically and dialogically, as a 'struggle' which turns the world into a spiritual battleground between the two opposing forces of love and malice. It resolves into two sets of equivalence relations counterposed in dramatic opposition: memory, commemoration, the bond between the quick and dead are illumined by the 'light of love', whereas worldly malice is a prison of darkness where the 'light of love' has been extinguished and from which the soul yearns to escape. Alyosha's arrival leads to the turning point in his life, but his quest is not allowed to end in an ideal conceived as an escape within the monastery walls. His finding of Zosima at the monastery is only the first stage in a journey which will put him and his life to a severe test, a life which is invested with more future significance than any other character in the novel. This emphasis on the hero's future begins just after the Epigraph, in the author's foreword.

'From the Author' is a direct appeal to the reader by the first-person narrator on behalf of his hero Alyosha Karamazov. For no other character in his entire *œuvre* has Dostoevsky used a narrator to intercede in this way. Five times in a text which barely covers two pages he calls Alyosha 'my hero'. He evidently finds it necessary to be emphatic about this because his hero is a man who is 'not at all great'. Because of this he employs one of Dostoevsky's favourite rhetorical topoi (procatalepsis): he anticipates various objections to his hero from a readership grown sceptical about heroes, or, who have a different conception of a hero, and answers them with a personal appeal. He foresees 'with sorrow' that his readers will not see the 'remarkableness' of his hero. He then asserts: 'For me he is remarkable but I very much doubt whether I shall succeed in proving it to the reader. The point is that he is, perhaps, a man of action, but only in a vague sort of way, in a way that has not become clear' (14,5). The author's vagueness about his hero's activity is not just a rhetorical evasion. He is speaking about a very young man in the process of formation, a man whose remarkable qualities cannot be summed up in so many words, but whose significance can only be left to the future to make clear.

With his next remarks, the narrator enormously broadens the context of his work:

Still, it would be strange to demand, in such a time as ours, clarity from people. One thing, perhaps, is fairly certain: he is a strange man, even an eccentric.[8] But strangeness and eccentricity are more likely to harm than to give one the right to attention, especially when everyone is striving to unite the particulars and to find at least some kind of general sense in the universal confusion. An eccentric in the majority of cases is a particularity and an isolated phenomenon. Isn't it so? But if you will agree that an eccentric is 'not always' an isolated harmful and irrelevant exception, then I, perhaps, will take heart concerning the significance of my hero. (14,5)

In the author's stress on his hero's eccentricity lies a key interpretative point for the novel's poetic memory. His view that his age is one of 'universal confusion' in which all are striving to find some unifying meaning to life underlies the whole novel. Against this background of rupture and disintegrating values, the author projects his eccentric hero onto the wider stage of history. Eccentricity, as Bakhtin says, is always a positive trait in the Dostoevskian world, and in this foreword Dostoevsky 'affirms even the special and vital *historical* importance of eccentricity'.[9] With his rhetorical question, the author may stimulate the reader's memory of history's great eccentrics who brought a new unifying message to the world. If so, he wins the crucial concession whereby the reader's sceptical expectations may be converted into affirmative ones. For the author's aim is precisely to create an eccentric who causes good, who has a right to be heeded, who will fulfil the task of uniting 'particulars' and finding meaning amidst the chaos. Such an eccentric would by any definition be a very remarkable man indeed.

The author then takes this idea to the limit:

For not only is an eccentric 'not always' a particularity and an exception but on the contrary, it sometimes happens that just he, perhaps, carries within himself sometimes the very heart of the whole, and the rest of the people of his epoch – everyone, has for some reason been temporarily torn away from it by some kind of gust of wind. (14,5)

We have arrived at the heart of the matter. As Børtnes remarks, the 'whole' is 'a synonym for Christ, a metonymy that corresponds to the remark in Dostoevskij's notebook that "Christ is the source of all"'.[10] Designating his hero as one who 'carries within himself' the 'very heart of the whole', the author brings Alyosha's image to the very limits of closeness to Christ, before it becomes identity or coincidence. And when he intimates that his eccentric hero bears within himself a message that no one of his epoch can see *yet*, he projects a great future revelation. Much of *The Brothers Karamazov* is given to identifying that 'reason' and to representing that 'gust of wind' which have temporarily led all Alyosha's contemporaries astray. Styling his hero as the unique man who embodies the 'whole', who can unite others, point a way out of the 'universal confusion', the author implies that only such a man as Alyosha can show a way out of the chaos and bring them back to their true place next to the 'heart of the whole'. Clearly, the author is preparing his hero for a messianic role. No eccentric could be more extraordinary.

For no other character in his *œuvre* did Dostoevsky open up the future so widely and conceive such a large role as he did for his messianic hero. Small wonder that he thought it would require 'two novels' to encompass Alyosha's life, and that he called his first novel 'not even a novel, but only one moment from the early life of my hero'. Several times he refers to Alyosha as 'my future hero', thus deferring his significance to the future unrealised novel. Even so, Alyosha's future path has been carefully prefigured in the novel we have, and his meaning far more developed than may appear at first sight. The narrative of Alyosha's childhood, demonstrably patterned on traditional childhood narratives of saints, is, like its canonical models, a preparation for great saintly deeds and his future theosis. Alyosha's quest for the 'light of love', then, is not just a quest for his personal salvation, but is designed as a mission to turn the reigning 'universal confusion' into universal harmony, to bring the 'light of love' into the 'world of malice' by rekindling the memory of the 'light of love' in the hearts of everyone in his epoch, when he has found it. This brings us to the centre of Christian prophecy.

REALISM AND FIGURAL INTERPRETATION

The real world of people and events always attracted Dostoevsky's passionate interest. The manifest sensory world was for him a real world in which real people live, talk, think, rejoice and suffer and die. Dostoevsky never succumbs to the idea that life, being so transitory and subject to suffering and decay, 'has neither worth or dignity'.[11] He never devalues reality nor belittles human dignity, but takes this world, in all its tragic and hopeful problematic complexity, with utter seriousness. But he saw reality in a different way than most writers since the nineteenth century. As he expressed it in his notebooks: 'Reality in its entirety is not to be exhausted by what is immediately at hand, for an overwhelming part of this reality is contained in the form of a still latent, unuttered future Word.'[12] On that majuscule 'W' hangs a whole interpretative tradition. Dostoevsky's consciousness, his artistic vision was coloured by his acute awareness of the 'antagonism between sensory appearance and meaning', which, as Auerbach says, 'permeates the whole Christian view of reality'.[13] His stories are never 'simply narrated reality'. In Dostoevsky's work concrete historical phenomena not only signify something more than themselves, something not immediately evident and calling for interpretation. This, after all, is true for many conventional realists, some of whom discover unconscious motivations in manifest acts and thoughts, others who discern causal relations between historical phenomena and various economic, social, or intellectual forces at work in the world. But Dostoevsky divines in these empirical and historical phenomena signs of something at once pre-existent and prophetic which links up through various stages to prototypes which were, are and ever will be. For the modern realist there is only this world. But for Dostoevsky this world, while it never loses its concrete historicity, reflects 'other worlds' which though invisible are just as real as this one, perhaps even more real, worlds which have been revealed in the Bible from which he took his prototypes. And just here is where Auerbach's analysis of figural interpretation proves so illuminating for the poetics of memory in Dostoevsky's last novel.

Phenomenal prophecy, or what Auerbach usually calls figural interpretation, arose from the need of the early fathers of the Christian Church to interpret the Old Testament 'as a series of figures prognosticating Christ' in order to bring it into correspondence with the events of the New Testament. In so doing, they took over the Judaic conception of universal providential history and developed it as a method of interpreting all historical events so as to bring them into the all encompassing context 'of one great drama whose beginning is God's creation of the world, whose climax is Christ's Incarnation and Passion, and whose expected conclusion will be Christ's second coming and the Last Judgment'.[14] Auerbach's definition of figural interpretation gives us the prime clue for understanding the relationship between memory and prophecy in *The Brothers Karamazov*:

Figural interpretation establishes a connection between two events or persons, the first of which signifies not only itself but also the second, while the second encompasses or fulfills the first. The two poles of the figure are separate in time, but both, being real events or figures, are within time, within the stream of historical life. Only the understanding of the two persons or events is a spiritual act, but this spiritual act deals with concrete events whether past, present or future, and not with concepts or abstractions; promise and fulfilment are real historical events, which have either happened in the incarnation of the Word or will happen in the second coming <...> figural interpretation is allegorical but it differs (from allegory) by the historicity of the sign and what it signifies.[15]

We may also follow Auerbach in applying this distinctive vision of reality to fiction, provided that the fictional persons and events have been constructed to reflect and correspond to biblical persons and events. Here we should remember that the Bible, besides being a sacred book, is also a record of the historical experience of the Jews and Christians. Its authors and those appearing in it are taken as historical people who played their part in the providential history of the world. Thus, figural interpretation is synonymous with biblical typology. We can see at once that foreshadowing or prefiguration as a literary technique for building up a narrative is not the same as figural interpretation. In the former, one fictional event represents incompletely beforehand another fictional event neither of which is based on a relation to, or an imitation of, a pre-existent model having both historical and revelatory authority. Figural interpretation is intertextual, it presupposes a correspondence to something outside the text itself. Foreshadowing and prefiguration are intratextual, they comprise those poetic correspondences the author establishes between the various levels and parts of his own text. Fictional prefigurations may remind us of the prototypes, but such associations are accidental, the relation to the prototypes is not systematically intended by the author nor subconsciously apprehended by the characters, the images are not constructed with any attempt to call them forth. They do not serve as reminders of the prototypes. In those prefigurations shaped by phenomenal prophecy, that relationship is there, profoundly so. We perceive the prototypes through biblical quotations, direct and indirect, and the presence of Christian symbols. Images and words which point to the future are thus joined with the memory of the prototypes of divine history. Specific to Dostoevsky is the way he artistically adapted this type of patristic interpretation to his work so that it becomes his particular variant of the poetic function, one which depends on an Urbild/Abbild structure. This must be what Forster sensed when he remarked:

In Dostoevsky the characters and situations always stand for more than themselves; infinity attends them, though they remain individuals they expand to embrace it and summon it to embrace them <...> Every sentence he writes implies this extension and the implication is the dominant aspect of his work <...> It is the ordinary world of fiction, but it reaches back <...> to be merely a person in Dostoevsky is to join up with all the other people far back.[16]

They frequently, though not 'always', reach back through memory to biblical prototypes. Dostoevsky was both a realist in the usual sense and 'realist in a higher sense'. He could create vivid images of reality (the 'earthly show'), and then, with a sudden turn of phrase, the insertion of a symbol or a semantically laden word or even a change of intonation, he could turn them into images of 'eternal verity'. He combined reality so seamlessly with Reality that we cannot tear them apart without doing violence to the artistic integrity of the whole novel.

Thus, the novel's most important memory, what we may call its macro-memory, lies outside it. This coincides with Bakhtin's concept of the macro-dialogue which transcends the text, just as figural interpretation transcends the text proper of *The Brothers Karamazov*. Figural interpretation, then, offered Dostoevsky the main way for bringing his text together with the texts of the Christian tradition and those modelled on it. Through poetic devices of metaphorical and symbolic equivalences and parallel patterning, Dostoevsky makes the connection between 'history', the realistic human events represented in his fiction, and the word of revelation in the Bible.

Several echoes from the author's foreword resolve into an ominous prefigurative pattern which gradually establish an identification of that 'gust of wind' sowing 'universal confusion' in his epoch. Just after he has witnessed Mitya's violent beating of Fyodor, Ivan takes his first step towards Alyosha with the suggestion that they soon meet, made, Alyosha feels, 'with some kind of intention'. Left alone, Alyosha is beset by indefinable anxieties and forebodings:

Alyosha left his father's house even more crushed and depressed in spirit than when he entered it. His mind too seemed shattered and scattered while he also felt that he was afraid to unite the scattered fragments and form a general idea from all the agonising contradictions he had experienced that day. There was something bordering almost on despair, something that had never before happened in Alyosha's heart. (14,132)

Just at this point, the narrator deftly introduces Ivan into Alyosha's troubled thoughts: 'There was something even enigmatic about it. His brother Ivan had taken a step towards him which Alyosha had long been wishing for. And yet he himself now felt for some reason, that this step towards intimacy frightened him' (14,132). Clearly, it is a menacing undercurrent of thoughts about Ivan's 'intention' which has undermined his psychic integration and induced fearful, nameless presentiments of evil. Here too the narrator holds back important information. Much later we learn that Alyosha, precisely at this moment realised that Ivan wished for their father's death. Since Alyosha is designed as a messianic hero, any intentions undermining his spiritual integration take on demonic meaning. The devil's aim is to throw people into doubt, to disintegrate their faith and their personalities. Here Dostoevsky subtly uses the 'poetry of grammar' by representing Alyosha's consciousness in perfective verbs and participles denoting completed processes of scattering and fragmentation. Alyosha's zigzagging thoughts and feelings mimic these rupturing, demonic influences on his soul and foreshadow the temptational word of the Inquisitor and the devil. The narrator rounds off Alyosha's train of thought with an image of darkness closing in: 'It was already seven o'clock and growing dark' (14,132).

Further echoes from the foreword occur in the last dialogues Alyosha has with Mitya, Fyodor and Ivan shortly before the murder. In each instance, similar ominous symbols are woven into their words. The gathering presence of evil in this novel is signalled at several critical moments by a rising wind on a dark night. All form a connection with Ivan. The first occurrence of the symbolic motif accompanies Mitya's despairing thoughts of suicide. As Alyosha approaches a deserted crossroads, Mitya suddenly appears and exclaims: 'Stop! Look at the night: you see what a gloomy night it is, those clouds, what a wind has risen! <...> Ah, the devil! <...> Yes, I'm a scoundrel! A thoroughgoing scoundrel!' (14,142). Parting from Alyosha, Mitya orders him: 'You go your way, and I mine', the same words which will be uttered by Ivan after the Legend. And just as Ivan will shortly reject Alyosha on leavetaking, so does Mitya now: 'And I don't want to see you any more, until some very last minute. Farewell, Aleksey! <...> Destruction and darkness' <...> Don't pray for me <...> I don't need it at all! Away!' (14,143–4) He too quickly walks away from Alyosha, leaving his brother standing looking after him.

Fyodor acutely senses evil in the air. The last time Alyosha sees his father, Fyodor's fear of Ivan has ripened into outright suspicion: 'He hasn't come here too to kill me in secret, has he?' (14,157). Fyodor defiantly swears to stick by the sure pleasures of sensuality, ridicules Alyosha's 'paradise' and denies the resurrection: 'In my opinion a man falls asleep and doesn't wake up, and there's nothing else', the same ideas Alyosha will soon hear from Ivan when he impersonates his Inquisitor. Fyodor shrewdly assesses Ivan's motives for spying on him, and exclaims 'Your Ivan is a scoundrel', exactly what Ivan will soon call himself (14,158). Fyodor's harangue against Ivan builds up to an ominous crescendo where very similar symbols now pass through Fyodor's speech:

Vanka is not going to Chermashnya – why? He has to spy <...> They're all scoundrels! And I don't recognise Ivan at all. I don't know him at all. Where did such as he spring from! He's not one of us in soul at all <...> Ivan loves nobody, Ivan isn't one of us, these people like Ivan, they, my boy [brat], are not our people, they're rising dust ... When the wind blows up, the dust will be gone. (14,159)

Indeed, the wind 'blows up' very soon and Ivan will be gone to Moscow. At the end of their talk at the tavern, after Alyosha watches Ivan walk away 'to the left' and notices his lower 'right' shoulder, fear overtakes him: 'But he too suddenly turned and almost ran to the monastery. It was already getting very dark and he felt almost frightened; something now was growing up inside him for which he could not have accounted. The wind had risen again as on the previous evening, and the age-old pines rustled gloomily around him' (14,241). Shortly thereafter, Ivan has his fateful talk with 'a clever man', spies on his father and abandons him. Thus, before the murder symbolic images of night, sudden rising wind and walking off in the darkness are combined with thoughts of suicide (Mitya and Ivan), devil curses, the label of 'scoundrel', fear and rejections of Alyosha and all he stands for, love, salvation and renewal.

The last evocation of these images occurs with redoubled force two months after the murder, hours before Smerdyakov's suicide, as Ivan sets out for their last meeting: 'In that part of town where Smerdyakov lived, there were scarcely any street lamps. Ivan Fyodorovich walked along in the darkness <...> Halfway there a sharp, dry wind rose up <...> and a fine, thick, dry snow began falling <...> the wind whirled it around, and soon a regular snowstorm rose up' (15,57). In folklore the devil's arrival is sometimes heralded by a gust of wind. This may also be a reminiscence from Pushkin's poem *Demons*, where a traveller, riding through a blinding snowstorm on a dark night, sees swarms of demons whose 'mournful scream and howling harrow' his 'heart'.[17] There are also biblical associations: 'The ungodly <...> are like the chaff which the wind driveth away' (Psalms 1:4). A whirlwind is a biblical symbol for the sudden destruction of the wicked (Psalms 10:25; Jeremiah 23:19). By now these parallel sequences will have prompted the reader to read the symbols of dust, rising wind and snowstorms on dark nights as prefigurations of evil whose fulfilments are the murder, Smerdyakov's suicide and Ivan's nightmare. These symbols are also fraught with prophetic, historical implications. Recalling the foreword, we may now see Ivan as a cautionary figure who stands for that 'whole generation' which has been torn away from the sacred source by a 'gust of wind', a motif we have now to interpret as a symbol for the devil. In this perspective, since Ivan did not, and never would, actually murder his father ('Not You, Not You!'), he can be understood as having been irresistibly blown astray by the devil who, says Alyosha, 'has got into a whole generation' (14,503).

Zosima embodies most fully the hagiographical topos of clair-voyance as well as the three major senses of prophecy: 'divinely inspired prevision and utterance', the 'inspired foretelling of future events' and the 'interpretation and expounding of Scripture or divine mysteries'. Thus, only he can further the author's highest aims by viewing the world and the brothers' lives from a vantage point which is above the criminal story, dignifying and solemnising their fates with a language per-meated by a hagiographical style and biblical reference. From the very beginning the narrator draws our attention to Zosima's instantaneous insight into what troubles the souls of those who seek him, from the nobility to the 'faithful peasant women', from the murderess's secret to the essence of Khok-hlakova's soul. He reveals his clairvoyance in a minor way when he accurately prophesies the return of a woman's long absent son. Thus Zosima's extraordinary gift for reading others' souls is well established before he turns his attention on the day of the monastery gathering to the personal futures of the novel's major protagonists, the brothers Karamazov, two of whom (Ivan and Mitya) he meets for the first time that day.[18]

Zosima is the first to divine Ivan's split soul, not, we note, fragmented amongst many possibilities, but divided between *pro* and *contra*, faith versus atheism. After Ivan affirms his thesis, 'there is no virtue if there is no immortality', Zosima says:

This idea has still not been resolved in your heart and torments it. But even a martyr sometimes loves to amuse himself with his despair, as it were also from despair. For the time being you too are amusing yourself with despair – with journal articles, society debates, yourself not believing your dialectic and with pain of heart mocking it to

yourself. In you this question is still not decided, and therein lies your great grief, for it insistently demands a solution ...
– Can it be decided in me? Decided in the affirmative? Ivan Fyodorovich continued strangely to ask, still looking at the elder with a kind of inexplicable smile.
– If it cannot be decided in the affirmative, then it will never be settled in the negative either, you yourself know this peculiarity of your heart; and in this lies all its torment. But thank the Creator that He gave you a higher heart capable of suffering such torment 'to mind high things and to seek high things, forasmuch as our dwelling is in heaven'. May God grant you that the decision of your heart reach you still on earth, and may God bless your path! (151,65–6)

Zosima has discerned the 'pain of heart' through Ivan's mockery, and heard the note of hope in Ivan's question 'Decided in the affirmative?' On these he bases his prognosis of Ivan's troubled spirit, and his blessing. The kernel of Zosima's prophecy is contained in his sentence 'If it cannot be decided in the affirmative, then it will never be settled in the negative'. His syntax is exceptionally telling. It contains one certain statement: 'it will never be settled in the negative'. His open 'if' carries the uncertainty, but only the uncertainty about arriving at an affirmation. The opposite syntax would explode any possibility of an affirmative resolution. The unavoidable implication is that once Ivan can decide in the affirmative, his decision will be stable, 'settled'. To aid him, Zosima attempts to sow the Word in his soul, drawing on two Pauline Epistles which he quotes in Church Slavonic. The biblical verses and their contexts are revealing. The first verse (Colossians 3:1–2) reads in full: 'And so, if ye be risen with Christ, then seek those things which are above [high things], where Christ sitteth on the right side of God; mind high things, not earthly ones'. This verse is set in Paul's warning on the perils of false teaching, the vanity of philosophy and his exhortations to the faithful not to trust in worldly wisdom, in the 'rudiments' of this world. The second fragment comes from (Philippians 3:20) which is an expression of faith in the Christian future, in the promised heavenly home and the Second Coming: 'And our dwelling is in heaven from where we await the Saviour, Our Lord Jesus Christ'. In the same epistle Paul speaks of his supreme ambition 'to know Christ' and the 'power of His resurrection and the fellowship of His suffering' and to attain 'by any means unto the resurrection of the dead' (Philippians 3:10–11). Zosima's biblical selections are finely attuned to Ivan's dilemma, oscillating between Christ and worldly philosophy, between the minding of earthly things and the heavenly image of his deepest longing. But Ivan's resolution of his dilemma, his escape from despair, can come only through his 'heart', a word Zosima repeats five times. Again, Zosima's syntax is telling, for with his last phrase, 'the decision of your heart', he conveys the all-important idea that Ivan's heart has already made the decision. Thus, right here Ivan's future path is structured to bring him to a fulfilment of what is already prefigured in his heart. Zosima concludes his prophecy with the priestly blessing in which the fingers form the four letters for 'Jesus Christ'. Ivan 'suddenly rose from his seat <...> received his blessing and, after kissing his hand, went back to his place in silence. His face looked firm and earnest' (14,66). As Golubov points out, Zosima's blessing is 'freely accepted' by Ivan and thus draws him, even if only for a moment, into Zosima's sphere, into the 'fellowship of humanity in Christ'.[19]

But it is only for a moment. The decision of Ivan's heart does not reach him in this novel, but his mental breakdown at the end devastatingly undermines the 'dialectic' in his head. However, if we believe Zosima, then we shall have to grant that Ivan's 'higher heart' may gain ascendancy over his negation. This is the most open and uncertain prophecy of the brothers' lives Zosima ventures.

To Mitya Zosima prophesies solely by gesture. His enigmatic genuflection before Mitya makes a portentous impression on all present. Later Zosima explains to Alyosha why he bowed to Mitya in terms which leave the matter obscure, though ominous:

I seemed to see something terrible yesterday ... just as if the look in his eyes expressed yesterday his whole fate <...> so that I was instantly horrified in my heart at what this man is preparing for himself. Once or twice in my life I have seen the same expression on

some peoples' faces ... reflecting as it were the whole fate of those
people, and their fate, alas, came true. (14,259)

Mitya's imminent ordeals are vivid corroboration of the clairvoyant horror in Zosima's heart. But then he adds: 'I sent you
to him, Aleksey, because I thought your brotherly face would
help him', whereupon he quotes the Epigraph. Zosima's
recollection of the Epigraph in association with his prevision of
Mitya's approaching trials will prove a true figural anticipation of Mitya's subsequent path.

Immediately after Alyosha's family leaves his cell, Zosima
sends Alyosha to them with the warning: 'Go, my dear boy
<...> make haste. You're more needed there <...> There's
no peace there. Wait upon them and be of use to them. If
demons rise up, say a prayer' (14,71). Zosima's identification
of the sources of discord as rising demons (*besy*) is another
example of one of the novel's governing hagiographical ideas,
namely, that evil is an active force with a malevolent will
which has to be countered by prayer (remembering God) and
service (remembering others). He follows this warning with
his first prophecy for Alyosha's life, one that is specific and
unambiguous for it is a combined prophecy and command he
lays on him as his elder.

And know, my son <...> that henceforth your place is not here.
Remember that, young man. As soon as it is God's will to call me to
Him – leave the monastery. Go completely. <...> Your place is not
here *for the time being*. I bless you for a great service in the world.
Yours will be a long pilgrimage. And you will have to take a wife, you
must. You will have to bear everything, *until you come back again*. And
there will be much to do. But I do not doubt you, that is why I'm
sending you. Christ is with you. Preserve Him and He will preserve
you. You will see great sorrow and in this sorrow you will be happy.
That's my testament to you: in sorrow seek happiness. Work, work
unceasingly. Remember my word from now on. (14,71–2) [my
italics]

Shortly thereafter, Father Paisy chimes in on the same theme,
quoting Zosima 'there is his place and not here for the time
being' (*poka*). He recalled you lovingly, with concern. This
means he foresees something in your fate! (14,145) In accord-

ance with the hagiographical pattern governing Alyosha's image, that 'something' would be his ultimate sanctification.

Just before his death Zosima again prophesies to Alyosha:

This is how I think of you: you will go forth from these walls, but will *sojourn in the world as a monk*. You will have many adversaries, but even your enemies themselves will love you. Life will bring you many misfortunes, but it is in them that you will be happy and will bless life, and you will make others bless life – which is most important of all. (14,259) [my italics]

To 'sojourn in the world as monk' is another hagiographical topos which orients the hero towards a future spiritual mission. But it is a sojourn which Zosima stresses (twice) is to be temporary, an arduous pilgrimage, full of trials and service to others, but one which will end with a return to the monastery.[20] Yet again the evidence of the 'memory of the genre' authorises an important inference for the hero's future.

And so does the word of prophecy. Later, after Alyosha has left the monastery, he prophesies to Kolya:

– Listen, Kolya, you will be a very unhappy man in life, – said Alyosha suddenly for some reason.
– I know, I know. How you know all this in advance! – at once Kolya affirmed.
– But all the same on the whole you will bless life.
– That's it! Hurrah! You are a prophet! (14,504)

The extraordinarily close parallels here between Zosima's prophecy for Alyosha and Alyosha's for Kolya testify to Alyosha's internalisation and imitation of Zosima, and his assumption of his elder's gift of prophecy. The two identical ideas, 'you will be unhappy', 'you will bless life', can only be a preparation for Kolya's future development after the model of Alyosha, and not Ivan.

Finally, Zosima, in parallel to his brother Markel many years before, accurately prophesies the approximate time of his own death. Sending Alyosha to find his brothers, Zosima reassures him: 'Know that I shall not die without saying my last word on earth in your presence' (14,155). And so it proved. By the end of the novel some of Zosima's prophecies have come true, others have yet to be fully tested, none has been falsified.

Prophecy strives to overtake the future, memory to recover the past. Both are determined by time, both are at any given moment rigorously separated on a temporal continuum which is relentlessly moving forwards. A crucial difference between memory and prophecy is that the past, while re-interpretable, is irreversible, and in that sense it is closed. At the same time, since memory statements are restrained by real or presumed facts, by lingering traces of the past, they enjoy greater authority. Whereas, the word of prophecy is necessarily speculative and freer since the future is unknown, full of potential and can be shaped by our actions and ideas. A prophecy at the time it is uttered is an article of belief or faith. Once uttered, a prophecy enters the past, it too becomes a memory. A prophecy can only be validated by memory, for the recognition that a prophecy has been fulfilled depends entirely on its having lodged in the memory. When such fulfilled prophecies are represented in a literary work, we can speak of prefiguration. Prophecy and prefiguration, then, are not the same, for prefiguration entails the combined notions of prophecy plus fulfilment. It is not always easy to distinguish prophecy from prefiguration in *The Brothers Karamazov*, since what may seem to be a prophecy at one point, turns out to have been a prefiguration. However we can be guided by the following distinction: a prophecy is something *spoken* or expressed by the characters, whereas prefiguration is something the reader understands after he has read the whole novel and is able to link the various parts with each other. Those prophecies which find fulfilment *in the text* are prefigurations, those which do not are prophecies pure and simple. Prophecy predicts the fulfilment, or non-fulfilment of a programme for the future. Moreover, every fulfilment of a prophecy within the text functions as a kind of proof of its validity. Since all the prophecies concern ultimate questions or conditions, their complete fulfilment is inevitably postponed. But all their partial fulfilments are constructed so as to suggest long range extensions. The questions then become, which prophecies are fulfilled, how are they represented and does the way in which they are depicted compromise or authorise one over the other? This brings us to the prophetic theories of history and eschatological visions represented in *The Brothers Karamazov*. All refer to futures *beyond the text*, but some are partially fulfilled in the text.

In troubled times of 'universal confusion' and disintegrating values, people often turn to prophecy in the hope of discerning a better future or to warn of 'catastrophe'. All the prophecies in *The Brothers Karamazov* have as their common theme the idea of a future paradise on earth. The very theme is symptomatic. Paradise denotes an ideal and an ideal by definition is an image of perfection to be actualised in the future. At the same time, an ideal image of the future presupposes an awareness of the present imperfect state of the world, of human suffering and injustice, and a programme for overcoming them, a goal towards which to strive. In Dostoevsky's art, prophecies cannot be discussed in the abstract but only in conjunction with the characters who believe them. Every prophecy is always filled with a person's response, and is evaluated from the way it impinges on his deepest concerns and on those among whom he lives. Thus we have to consider them as the characters' conscious, intentional prophetic utterances.

Two opposing variations on the theme of 'paradise on earth' are represented and embodied in their fictional proponents. Since they proceed from radically different attitudes towards the past, they inevitably advance radically different views of the future and programmes for arriving there. On the one side there are the views of Ivan and his birds of an ideological feather which are grounded on atheism and ideas of progress. On the other side are the views of Zosima and his followers which rest on faith in God and immortality. The socialist utopia of atheistic humanism collides with the Christian prophecies of the New Jerusalem. Both have negative variants: the progressives are debased and ridiculed in the shallow Rakitin and pompous Miusov, while the hallucinatory fanaticism of Father Ferapont represents the dead end of Christianity. Most of the controversial heat provoked by *The Brothers Karamazov* is concentrated in the turbulent ideological battleground where these diametrically opposed interpretations of history and meta-history clash in unceasing struggle. There is no merging nor synthesis of these antithetical views. Their various representatives all interact, all sound 'alongside' each other in the great unfinalised dialogue of the whole novel.

Almost everyone in the novel sees that the present is far from ideal. Smerdyakov, totally lacking compassion or any awareness of the suffering of others (and animals), has no notion of a better future for humanity, apart from the debased idea of Russia as a colony of France. Fyodor stands for a continuation of the status quo. Mitya, the instinctual man, has no theories about the future, but, after passing through a phase of cathartic suffering he attains a prophetic vision filled with hope, love and compassion. Ivan and Alyosha have far more developed ideas about the future, ideas based on well known but radically divergent and historically fraught world views. It is they who are the main proponents of the two opposed versions of 'paradise on earth'. Following the narrator we begin again with the 'future hero'.

ALYOSHA'S PROPHECY: VARIATIONS ON THE BIBLICAL KINGDOM

Going back over the year Alyosha had been spending at the monastery, the narrator recalls that it was Alyosha's habit to accompany Zosima while his elder blessed the simple people who flocked to him in the belief that he would alleviate their suffering. He remarks Alyosha's deep sympathy for the people, overburdened by hard labour, injustice and sin, and his understanding of their need to bow to something holy. He then lets the compound 'voice of the people' speak: 'If there is sin, injustice and temptation among us, yet there is somewhere on earth someone holy and exalted; he has the truth [*pravda*], he knows the truth: that means it is not dying upon the earth and will therefore one day come to us, too, and it will rule over all the earth, as it was promised' (14,29). In the midst of their misery, the people remember the promise and believe in its ultimate fulfilment 'over all the earth'. With this *vox populi* the narrator merges the voice of his hero, even to equivalence of vocabulary and phraseology, in order to make the dream of the people and hero one. Beginning again with his word, he leaves it to Alyosha to speak his dream for the future and to identify the promised 'truth' that will come:

And all the time of late a kind of deep, flaming inner ecstasy was flaring up more and more strongly in his heart. That this elder however stood before him as a single example did not trouble him in the least: 'it doesn't matter, he is holy, in his heart is the secret of renewal for all: that power which will, at last, establish the truth [*pravda*] on earth, – and everyone will be holy, and will love each other, and there will be no rich nor poor, no exalted nor humbled, but everyone will be as the children of God, and the true Kingdom of Christ will come'. That's what Alyosha's heart dreamt of. (14,29)

The narrator displays Alyosha's dream for the future just as he did his hero's iconic memory from the past. Only here we are invited to contemplate not an iconographic scene, but a collective memory of a promise stretching back two millennia, the memory of Christ's promise to return and establish His eternal Kingdom where all the resurrected will dwell. When Alyosha identifies the future to come as the 'true Kingdom of Christ', he reaches the ultimate syntactic and semantic end-point of his utterance: his 'dream' of the future closes (in the Russian text) on the word 'Christ'. The memory of Christ and His promise resides in his heart, the metaphorical seat of love, as the subject of his deepest dream. The coming 'true Kingdom of Christ' cannot be temporally pinpointed, only affirmed and believed. But it is not an abstract idea. Rather, it is a promise personified in the image of Christ, Who in His incarnation once lived on earth within the stream of human history, Who was Himself a fulfilment of the covenant made at the beginning of the world and Who, in His life and teachings, left behind a personified image of the Kingdom to come, facts of cardinal importance for the author and the poetics of his last novel. For in terms of figural interpretation, Alyosha's dream of the

Kingdom is not utopian, but the goal and consummation of all historical development.

Dostoevsky's interpretation of the culminating New Testament prophecies emerges from those elements he selected to create the contents of the peoples' faith and his hero's dream. In the first place, they contain the fundamental ideas that there exists an absolute, eternal truth, a real, objective 'structure of things', that this truth constitutes a standard of virtue for guidance in life, and that it is located in Christ. The remaining ideas are an amalgam of Christ's canonical teachings and promises, Orthodox spirituality, and faint resonances of the Christian socialist, utopian ideals of Dostoevsky's youth. The idea that there are holy individuals keeping the truth pure is a favourite hagiographical topos of the Eastern Church. The phrase 'everyone will be holy', with its stress on 'everyone', is a slightly heretical expression of the Orthodox ideal of the deification of creation (theosis) through union with God. The primacy of universal love, which derives from Christ's 'new commandment', and the promise of the Second Coming are canonical (John 13:34). An end to injustice and the causes of dissension (pride and poverty) and the equality of all in perfect brotherhood as the 'children of God' under the kingship of Christ are a mixture of canonical and nineteenth-century Christian socialist and sentimental interpretations of Revelation. Distinctive to Dostoevsky are two crucial prophetic ideas, not part of Orthodox dogma, which he attempted to affirm poetically and rhetorically in this novel. The first is the idea that paradise can be realised *on earth* through following Christ's truth (the phrase 'on earth' is repeated throughout). The second concerns hell. Significantly, Dostoevsky gave no place in his hero's ideal dream to the Last Judgment when the final separation between the chosen and the damned will occur. The great Christian promise of resurrection has been maximally expanded with the universal quantifier in Alyosha's phrase 'renewal for all'. Dostoevsky's vision of divine justice was ultimately a merciful one, one which stipulated 'renewal for all'.[21] In Ivan's objection to a final harmony that leaves the sinners in eternal hell – 'What sort of a harmony is it if there is a hell' – we can hear Dostoevsky himself (14,223). Images of hell, eternal punishment and terrifying motifs of apocalypse were assigned to the adversaries, as the contents of their fantasies and experiences. For the hero (and Zosima) were reserved only images of love, harmony, brotherhood and universal participation in the Kingdom.

Dostoevsky's very placing of voices in this indirect exchange lends poetic support to the message. These two passages contain what Vitz designates as the three narrative subjects essential for hagiography: the people, the saint and God (here, the 'truth' that will come).[22] The people are necessary because without 'the prayers of the faithful inscribed in the text', without a '"we" desiring salvation' and the Kingdom, we would have only a religious biography or romance, it would be just Alyosha's personal story. Without God, 'we are very likely to have some sort of "study in psychopathology"', the saint would appear to be talking only to himself and hence a victim of delusional fantasies. This is why Alyosha and Zosima are often represented praying and in company with those who 'thirst' for spiritual guidance and consolation, who yearn for salvation. In fact, all Zosima's discourses constitute one great prayer. (The linking of Mitya and Grushenka with religious folk legends is another variation of the same idea.) Conversely, it is also why Ivan, the Inquisitor and the devil are alone, their words are devoid of prayer and find no acknowledging response from the people. Here, Dostoevsky gathers together the words of the people, narrator and hero, and joins them in a common prophetic theme. And they are pure extra-plot, they do not arise out of any specific event or time. Their three-way dialogue floats free above the times and locales of ordinary life, their voices sound outside the pragmatic events of the story. For in terms of figural interpretation, this is a memory of the future which transcends the concrete sequential events of history, which always was, is and shall be. Alyosha's dream of the Kingdom would appear to be a prophecy pure and simple. And yet it turns out to be a prefiguration of various passages in which momentary fulfilments are realised 'on earth'. Indeed, the hero's dream of a remembered future is the ideal dream by which every future vision in the novel is measured. This is the hopeful prophecy Ivan attempts to subvert.

But on the day preceding the meeting between Ivan and Alyosha, Father Paisy seeks to forearm Alyosha against the 'severe temptations' of the world he is soon to enter in a discourse which is a generative paradigm for the great ideological struggles ahead. Paisy's word is shaped by two poetic structures; a central metaphorical opposition of whole versus parts, and prefiguration. The moment Paisy speaks there is a sharp stylistic shift to biblical kerygma which perfectly accords with the resonant urgency and hagiographical function of his word: 'Remember, young man, unceasingly <...> that secular science, which has grown into a great power, especially over the last century, has analysed everything in the holy books bequeathed to us from heaven. And after the cruel analysis by the learned scientists of this world, absolutely nothing has remained of the former sacred testament' (14,155). Paisy presents secular science as a powerful force whose practitioners are not simply analysing, but cruelly annihilating the sacred testament to 'absolutely nothing' (*reshitel' no nichego*), a phrase which is synonymous to Ivan's 'absolute zero' and thus allows us to identify Ivan as one of the 'cruel' analysts. By using the plural, Paisy conveys a sense of pervasive, wilful evil relentlessly at work in the world. But the phrase the 'scientists of this world' implies that there are other worlds, and that these scientists are confined to the parts, to the narrower compass of this world. Father Paisy expands his metaphor: 'But they have only analysed the parts and have overlooked the whole, and indeed their blindness is amazing. Meanwhile the whole stands before their very eyes, unshakeable as before, and the gates of hell shall not prevail against it' (14,155–6). Nowhere else is one of the novel's central metaphorical oppositions – parts versus whole – so sharply and passionately marked. Paisy's attack rests on the idea of blindness, and an assertion of divine, invincible omnipresence. It echoes those biblical passages where mocking unbelievers fail to see the one divine truth because they are spiritually blind. Paisy's choice of biblical quotation (Matthew 16:18) prefigures those 'gates of hell' in the novel trying to prevail against the divine whole. But if there are the 'gates of hell', there are also the 'doors of paradise', and later in the novel they too are variously invoked. Those familiar with the biblical verse may recall the famous preceding lines – 'I say unto thee, thou art Peter, and on this rock I shall build My church' – and, given that Paisy's word is addressed to Alyosha, may subsequently see his biblical allusion as a subtle prefiguration of Alyosha's speech by the stone to the twelve boys which marks the beginning of his ministry to found his new church on the rock of sacred memory, the 'former sacred testament'.

Paisy, now merging scientists with atheists, gives the agenda for the struggle ahead and utters the fundamental prophecy which the novel will go on to fulfil:

Even in the souls of those very atheists, who are destroying everything, it [the whole] lives as before, unshakeable! For even those who have renounced Christianity and who are rebelling against it, are, in their innermost being, cast in the image of Christ and such they have remained, for hitherto neither their subtlety nor their ardour of heart has been able to create a higher image for man and his dignity, than the image shown to us of old by Christ. And whenever it has been attempted, the result has been only deformities. (14,156)

Paisy prophesies the inevitable defeat of the annihilators because his metaphorical definition of a human being and Christ's image precludes their separation. Paisy's insistence on the term 'image' is telling. Christ's deeds, His thoughts and teachings, are not singled out for mention. Christ as icon is the dominant authentic representation of Him in this novel. The destroying atheists' substitutions of this icon are also expressed in the pictorial term 'deformities'. Here we have a fine prefiguration of Smerdyakov's squinting left eye, of Ivan's strange gait with his longer left leg, and of his attempt to create a better image for man in his 'Golden Age' vision of the future where secular science promotes the ascendancy of the man–god, and which that ultimate deformity, the nightmare devil, quotes back at him as his final taunt. And the final fulfilment of a 'deformity' comes when, giving evidence at the trial, Ivan invokes his absent 'witness' who has a 'tail' and turns to the

public and sees not human faces but 'ugly m-mugs!' (*r-rozhi!*).
Minutes later he himself is transformed into an image of a
demon when, uttering a 'furious howl', he leaves the novel
being carried out of the courtroom, and 'all the while he
screamed and shouted something incoherent' (15,117–18).

The metaphor of parts versus the whole, then, resolves into
two sets of antonymous terms: to 'parts' belong the notions
temporal power, this world, annihilation, nothingness, blindness, absence, transcience, atheists, rebellion, destruction,
deformities, hell; to the 'whole' belong bequeathal, the sacred,
other worlds, the Bible, image, vision, presence, human
dignity, eternal, heaven, Christ. The distribution of these
antithetical ideas is systematically maintained throughout the
novel on the two axes of its fundamental opposition, faith and
atheism. The prefigurative pattern outlined here points to the
subsequent development of these oppositions as they dramatically unfold and interact in words and events laden with
prophecy and fulfilment. Alyosha is shortly to face the temptations of the rebellious, atheistic intellect when he meets Ivan,
the natural scientist who sees only parts, who attempts to strip
Christ of His divine nature. Paisy's warning proves to be a
prefiguration of the intellectual activities of Ivan, Rakitin and
the devil.

IVAN'S UTOPIAN PROPHECIES: (1) THE GRAND INQUISITOR

The two chief prophets of *The Brothers Karamazov* are old men
whose prophecies are for the most part represented in the
compositions of the two young author–brothers, Ivan and
Alyosha. Each brother creates his image of a father-prophet
whose word he takes to be authoritative. The many different
ways they represent their prophecies, contextual, stylistic,
rhetorical and aesthetic, crucially influence our moral assessments of their words. Alyosha's dream, developed by Zosima
in the Life, is all of a piece, whereas Ivan's prophecies typically
bifurcate into two distinct strands of atheism from which he
mounts a double pronged attack on the ideas of God and

immortality. We consider Ivan's first strand of atheism and its utopian product.

Ivan is keenly, even exclusively, aware of the world's injustice and suffering. His unappeaseable indictment of God is powerfully deployed in his 'Rebellion', the chapter preceding the Legend, where he attempts to demonstrate with his collection of facts that history is little more than a record of meaningless suffering, and hence provides incontrovertible proof that man is, was and always will be 'a savage and vicious animal'. Nevertheless, he sincerely exlaims: 'I want to forgive, I want to embrace, I don't want any more suffering' (14,223). However, Ivan does not offer a single idea in his own direct speech for eliminating suffering. Rather, he leaves it entirely to his fictitious Inquisitor to set forth a programme for establishing an earthly order which will guarantee the future universal happiness of humanity.

The Inquisitor's discourse is in essence a prophetic diatribe on history, past and future. For him, history was long ago foretold by the 'dread and clever spirit, the spirit of self destruction and non-being'. Satan's three temptations of Christ express 'the whole future history of the world and humanity. For in these questions all subsequent human history has been foretold and joined into a single whole' (14,230). Christ was able to reject Satan's temptations, but history infallibly proves that humanity is too weak, vile and rebellious to resist them. With this as his axiom, he constructs his future eternal reign by providing humanity with the devil's offerings, with 'miracle, mystery and authority'. Thus, for the Inquisitor the future of humanity is closed off, finalised once and for all: 'And so it will be until the end of the world' (14,231).

The Inquisitor's dogmatic view of history is forcefully supported by the grammatical structure of his speech. He uses an unusually large number of future perfective verbs, the verbal aspect in Russian which specifies a single termination and completion of the action in the future.[23] They follow one another like relentless hammer blows, imparting a sense of finality, of absolute closure to the future, which perfectly accords with his totalitarian plan and his view that human nature is eternally irredeemable.

The Word is finished, not subject to any further interpretation or renewal. Significantly, the Inquisitor begins his tirade with a command to his Prisoner: 'Don't answer, be silent <...> Thou hast no right to add anything to what was already said by Thee before' (14,228). The Inquisitor's demand that 'nothing should be added' is his attempt to capture and freeze the Word, to close it off forever from the future, to insure that that 'latent, future Word' is never uttered. The dialogue between human words and the divine Word, and hence between this world and other worlds, is over. And if the Word is imprisoned, or turned into a dead letter, so is the freedom to choose the redemptive path Christ offered the world: 'but we've at last finished this business, in Thy name. Fifteen centuries we've been tormenting ourselves with this freedom, but now it's finished and finished for good' (14,229).

The Inquisitor's scheme for a future world order is an inversion of the Kingdom prophecies which is systematically structured on negation and diabolic substitutions. The idea that 'all will be holy' is nullified by his fundamental axiom that man is, and ever will be, incorrigibly 'weak and vile', with rare exceptions. Instead of all loving each other, everyone will love the Inquisitor and his coterie ('they will love us like children'). Rather than all being the children of a divine Father, all will be the children of an earthly tyrant: 'we shall arrange life for them like child's play, with children's songs, chorus and innocent dances' (14,236). The most important promise of Christianity (and of the novel), the promise of 'renewal for all', is negated absolutely. All people are destined only for the eternal oblivion of extinction after their short span on earth: 'Peacefully they will die, peacefully they will fade away in Thy name, and beyond the grave they will find only death' (14,236). Thus, he strives to destroy the redemptive meaning of the Epigraph, the master prophecy of the novel. The ideas of equality and harmony are also stood on their heads. Except for the Inquisitor's circle, all will be slaves. Christ rejected power over all the kingdoms of the earth, but the goal of the Inquisitor's elite is to establish a universal totalitarian state over which they will rule forever: 'We took from him [the devil] Rome and the sword of Caesar, and proclaimed ourselves the rulers of the earth, the sole rulers' (14,234). The Inquisitor is a usurper of the divine prerogatives and thus is playing the devil's role. Indeed, he unequivocally declares that he and his elite are with the devil: 'we are not with Thee, but with *him*, that is our mystery! For a long time now we have not been with Thee, but with *him*' (14,234). In a religious system, any inversion of a divine motif yields its exact opposite and therefore has to be interpreted as a perversion, a wilful turning aside from the true course. Thus, instead of the 'true Kingdom of Christ', Ivan's Inquisitor offers the false Kingdom of *him*, the Antichrist. But their work has not yet been brought to 'total completion'. Looking far ahead, the Inquisitor prophesies:

> Oh, this work up to now is still only in its beginning, but it has begun. We shall have to wait a long time for its completion and the earth will have yet much to suffer, but we shall reach our goal and we shall be Caesars, and then we shall think about the universal happiness of people. (14,234).

In the Seville of the Inquisitor, where the 'work has already begun', we are given an accomplished image of the Inquisitor's future, a future conceived as the eternal status quo of his elite. And since it is a state ruled by slavery and terror, it thus becomes in itself a damning and cautionary prefiguration of universal totalitarianism, in Sandoz's term, an earthly 'political apocalypse'. Eventually everyone, he prophesies, will come to their side. 'With us everyone will be happy'. There will be a further rebellion, but in the end: 'the herd will gather together again, and again it will submit, and then once and for all. Then we shall give them a quiet, pacified happiness', a 'happiness' which entails their final submission to the Inquisitor (14,236). He concludes his harangue on a note of apodictic prophecy: 'What I say to Thee will come to pass and our kingdom will be established' (14,237).

In essence the Inquisitor denies the figural interpretation of universal history by trying to reduce Christ's appearance to an historical event, stupendous and miraculous in its uniqueness, but now past and done with like all others. He does not believe in the Bible, its prophecies are false, Christ's promises were mis-addressed, they will never come true. In this world of weak, contemptible humanity, the Incarnation and Passion were to no avail or purpose. Thus, he breaks the connection between the poles of figure/fulfilment by severing the figure from its future fulfilment. So when He appears again, threatening to overturn the Inquisitor's future, He must be burned. And in this the Inquisitor betrays his deep fear of the Word, of its great generative and regenerative potentials. Whatever is capable of infinitely generating new responses, contains a free, creative potential. The Inquisitor sends Christ away in order to prevent Him from interfering with his grandiose totalitarian plan ('For Thou hast come to hinder us and Thou Thyself knowest it' (14,228)). In sending Christ away, he sends away the promised future of the Kingdom, the 'dream' of Alyosha. Thus, given the novel's bipolar system, the only future left for humanity is the one begun and envisaged by the Inquisitor. And it is a vision of hell on earth, a complete inversion of Alyosha's dream and Zosima's teaching that all people are children of a heavenly Father, capable of love, renewal, spiritual growth, and destined for resurrection to eternal life.

The Inquisitor's prophecies are in fact Ivan's modern prophecies projected into a vanished historical period allegorised by his own imagining. But such men as the Inquisitor exist 'now', maintains Ivan, and 'must exist'. And so they do. Indeed, the Inquisitor's ideas still live, only in different forms, under different banners. Dostoevsky saw atheism and socialism as having originated in catholicism and protestantism.[24] It was the new views based on atheism which were far more worrying to the author, and which were coming to fruition in his own time. In this perspective the Legend turns out to be a prefiguration of Ivan's modern atheism as expressed in his conversation with the devil where it will re-emerge shed of any Christian foundation.

ZOSIMA'S PROPHECIES

Zosima is depicted as a real living person, as the hero's spiritual father whom he has known, loved and with whom he has lived in closest proximity. Zosima's prophecies are represented in two contexts; by the narrator in the 'here and now' of his story where Zosima prophesies to various circles of people (pilgrims, visitors, his monastic brethren and beloved novice), and by Alyosha in the Life where they are preserved in writing so that they may continue to live in the world for future generations. Thanks to this compositional arrangement, Zosima's prophetic word opens out into the world so as to insure its extensive dissemination. Thus as transmitters of Zosima's prophetic word, both Alyosha and the narrator bear mutual witness for Zosima. The narrator offers no such support for the Grand Inquisitor but leaves him strictly to Ivan, sealing his discourse off from all the other characters save Alyosha. Ivan's totalitarian father is a fantasy figure from a distant history whose prophecies are transmitted by Ivan in his conversation with Alyosha, and that is the only time we hear them. The compositional isolation of the Inquisitor's discourse reflects the closed obsessional system of his thoughts and mirrors the self-sufficient isolation of its author, Ivan himself. Thus, while the Inquisitor's ideas enter the novel's dialogue, the fact that he himself is only Ivan's fantasy has the effect of undermining his prophecies. This contextual opposition of Zosima's and the Inquisitor's utterances between reality and fantasy inevitably affects the way we evaluate their prophecies. We tend to take more seriously those utterances, and events, which come from reality than from fantasy. This is all the more important since the word of prophecy is necessarily speculative and it is Zosima's prophecies which the author aims to affirm and validate.

Zosima's prophecies would appear to have little relation to the novel's tragic events, while Ivan's ideas cannot be extricated from them. However, the links between Zosima's word and the story depend largely on patterns of prefiguration, and on indirect answers to the events and dilemmas depicted in the novel's 'outside' world. Memory and prophecy are Zosima's two great modes. And given the Christian context of his image, they are really two sides of the same coin, the coin of figure fulfilled and figure to be fulfilled. Zosima's prophecies are first spoken in the immediate world of the story and then in the timeless world of the Life where all his words are uttered *sub specie aeternitatis*. He is now positioned at a point from where he can view his whole life as a fulfilment of what came in the beginning. In his searching attempt to penetrate the shape of the future, Zosima takes his bearings on the Word held in memory. The sphere of Zosima's life presents a living chronological chain between three men whose crises bring them to a new revelation, a new interpretation of the Word, which fundamentally alters their vision of reality and the future. Each, on the threshold of death, sensing his approaching end, speaks of a future paradise on earth. First Markel, Zosima's dying brother, speaks of this world as already transfigured into an image of paradise ('life is paradise'). The chain of prophecy continues with the Mysterious Visitor (who 'taught' Zosima so much) and who interprets the modern malaise in the light of the New Testament prophecies. Life is not yet paradise, but it will be when the period of human alienation ends, when all individually change spiritually and become brothers, bringing with it an end to injustice, evil and suffering on earth. Then there is Zosima in whose words we can see the fullest flowering and expansion of this idea. The whole Life can be read as Zosima's interpretation and re-affirmation of the Kingdom prophecies and an exhortation to hasten their fulfilment now, on earth.

Zosima also gives the memory of the Word a social, missionary significance. He urges his followers to read the Bible to the simple people, to sow the seed of the Word in their souls for the future:

Only a small seed is needed, a tiny one: cast it into the soul of the simple people and it will not die, it will live in their souls all their lives, will lie hidden inside them amidst the darkness, amidst the stench of their sins, like a bright point, like a great reminder. (14,266)

The Word is to be the ideal of the communal memory, the collective light out of darkness, just as it is individually for the hero. Zosima projects the prophetic revelations of the New Jerusalem into the relatively near future. 'The time is at hand' (*vremia blizko*), where the 'time' denotes that regenerative spiritual revolution which will soon take place on earth where 'the Truth will be fulfilled'. Of this 'time' only God knows the 'hour and the day'. But the conviction that it will be 'soon' ('So Be It, So Be It!' as the chapter heading has it) permeates Zosima's utterances with that sense of impending Apocalypse which fills Revelation, the Book which deeply coloured Dostoevsky's prophetic thought. In the Life, Zosima also prepares Alyosha for his future mission 'in the world'. In a passage addressed to his novice, he says: 'You are working for the whole, you are acting for the future <...> be a light unto the world' (14,292). Alyosha, the 'angel'/messenger is the future carrier of Zosima's message into the world both in word, through the Life, and in deed, through his practice of 'active love'. Thus, Alyosha's face for him is 'a reminder and a prophecy', a reminder of Markel whom he spiritually resembles, and of another, the divine prototype, a *figura Christi*. Through his chosen disciple, Zosima's prophetic discourses radiate out into the novel's world. The last scene of the novel, where Alyosha begins his work (*delo*), is Dostoevsky's attempt to fulfil and accelerate the coming spiritual revolution by creating a poetic example.

MITYA'S DREAM

At the end of his interrogation, Mitya falls asleep and has a 'strange dream' in which he is driving through the barren steppe in damp falling snow. He comes upon a burnt out village and sees a group of emaciated peasant women with 'brownish faces'. One in particular stands out, holding an infant, blue with cold and crying from hunger. Insistent, urgent questions rise up as Mitya asks his coachman: 'Why are the people poor?', 'Why is the babe crying?', 'Why don't they hug each other and kiss?' The narrator then shifts to Mitya's inner thoughts and feelings, retaining the present tense of the dialogue, (a significant grammatical nuance ignored in English translations) and here an answer emerges which is another variation on the Kingdom prophecies:

He feels surging up in his heart a kind of tender emotion (*umilienie*) such as never before, so that he wants to cry, he wants to do something for them all so that the babe should weep no more, so that the babe's blackened, dried-up mother should not weep, so that no one should shed any tears from this very minute, and that he ought to do this at once, at once, without delaying, regardless of anything. (14,456–7)

This is an echo from the biblical vision of the New Jerusalem: 'And God shall wipe away every tear from their eyes: and there shall be no more death, neither sorrow nor crying, neither shall there be any more pain: for the former things are passed away' (Revelation 21:4). The present tense reflects Markel's and Zosima's belief that the Kingdom can be fulfilled now, on earth. When Mitya longs to put this vision into practice, 'to do something for them all this very minute', when this memory of the future becomes a present wish for him, then his catharsis is at last achieved and he finds a 'new man' in himself.

Mitya's dream is also subjected to an attempt at subversion. Visiting Mitya on the eve of the trial, Alyosha finds him fraught, confused and despondent:

Well, Aleksey, now I'm done for (literally 'my head's lost') but not because of the trial. It's not my head that's lost, but what was sitting in my head, that's what is lost ... Ideas, ideas, that's what's the matter! <...> Ethics. What is ethics? Yes, a science, but what kind? ... Claude Bernard. what's that? Chemistry or what? ... they're all scoundrels ... Ugh, Bernards! They've bred in large numbers! <...> Alyosha, my cherub, these different philosophies are killing me, the devil take them! <...> Why am I done for? Hmm. The main reason is ... if you take it all as a whole – I'm sorry for God, that's what! (15,27)

What has brought Mitya to his lament for God? It quickly emerges that Rakitin, a shallow emissary from Ivan's ideological sphere, has been giving Mitya lessons in scientific materialism and determinism. Explaining it to Alyosha in his own words, Mitya fills them with his own passionate beliefs and emotional response. In a short speech interspersed with three devil curses, Mitya describes human nerve endings as 'little tails' (*khvostiki*). Coming to the heart of the matter he says: 'that's why I see and then think ... because of these little tails, and not at all because I have a soul and that I am some kind of image and likeness ... This science is splendid, Alyosha! A new man is coming, that I too understand ... But all the same, I'm sorry for God' (15,28). Rakitin has been promoting the scientific discoveries of Claude Bernard to undermine Mitya's faith, the 'new man' he has found in himself since his dream of the babe. In the space of two scant pages, Mitya twice calls Rakitin 'a swine' (*svin'ia*), and utters nine devil curses, including a fourfold repetition of 'the devil take him!' Significant for symbolic analysis is the profusion of plurals, 'ideas', 'scoundrels', 'Ugh, Bernards! They've bred in large numbers!', 'philosophies', 'little tails'. Discussing the parable of the Gadarene swine, Starobinski observes: 'evil is always on the side of plurality: whether it be a matter of illness, demonic hostility, or unbelief, the adverse element is always plural'.[25] So, a scientific fact, refracted in Mitya's language, has become a metaphor for demonic invasion of the human nervous system. This gives rise to the correlation: Rakitin, in attempting to replace the soul, 'the image and likeness', with chemistry, and the old morality with a secular ethics, is doing the devil's work. The 'science' of ethics, which Rakitin preaches, is effectively compromised and dissociated from morality when we learn here that Rakitin has given up the monastic life. Rakitin's hatred of God 'And Rakitin hates God, ugh he hates him!' allies him too with the devil (15,29). Now Rakitin's talks with Kolya, the precocious, 'young Ivan' who asserts: 'I respect only mathematics and natural sciences', and who enthusiastically mouths fashionable radical ideas and socialist slogans ('I'm an incorrigible socialist!') also take on demonic meaning (14,497). When Alyosha tells Kolya that the devil 'has crawled into the whole generation' we can now identify the devil's offspring and the ideas they are spreading (14,503). The proliferation of Bernards (and Rakitins) harks back to Father Paisy's warning about the proliferation of atheistic scientists destroying the sacred 'image of Christ' with their cruel analysis. One section of the text projects forwards, its complement echoes back and the reader makes the join in 'an act of spiritual understanding'.

Rakitin, a polemical figure of the radicals of the 1860s, and Miusov, a leftover of the liberals of the 1840s, also join in espousing the 'new' ideas. What they all fundamentally share is the belief in human progress, the conviction that 'paradise on earth' can be created on the basis of scientific and socialist principles purged of any transcendental faith or values. The whole idea of progress is very problematic. If one believes in progress, then any new stage will be a better stage. Therefore the past may be forgotten or in any case depreciated. In *The Brothers Karamazov*, all those who believe in secular utopian ideas of progress are possessed by an intense wish to leap clear of memory, to shake off once and for all the experience of the past, especially the religious tradition and its 'old morality'. Only the new tendencies from Western Europe, scientific, atheistic and socialist, are judged to show the way to humanity's best future. The residues of the past, particularly the Russian religious past, its cultural memories and values, are branded as superstitious 'mysticism', as harmful obstacles standing in the ultimately triumphant way of progress. These remnants are to be destroyed and rooted out as quickly as possible. Everything will be reshaped by man alone who will find strength solely in himself to change the world, unaided by any transcendental support, says Rakitin, one of the most compromised and unattractive characters of the novel. But Rakitin is a petty demon, so far sowing no more than mischief. And a small prophet; his views of a new future world remain within the clichés circulating in Dostoevsky's epoch. He fails, just as Ivan failed with Alyosha. Various shades and degrees of these modern utopian ideas are also reflected in the speech of Miusov and Kolya, but the chief prophet–ideologist of a radically secular utopia is Ivan. Mitya's meetings with Rakitin are a prefiguration of Ivan's meeting with the devil when the former seminarian's ideas about the 'new people', the 'Bernards' and the new science will return in the darkest register.

IVAN'S UTOPIAN PROPHECIES: (2) THE DEVIL AND THE FUTURE GOLDEN AGE

With his first version of atheism, the Legend, Ivan attempts to subvert Christianity on its own grounds by showing that all the clever leaders of the church are really atheists who heroically take upon themselves the necessary deception of their 'herd' in order to organise its future for its own good. The Inquisitor, though, speaks only from a recognisable past; he is located in, and limited by a specific time and place, on the familiar territory of European history, in a Spain still living in the Middle Ages, well before the social, industrial and scientific revolutions which ushered in the modern age.

The second strand of atheism in Ivan's views is explicitly based on recent scientific and socialist utopian ideas which do not have a long tradition in the collective memory. These ideas are far more threatening than those of the Grand Inquisitor because they are 'new', persuasive and were gaining ever more adherents among the young generation of Dostoevsky's epoch. It is in the conversation between Ivan and the devil that we receive a picture of reality familiar to our age. New scientific and mathematical concepts of space and time have entered the human consciousness resulting in a fundamental reordering of the old categories and in new perspectives on the future. They are developed in the most concentrated poetic form in the context of a nightmare and in the discourses of the devil.

We recall that Ivan's most radical attack on God and immortality only emerges at the end of his nightmare as a quotation by the devil. But first the devil puts forward certain cosmological views which, while not explicitly attributed to Ivan, fall within the sphere of his thought. The devil uses Ivan's education by selecting various fragments of scientific facts which Ivan would have learned in his natural science course at university. Cosmology, while explaining the past of the universe, is at the same time necessarily prognosticating its future. The devil insinuates four closely related cosmological ideas into his discourse, absurdity, indeterminacy, replication and infinite repetition.

The devil, when speaking of space and time, queers his descriptions by mixing bizarre, banal and fantastic details with sober, neutral scientific facts. Once, he tells Ivan, he caught a cold while rushing to a diplomatic reception. As he set out, he says, 'I was still God knows where'. To get to earth he had to fly over a vast distance which for him is a matter of 'just one moment', and adds: 'but even a ray of light from the sun takes a whole eight minutes', ending with the absurdly ingratiating, 'and just imagine, in a tail-coat and open vest' (15,75). The devil catches a cold because he is not warmed by the sun, but comes from some region far away from it. The sun, the source of earthly light and life, is Dostoevsky's recurrent symbol of Grace, resurrection and the divine, uncreated light. In the shedding of its rays, the distance between heaven and earth is symbolically overcome. Hence, everything contrary to the symbolic attributes of the sun, and everything which increases the distance from it, would fall into the negative symbolic system. Thus, the devil is imbued and surrounded with images of cold, darkness and inconceivable distances. The contrast between the literal, banal details, the Khlestakovian empty talk, and the celestial solar symbol and cosmic distances creates that dominant impression of an absurd universe for which the devil is aiming.

The devil goes on, trying to impress Ivan with the extreme frigidity of outer space: 'and you know, in those empty spaces, in the ether, in that water *which is above the firmament*, – why there's such a frost ... that is, such a frost that one cannot even call it frost, you can imagine: one-hundred-and-fifty degrees below zero!' [my italics] (15,75). Into his modern image of outer space, rounded off with a precise scientific measurement, the devil slips in a fragment from Genesis 1:7: 'And God made the firmament from the waters which were under the firmament from the waters *which were above the firmament*'. But he omits the subject of the biblical sentence thereby playing on Ivan's haunting sense of the *Deus absconditus*. The temperature 'above the firmament' has been exactly measured and God obliterated, frozen out. Here then is Smerdyakov's true inspirer of his clever perversion of Genesis.

Next, invoking 'de Sade', the devil reminds Ivan of a custom of country girls who persuade oafish dupes to lick an axe at thirty degrees below zero, inserting images of a bleeding tongue and amputated fingers. He further decontextualizes the biblical quotation and integrates it into his own picture of an absurd universe by insinuating the axe into outer space. The axe excites Ivan's furious curiosity to find out what happens to it 'there'. The devil replies: 'What will happen to the axe in space? *Quelle idée!* If it would fall a little further, it would begin, I think, to fly around the earth, itself not knowing why, as a satellite. The astronomers would calculate the rising and setting of the axe, Gattsuk would enter it in his calendar, that's all' (15,75). The juxtaposition of an axe, an instrument for chopping, splintering and murdering, rising and setting in company with the life giving sun, the novel's symbol of Grace, is particularly malevolent. The inclusion of the axe in Gattsuk's calendar is another malicious flourish. Gattsuk's publication was a popular saints' calendar which marked the anniversaries of Orthodox saints and holy days as well as astronomical phenomena. The devil, with his grotesque orbiting axe reduces the saints and 'God's other worlds' to inexorable scientific laws represented by those astronomers who will duly and impassively 'calculate' the axe's times of rising and setting. In the future of the scientists–materialists, when their 'cruel analysis' will prevail, there will be no essential difference between saints, celestial bodies and axes. The devil's final phrase, 'that's all', concludes his flight of cynical fancy on a note of *reductio ad absurdum* and *ad nihilum*. This bizarre image of the axe endlessly orbiting the Earth is diametrically opposed to Zosima's vision in which all creation, animate and inanimate, is touched by God and is part of His unified purpose.

Next, the devil torments Ivan with the cosmological idea of replication: 'Everything you have – we have too, I'm revealing one of our secrets to you out of friendship, although it's forbidden'. (15,78). The devil's 'revelation' that his realm is a replica, a mirror image of this world, complements the fact that his entire discourse is a mocking mimicry of Ivan's ideas. Here he substitutes the sacred Urbild–Abbild structure with a demonic one. As we have seen, any Abbild of a sacred Urbild will be sacralised. A demonic world Urbild will demonise the world. (A similar structure shapes the Ivan/Smerdyakov dyad.) But is the devil merely repeating Ivan's ideas, or has Ivan been repeating the devil's? Either the devil's realm is an imitation of this world, in which case it is a derivative of this authentic original world, or his realm is the real original one and the earth is a diabolic imitation of it and not the creation of God. Of the two possibilities, the last is most horrific for it projects the whole future of humanity hopelessly trapped into dancing to the devil's tune, 'itself not knowing why'.

The idea of repetition is far deadlier because the devil adds the idea of an infinitely repeating series when, continuing his torment of Ivan, he advances an image of cosmic palingenesis:

> Oh, but you keep thinking of our present earth! Why, the present earth may have been repeated a billion times; why, it's become extinct, frozen, cracked, fallen to pieces, disintegrated into its component elements, again the water *which is above the firmament*, then again a comet, again a sun, again from the sun an earth, – why, this evolution, you know, may have already been infinitely repeated, and all in exactly the same way, to the smallest detail. A most indecently tedious business! [my italics] (15,79)

The main impression this passage makes is one of total inanimate desolation, the absolute absence of the human and divine. These are images of dead worlds, cosmic graveyards from which no seeds could come. Omitting again the biblical subject, God, and the transitive verbs which signify His cosmic creative acts, the devil covertly replaces God the Creator with a positivist, self-existent, self-acting and self-perpetuating cosmogony. In such a scheme, everyone is trapped forever in a cycle which cannot be altered in the 'smallest detail', condemned eternally to re-experience their earthly misery. There is no love, no salvation, no divine mercy, only the relentless cycles of doomed repetition in which Ivan himself is mentally ensnared. Suffering will never end, nor sin be atoned, rather it will be eternally repeated 'to the smallest detail', including Ivan's appalling cases of maltreated children. The Inquisitor's scheme of a future earthly order without God has now been maximally extended by the devil to an image of the whole universe without God. With his repetition of the biblical fragment, the devil debases the Word, reducing it to a banal figure of speech, a cliché. God is no more than the palest reminiscence, a dying memory without any future. Nietzsche considered the idea of 'eternal recurrence', 'without sense or goal', to be 'the extremest form of nihilism'.[26] The devil's vicious circle view of the future represents Ivan's worst fears. It would be hard to imagine a more hellish vision of the universe.

But these are the devil's projections, or Ivan's current re-evaluations of his former ideas. Ivan has composed what he took to be a highly positive programme for the future. Towards the end of their conversation the devil reminds Ivan of his 'poem', 'The Geological Cataclysm'. It is most characteristic and symbolic that Ivan chose to name his future human utopia after a science whose object of study is inanimate nature. In this respect Ivan's title prefigured the devil's depiction of the repeating universal cataclysms of inanimate matter.[27] Ivan is drawn to the inanimate; he wants 'to kiss' the old gravestones of the European 'cemetery'. Ivan's Legend was narrated by him. Here we are only given the devil's summary of Ivan's essay. And this chimes in with the fact that Ivan is ideologically on the retreat and consequently he is on the retreat from his own words, trying now to disown them, to distance them from himself.

We recall that Ivan's necessary and sufficient requirement for ushering in a future utopia is the permanent destruction of the very idea of God from human memory. Ivan mocks the 'new people' among his contemporaries who propose to start anew by universal destruction. The devil quotes Ivan: 'The stupid fellows, they didn't ask me <...> Oh, blind race of men who have no understanding!' The devil then elaborates Ivan's utopian prophecy:

Man will be exalted with a spirit of divine titanic pride and the man–god will appear. Every hour conquering nature without limits by his will and science, man by that very fact will feel every hour so lofty a joy that it will make up for him all the former hopes of the joys of heaven. <...> Everyone will know that he is entirely mortal, without resurrection, and will accept death proudly and serenely, like a god. (15,83)

This is the modern myth our world lives by with its dream of technological progress and omnipotent science. The emphasis on 'titanic pride', 'man–god' and 'will' is particularly symptomatic. Romanticism has become allied with science. When the devil mocks Ivan with 'there is that romantic strain in you', he hits on a revealing point personally and ideologically (15,81). Ivan himself wishes to be 'like a god'. For in Ivan's future utopia (a modern variation on the classical Golden Age) there emerge two chief characteristics of romanticism elucidated by I. Berlin.[28] The first is the idea that there is 'no structure of things', no objective standard of truth, virtue or knowledge; the age old patterns of the classical and Christian views are fragmenting, breaking down. The second, which is a response to the first phenomenon, is the belief in the indomitable self-will of the individual, thrusting against the old limits. Man alone will create his own truths, his own myths and views of the universe. Ivan's Inquisitor still invokes the Christian pattern to sanction his rule, though he perverts it by turning it into a myth. In Ivan's humanist, scientific utopia this old structure is completely replaced by the will. Ivan advances the 'titanic pride' of the new men–gods who will supplant the pathetic former men–slaves constrained by the old religious morality. Rather than all being God's children, there will be no fathers and children, only 'men–gods'. The 'secret of renewal' will reside in science so that instead of immortality in heaven, there will be longevity on earth. In his fantasy utopia of free will, Ivan offers the joyous conquest of nature as a substitute for 'all former hopes of heavenly bliss'. The devil's parody of Ivan's future Golden Age would be the fulfilment of the Legend, only now in a modern scientific version of an atheistic socialist Utopia. The seedy modern devil is himself a parodic fulfilment of the Inquisitor's master minds. The devil quotes Ivan's statement which rings with the same certitude and in words almost identical to the Inquisitor's: 'and I believe that this period, parallel to the geological periods, will come to pass' (15,83). But Ivan is no longer capable of prophesying that this period 'will come to pass'. His most recent prophecy has become a terrifying mockery.

In the Revelation of St John (Ivan's namesake), the New Jerusalem descends *from* heaven to earth. The coming of the messianic Kingdom, of 'a new heaven and a new earth', is a vision of heaven restored, it is rooted in memory. Ivan proposes to 'make all things new' without God, by deleting this memory of the future entirely. But the whole gist of the novel's poetics of memory is based on the idea that one cannot make 'all things new' without the eternally regenerative Word.

The devil insinuates cosmological motifs which emphasise humanity's insignificance, its total impotence in the face of an absurd, meaningless universe in order to mock and undermine Ivan's humanist Golden Age prophecy where people would be the proud, god-like masters of themselves and nature. The devil's ideas and images are not just inversions of the Kingdom prophecies (an inversion may be reversed), they are not built on the old oppositions (God/devil), but on different terms altogether. Every aspect of phenomenal prophecy, the divine promises, the beginning and the ends, are here dissolved into images and ideas of a universe governed by indeterminacy, absurdity and cold indifference. It is a future vision without a history, without a text, without a memory. The devil's future is not a programme but a mockery of any programme, human or divine, utopian or providential. Thus, when the devil effaces the subject 'God' in his partial quote of Genesis, he deletes the divine plan of salvation and providential history which began with God's creation of the universe and projects a universe without a plan, hence absurd, indeterminate. The divine plan directed by a providential consciousness is replaced by the cycles of nature. History is a record of unique, unrepeatable events enacted by unrepeatable unique individuals. While the principle of coexistence and simultaneity governs Dostoevsky's compositional arrangements of the dialogues, the speakers of the dialogues are keenly aware of history, their consciousnesses are saturated with a sense of history. Indeed Dostoevsky's mode of thought was, as Mirsky said, 'eminently historical', ever 'concerned with the drama that is being played out in human history by the supreme forces of the universe'.[29] But nature is indifferent to history, to human fate; it absorbs, swallows up and renders insignificant human events. History and human fates cannot be adequately described by nature or myth. They can only unfold in historical time, the time of unrepeatable, irreversible events, whereas myth and nature are closed, their ends predetermined, endlessly repeating. This is equivalent to killing the very ground of prophecy. As Cassirer says, 'Nature can offer no support to the prophetic consciousness'.[30] Thus, when the devil dissolves familiar spaces and time (he does not wear a watch), he obliterates the very matrix of history, and memory. This is not mythical time or even biological time, but geological, or rather, cosmological time. The collapse of the 'Golden Age' idea coincides with Ivan's total mental breakdown when minutes later Ivan, echoing Luther, hurls his glass at the devil. Alyosha finds him shattered, barely coherent.

The appearance of Alyosha, the 'pure cherub', at this critical juncture points to a salvational potential for Ivan: a cherub indicates the presence of God. In fact there are compassionate loopholes pointing to the ultimate salvation for all the novel's negative characters. They can be discerned in those subtle embeddings of prefigurative patterns which combine ominous with ironic and sublime motifs. And here we can observe a progression typical of Dostoevsky's poetics whereby an event on the empirical level receives its realistic, concretely vivid representation, is then taken through the ideological level where it reveals its ideational significance and finally receives its fullest highest meaning on the figural level. This is one way Dostoevsky achieved the extension of his world on the vertical, an achievement which Bakhtin designated as a distinctive feature of Dostoevsky's poetics and worldview, equalled only by Dante.[31]

For our first example we take the scene depicting Fyodor's reaction to the news of his first wife's tragic death, an event which provokes his communal performance on the streets as a repentant sinner. Although memory dominates this passage – indeed we are never far from memory in *The Brothers Karamazov* – the author amplified its poetic effect by combining an ironic prefiguration with a veiled figural prophecy:

Fyodor Pavlovich found out about the death of his first spouse when he was drunk, and, they say, ran along the street and began to shout, raising his hands in joy to heaven: 'Lord now lettest Thy servant depart in peace', and according to others – he wept unrestrainedly like a little child so much so, they say, that it was pitiful even to look at him in spite of the disgust he inspired. It is very possible that both versions are true, that is to say, that he rejoiced at his release and wept for her who had released him – at one and the same time. In the majority of cases people, even evil-doers, are much more naive and simple-hearted than we generally suppose. And we ourselves are too. (14,9–10)

This image of a drunken reprobate running down the street, arms raised in mock ritual gesture, shouting a solemn prayer from the Orthodox service is a carnivalised image, a vivid example of a Dostoevskian *parodia sacra*, which Bakhtin defines as a 'parody of sacred texts and rituals'.[32] Many of Dostoevsky's Russian readers would have recognised the phrase 'now lettest Thy servant depart' from the *Song of Simeon*, the old man, 'just and devout, waiting for the consolation of God' to whom it was revealed that he should not see death before he had seen the Lord's Christ (Luke 2:26–30). The juxtaposition of death and grotesque comedy is typical of carnivalisation (and of many motifs in Dostoevsky's art). Fyodor brings the high low and turns the tragic into farce. But, like all profoundly carnivalised motifs, this is also a deeply ambivalent image (Fyodor 'wept' and 'rejoiced'). For while Fyodor travesties the highest word of all, the divine Logos, he also remembers it, and invokes it at a moment of loss and death. His biblical quotation is, in his burlesque way, his prayer, his hymn. And in the context of the whole novel, the Word is not debunked, but vindicated. It is not the biblical phrase which is the object of the narrator's irony but Fyodor who prophesies more than he knows of himself. Although these words were uttered many years ago, they are recalled and reported at a point when Fyodor will himself soon 'depart', though not 'in peace'. And not before he has 'seen' his 'angel' Alyosha. When seen in its immediate context the biblical phrase is not prophetic, but when read together with the murder it acquires an ironic prefigurative function. When combined with Alyosha's transforming appearance in Fyodor's life, it acquires a sublime figural meaning.

The briefest events, the most fleeting gestures, unconscious thoughts and half-spoken words can be heavily weighted with prefiguration in Dostoevsky's art. The last time Alyosha sees his father alive, the day before the murder, he suddenly makes a striking gesture which simultaneously combines an ominous and sublime prefiguration. Just before he leaves the house:

Alyosha went up to say good-bye and kissed him on the shoulder. – Why did you do that? – asked the old man with some surprise. – We'll see each other after all. Or do you think we won't see each other? – Not at all, I just did it without thinking. – I didn't mean anything either, I, too, said it without thinking, said the old man looking at him. (14,160)

Alyosha's parting kiss on his father's shoulder has a solemn religious significance of filial reverence and forgiveness.[33] Both seem moved by some mysterious unconscious knowledge. The son's kiss and the father's anxious queries occur of themselves, 'without thinking'. And yet each subliminally recognises something final and solemn in this seemingly modest prophetic gesture of farewell whose fulfilment is the murder of Fyodor and, perhaps, his salvation. Shortly before his violent death, Fyodor receives from his 'angel', his 'only son', a final, angelic kiss of grace which complements Alyosha's quiet assurance in the novel's first dialogue that 'there are no hooks' in hell.

Our next example features Smerdyakov. In the chapter devoted to Smerdyakov's biography, the narrator mentions Smerdyakov's taciturnity ('Seldom would he begin speaking') and his impenetrable visage which gives away nothing of his real interests or feelings. Remarking Smerdyakov's habit of suddenly stopping in his tracks, sunk in thought for minutes at a time, the narrator, as if at a loss to understand him, appeals to the opinion of an expert, a physiognomist, who would say that Smerdyakov is not thinking but 'contemplating'. Rather than entering Smerdyakov's mind directly, the narrator attempts to do so through a painting by Kramskoi, 'The Contemplator' (*Sozertsatel'*), which he re-paints for the reader:

a forest in winter is depicted, and in the forest, on a roadway, a little wandering peasant in a torn little caftan and bast shoes is standing all alone in the deepest solitude, and he stands as if lost in thought, but he is not thinking, but 'contemplating' something. If you were to nudge him, he would give a start and look at you as though he had woken up, but without understanding anything. He would, it is true, have immediately come to himself, but if you asked him what he was thinking about while standing there, he most certainly would not remember anything, but he most certainly would have been hiding in himself the impression under which he was dominated during the time of his contemplation. These impressions are dear to him, and he is most likely storing them up imperceptibly, and even without being aware of it, – for what and why, of course he does not know either: perhaps, after saving up impressions for many years, he will suddenly abandon everything and go off to Jerusalem, to wander and seek salvation, or, perhaps he will suddenly set fire to his native village, or perhaps, both one and the other will happen together. There are a good many contemplators among the peasantry. And Smerdyakov was most certainly one of them too, and he, too, no doubt, was greedily storing up his impressions, hardly knowing why himself. (14,116–17)

The immediate purpose of this painting as trope is to leave the reader with a sense of ominous foreboding about Smerdyakov. The isolation of the figure in the painting ('in the deepest solitude') is an analogue to Smerdyakov's isolation in the world of the novel. Isolation is always both sinister cause and symptom of spiritual illness in Dostoevsky's fiction. The poor clothes of the peasant stand in contrast to Smerdyakov's dandyism thus suggesting that underneath Smerdyakov is just such a peasant. A man who is ever 'storing up impressions' for which he has no words, himself not knowing why, cannot be trusted. He might do anything. Later when we learn of Smerdyakov's cunning execution of the crime, we recall 'The Contemplator'. Then, projecting backwards, we metaphorically substitute those unspoken thoughts the anonymous figure is 'storing up' with plans for murder. Then too Fyodor's sensations of 'spiritual terror' and need for protection from 'someone unknown but frightening and dangerous' when alone at night acquire a prefigurative function (14,86–7). This painting is a silent sign premonitory of evil which later comes to pass, a 'chilling' prefiguration of the murder, and of Ivan's nightmare.

The lonely winter scene in the painting prefigures the lonely winter night when Ivan, on his way to see Smerdyakov for the last time, knocks down just such a peasant, deliberately leaving him to a solitary white death in the freezing snow. (This gesture, itself so revealing of Ivan's inner violence, was foreshadowed early in the novel when Ivan viciously shoved the inoffensive Maximov from the coach.) On that same night, after telling the truth to Ivan, Smerdyakov ends his life. And on that same cold wintry night the devil comes to visit Ivan from the frigid empty expanses of dark space. White, cold, isolation, night, darkness, all are symbolic of evil, of the devil's presence in this novel's world. The painting of 'Smerdyakov' standing in the cold snow on earth may now be understood as a prefiguration of the devil flying through the extreme cold of the universe. And since Smerdyakov takes his life while the devil is visiting Ivan, it is also a prefiguration of his own death. Those scenes are still far away, but the painting's prefigurative function can only be seen in retrospect, in relation to those far-away scenes.

The painting is also a prefiguration of Smerdyakov's immediate future. The narrator speculates on the 'contemplator's' future, before whom lie two totally opposite paths: he might take a religious path – go on a pilgrimage to Jerusalem to save himself, or, he might take a criminal path – burn down his native village.[34] Then again, he might do both. In Dostoevsky's fiction *les extrêmes se touchent*. But their order is crucial. Tracing Smerdyakov's spiritual development from this painting, we find just this pattern emerging. First, Smerdyakov murders. Then, in his last scene with Ivan, we learn that he has been reading Isaac of Nineveh, the very book his adoptive father Grigory loved to read. Saint Isaac teaches how every soul may reach God and he believed in the eventual disappearance of hell. Now, too, the first stirring of a good childhood memory moves Smerdyakov to say to Ivan when recalling his stepmother Marfa's care during his bouts of epilepsy: 'she was always very affectionate to me right from my very birth' (15,62). The third meeting is Smerdyakov's confession not only because he now realises that it is not true that 'all is permitted', but because this discredited idea has been replaced by intimations of divine justice:

– You know what: I'm afraid that you're a dream, that you're a phantom sitting in front of me, – he [Ivan] murmered.
– There's no phantom here, sir, except both of us, and a certain third one besides. Without doubt he's here now, that third one, between us two.
– Who is he? Who's here? Who's the third one? – Ivan uttered in fright, looking around and hastily searching with his eyes for someone in all the corners.
– The third one's God, sir. Aye, Providence itself, sir. It's here now beside us, only don't search for it, you won't find it. (15,60)

Smerdyakov is on his way to 'Jerusalem'. In his own sectarian way, he has been seeking God, he has returned to the sources of sacred memory and dimly discerned God's providential design.[35]

And Ivan, again in rhythm with Smerdyakov, for the first time also invokes God with an appeal to His justice. Vowing to reveal all at the trial, he exclaims: 'God sees (Ivan raised his hand upwards)' (15,66). This is a subtle vindication of Father Paisy's word, for to whom can the two murderers, now desperate, turn for mercy and justice if not to that image in whose likeness they were created and on whom no one can ever improve?

Passages of prefiguration and partial fulfilment also suggest the fulfilment of Ivan's ideological prophecies beyond the text. For Smerdyakov has also to be read as a prophetic figure on the broad historical scale, a figure of all those future Smerdyakovs from the mass of the Russian peasants who will serve as the Lichardas of the Ivans, as the willing tools of murderous ideologies, the cunning minions of clever leaders. Indeed, we get a glimpse, and only one, of Ivan's revolutionary nihilism, when, 'over the cognac', Fyodor asks Ivan why Smerdyakov has taken it into his head to respect him, Ivan replies: 'he's a lackey, progressive flesh when the time comes' (14,122).[36] Thus, the parricidal 'catastrophe' prepared by Ivan and Smerdyakov in a Russian provincial town points to a future catastrophe being prepared by the Ivans and Smerdyakovs for all Russia, by the sons for the fathers.

But Dostoevsky shows a way out of this threatening mayhem through a motif of biblical typology. Returning from his last meeting with Smerdyakov, Ivan partially atones for the ruin of Smerdyakov, the peasant – 'contemplator' standing stock still 'on a roadway' in the winter forest, by saving the drunken peasant he left to die 'lying motionless, on the road' in the freezing snow. For when Ivan unconsciously re-enacts the prototype of the good Samaritan, Dostoevsky, so to speak, goes over Ivan's head in order to introduce this biblical memory as a future paradigm for all Russia's alienated intellectuals, to remind them to be the brother–keepers of their compatriots, of that great mass of peasants from which Smerdyakov springs. Thus the Kramskoi painting of 'The Contemplator/ Smerdyakov' gains its fuller significance in retrospect, only after the last meeting with Smerdyakov and Ivan's nightmare, when its symbolic meaning can be divined by the reader's 'spiritual act' of understanding. Such a sequence characterises a poetics of memory and is all pervasive in *The Brothers Karamazov*.

One further, more obscure prefiguration emerges concerning Smerdyakov's death and redemption. In his 'jesuitical' argument about the Christian martyr skinned alive by the Mohammedans, Smerdyakov invokes the Russian Orthodox tradition according to which the world is saved by one or two hermits of great faith praying somewhere in the wilderness. 'Knowing <...> that I shouldn't attain altogether to the Kingdom of Heaven <...> therefore, putting my trust in God's mercy, I can only hope, sir, that one day I shall be altogether forgiven <...> if I shed true tears of repentence'

(14,120). This was a casuistic performance played for Ivan, still, there is now a tragic pathos in Smerdyakov's account, given in a 'trembling voice', about his former 'dream', now totally shattered, of 'starting a new life' in Moscow. The pathos is further accentuated when we realise, as Terras points out, that Smerdyakov wants to part friends with Ivan, the last person he sees before taking his life. As far as we know, he fails to 'shed tears of repentance' whose result, in this novel's artistic system, would be rebirth in faith. Instead, he aborts the endpoint of the salvational sequence with suicide. Still, even here a small compassionate loophole exists earlier in the novel, in Zosima's sermon on hell where it emerges that there is at least one holy man who has been praying for those like Smerdyakov:

> But woe to those who have destroyed themselves on earth, woe to the suicides! I think that there can be none more unhappy than they. It is a sin, they tell us, to pray to God for them, and outwardly the Church, as it were, rejects them, but in the depths of my soul I think that one may pray even for them. For love, Christ will not be angry. For such as those I have prayed inwardly all my life, I confess it to you, fathers and teachers, and even now I am praying for them every day. (14,293)

One passage turns out to be an 'indirect' answer to another. Everything is connected in this novel when read retrospectively, which is to read it poetically.

The biblical Satan, condemned to roam because of his rebellion against God, was deprived of all hope of futurity, in the sense of a final transformation to his former angelic state. Ivan's devil, though, entertains a faint glimmer of hope which emerges when he implicitly relates to himself Ivan's anecdote about the philosopher who finally reached paradise. Portraying himself as a long suffering victim who has been assigned the onerous, inescapable role of leading people into temptation and ruin, he says:

> I know, you see, that there's a secret here, but they don't want to reveal this secret to me for anything, because then perhaps, having guessed what it's all about, I might roar out 'hosannah' and at once the necessary minus would disappear and good sense would reign in

all the world <...> I know, after all, that in the end I shall become reconciled, I shall reach the end of my quadrillion and find out the secret. (15,82)

'Necessary' implies a plan. If the devil is 'necessary', it can only be a divine plan. And since the devil has not been let in on the 'secret', he is admitting that he is not all powerful, that there is some sentient being greater than he who knows, someone who could only be God. It is essential to stress that the devil is not an atheist but an agnostic, and in this he mirrors Ivan's problem of not knowing. He is only sure that there is a plan, a 'secret', which will be revealed in the unimaginably distant future. The devil's parenthetical remark about the disintegration of the philosopher's watch reminds us of the narrator's earlier, seemingly casual comment that the devil was not wearing a watch. Putting this fact together with the devil's concessionary admission that he will one day reach the end of his 'quadrillion', we may fairly conclude that the author's conception of the divine plan was ultimately a merciful one. Even the devil will be saved and forgiven; he has just stopped for a moment on his inconceivably long trek to paradise. Ivan's salvation is not represented in the novel, though it is hinted at, just as the devil here hints at his own. The devil's long walk prefigures Ivan's, beyond the novel. Or rather, Ivan prefigured his own walk in the anecdote he composed in his first youth.

But Ivan is not yet sure about the plan, the 'secret'. He tells Alyosha who stays to tend him just after his nightmare: 'He was frightened of you, you, a dove. You're a "pure cherub". Dmitry calls you a cherub. A cherub ... The thunderous howl of ecstasy of the seraphim! What is a seraph? Maybe a whole constellation. But maybe the whole of that constellation is just some kind of chemical molecule ... ' (15,85–6). Doubt steals in on Ivan's (accurate) quotation of the devil's phrase mocking the mystery of the Resurrection, then on a question and a 'maybe', on an implicit 'either/or'. Perhaps no other passage captures so succinctly and beautifully how easily Ivan slides from an animated paradisiacal image of God's other worlds to an image that is utterly 'other' and reductive, one of totally indifferent inanimate matter, but which has been demonised by the devil's discourse. The tension here between two views of the universe and origins, between the waning transcendental creationist and the ascendant materialist scientific is a fine prefiguration of the modern consciousness.

Praying for Ivan after his nightmare, Alyosha says: 'the torments of a proud decision, a deep conscience!' However, Ivan's conscience is still ambiguous. As Alyosha immediately adds: 'Either he will rise in the light of truth, or perish in hatred, taking revenge on himself for having served what he did not believe in' (15,89). With Ivan it is always either/or, *pro* or *contra*. Dostoevsky left Ivan at the point where the voice of 'Christ's law' was only beginning to claim his conscience, at the first stage of necessary inner suffering. In a note written just after he completed *The Brothers Karamazov*, Dostoevsky said: 'Conscience without God is a horror, it can go astray to the most immoral things'.[37] Ivan, in his doomed struggle to reconcile his 'deep conscience' without God is, more than anyone else, a vivid example of his author's aphorism.

IMAGES OF THE KINGDOM FULFILLED

Neither of Ivan's utopian fantasies is really fulfilled in the novel's world. Rather, they are indirectly fulfilled locally, in unintended and horrifying ways. Thus they have a cautionary and didactic function. Alyosha's dream of the Kingdom is fulfilled in a multitude of fleeting but real events which take place in the novel, true, only partially, only for a moment, but fulfilled nonetheless, and thus validated in life. Alyosha's epiphanous encounter with Grushenka, the love between her and Mitya, between Snegirov and Ilyusha, the ideal father/son relationship between Alyosha and Zosima, the spiritual community in the monastery, the pilgrim woman who gives a coin to help 'someone who needs it more than I', are all variations on the Kingdom paradigm. It is in Alyosha's relationship with the children that these ideas receive their most vivid future significance.

It is a striking fact that Dostoevsky devoted a whole book

plus two chapters of his novel to representing the world of
children and that two children, Ilyusha and Kolya, are among
the novel's prominent characters. This alone demonstrates
Dostoevsky's concern for the future of which children are the
new seed and inheritors. Still more striking is the way he
artistically integrated their lives into the novel's larger spiritual and ideological themes. Two salient fulfilments of the
Kingdom ideas are represented within the children's world.
Indeed, the seed planted by Alyosha has already born fruit in
Kolya; he undergoes a significant change of heart. Rather than
trace this process, let us take two scenes which represent its
fulfilment.

Just after they learn that Ilyusha will die, Kolya and
Snegirov go to Ilyusha's bed while Alyosha stands silently by.
The ensuing scene is the culminating tableau towards which
the book 'Boys' has been leading:

'Papa, papa, come here … we … ', Ilyusha murmured in extreme
agitation, but evidently not having the strength to go on, he suddenly
flung both his wasted little arms forward and, as firmly as only he
could, embraced both of them at once, Kolya and his papa, joining
them in one embrace and hugging them tightly to himself. The
captain suddenly shook all over with wordless sobbing, and Kolya's
lips and chin began to tremble <…> 'Oh, how I curse myself, that I
didn't come sooner', murmured Kolya, weeping and no longer
ashamed that he was weeping. (14,506–7)

Alyosha's future is only just coming to fruition, most of it
remains to be fulfilled. But in the final scene of the novel, he is
depicted 'in the world', founding his new brotherhood of the
boys in memory of Ilyusha, in accordance with his elder's
prophecy. The very last sentence contains Kolya's exultant
'Hurrah for Karamazov!' This is a promise that the seed will
not die, that the providential chain which began with Markel
and Sophia will not be broken. Kolya will carry the seed
further after Alyosha who, by the novel's end, has become
Kolya's ideal. Through the boys, and especially through the
young Kolya, Alyosha's word will find continuing life in the
new generation.[38] Children are the inheritors and figures of the
Kingdom ('of such is the Kingdom of heaven' Matthew 19:14).

The 'gust of wind' has blown away and the novel ends with an image of the Kingdom fulfilled on earth.

The most important figural motif of the Kingdom is fulfilled in a sublime vision of heaven, in the mystical culminating point of the novel. It is prepared for in one of Zosima's sermons addressed to Alyosha. This requires a fuller scrutiny of those elements which take us to the 'very heart of the whole' of the novel's poetic memory system.

CHAPTER 8

The Christocentric poetic memory system

And He took bread and gave thanks, and broke it, and gave unto them, saying, This is My body which is given for you: this do in remembrance of Me.

(Luke 22:19)

This cup is the new covenant in My blood. Do this whenever you drink it, in remembrance of Me.

(I Corinthians 11:24)

IMITATIONS OF CHRIST: VARIATIONS ON A THEME

The ideal of Christ was the final cause and aim of Dostoevsky's poetic work and aesthetic thought. When Bakhtin said that the voice and image of Christ 'must crown the world of voices, organize and subdue it', he added in an interesting footnote that 'such an ideal, authoritative image which is not contemplated, but followed' was 'never realised' in Dostoevsky's work, but was 'only envisioned by Dostoevsky as the ultimate limit of his artistic projects'.[1] Not perfectly realised, true enough. For a limit, by definition, is some ultimate point, or fixed value to which a series progressively converges but can never reach or equal in a finite number of terms. But this ideal limit was most closely approximated in *The Brothers Karamazov*. Every aspect of poetic memory ultimately leads to the memory of Christ. We may designate this master memory as the 'dominant', which Jakobson defines as 'the focusing component of a work of art: it rules, determines and transforms the remaining components'.[2] And given that we have to do with a

273

dominant that is a divine ideal, it also transcends all the novel's components. Every time Dostoevsky transcends the structure of prose, he transcends it towards this invariant prototypal ideal. Ideal should be understood not in the sense of something existing only as an abstract idea, but as an eternal model of spiritual perfection which refers to something real and realisable in the sense of being susceptible to imitation or assimilation.

But it is an ideal which by Dostoevsky's time had become problematic. It had to compete with other newly emergent ideals which challenged or denied its claims to the highest truth. As Grossman remarked: 'All Dostoevsky's post-Siberian works are dedicated to the problem of Christ in contemporary life'.[3] Contemporary life is the nub of the matter. For the incarnate Christ has long been absent from the world, His Incarnation is itself a memory and can only be a memory. And this is no ordinary absence as of someone once part of a familiar world, but an absence of whole contexts. Christ lived and spoke in a very different world from that represented in Dostoevsky's novel. This presented Dostoevsky with the problem of representing an absent ideal and integrating it into a cultural, spatio-temporal and historical context inherently alien to it. Dostoevsky aimed to make that memory alive, active and dynamic by incorporating it into mimetic images of contemporary people, into the dramas of their lives, into their waking acts and thoughts, their dreams, fantasies and visions. This he achieved by establishing various poetic relationships between this ideal and his fictional characters, by quotations or allusions to canonical sources, the use of Christian symbolism and evocations of the divine prototypes through iconographic images. The figure of Christ is also powerfully evoked by the poetic principle of symmetric contrast, by making it interact with its negative inverse, with various images of Antichrist. This mode is among Dostoevsky's strongest artistic suits. The all encompassing interpretative concept of figural interpretation was, as we have seen, the most important way of unifying his novel's form and content; it simultaneously offered Dostoevsky the prototypal Christian motifs and the prefigurative structures for realising his own poetic variations and interpretations of them.

One major authorial clue to Christ's pre-eminence lies in the Epigraph, that conspicuous foregrounding of His word. Another resides in Alyosha's parting speech in the Epilogue from where we can see that the novel has fulfilled and affirmed the meaning of the Epigraph. In between these two extremities are numerous biblical allusions and Christian themes, motifs and symbols. But by far the most important events of Christ's drama for *The Brothers Karamazov* are the Passion and Resurrection. This is the pattern Dostoevsky attempted to realise by depicting the most essential experiences of his protagonists as a set of various imitations of Christ. Moreover, Christ not only embodied a pregiven image and Word, but offered His Own activity as a model for a new way of thinking and seeing – a new way of living in the world. Each brother has his own view of Christ; each is explicitly associated to a particular image of Christ, and in very different ways. Our present aim is to show how this idea is realised in *The Brothers Karamazov*, to inquire what precisely are the characteristics of Dostoevsky's ideal Christ as we find them in his last novel, and how and to what extent this ideal is not merely 'contemplated' but 'followed' as an imitation.

MITYA'S IMITATIO CHRISTI

Before the murder, Mitya is mainly depicted as a character from European romantic fiction, as a wild young officer and spendthrift who has the usual adventures (women, gambling, drink and duels). His imagination, spontaneity of thought and feeling, and lyrical mode of expression are permeated with the idiom and exalted spirit of German Idealism and Pre-Romanticism. We recall that in early childhood he learned the divine names in German. He styles his first 'confession of an ardent heart' to Alyosha 'a hymn to Schiller's joy', and thanks the 'gods' that Alyosha has turned up. He expresses his love and praise of God in an image borrowed from Goethe: 'let me kiss the hem of that garment' (14,99). He voices his joy in God's creation with extended quotations from Schiller's *An die Freude*, including the lines: 'Joy everlasting <...> flames the cup of life [*kubok zhizni*]' (14,99). This, then, is the context of cultural memory in which Mitya is initially situated.

After he fells Grigory and flees from his father's garden, a fundamental contextual shift takes place. It is then that Christian prayers and symbols begin to flood into Mitya's language while German and classical allusions (Ceres, Phoebus) disappear entirely. This can be seen most clearly by following the changes in Mitya's repeated figurative allusions to the sun. Convinced that he has killed Grigory and lost Grushenka forever, Mitya resolves to shoot himself at dawn, when the 'sun flies high' (14,358). But first he decides to rush off to Mokroe to see his *tsaritsa* for one last time. In the midst of ordering the food and drink for his last spree, Mitya alludes again to his decision to commit suicide at sunrise, now expressing this solar time in a classical metaphor: 'as soon as Phoebus, ever young, flies upwards' (14,362). Next, he imbues the metaphor with his own feelings: 'I love golden-haired Phoebus and his hot light' (14,363). Then, shortly before setting off to Mokroe, Mitya metaphorically identifies himself with Phoebus and in the same breath alludes again to suicide in his Schilleresque: 'drink this glass to me, to Phoebus, the golden-haired, of tomorrow morn' (14,366). Finally, as Mitya is speeding to Mokroe, the narrator takes up the metaphor when he mentions Mitya's plan to end his life at the 'first hot ray of golden-haired Phoebus', adding now the image of a 'ray' but still fusing it to the classical image (14,370). Thus, Dostoevsky has connected the classical solar metaphor with suicide and hopelessness, with irreversible tragedy.[4]

On the way to Mokroe, the redemptive turning point occurs. Significantly, the catalyst is an encounter with one of the Russian folk. Mitya and the coachman Andrey fall into an eschatological dialogue which marks the first stage for bringing Mitya fully into the novel's encompassing collective memory of the Russian Christian tradition. In response to Mitya's sudden question, 'will I go to hell?', Andrey tells the 'folk legend' of Christ's 'harrowing of hell'. Christ descends 'straight from the cross' into hell, frees all the sinners and promises to come once more to empty hell forever. 'The Lord will forgive you', Andrey says to Mitya, hell is not the place for him because 'you're like a little child, sir'. But Mitya needs some good soul to forgive him right now. When he importunes Andrey 'Will you forgive me <...> for everyone, for everyone you alone, here now, right away, here, on the road, will you forgive me for everyone', he herewith turns the coachman into a figure of Christ (14,372). In this novel's world anyone, including, or especially the most humble and episodic, can momentarily be an imitator of Christ. The coachman's response, 'God will forgive you' and the image of the infinitely forgiving Christ it evokes, inspire a prayer in which echoes of Christ's Mount of Olives prayer can be heard:

Lord, receive me with all my lawlessness, and do not condemn me. Let me pass by Thy judgment <...> for I love Thee, O Lord <...> If Thou sendest me to hell, I shall love Thee there, and from there I shall cry out that I love Thee for ever and ever. But let me love to the end, here and now, to the end, for just five hours till Thy hot ray. (14,372)

Mitya's solar image has moved into Alyosha's and Zosima's Christian symbolic sphere; the sun's rays are now 'God's rays', as Alyosha remembered Zosima recalling them from childhood and set down in the Life.

It is at Mokroe that Mitya's path of suffering assumes an explicit similarity to Christ's path to Golgotha through a series of striking parallels. Tormented by the thought that he has killed Grigory, Mitya withdraws from the revellers to be alone and prays: 'God, restore to life the man I knocked down by the fence! Let this fearful cup [*chasha*] pass from me!' (14,394). The last phrase makes the figural join between Mitya and Christ Who, when He withdrew from His disciples to pray, alone in His agony in the Garden of Gethsemane, implored God: 'My Father, if it be possible, let this cup [*chasha*] pass from me.' Mitya's cup of life (*kubok zhizni*) from Schiller has now become the canonical cup (*chasha*) of suffering. But so far Mitya has only taken into himself the first half of Christ's prayer, the plea to be spared the cup. He has not yet accepted the second half,

Christ's submission to god's will: 'However, not as I will but as Thou wilt' (Matthew 26:39). Mitya's prayer is soon followed by his arrest, the arrest of the imperfectly innocent man just as Gethsemane was followed by the arrest of the perfectly innocent One. Continuing the pattern of the Passion, Mitya now rapidly descends through the trials of betrayal (by the innkeeper Trifon), the false accusation, the public humiliation of having his clothes removed and his indictment. Dostoevsky accommodated this stage of Mitya's ordeal under the heading 'The Journey of a Soul Through the Torments' thereby bringing Mitya's suffering into an Orthodox eschatological context according to which evil spirits subject the soul to many trials or 'torments' (*mytarstva*) as it ascends heavenwards after death. But, distinctive for the eschatology of *The Brothers Karamazov* is the idea that this journey is no longer otherworldly, that paradise is not only celestial but terrestrial, that it can be realised in this world. Thus, this heading simultaneously announces that a spiritual testing is in progress and prefigures Mitya's journey of ascent and spiritual rebirth on earth.

It is Mitya's compassionate dream of the babe which opens his way to spiritual renewal, to his re-enactment of the last scenes in the drama of the Passion, the Resurrection. 'And his whole heart blazed up, and strove towards some kind of light, and he wants to live and live, to go on and on towards some kind of new path, to the beckoning light, quickly, quickly, now, right away!' (14,457) Shortly after this revelatory dream, the theme of catharsis through redemptive suffering first sounds in Mitya's words when he exclaims to his interrogators: 'I accept the torment of accusation and my public shame, I want to suffer and by suffering to cleanse myself!' (14,458). Even though he is innocent of the actual crime, he accepts punishment because he wanted to kill his father, and perhaps would have killed him.

Two months later, on the eve of his trial when Alyosha visits him in gaol, Mitya's dream and his acceptance of suffering gather a far larger significance. His dream of the babe has been growing in his memory. He exclaims to Alyosha: 'It's for the babe I'm going. Because all are to blame for all ... I didn't kill father, but I've got to go, I accept it!' (15,31) The reader will at once recognise Zosima's main precept embedded as a hidden quotation in Mitya's word. Mitya never heard it from Zosima. He has discovered it independently, it has become part of him, and he has confirmed its truth through his own inner experience. Now Mitya accepts suffering not just for the sake of his personal redemption ('to cleanse myself'), but for the sake of 'the babe', symbol of all helpless and innocent sufferers. When he sees his ordeal in this universal light, he becomes a figure of Christ, an Abbild of Christ's redemptive suffering for all humankind. His new found spiritual insight leads to his rebirth: 'I've felt a new man in myself resurrected' (15,30). Mitya has become an embodiment of the same ideal that is also expressed in Zosima's teaching of 'active love', for he does not just passively accept but freely chooses this role: 'I shall go for everyone, because someone has to go for everyone' (15,31). Mitya has accepted the cup of suffering. This is the height of his *imitatio*. And he expresses it with the central symbol of the Passion, the cross: 'I ran away from crucifixion! <...> kiss me and make the sign of the cross over me, my dear fellow, sign me with the cross for the cross I have to bear tomorrow' (15,34,35). Even small details become part of Mitya's *imitatio Christi*. In the prison hospital, Alyosha finds Mitya sitting on his bunk, his 'head wrapped in a towel moistened with vinegar', a reminiscence of the sponge soaked in vinegar offered to Christ on the cross (15,183–4).

However, Mitya is not a saint or a martyr; he only knows that the 'sun is', and 'there's a whole life' in just knowing that. In the Epilogue, Alyosha sanctions the plans for Mitya's escape because he is innocent and 'such a great martyr's cross' is too heavy for him to bear. He 'doesn't need it', he is 'unprepared'. Speaking now with the assurance of his elder, Alyosha tells him: 'remember only for your whole life this other man. That's enough for you' (15,185). And that is enough for most people. Mitya's *imitatio* breaks off when he is spiritually cleansed through suffering, when he has found the 'new man' in himself. His spiritual drama is over, and his story proceeds to a conventional ending.

Before his conversion Mitya had projected himself into his memory of German Romanticism. But this context does not function within *The Brothers Karamazov*: 'I always read that poem about Ceres and man. Has it reformed me? Never!' (14,99). It is only when Mitya identifies himself with the Christian collective memory that he, to paraphrase Colossians 3:10, puts on 'a new man' and is 'renewed in the knowledge and after the image of Him'. Then, Schiller's hymn to joy, *An Die Freude*, gives way to Mitya's communal 'tragic Hymn to God, with Whom is joy' sent up from underground by the Russian prisoners. 'I love Russia, Aleksey, I love the Russian God', he exclaims in the Epilogue (15,186). This is where the author has been aiming to bring Mitya all along. Thus, Mitya only realises his true potential when he remembers Christ as the model for his own life. Mitya's path of suffering and rebirth, then, resolves into a metaphorical representation of Christ's last days. The death of the old man and the birth of the new man in Mitya is a spiritualised metaphor of Christ's historical suffering and Resurrection.

IVAN'S IMAGE OF CHRIST

There are two other explicit representations of Christ in the novel, the first is composed by Ivan, the second is associated to Alyosha. From their similarities but most of all from their differences, the novel's ideal Christ emerges. Ivan's representation occurs first and is much the longest.

Ivan's image of Christ is transmitted through two different speakers in two very different contexts. The first is Ivan himself, the second is Ivan impersonating another, his Grand Inquisitor. Here I should like to use an idea from pure mathematics, not in any attempt to reduce a literary work about human beings to mathematical abstractions, but in order to make Dostoevsky's poetic use of language in building up his images and hence our interpretations more precise. The idea is called a mapping which presupposes the fundamental notion of a set. A set is made up of the things which belong to it and is characterised by all those things and only those things which belong to it. The New Testament is the set of all those words and images contained in it. This set has a unique status as the primary source for Christ's life and teaching; it contains the canonical representations of His verbal image. Every departure from this canonical image is inevitably an interpretation of it. From this ready-made set, Ivan selects and combines certain elements in order to create his new set, that is, his representation of Christ, which is the set of all words pertaining to Christ from the end of 'Rebellion' to the end of the following chapter, 'The Grand Inquisitor'. Now Ivan has his own ideas about Christ. He does not limit his selection to elements from the Bible, but draws on many other sources. In mathematical terms he performs a number of mappings taking a elements from one set, b elements from another, c from another, and so on, and combines them in a certain order to form his own set $(a, b, c, \ldots)$. This new set is his interpretation just because it is his selection and his ordering of the aggregate. The beauty of the set/mapping idea is that every set is uniquely characterised by its inventory of elements. Literary art is very much about concrete images uniquely selected and combined. The elements of this set Ivan distributes among two voices, taking some for himself, others for his Inquisitor. All the Inquisitor's words comprise his set, his image of Christ; all Ivan's words belong to his. And they are not the same. As Ivan imitates the old tyrant, his natural voice undergoes various changes, and so does his selection of words, meanings and memory contexts. When Ivan speaks in his own voice, we retain our awareness that Alyosha is his interlocutor and that a contemporary dialogue between two young brothers in a Russian provincial tavern is in progress. When he speaks as the Inquisitor, the world of the Karamazovs recedes, we become absorbed in the Inquisitor's world and time, and we hear a ranting voice in a 'dark prison' addressed to a totally silent listener, his Prisoner. The distinctions between these two discourses, and their dialogic and historical contexts of memory, are crucial for our understanding of Ivan, his image of Christ and for a poetic interpretation of one of Dostoevsky's most celebrated artistic passages.

Ivan sets the scene for Christ's reappearance with biblically alien elements taken from his fantasied re-creation of sixteenth-century Spain at the height of the Inquisition's reign of terror. Ivan combines this setting with a reference to the Reformation, also a time of terror and torture, which he interprets as having been inspired by the devil: 'But the devil does not slumber <...> there appeared then <...> in Germany, a terrible new heresy' (14,226). These historical contexts are very important ideologically for Ivan's representation. They are not just a question of creating a dramatic atmosphere, important as that is artistically, but an attempt to undermine Christ with the indisputable facts of history. Ivan brings Christ back to earth during the worst period in the history of the Western Church, at a time of hell on earth instituted by the Catholic Church in His name, and then sends Him away, nothing having changed, precisely in order to demonstrate Christ's impotence in the face of secular power and human suffering.

In addition to these anachronous historical elements, Ivan selects secular literary references in building up his image of Christ. One is a quotation from Schiller's *Sehnsucht*, a poem imbued with the spirit of German romantic idealism. He evokes the evening air of Seville with a quotation ('it smells of laurel and lemon') taken from Pushkin's 'little tragedy' on the Don Juan legend, *The Stone Guest*, not an allusion guaranteed to call forth pious associations. To these Ivan adds contemporary literary interpretations of Christianity by other nineteenth century poets such as Tiutchev's poem on the kenotic Christ and Polezhaev's poem on the Inquisition. Ivan depicts His appearance as follows: 'The sun of love burns in His heart, rays of Light, Englightenment and Power shine from His eyes and, pouring over the people, stir their hearts with a responsive love. He stretches forth His hands to them, blesses them, and from His touch, even from His garments, issues a healing power' (14,227). This is a problematic and ambiguous image. Komarovich finds that the images of the sun burning in His heart, His extended hands and streaming rays owe something to Heine's vision of Him in *Die Nordsee* lyrics.[5] If so, then this is another ambiguous element since later on the devil, after composing his image of the 'thunderous squeals' of the seraphims' Hosanna at the Cross, boasts of his 'sarcastic tone *à la*

Heine' (15,83). Perhaps more important is A. Johae's remark that a 'love which burns is excessively passionate and tends to destroy' while 'power threatens to impose itself on men' and was disdained by Christ at the temptation.[6] 'Enlightenment' is altogether ambiguous. Pushkin, Schiller, Tiutchev, Heine, these nineteenth century elements, anachronous with respect to Christ, form another superimposed set containing Ivan's modern ideas, his contemporary literary and aesthetic culture. Ivan's new set only marginally overlaps with the biblical set because he has embedded his image of Christ amongst so many secular accretions. Thus we have manifold mappings from extra-canonical sources, sixteenth-century Spain, the German Reformation, nineteenth-century Russian and European culture, all selected under the pressure of Ivan's 'intention', his ideological conflict, and 'despair'.

There are other touches which subtly convert Ivan's image of Christ into a figure with vaguely pre-Raphaelite overtones. Ivan's introduction of weeping people kissing the earth and singing children throwing flowers at Him as He walks through Seville are theatrical sentimentalised deviations from the biblical account, as are the white coffin full of flowers and the 'bouquet of white roses' in the dead girl's hands. The Gospel accounts of Christ's entry into Jerusalem are spare, austere, without flowers, children, singing and weeping. The emphasis is on the glorification of Christ, on the people's acknowledgment of His Kingship.

After taking into account all the extra-biblical elements, what remains of the original source is a jumbled, not overly large, and not always accurate portion. Ivan's set emphasises Christ's superior human traits, it is stamped with currents of romanticism, idealism, sentimentalism and humanism. Ivan's Christ comes very close to the de-Christianised Jesus of the nineteenth-century thinkers, in particular Renan, Strauss and the Utopian Socialists who tried to humanise Him, and in the case of the former, to sentimentalise Him. Ivan calls Him the 'great idealist' who 'dreamed of his harmony' (14,238). The very terms 'idealist' and 'dreamed' strip Christ of His divinity and reduce Him to the level of a great man, a romantic dreamer. Says Ouspensky in words which can be applied to Ivan's artistic image of Christ:

In true sacred art there is no place for idealism or idealization <...> just as there is no place for them in the liturgy or in the Scripture <...> since all idealization, even if it is not an illusion or a lie, has a subjective element and is, therefore, limited. It inevitably limits reality, more or less deforming it. Indeed, one can say that an image, once it is marked with idealization, ceases to be an icon.[7]

The most problematic aspect of Ivan's Christ concerns His identity. The first doubtful point is that the appearance of Ivan's Christ 'quietly, inconspiciously' is contrary to His promise to return in a great flash of lightning (Matthew 24:27, Luke 17:24). A Christ Who does not fulfill His own prophecy cannot be He. Perhaps the most ambiguous feature of Ivan's representation is his absolute refusal to call his Christ-like figure by His divine names. Never once does Ivan utter the names Christ, or Jesus, referring to Him instead by the pronoun 'He'. Yet, Ivan describes His entry by making the very sight of Him instantly inspire an ecstatic worshipful response. Precisely this phenomenon intrigues Ivan: 'This could have been one of the best places of the poem, that is, just why do they recognise Him?' (14,226) Ivan never answers his question. It is as if once Ivan would identify Him by name, that would be to recognise him, which is one step away from accepting Him. We have to recognise the Christ-like figure in the Legend as Ivan's creation and then we can see that his use of 'He' is yet another aspect of his wavering doubt. Ivan's 'He' is a variant of the Urbild, but only of its 'human nature'. Had his figure been based solely on the canonical Christ, He would have transcended the Christ of the Legend. By referring to Him only as He, Ivan only refers to the figure in his Legend, and he never makes any reference to Him outside it and its immediate context. The very name 'Jesus Christ' expresses His unique essence; to withhold His name is to deny Him that essence. In the New Testament, the criterion of faith is the recognition of Jesus as Christ, the son of God, and the acknowledgement of His divinity entails calling Him by His divine names (to 'believe on the name of His Son Jesus

Christ'). This question of identity and hence of authenticity dogs the whole discourse.

Significantly, Alyosha does not at once recognise Ivan's Christ as *the* Christ. Just as the Inquisitor is launching into his tirade, Alyosha interrupts: 'I don't quite understand, Ivan, what does it mean? <...> Is it just a wild fantasy or some mistake of the old man, some kind of impossible *qui pro quo*?' (14,228) Ivan replies:

> if our modern realism has so spoiled you and you can't bear anything fantastic – if you wish a *qui pro quo*, then let it be so. It is true, the old man is ninety and he might long ago have gone mad over his idea. It could be, in the end, simply a delirium, an apparition of a ninety-year-old man before his death. (14,228)

But this is doubly ironic. It is Ivan who has been spoiled by the 'fantastic'. The Inquisitor's mad *idée fixe*, his 'delirium' and 'apparition' are ironic prefigurations of Ivan's eventual unhinging over his 'idea', of his own 'delirium' and visitations by a diabolic 'apparition'. In the light of this, the diabolic distortion in Ivan's mapping is more evident.

As soon as Ivan begins impersonating his Inquisitor, the dialogic situation changes radically. And so does the substance of the dialogue. Instead of Ivan talking to Alyosha about an absent Him (an 'I/thou' exchange about 'Him'), Ivan speaks through his imaginary Inquisitor to address directly a present but silent 'Thou' (a one-way 'I' to 'Thou'). Into this 'I' Ivan puts his accusation against Christ. Consequently all his most negative thoughts about Him he leaves to his Inquisitor. Since all the Inquisitor's words are dialogically addressed to his Prisoner, he is inevitably creating an image of Him as he speaks to Him. And since the Inquisitor puts Him on trial and assumes the role of His prosecutor, he inevitably strives to project an image which emphasises His blameworthy qualities. The Prisoner does not utter a single word in self-defence throughout the Inquisitor's whole diatribe. This fact partially associates Him with His biblical image in so far as this scene mirrors the silence of Christ in the Synoptic Gospels when He is brought to trial before the high priests and Pontius Pilate precisely on the issue of His divine identity, His kingship.

The passages the Inquisitor selects from the Gospels in projecting his image of Christ are the Synoptic accounts of the three temptations. Precisely Christ's struggle with Satan fascinates the Inquisitor (and Ivan), for it is their struggle too. As we have seen, his accusations stem from his own wilful perversion of the canonical episode. The Inquisitor falsely accuses Christ of having imposed too great a burden of freedom on man. Leaving behind only His image as a guide, He bequeathed to humanity nothing but 'restlessness, confusion and unhappiness'. He set people an impossibly high goal and example which they could never live up to, save a few elect. In essence, the Inquisitor projects an image of Christ as an eccentric Who caused nothing but harm, exactly the opposite of the sort of eccentric (*chudak*) the author wished to create for the hero of his novel. Moreover, the Inquisitor's branding of Him 'as the most evil of heretics, and his closing condemnation 'if anyone most deserved our fire, it is Thou' reveal the Inquisitor's own dialobic perversions (14,228,237). The image of Christ as a heretic, from the point of view of the Inquisitor (the Catholic Church) is a topos which shows the ambiguity of Ivan's Christ. That Ivan could even fantasise about having Him burnt alive should alert interpreters to the diabolic strain permeating the whole passage. He may be Christ-like, but He is still a distortion.

Here too the problem of identity persists. Beginning his tirade, the Inquisitor declares: 'I don't know who Thou art, and I don't want to know' (14,228). However, throughout the whole scene the Inquisitor speaks to Him 'as if' He were Christ. Indeed, so great is his need 'to have his say' to Him, that it overrides any necessity of establishing an accurate identification. Gradually the Inquisitor unintentionally projects an image which comes closer to that of the authentic Christ. Indeed, every point of his case for the prosecution actually speaks in favour of Him (His great rejection of Satan's temptations, His boundless love and respect for man). For during this whole encounter an intense dialogic process is taking place. All the while, the silent Prisoner is exerting a powerful influence on the Inquisitor's every word, his every thought and feeling. Towards the end of his tirade the Inquisitor slips in a revealing autobiographical reminiscence which casts his whole discourse in a different light. Then we learn that he was once one of those who longed to be among Christ's elect, who fed on 'locusts and roots in the desert', who also once 'blessed freedom'. But he got tired of waiting, he did not want 'to serve madness' and so 'joined those who had corrected' Christ's feat (*podvig*) and allied himself with *him*. Now we may see his impassioned polemic as an exercise in self-justification which springs from his need to justify his having left off the 'madness' of serving Him and joining the clever people who were correcting His image. Thus, the Inquisitor projects the highest listener to hear his most secret, long-concealed thoughts out of his own need to confess, to be forgiven and absolved by Him. It is the Inquisitor who urgently seeks an intimate dialogue with his Prisoner. There is something gnawing him inside, some powerful inner impulse, driving him out into the night to visit Him alone in prison, giving him no rest, something, like Fyodor, long ago 'smothered'. And since his accusation turns into a confession, his 'blame' turns into 'praise', for a freely offered confession is one of the highest marks of respect. Clearly, 'He' has stirred the Inquisitor's memory of what he once long ago served and ardently loved, that old memory which he still reveres with his heart.

For one moment the Inquisitor betrays his awareness of the offer of love expressed in his Prisoner's gaze. This he categorically rejects: 'I don't want Thy love because I myself don't love Thee', and he defiantly declares his allegiance to the devil: 'We are with *him*'. Here is a key difference between Ivan's set and his protagonist's. It is the Inquisitor who categorically rejects Christ and sides with *him*, not Ivan, ever. And while Vetlovskaia rightly points out the diabolic streak in that laugh which is Ivan's sole answer to Alyosha's anxious question – 'And are you with *him* too, you? <...> Ivan laughed' – it is not purely diabolic (14,239).

Ivan, the ambivalent author, unconsciously subverts his intention with his own set of words and images, to which we now return. Several clues reveal this process. The first emerges

in a small grammatical mistake. Ivan's accusation against God
is that He appeared long ago and has not come back, has
forgotten mankind. Speaking of the ardent prayers sent up by
the patient faithful over 'so many centuries', Ivan misquotes
and misconstrues a phrase from Psalms 118:27 sung in the
Orthodox liturgy. The phrase should read: 'The Lord God
appeared to us [*Bog-Gospod', i iavilsia nam*]'. Ivan gives it as; 'for
Lord appear to us! [*bo Gospodi iavisia nam!*]' (14,226). Ivan
misreads a Church Slavonic aorist (appeared) for an imperative (appear!), deletes 'God (*Bog*) and substitutes it with 'for
(*bo – ibo*) and turns 'Lord' into a vocative. As the editors of
the *PSS* point out, the word 'for' together with the vocative
'deprives the phrase of any sense' (15,557). Of any grammatical sense, true, but not of any poetic sense. By turning the
statement subject 'Lord' into a call to the subject and by
misconstructing the past tense as an imperative, Ivan
expresses his own longing, his own imperative wish that He
appear. Indeed, Ivan's whole discourse is a veiled expression of
his longing to see Him and His harmony: 'I want to see with
my own eyes the doe lie down with the lion' (14,222). The
whole Legend is built on the Christ returned to earth topos.

There is another clue in Ivan's discourse. Ivan's Christ,
unlike the inquisitor's, is not totally silent. After He restores
sight to a blind old man, He performs another miracle, the
most important one, when He resurrects the little girl in the
white coffin saying 'Talitha cumi' (Damsel, arise).[8] These are
sole words of the canonical Christ which Ivan quotes, and he
quotes them exactly. For his Inquisitor, Ivan selected biblical
passages dwelling on the temptation and hell, but for himself,
Ivan chose to create a variation on the miracle of the raising of
Jairus's daughter in Mark's version (5:41–2), the Gospel which
contains one of only two utterances of Christ in His Own
language (Aramaic). The knowledge that these are the actual
untranslated words Christ said at this miraculous moment
creates an instant, mysterious contact between the divine
speaker and listeners. This direct unmediated word of Christ,
His call to resurrection, the word which affirms the most
important memory in the novel, Dostoevsky gave to Ivan alone

to remember, and to quote to Alyosha. Alyosha told Ivan that he needs to 'resurrect' his dead. With this quotation, Ivan expresses his own yearning to believe in the reality of resurection. Ivan's memory of the Bible is a memory of the dead who were resurrected by Christ. With these he identifies himself. His deepest unconscious desire, then, is to reject the Inquisitor's ideology. As it soon emerges, Alyosha reads it correctly.

Alyosha's cry, 'Your poem is in praise of Jesus, and not in blame ... as you wanted it to be', is the correct reading of the Legend (14,237). This implies, as Børtnes says, 'that Ivan's "voice", too, is governed by "the highest of voices", the voice of Christ'.[9] And given Ivan's sources (the Spanish Inquisition and the New Testament) there was no way that he could have constructed a recognisable representation of his Inquisitor and his 'Christ' without the diabolic qualities of the former and the divine attributes of the latter emerging.

But it is not Dostoevsky's highest image of Christ. It is a flawed ambivalent image and has to be because it reflects Ivan's flawed, alienated self. Dostoevsky put in just enough of the authentic, original Christ to make the poem convey a final impression of 'praise', to make a positive reading possible. So potent is Christ's image, so appealing His Word of love and mercy, that even when fragmented and admixed with other elements, it reconstitutes itself, gradually incorporating and subduing its invaders. What we are meant to witness here is the inherent power of the incarnated Logos, a power which derives from its eternal truth, from its perfection as the divine prototype. Ivan's image of Christ is a heavily mediated mosaic, but the biblical pieces retain the impress of their original. Such is the numinous power of the highest voice and image that it triumphs over Ivan's distortions and nihilistic intention. Neither the subversions of rhetorical arguments nor the substitutions of earthly ideologies can destroy it. Even if broken into parts, the 'whole' absorbs them into itself; the smallest genuine fragments from the canonical incarnate Word are sufficient to break through the lies of a tyrant and the distortions and defences of Ivan, the adversaries, the annihilating analysts. Father Paisy's word is fulfilled: 'They have analysed in parts, but overlooked the whole <...> they could never create a higher image for man and his dignity <...> The whole [Christ] stands before their eyes unshakeable, as before, and the gates of hell shall not prevail against it' (14,155–6). Ivan cannot see 'the whole' because he has fragmented, distorted and overlaid it with so many secular accretions, with so many rudiments of worldly art and philosophy.

Ivan crowns his poem with the Prisoner's silent kiss, the result of which is that the Inquisitor frees Him. Christ is never shown kissing anyone in the Bible, let alone 'on the lips'. This is another theatrical, even heretical, stroke of Ivan's. Ivan's Christ, and the one he created for his Inquisitors, is a figure which bears stylistic traces of nineteenth-century melodrama. Still, His farewell kiss emphasises His mercy, forgiveness and love, and hence expresses Ivan's veiled wish to receive them. Ivan cannot bring himself to kill Him even in a 'stupid poem, written by a stupid student'. But he did in his latest work ('The Geological Cataclysm') where he called for killing the very 'idea of God'. This 'poem' he does not recite to Alyosha. Only now does the 'decision of his heart' momentarily reach him while 'still on earth' when his Inquisitor finds himself unable to burn Him. But Ivan's ending to the Legend is provisional ('I wanted to end it'). Christ's love has conquered the old man's heart, but not his head. 'The kiss glows in his heart, but the old man sticks by his idea' (14,239).

Ivan too will stick by his 'idea'. He winds up his poem with a threat of suicide – 'dash the cup to the ground!' – the threat with which he began his narration. To Alyosha's silent gaze, Ivan makes a genuine confession:

I thought, brother, that going away from here I have in all the world at least you, – Ivan said suddenly with unexpected feeling, – but now I see, that you have no place for me in your heart, my dear hermit. The formula 'all is permitted' I shall not renounce, well and what of it, for that you will renounce me, yes, yes? (14,240)

Alyosha hears at once the lonely despair and wish for love in his brother's words. Consequently he rightly relates the ending of the Legend to Ivan and, imitating Ivan's Christ, kisses him.

Ivan, though moved, reverts to his self-contained pride, abruptly remarking that it is time for them to go. But just before parting he makes a concessionary revelation:

Look here, Alyosha, – said Ivan in a firm voice, – if I really will be able to care for the sticky little leaves, then I shall love them only remembering you. It's enough for me that you are somewhere here and I shall not stop wanting to live. Is that enough for you? If you like, take at least this for a declaration of love. (14,240)

Clearly, Alyosha's kiss glows in Ivan's heart, so much so that Ivan exclusively links his anticipated remembrances of Alyosha with his ability to love. Still more unusual, in terms of 'modern realism', is Ivan's conviction that his mere knowledge that Alyosha exists 'somewhere here', and to know this will be to remember him, will in future suffice to make him wish to live. Earlier in their conversation, Alyosha told his brother: 'But really there is a lot of love in humanity, and almost Christ-like love, this I know myself, Ivan ... Well, I don't know this yet and can't understand' (14,216). Ivan needs to know that a Christ-like love really exists in this world for his own salvation. Indeed, it is a fundamental idea of this novel that no one can love and live without the memory, conscious, subliminal or intuitive, of divine love. Love of an other and love the Other are inseparable. Later, in the Life, Alyosha will quote Zosima's expression of this idea: 'Without Christ's image before us, we would perish <...> everything <...> lives and is alive only by its feeling of contact with other mysterious worlds <...> if that feeling is destroyed in you, you'll grow indifferent to life and will even hate it' (Ivan's threat of suicide) (14,290–1). Yet again, reminiscences of divine love and salvation draw together in Alyosha's image.

In the Legend Ivan projects half his thoughts into his Inquisitor, but the remaining half associates him with Alyosha. His Legend is a dialogically directed polemic in which a continuous interference takes place between his spokesman's openly stated views and his own secret wish to have them refuted. All Ivan's compositions were composed before he came home and became re-acquainted with Alyosha after a separation of many years, before he felt for 'three months' his brother's quiet 'continuous expectant gaze' on him. At first Ivan could 'not endure it'. But, 'in the end your expectant gaze became not at all offensive to me: on the contrary, I came at last to love your expectant gaze ... You seem to love me for some reason, Alyosha? – I love you, Ivan' (14,209). Alyosha's waiting silence, his loving look turned on Ivan, forms a poetic analogy to the Prisoner's meek, silent searching gaze at the Inquisitor. And so Ivan chose Alyosha as his confessor, whom he had already prefigured 'about a year ago' when he composed his Legend, the only one who could refute his ideas, not in words but in a gesture and image of love. What we witness here is the slow crumbling of Ivan's intellectual defences under the influence of Alyosha's loving presence, under the irresistable response of his 'higher heart' to the 'very heart of the whole' which his younger brother 'carries within himself'.

For the meantime though, Ivan withdraws from Alyosha and chooses the sinister direction ('now you go to the right, I to the left'), symbolically and unconsciously foreshadowing his imminent sinister abandonments. He testily asks Alyosha not to speak with him anymore 'on these themes'. Unlike his Inquisitor, though, he does not send Alyosha away forever, but promises that towards his thirtieth year, should he want to 'dash the cup to the ground' (his third threat of suicide), he will seek him out. Ivan's 'cup' (*kubok*) is the secular 'goblet', and not the canonical 'cup' (*chasha*) of suffering which Mitya accepts. Thus, his threat to dash the goblet is at once a refusal to accept the redemptive way and a hidden rejection of a secularised life. But here too, at the very end, his heart momentarily relents. He, who did not want to let his brother go to his Zosima, now urges him to return to his dying 'Pater Seraphicus', and asks him to kiss him 'once more'. Ivan's request for Alyosha's parting kiss and his concluding metaphorical elevation of Zosima to the celestial apotheosis of St Francis at the end of Goethe's *Faust* are at once a finely allusive admission of his ideological defeat and an indication of his potential for salvation.

Ivan's pride, though, overpowers all. When at the end of their meeting Ivan withdraws from Alyosha, he rejects the only interlocutor who can support his 'higher heart'. Then he is ripe for deadly 'clever' games with his half-brother Smerdyakov, the shadow of his evil half. Smerdyakov, though, with the 'sideways' glance and the sleepwalker's gaze of the 'contemplator', is no fantasy.

THE IMAGE OF CHRIST: ALYOSHA

It was in Siberia, remarks Grossman, that Dostoevsky's 'evangelical worldview' deepened and determined his conception of his future artistic tasks: 'He now needs the authentic Christ, original, absolute and complete, not corrected by Saint-Simon or Pierre Leroux, not renovated in the spirit of the demands of the time.'[10] This was the Christ Dostoevsky attempted to represent and attach to Alyosha in 'Cana of Galilee'. The Christ 'corrected' 'in the spirit' of the times was left to Ivan and his Inquisitor ('we've corrected your *podvig*'). The set of all those words pertaining to Christ in this chapter constitutes the representation of His image reserved for the hero. It is very different from Ivan's, and it is represented with very different poetic means.

The telling of 'Cana of Galilee' represents a high point in Dostoevsky's narrative art. He called this chapter 'the most essential one in the whole book, and perhaps in the novel as well.'[11] Perlina calls it 'one of the great achievements of world literature'.[12] Bakhtin was also moved to comment on this chapter, assigning it a unique place in Dostoevsky's verbal art. He defines the hagiographical word as 'a word without a sideways glance, calmly sufficient unto itself and its object'.[13] In Dostoevsky's works, it begins to be heard whenever 'a hero comes close to the truth about himself, makes peace with the other and takes possession of his own authentic voice'. 'Words about paradise' are also represented in a hagiographical style, 'but in tones of fulfilment'. All the instances he cites are from *The Brothers Karamazov*. He finds that while 'tones of fulfilment sound in the speech' of Markel, Zosima and the Mysterious

Visitor, all their speeches are 'subordinated to the stylised tones' of a hagiographic or confessional style. 'In the narration itself these tones appear only once' in 'Cana of Galilee'. In 'the narration itself', then, we shall have to seek that singular fulfilment of which Bakhtin speaks. But not only the mode of narration emptied of its crucial content. Fulfilment, formally and logically, has to be prefigured. Hagiographical discourse is more than a 'tone of voice', more than a psychological process of discovering the 'truth about oneself', of mastering one's 'own authentic voice'. The literary model of this chapter is the 'vision' of the Lives of the Saints which takes as its theme a divine revelation that transforms the saint's life.

Viewed as a whole, the narrative of 'Cana of Galilee' forms an iconic triptych consisting of two subordinate lateral scenes and an hierarchically superior centerpiece, marked by two correspondingly different modes of narration. The triptych is structurally and thematically linked by a rite of passage beginning with preparation, vision and the passing of the test. In the first lateral segment, the narrator begins by performing his usual narrational tasks; he represents the setting in Zosima's cell and his hero's thoughts and feelings. It is evening (again a picture compels the present tense), 'the hour of communal rest and peace after such a disturbing day for everyone'.[14] Father Paisy is reading the Bible over Zosima's coffin. Alyosha enters, falls on his knees and begins to pray. Only Paisy, Alyosha and the dead Zosima are present; Paisy awake, reading, Alyosha, first awake and conscious, then gradually sleepy and semi-conscious, and Zosima, asleep, in earthly terms, unconscious forever. This is a 'threshold' situation in which Alyosha is suspended between two worlds and the possibility of any mundane, earthly dialogue is eliminated. Although this is a scene of mourning, Alyosha's 'mind' and 'heart' are full of 'joy'. This oxymoronic combination is of the essence of Christianity, a system which is built on the dynamic suspension of paradoxical oppositions (life from death, the 'crown of thorns'). And, as it soon emerges, it accords with the meaning of the chapter. Mourning can only be joyous when death is no longer the final separation. In metaphor and simile the narrator conveys the contents of Alyosha's soul where one emotion, one thought follows another, none dominating:

His soul was overflowing, but vaguely somehow, and no single sensation stood out distinctly, on the contrary, one supplanted another in a kind of quiet, even rotation <...> joy, joy shone in his mind and his heart. Fragments of thoughts flashed through his soul, caught fire like little stars and at once died down, giving way to others <...> but then something whole, firm, soothing reigned in his soul, and he was aware of it himself.

The 'little stars' to which Alyosha's thoughts are likened here, are symmetrically echoed and boundlessly extended in the third segment of the triptych where Alyosha sees the distant real 'stars' of the night sky: 'Above him the vault of heaven, full of softly shining stars stretched wide and vast.' In this way the author creates a link between Alyosha's thoughts and God's creation, His 'other worlds' strewn over the heavens. Alyosha's soul, temporarily fragmented and scattered by the day's disturbing events, has reconstituted itself after the episode with Grushenka. 'Something whole' now reigns within. The hero is now recovering the 'very heart of the whole' in preparation for becoming that 'eccentric' who will unite others and show them the way out of the 'general confusion'. He starts listening to the reading, but 'little by little' begins 'to doze'. At this point the narrator, that constant counter of time and reminder of place, effaces himself. Alyosha's soul is now prepared for the great turning point of his dream–vision. Let us return to the idea of a set.

The centrepiece of the triptych is the symbolic centre of the novel. Now the narration alternates between the reading of a Gospel passage and the direct, mimetic representation of Alyosha's inner speech expressing his reactions to the sacred verses. Applying the idea of a mapping, we at once notice a striking difference between the Christological representations associated to Ivan and Alyosha. Almost the entire account of Christ's first miracle (John 2:1–11) has been inserted into this short chapter and highlighted in italic type. For Alyosha, then, a proper subset of the New Testament has been mapped directly into the novel's text through the device of Paisy's reading. This proper subset, let us call it (C), consists of the words of Christ, His Mother, the steward and the narrator-evangelist, St John. Unlike Ivan's representation, this verbal image of Christ is whole, the inserted verses are preserved intact.

The words of (C), which belong to the novel's hierarchically highest words, inspire the creation of a second set (A) which consists of the thoughts and feelings they arouse in Alyosha. Alyosha's responses to the *cantus firmus* of (C) are antiphonally set into the text. The biblical words are not broken up into the incorporated bits of speech by one who appropriates them in order to bend them to his diabolical intention, but here preserve their artistic integrity, their linguistic autonomy and semantic authority. They are not mapped centuries backwards into the diabolic mouth of a fantasised surrogate speaker in his context of horror, but penetrate directly from the ancient original source into the novel's present. No other spokesman stands between the Word and the receiver of Its message. We receive the unmediated transmission of the Logos together with the hero's ecstatic response to It. The biblical words inspire joy, love and faith directly, they do not need reprocessing.

The same device of a reading from the New Testament was used in *Crime and Punishment*, only here the biblical word is transmitted not by a saintly prostitute in the vernacular but by a monk in Church Slavonic, the language of liturgical ritual and worship (a key nuance lost in English translation). As such it is bound to sound more ancient, solemn and mysterious to Russian ears. The old language of Russian Orthodox worship conveys an image of Christ which has been transmitted over the centuries, and consequently brings the listener into communion with the original image, 'not corrected in the spirit of the time'. Such linguistic and contextual associations were just what the author needed for his conception of the Orthodox Christ as the true apostolic ideal, and for attaching it to his hero. For the resonant biblical words which are being solemnly intoned in Church Slavonic alternate with Alyosha's dozing thoughts expressed in a simple, exclamatory, transparent

Russian, thus forming a link between the divine words and the hero's human thoughts.

The events of the troubling day, as they tumble about in Alyosha's mind, take on new meaning as they interpenetrate with the biblical words. Initially, his thoughts are peopled with those he loves and knows. Then his memory of this biblical passage is stirred – 'I love that passage'. He remembers Zosima's words 'He who loves people, loves their joy too', and Mitya's 'Without joy one cannot live'. Joy and love dominate the whole dream. The counterpoint between the two sets (C) and (A) generates a new set (C,A) thanks to their juxtaposition and to the connections which the author (and reader) make between them. Additional elements, personal and sacred, begin streaming into (C,A) as Alyosha's dream–vision enlarges. He imagines the biblical scene, the lake, the poor people, the Mother of God (again Alyosha is associated with her image) 'that other great being' with a 'great heart'. Interesting here are the author's own interpretations of the biblical set as they emerge through his hero's voice. Alyosha softens Christ's abrupt remark to His mother ('Woman, what have I to do with thee; Mine hour is not yet come.') with: 'He certainly smiled gently at Her'. A comparison of (C) with (A) reveals the absence in (C) of any mention of joy or love. Juxtaposing his hero's ardent responses, Dostoevsky follows his tendency to modify the austerity of the Bible with motifs of joy and accents of tenderness.

Just after Paisy reads the governor's confirmation of the miracle, the high point in the biblical story, Alyosha's dream–vision begins. The room 'spreads apart', the vision opens up, enlarges, transforming itself into an icon of the marriage feast at Cana. In Alyosha's words: 'Why is the room expanding ... Ah, yes ... it's the marriage, the wedding ... yes, of course. And here are the guests, and here the young couple are sitting and the merry crowd and ... '. Discussing the inverse perspective of the icon, Ouspensky says that 'the point of departure of its perspective is not found in the illusory depth of the image which attempts to reproduce visible space, but *before* the image, in the spectator himself <...> It is as if man were standing

before a path which, instead of losing itself in space, opens on
to infinite fullness.'[15] The iconic vision expands again, pushing
the frame of the room to the periphery: 'Again the room
expanded ... '. A figure comes towards Alyosha (and the
reader), or, in terms of inverse perspective, a figure is brought
forwards as the icon's background becomes the visual foreground. On Alyosha's exclamation 'But he's here too ... he got
up, he saw me, he's coming here ... Lord! ... ', the narrator
re-enters to confirm his hero's vision of Zosima resurrected –
'yes, he came up to him, to him' – and then leaves Zosima to
speak. Alyosha hears the 'soft voice' of his elder which 'sounds
above him' inviting him to the marriage feast. Zosima lifts
Alyosha up from his kneeling position. Minutes later Alyosha
will lift himself up from his prostrate position 'a firm fighter for
his whole life'. Zosima introduces Alyosha into the Kingdom of
Heaven where he now appears to dwell. In Linnér's words:
'the scene is transformed from the earthly wedding in Cana
into the heavenly banquet, whose host is the Lord resurrected'.[16] Zosima speaks of the 'new wine'. Images of welcoming,
calling and sharing prevail in the remainder of the vision.
Zosima, recalling the onion as though he had witnessed the
scene with Grushenka, seems to testify to the supernal vantage
point of his resurrected vision. He urges Alyosha to begin his
work (*delo*) because his novice has the rare gift of aiding others
to redemption, of exorcising their demons and thus turning the
earth into this image of paradise.

The dream culminates in a combination of utterance and
vision: 'And do you see our Sun, do you see Him? – I'm afraid
... I dare not look ... – whispered Alyosha. "Do not fear Him.
He is terrible in His grandeur before us, awful in His sublimity,
but infinitely merciful".' The young hero has escaped from the
'darkness of earthly malice' and found the 'light of love'.
Alyosha beholds, if only for a dazzling moment, the Lord 'face
to face'. The sun is a canonical and patristic symbol of Christ.
The solar image comes from two biblical verses. The first, at
the Transfiguration, contains the only description of Christ's
physical appearance in the Gospels: 'His face did shine as the
sun, and His raiment became white as the light' (Matthew

17:2). This is traditionally held to be the most sublime image of Christ on earth, one beheld only by His disciples in order to give them an image of the glory of heaven. The second is an image of Christ in heaven where: 'His countenance was as the sun shineth in his strength' (Revelation 1:16). In a patristic source we find: 'The Son was born of the Father by some incomprehensible birth, as the ray from the sun'.[17] This, then, is not an image of the Jesus of the Gospels but a vision of glory, of Christ Pantocrator, Sun of Justice, reigning in heaven and celebrated in His divine majesty. It is also a prefiguration of His second coming when He will return in all His glory to establish the Kingdom. This 'ancient apostolic' image, 'infinitely merciful', is the authentic Christ of the novel. Alyosha's childhood memory of the 'rays of the setting sun' can now be seen as a variation on and prefiguration of this image of the uncreated Light. From a child held up to the sacred image, Alyosha has now broken into the non-Euclidean space of the icon, he has entered the memory of the future and become a part of it, a part of the 'whole'. The two iconographic representations of Alyosha are based on contiguous juxtapositions to the 'highest image', Child and Christ Pantocrator which, taken together, traditionally encompass a recapitulation of all creation. Thus, Alyosha's path is one of increasing proximity to Christ; it describes a metonymic ascent as he approaches and approximates to the divine. He *is* the brother closest to the authentic Christ.

'He hath made Himself like unto us from love and rejoices with us', continues Zosima. 'He is turning the water into wine so that the gladness of the guests may not cease, He is expecting new guests, He is calling new ones unceasingly and forever and ever'. The iconic vision has become infinitely full. The author has created a movement from the Word of Christ to the image of Christ Pantocrator. This ideal image of Christ emphasises His majesty, compassion and love of joy as He presides over the universal feast in heaven; He remembers everyone and keeps a place for all. The biblical subtext here is surely John 14:2: 'In My Father's house there are many dwelling-places <...> I go to prepare a place for you'. Thus,

Alyosha's vision is of a future remembered, of the fulfilment of Christ's promise of eternal life for all. The small set of the biblical excerpt has, like a seed, generated a greatly expanded set, the result of which is that from the enlarged perspective of (C,A), the hero's image has become intermingled with that of Christ. The canonical set has engendered a vision of paradise.

The Orthodox *kontakion* concludes with the declaration: 'We confess and proclaim our salvation in word and image'. Dostoevsky's intention to answer Ivan and the Grand Inquisitor 'in an artistic picture' is realised here in a most condensed and climactic manner. This is the heavenly fulfilment of Alyosha's 'dream' of the Kingdom. The beginning of its earthly fulfilment occurs in the novel's final scene.

If the centrepiece of the triptych is an icon of the resurrected Zosima culminating in an image of Christ and the beholding hero, the third compartment is an iconographic representation of Alyosha's 'resurrection' in the monastery garden, itself a reminiscence of the archetypal Garden of Eden and a prefiguration of the paradisiacal garden to come. As Alyosha awakes, the narrator takes full control of the remainder of the chapter. Alyosha runs outside, stops to take in the majestic beauty of the night sky and suddenly falls to his knees. Alyosha experiences his ecstasy while fully awake in the 'here and now', but it is memory which gives his rite of passage a sense of fulfilment.

In the second of Zosima's two sermons addressed to Alyosha, he enjoins his novice: 'fall on the earth and kiss it <...> Water the earth with the tears of your gladness' (14,291,292). After Alyosha falls to the earth:

He did not know why he was embracing it, he could not have explained to himself why he longed so irresistibly to kiss it, to kiss it all, but he kissed it weeping, sobbing and watering it with his tears, and frenziedly vowed to love it, to love it forever and ever. 'Water the earth with the tears of your gladness and love these tears of yours ...' rang in his soul.

Here Alyosha's mystical ecstasy resonates with his memory of Zosima's words resounding in his soul. Then a paraphrase from Zosima's great passage on our connection with 'other mysterious worlds' comes floating into Alyosha's soul: 'It was as though the threads from all those innumerable worlds of God met all at once in his soul, and it was all trembling "as it came into contact with other worlds"'. Zosima's mystical teachings are now fulfilled in Alyosha's mystical experience. Alyosha committed Zosima's words to writing some time after this event, but he did not write about it in the Life. This the author took charge of, but first he inserted the Life, then he depicted Alyosha's experience. Had we first read Alyosha's dream vision and then Zosima's discourses, the sense of prefiguration, of that 'indirect picture' favoured by Dostoevsky, would have been hopelessly lost. The dream vision comes with memory behind it, with Alyosha's (and the reader's) memory of Zosima's word whose prefigurative function now comes to life in its incarnate fulfilment.

As the narrator ends his representation of the third side of the triptych, he transfers his hero's rite of passage into a permanent memory of the future:

But with every moment he felt clearly and almost palpably that something firm and unshakeable, like that vault of heaven had descended into his soul. Some sort of idea had established sovereignty in his mind – and that for his whole life, and forever and ever. And never, never could Alyosha forget for his whole life afterwards this minute. 'Someone visited my soul at that hour!' he used to say afterwards with firm faith in his words.

Yet again, the remembering narrator can verify Alyosha's memory of 'that hour', of his rebirth in faith for his 'whole life'. Since the 'someone' who visited Alyosha's soul expresses an encounter with the divine, it is left unspecified. However, those familiar with the Christian tradition can identify that 'someone'. Alyosha's vision is inspired by the reading of 'Cana of Galilee', one of the three canonical epiphanies (the other two are the homage of the Magi and the baptism of Christ). An epiphany in its New Testament meaning is 'a manifestation of Christ'. The Eastern Church retains for them the ancient term 'theophany': 'a manifestation or appearance of God to man'. The concluding verse of the miracle at Cana, omitted by

Dostoevsky, contains the Evangelist's interpretation of the event. 'This beginning of the miracles did Jesus in Cana of Galilee and manifested His glory; and His disciples believed on Him'. 'Begin, dear one, your work, begin gentle one', Zosima urges Alyosha in the dream. Yet another parallel transforms Alyosha and his future work into a figure of Christ and His mission.

Reverting to the sober tone of a chronicler, the narrator closes the triptych: 'After three days he left the monastery in accordance with the word of his late elder who had bidden him "sojourn in the world"'. Alyosha's brief rebellion over, he obeys his elder's command. The quest has been fulfilled with a vision of the uncreated Light, the test passed as Alyosha leaves firm for life to sojourn in the world.

Once we see the memory of Christ as the dominant of the novel, we gain another perspective on the narrator's role. The Gospels are memoirs, retrospective testimonials to Christ's mission in the world. The narrator occupies with respect to Alyosha a position analogous to that of the Evangelists. Only he lives in an epoch which compels him to 'prove' the remarkableness of his hero, whereas the Evangelists could openly proclaim and glorify Him. But Dostoevsky could not create a narrator who was an evangelist. Neither his hero, nor his tale, was commensurate with such an aim. He had to find other ways. This is a rhetorical problem, but it is also a poetic one. Evdokimov pinpoints Dostoevsky's aesthetic solution to this problem when he remarks that 'Dostoevsky consciously replaces the classical principle of description with the principle of *iconographic expression*'.[18] In his depiction of his hero, Dostoevsky carried this principle to its fullest extent. In the Orthodox Church the icon is part of the liturgy and a major object of veneration. Thus, in the iconographic scenes the narrator 'paints' for the reader, he as if beholds and venerates what they symbolically represent. Indeed, the very painting of an icon is an act of veneration. The narrator invites us to behold the icon with him and in this way to take us into the image, to bring us into direct communion with 'Christ the icon of God'. The narrator carries out his expository tasks in many guises, as chronicler, biographer, historian, hagiographer, but when he becomes an iconographer he reaches the summit of his narrative tasks.

Cana of Galilee was a beautiful choice. It is traditionally a figure of Paradise. Of all Christ's acts, it is most susceptible to combining faith and miracle with motifs of joy, love and communality. It is also the miracle which lays the greatest emphasis on His Synthetic nature, human and divine, while conveying an image of the social Christ as the communal ideal. Moreover, as the first miracle marking the beginning of Christ's mission, it provided a perfect analogy for marking and sacralising the beginning of his hero's 'work'. But the way Dostoevsky poetically integrated it into his novel was perhaps one of his greatest artistic moves. Indeed, a reading is a brilliant hagiographical device for incorporating a sacred text because it imposes the closest adherence to the order of a text, (what is called in set theory a well ordered set). Since it best preserves the original textual order, it best preserves its aesthetic and semantic pattern. This is of cardinal importance for this novel. For the author most wishes to affirm the idea that there is a divine pattern, a highest truth and a highest reality which, if we try to grasp it, will make sense of our world and our lives. Fidelity to this pattern, to this memory, is, for the author, piety in its highest sense. And the denial of that pattern, the fragmentation of that structure is in essence the main project of the novel's self-willed characters. Dostoevsky's last novel is very much about the intense modern struggle between a pregiven, absolute standard of virtue and truth and the shifting, relative values asserted by self-willed individuals, between a divine plan and an endlessly self-creating universe, between piety and romanticism.

THE LEGEND AND THE LIFE AS PREFIGURATIONS

The two different images of Christ give rise to a series of contrasting parallels which form the novel's pervasive pattern of prefiguration. The very chapter headings are revealing: Ivan's Christ is subsumed under 'The Grand Inquisitor', whereas Alyosha's appears in the chapter named after a canonical epiphany, the first miracle. Contexts and atmosphere are also determining: the Inquisitor appears in a context of terror and mass murder, the literal consuming of people in flames, whereas Alyosha's vision takes place in a situation of worship, salvation and commemoration. The Grand Inquisitor's nocturnal visit to the 'dark' prison where 'heretics' are confined prior to being burnt to death is a world away from the nocturnal monastic scene of peaceful mourning and silent prayer followed by the exultant freedom of the starry night sky. The Inquisitor is projected backwards 300 years in a quasi-fantastical setting inhabited by phantom figures. The monastery is a contemporary setting where the novel's 'real' people have their being 'now'. A mystical symbolic dimension is more likely to convince when it is incorporated into a familiar reality and is seen to be engendered by the 'real' events of an absorbing story; hence the realistic frame of the triptych's lateral scenes.

Contrastive ideas and images are also crucial. Instead of the Inquisitor's (and Ivan's) accusatory argumentation against Him, there is Alyosha's (and Zosima's) loving acceptance of His message. Rather than a diatribe in a gloomy prison, there is a dialogue in heaven. Instead of Christ being sent away from this world, the Christ-like Alyosha is sent into it. Instead of the apocalyptic 'star of heresy' threatening the world with devastation, there are the majestic stars, the beneficent visible signs of 'other worlds'. Rather than the bitter waters of the Apocalypse, Alyosha's vision offers the new wine of gladness. In place of a small totalitarian elite, there is the Kingdom where all are elected. Instead of *autos da fé* ordered by a tyrant, there is the eternal feast in heaven to which all are invited by the Lord of Hosts. Instead of an image of hell, there is an image of paradise.

Since *The Brothers Karamazov* is addressed to the future, these different images of Christ have significant prophetic implications. The Life follows the Legend compositionally and chronologically. Apart from the narrator's word, the Life is the most recent word in the novel, thus giving Alyosha the last word on two levels. This is important both rhetorically and from the viewpoint of poetic memory. Rhetorically the one who comes after his opponent always has the advantage because he has been able to think over the opponent's arguments. Moreover, had Ivan's Legend come after Zosima's Life, that would have been to give the last word to despair. Alyosha, after some lapse of time, answers Ivan through the mode of reminiscence, through the power of cherished memories. If the Life is Zosima's 'answer' to the Grand Inquisitor, as Dostoevsky said, then it is in fact Alyosha's answer, not only because he is its author, but because he heard the Inquisitor's words and Zosima did not. Thus the two compositions are really a conversation between the two brothers through the reader's point of view.

This is very significant for the relationship of the Legend to the Life. Ivan's Legend is a veiled prophecy projected into an evil past. At the same time it forms a relationship with Ivan's present since the Legend is the fulfilment of what is prefigured in Ivan's contemporary atheism. The Legend, then, can be viewed as a memory of the future projected into the past, the Life, a memory of the recent past preserved as a model programme for the future. The Legend is created out of a memory of evil and terror, the Life is created out of a memory of mercy and love.

These contrasting parallels and figural patterns are carried through the novel's whole length. Ivan's Legend is a prefiguration of a future without God which is fulfilled in his parodic nightmare, and in his own breakdown. Ivan's relationship with Smerdyakov, his fantasied Inquisitor and his phantom devil are images of hell, evil and oblivion which form the closed system of a vicious circle. Alyosha's life, his memories, dreams and loving relationships are images of goodness, hope and heaven which form an open system of growth, spiritual renewal and resurrection. Alyosha's Life of Zosima is a reality with a future fulfilment, in the novel and beyond. For the final scene in the Epilogue is a symbolic fulfilment of Alyosha's first dream of the Kingdom. Here, after the chaos of the novel, Alyosha founds a new order.[19] This scene, in turn, prefigures a transcendent 'true Kingdom of Christ' of which it is an anagogical representation.

We may thus regard *The Brothers Karamazov* as a poetic experiment in imitations of Christ with three major variations (and many minor ones). We end up with one variant which, from Dostoevsky's point of view, is the positive interpretation, Alyosha. The other two are broken off (Mitya) or rejected, frustrated (Ivan). Initially, Mitya identifies with the Dionysian myth of death and regeneration. He speaks in the syncretic idiom of Romanticism and Romantic Theology which aimed at uniting and reconciling this ancient myth with Christ's suffering and Resurrection. As he undergoes his inner transformation, he sheds this cultural context. By alluding to the cup, his image becomes Christological. He then identifies with Christ's Passion, with the idea of sacrificial suffering, to take up his cross 'for the babe'. Once he has taken into himself a true *imitatio Christi* as an ideal to remember for the rest of his life, his imitation breaks off, comes to an end.

Ivan, unlike Mitya and Alyosha, does not imitate Christ, or rather, his imitation is at one remove to an *imitatio* since he only gives it a literary form (a text) in which he represents Christ as a fictitious person. It is a kind of imitation but only in art, and it is only hypothetical; his whole 'poem' is governed by the subjunctive (past conditional) mood. Therefore, his imitation does not enter his own life, it is not an existential imitation and consequently is not, and cannot be a true *imitatio Christi*. It remains on the plane of reflection, in Bakhtin's terms, it is 'contemplated' and not 'followed'. By composing the Legend, by making up a fantasy in which Christ is represented, Ivan attempts to control Christ, to impose his own ideas on Him, to create Him in the image and likeness of himself. By giving Him a literary representation, he brings Him into the sphere of German Idealism, into the plane of reflection instead of the existential plane of an imitation of Christ in life. In this, he is a typical German Romantic hero who lives so much in his head, in his ideas and dreams, that he cannot love his neighbours, he can only love humanity 'in the abstract'. And so he withdraws from human society into a realm of fantasies, dilemmas and paradoxes until he finally loses contact with the real world, hallucinating the devil and seeing phantoms of the dead. He is haunted by Christ, but he shies away from personal involvement which, in Christianity, is everything. All this tells on his literary image of Christ and hence on his *imitatio*, Ivan, in contrast to Mitya and Alyosha, refuses to take Christ into his own existence, as a model for his life, or he is at most very hesitant to do so. This has also to do with his relationship with his father. Because Ivan rejects his own father, he rejects God the Father and His creation. Thus he does not, or cannot, regard himself as a son of God. He creates a miracle-working Christ Who is not the Son of God, but God Himself. He leaves the Father out of his image, he forgets Him, as he forgot his own father. Mitya makes the transition from the carnal to the spiritual Father because he has an idea of God and has consequently formed a relationship with the Father: 'I love God! <...> I am Thy son, O Lord, and I love Thee' (14,99). This is why he does not kill his father.

Ivan takes as his prototype the miracle-working Jesus of the Gospels. The Christ Whom he wants to imitate is the wonder-working Christ in Whom he can no longer believe. Ivan is a variation on the biblical doubting Thomas who wants proofs in order to believe, hence his fascination with miracles. He longs for a human Christ performing miracles, or to be Christ himself, to be invested with power, with the gift of working wonders in order to relieve people of suffering. Ivan cannot accept suffering, and in this he is very modern. And he does not accept that Christ suffered for him. However, man is not meant to imitate Christ by working miracles, but by trying to realise His Word in the world. The consequence of an imitation based on a humanised, miracle-working Christ is the Grand Inquisitor who gives the people its faith in miracles and who can throw Christ into prison. Ivan is fascinated by power. Ivan remembers Him as the miracle-working Jesus of the Gospels, before the Resurrection, before the culminating event of the New Testament which, according to Christian tenets, established His transcendent divinity once and for all. This is the idea Ivan rejects in his head, but which burns in his heart. Furthermore,

Ivan's imitation, in contrast to the other two, is perverted, mixed with demonic elements. We can see them everywhere, in his temptation of Alyosha, his Inquisitor, the devil and in Smerdyakov, his spiritual offspring, who is doubly perverted. Thus, Ivan's path is a fulfilment of the redemption frustrated pattern Christ outlines in the Epigraph. He is one of the 'contemporary dead men' who can neither die nor live. His *imitatio* is still at the stage of Christ's agony in the garden: 'My soul is exceeding sorrowful even unto death' (Matthew 26:38).[20] Only when Ivan will be able to carry his *imitatio* to the next stage, only when he will accept the cup with humility ('nevertheless not as I will'), will his regeneration be achievable.

Alyosha's imitation is the most differentiated and poetically elaborated one. His path bears the closest similarity to the regenerative pattern of the Epigraph. He falls into doubt, but he rises in triumph to become a living sower of the Word. Alyosha believes in a Christ by Whom one can be redeemed. His *imitatio* takes place on the plane of action (active love), not just words. His is the only Urbild truly realised in the novel. Alyosha is sent by his elder to promote redemption through brotherhood, to save the earth through Christ-like love. His *imitatio* is what the world needs. This is why of all the characters Dostoevsky invested him with the greatest future dimension. For the others, their earthly future is either over (Smerdyakov), broken off (Mitya) or uncertain (Ivan).

It is not only the brothers Karamazov who reflect an *imitatio Christi*. Everyone in this novel can at certain moments realise the ideal of Christ. Markel, in his last days, took communion (the cup). The liturgical term 'lover of man' (*chelovekoliubets*) is applied to Dr. Herzenstube in connection with his treating the poor without payment. Fyodor returns the icon to Alyosha. Ilyusha stands up for truth and his father. And, at the very end of the novel, Kolya, the seed of the new generation, says 'I want to suffer for all people' (15,195). 'We are not always sinful', said Dosteovsky, 'on the contrary, we are sometimes holy too. And who could live if it were otherwise'.[21]

Since the Kingdom is held to be present in Christ's

behaviour, all the characters' imitations bear directly on the central question of the novel, how to redeem the fallen in order to achieve paradise, on earth and in heaven. Dostoevsky sought answers in the sacred tradition, in memories held in sacred texts (the Bible, legends, apocrypha). On the metaphorical, symbolic level, Dostoevsky introduced, through his characters' memories, three eschatological folk legends describing a merciful visit to hell by divine beings in ascending order and gradations of divine power and compassion: in Grushenka's fable, a Guardian Angel tries to pull a sinner up to heaven; in Ivan's apocrypha, the Mother of God obtains for all sinners annual respite from suffering; and finally, in the harrowing of hell told to Mitya by the coachman, the 'infinitely merciful' Christ promises to return and empty hell forever.

Ways to paradise are also indicated existentially, in the characters' own words and experiences. Each brother has a vision of paradise. For Mitya and Alyosha the vision comes to them at a time of personal crisis, in their revelatory dreams. Mitya, in his dream of the babe is seized by an overpowering wish to 'do something for the babe now', after which he sees a great light. (Grushenka's fable gives an analogous message, namely, do a good deed, no matter how small.) In his dream, Alyosha enters the beatific vision of 'our Sun'. Ivan, unlike his brothers, makes up a fictitious 'other' who has a glimpse of paradise (the atheistic philosopher in his anecdote). Ivan's vision, just as his *imitatio*, is only at second remove, it does not enter his own intimate experience. He gives it a literary text, just as he does his Christ. His view of paradise thus remains at the level of ironic detachment, weighed down with intellectual reservations. Ivan's failure to attain a heavenly vision himself is reflected in his ideological preoccupations, in his fantasy of a future earthly utopia where 'men–gods' will obtain a natural beatitude by their own unaided powers. This is the essence of the devil's sin of pride which caused his fall. Just this idea, more than any other, Dostoevsky aimed to undermine maximally by having the devil deliver it in mockery of Ivan. In *The Brothers Karamazov*, the ultimate meaning and function of poetic memory, then, is to affirm the idea that paradise, celestial and

terrestrial, is attainable only through remembering and imitating Christ, through taking Him as one's model and trying to
realise the Word in one's life. There is an intriguing clue in the
devil's discourse that Ivan knows this and yearns for it,
subconsciously.

IVAN AND THE DEVIL: A POTENTIAL IMITATIO

Beginning with the symbol of the seed, another echo of the
Epigraph, the devil utters a remarkable prophecy to Ivan:

But my aim is noble. I shall sow in you only a tiny little seed of faith,
and out of it an oak will grow, and such an oak tree that, sitting on it,
you will long to enter the ranks of 'the hermit monks and chaste
women', for in secret you want that very, very much, you will feed on
locusts, you will drag yourself off into the wilderness to seek
salvation! (15,80)

This is one of the two most important statements about Ivan in
the novel, the first being Zosima's. It is supremely typical of
Dostoevsky's dialogic art that both the devil and a saint say the
truest words about Ivan, thus reflecting the two extremes of
Ivan's split soul. The devil quotes the first line of Pushkin's
great paraphrase of Saint Ephraim the Syrian's Penitent
Prayer (*Ottsy pustynniki i zheny neporochny*). The Prayer is read
out in the Orthodox liturgy during Great Lent and is well
known to Orthodox Russians. The devil's association of Ivan
to this poem is highly telling. In Pushkin's prothesis to the
paraphrased Prayer, the lyrical subject speaks of the saints
who composed 'many divine prayers' in order 'with the heart
to ascend to invisible regions' and 'to strengthen it' midst the
'storms and battles' of earth.[22] The lyrical hero of Pushkin's
poem is a 'fallen man' who in his role as penitent sinner calls on
God not to allow the 'hidden serpent' to enter his soul. He asks
God that he may see his own sins so that he will not judge his
'brother', and he implores Him to 'revive' in his 'heart' the
Christian virtues, the 'spirit of humility, patience, love and
chastity'. Ivan is still struggling to expunge the 'hidden
serpent' within him. He cannot yet say this prayer directly,
from his own lips. But if, as the devil says, he longs 'in secret' to

enter the ranks of 'desert fathers and chaste women', then his deepest wish is to compose 'many divine prayers' and not an Inquisitor's Legend, to take a Christian vow of poverty, chastity and obedience rather than the side of atheistic rebellion. And this would mean that Ivan wishes to address Him as Thou with a prayer rather than through a fictitious intermediary who addresses Him as Thou with an accusation. And he not only seeks penance and spiritual rebirth, but, says the devil, saintly martyrdom. The devil's images of 'locusts' and the 'wilderness' associate Ivan to his biblical namesake, St John the Baptist. Alyosha divined this early in the novel when, rejecting Rakitin's cynical imputations that Ivan only wants Katerina and her money, he countered: 'Ivan looks higher <...> Perhaps he is seeking suffering' (14,76). The word Alyosha uses for 'suffering' is *muchenie*, traditionally invoked to signify the torments of martyrs and saints. Ivan has already said as much himself, of course, indirectly and unconsciously.

Beginning the narration of his 'Rebellion', Ivan tells Alyosha that he has never understood how it is possible to love one's neighbours, especially them. He recalls having read about a certain saint 'John the Merciful' (Ioann Milostivyi) who warmed 'a hungry, frozen passerby' with his own body, and breathed in his mouth, 'festering and putrid from some awful disease' (14,215). Ivan is convinced that the saint's mercy was not an act of love but penance. But he has confused two different saints. The act he describes was performed by St Julian, a man who by mistake killed his father and mother and then spent his life atoning for his crime.[23] The editors of the *PSS* rightly remark the importance of this in view of Ivan's complicity in the murder of his father (15,551). But Ivan's misnomer is equally revelatory of his own deepest wishes 'on the positive side'. Replacing 'Julian' with 'Ioann' (the Church Slavonic version of his name), Ivan unconsciously prefigures his rescue of the peasant he left freezing in the snow. At the same time he associates himself to St John the Merciful who championed the poor and oppressed and who took the humble kenotic Christ as the model for his life.[24] That the devil says the same thing to Ivan as Zosima and Alyosha is by now not so surprising, or even paradoxical. For the devil remembers the Prayer, God has entered him too and subdued his intention to do evil. He wants to do something 'noble' in spite of himself. He takes Zosima's prophecy for Ivan to the limits of the 'positive side'. Ivan will have a great faith. He will seek salvation in the wilderness and eventually become an imitator of Christ. Indeed, Ivan's impassioned wish to know God, to see Him and His harmony with his own eyes is not just a Christian wish but a saintly desire. When he reaches the highest ranks of saints and martyrs, he will realise his true calling and the meaning of the Epigraph. Ivan is a saint *manqué*. But one 'little seed', one turn of the hinge and he could be not only an ardent believer, but an ascetic saint, a *skhimnik*. Ivan and Alyosha are at bottom very close after all. That they share the same mother is no longer an enigma. Father Paisy was right. Christ the ideal is in his heart, no matter how fragmented. In this novel's world, Christ's image is inescapable. Ivan's atheism is not absolute. In fact, there is no absolute atheism in *The Brothers Karamazov*.

ALYOSHA, THE CHRISTOLOGICAL HERO

Vetlovskaia traces Alyosha's literary origins to the popular Russian saint, Aleksei Man-of-God. Perlina rightly objects that 'in his biographical plot Alyosha Karamazov does everything opposite to the saint of the hagiography: he does not seek solitude, but goes into the world; he does not abandon his bride, but intends to marry; he does not run away from the parental home, but sets off for there'.[25] Belknap makes the cardinal point: 'The Christ figure not only generates the common features of Alёša's sources, it also underlies Alёša directly'.[26] Dostoevsky's conception of his 'hero' was determined by the Christian conception of sainthood. Every saint is understood to be enacting an imitation of Christ. Of course, the differences between Alyosha and Christ are also important for establishing those similarities most essential to the author. In order for an artistic image based on a model to be convincing, it must have differences from the prototype. The similarities can never be so great that the differences become obscured, or are not even greater. 'With a basis of similarity there should be many dissimilarities', said Petrarch apropos imitation.[27] The 'basis of similarity' is the key point. The dissimilarities are there. Most importantly, Alyosha is not divine and he bears the mark of the Karamazovs. But the 'basis of similarity' from which they diverge is Christ.

There are numerous metaphorical and metonymical correspondences between Alyosha and Christ. Most important are the symbolic ones. We may take as a definition of a symbol Losev's idea that a symbol contains a 'generative principle'.[28] Once we know this principle, then all its various individual representations remind us of what it symbolises. In *The Brothers Karamazov* Christ is the dominant transcendental generative symbol whose many-faceted features can be reflected in an infinite series of representations. This means that every Christological feature of Alyosha will remind us of Christ, the prototype. We can indicate only a few.[29]

A number of direct and hidden biblical quotations associate Alyosha with Christ, for example, Rakitin's sarcastic taunt that Alyosha has 'turned the sinner' (Grushenka). The narrator's emphasis on Alyosha's refusal to judge others is a reminiscence of Christ's declaration: 'I came not to judge the world but to save the world' (John 12:47). Then, the author reserved for Alyosha (and Zosima) the most transcendental episode of the novel where his hero beholds 'our Sun'. One outstanding Christological trait of Alyosha is his innate gift ('from the cradle') for arousing universal love and respect. Others are his role as an absorber of others' suffering and his loving involvement with children. Also of particular importance is his singularity.

We recall that the author stresses Alyosha's singularity at the outset. The characters go on to confirm it by recognising it as well. Miusov pronounces him 'the only man in the world' who, left alone in a strange city, would be immediately taken care of. Fyodor calls him his 'only son' and 'the only one' who never judged him. Grushenka tells him she 'has been waiting for him' all her life. Everyone believes 'only' him. This emphasis on the hero's beneficient singularity yields another synonymous parallel to Christ. As Starobinski says: 'Jesus, permanent hero of the evangelical narrative, is the immutable representative of the singular'.[30]

Alyosha's appellations are another symbolic aspect of his Christological representation. Besides 'angel', he is also called 'cherub' and *skhimnik*. A *skhimnik* is a monk who has taken on the strictest rules, the *skhima*, which Dal' defines as the 'great angelic image'. In the Orthodox Church the image of *le Christ-Ange*, says Meyendorff, 'designates his mission in the world: it is in so far as it is incarnated that the Logos is a 'messenger' of God'.[31] Grushenka's calling him "prince" is clearly a Christological reminiscence (14,314,316). The name of Alyosha's mother is another facet of Christological iconography: 'Sophia was also considered a figure of Christ'. Alyosha's extraordinary resemblance to his mother is an additional Christological component of his image; Christ became incarnate and hence representable only through His mother whom He naturally resembled. Introducing Alyosha in his hagiographical childhood memoir, the narrator calls him an 'early lover of man' (*chelovekoliubets*). The Russian word not only has, as Børtnes says, 'strong Christological overtones', but is one of the synonyms of Christ.[32] In the Orthodox Prayerbook, we find it in various formulaic invocations to Christ which would have been well known to Dostoevsky.[33] Alyosha's face is also a reflection of the symbol of Christ. Volynsky long ago observed that it is the face of an icon.[34] We may take this observation further. Alyosha's radiant face is repeatedly seen by others as a salvational visage. Zosima sends Alyosha to Mitya because, he says, 'I thought your brotherly face (*lik*) would help' (14,259). After his nightmare Ivan says to Alyosha: 'Yes, you drove him away: he disappeared when you appeared. I love your face, Alyosha. Did you know that I love your face?' (15,87) This suggests a face reminiscent of Christ the icon of God, the canonical source being: 'he that seeth Me seeth Him that sent Me' (John 12:45, 14:9). All these features are symbolic figures of Christ.

Another Christological motif is 'the one who is sent'.

Alyosha is no ordinary messenger. In his 'Confession of an Ardent Heart', Mitya tells Alyosha: 'I could have sent anyone, but I needed to send an angel <...> You're an angel on the earth', phrases which echo the well known hagiographical formula of the saint as 'a heavenly man and an earthly angel' (*nebesnyi chelovek, zemnoi angel*), as a mediator between the two spheres and thus a figure of the divine Mediator (14,97).

Later, Dostoevsky extends this idea. In the chapter 'Not You, Not You!', Ivan's obsessional inner conflict has become dangerously acute, leading him to the onset of madness. Now Alyosha speaks urgently to Ivan's better side:

But he was already speaking, as it were, outside himself, not of his own will, as though obeying some irresistible command. – You've been accusing yourself and confessing to yourself that the murderer is no one else but you. But you didn't murder, you are mistaken, you're not the murderer, do you hear me, not you! God sent me to tell you this. <...> I said this word to you for your whole life: it was *not you*! Do you hear, for your whole life. And it was God who put it into my soul to tell you this. (15,40)

Here the action of God in the text is laid bare. For there are two subjects here: God, Whose will guides Alyosha's words, and Alyosha who does God's will. God is the transcendent subject, absent in His person but present in spirit. But because Alyosha is present in person, he can carry out that 'irresistible command' in the world. This transforms him at once into protagonist, hero and a figure of Christ. Christ is pre-eminently the One Who is sent. Alyosha's 'God sent me', and 'God put it into my soul' are hidden quotations of Christ's frequent references to His having been sent by the Father (John 8:18, 12:45). As such, they have been internalised, completely integrated into Alyosha's inner life. Thus Alyosha forms a synecdochical relation to Christ, a part of the 'whole'. Here Alyosha sees himself as a divine messenger giving us the analogy as God sent Christ so He sent Alyosha and thus another important similarity relation between Alyosha and Christ. Moreover, Alyosha is not simply a passive vessel of the Word, a neutral deliverer of a message, but he actively strives, as Bakhtin puts it, to interfere in Ivan's tortuous inner dialogue, helping him to find a way out from hell. And since Alyosha is trying to save Ivan according to God's 'command', this means that God is not absent, that He has, so to speak, been watching over Ivan, that He forgives, loves and remembers Ivan too. Zosima sent Alyosha from the monastery to save his brothers, and later a wider world. But there has been a fundamental shift in the sender; the 'someone' who visited Alyosha's soul after Zosima's death has taken the elder's place. Alyosha now speaks with the consciousness that he lives solely under God's 'command'. He alone thus assumes one of Christ's greatest functions, that of the Saviour.

This brings us back to the question of how we are to see fulfilment in this novel. Fulfilment implies a lack supplied, the satisfaction of a desire. Here we may apply Vitz's analysis of the 'sacred subject' to Alyosha. As Vitz has shown, a hagiographical hero is created with a different conception of desire/fulfilment, and consequently of subject/object, from the protagonists of modern narratives and secular stories.[35] The object of the saint's deepest desire is God, he wishes to love Him, to serve Him, to do His will and ultimately to see Him 'face to face'. However, his relation to his object, his desire for it, is paradoxical. For his 'Object is both absent and present; hidden, to be enjoyed fully only in the future, in paradise, yet constantly possessed, through prayer or meditation'. Alyosha desires above all to find a way to the 'light of love' and to see the 'true Kingdom of Christ' on earth. But these are not just passive wishes. He made a conscious choice to 'live for God and immortality'. And since he willed this path, he is a full subject in his own right. At the same time, he is always a subordinate subject because he subordinates his will to the will of God. God is the subject and object of his life, absent and present. Without Alyosha's love for God and his will to prayer and service, his epiphany in 'Cana of Galilee' would be only a 'manifestation of God's power'. Without God as the subject of his life, 'we may have a hero <...> but we cannot have a saint'. Therefore Alyosha's willing, loving service to God entails a double subject. In fact, a saint always forms a double subject with God; they cannot be torn apart without destroying the hagiographical structure and idea. In so far as others in the novel share this desire, they too form a double subject with God. When they reject Him, Dostoevsky supplies them with the devil as their twin subject. 'We are with *him*', says the Inquisitor, and so are all those who will to serve '*him*'. No one is alone in *The Brothers Karamazov*, no one is separate from other powers, good or evil.

There are also suggestive narrative arrangements underlying Alyosha's Christological image. The narrator's repeated comments that Alyosha remembered something 'for his whole life' could simply mean what it logically implies, namely, that he can see his hero's 'whole life' because he has outlived him. If so, then further interesting inferences suggest themselves. The narrator is relating the events of 'exactly thirteen years ago' when his hero was twenty-years old. Alyosha's Life of Zosima breaks off abruptly, to be immediately followed by the narrator's account of Zosima's last moments. Hagiographers usually represent the deaths of their subjects. Did Alyosha's sudden death intervene before he could complete the Life? There is a well established literary convention of narrators obtaining manuscripts of deceased persons which they pretend to pass on to the reader. Indeed, Dostoevsky used this device in *The House of the Dead* which begins with the fictitious narrator finding the hero's posthumous manuscript containing his 'disconnected description' of his ten years in the prison camp. The 'author' of *The Brothers Karamazov* calls himself the 'biographer' of his hero, but a biography is usually written after the subject's death. If Dostoevsky did consider having Alyosha die in his second novel, this would mean that he died in his thirty third year, the same age as Christ when He completed His mission on earth. This is not a matter of drawing inferences solely on the basis of coincidental chronologies. The age thirty-three is another particular aspect of the symbol of Christ. An author who surrounds his hero with 'twelve' boy-disciples at the end of his novel would hardly be averse to having him die at thirty three. Symbolic parallels inevitably generate such associations.

One of Dostoevsky's cherished projects, which he did not

live to accomplish, was to write a book about 'Jesus Christ'. *The Brothers Karamazov*, more than any other of his works, bears evidence of this ideal artistic project coming to fruition. Dostoevsky's transfigurations of his characters into figures of Christ, are really postfigures who in various ways fulfil the prototype. But they always and inevitably fall short of it. Their fulfilments can never be perfectly realised since Christ alone is the perfect fulfilment of what was prefigured in the Old Testament and, at the same time, the perfect prefiguration of what is to come 'in the fullness of time'. Christ is the hero of Dostoevsky's ideal novel which did not get written, but which symbolically structures his last novel. Alyosha most closely approximates a fulfilment of that ideal. Dmitry may be the hero of the story, Ivan the great ideological protagonist, but Alyosha is the hero of *The Brothers Karamazov*, as the author said.

CHAPTER 9

Afterword

The importance of memory in *The Brothers Karamazov* gains an added dimension when seen against the background of Dostoevsky's notes and diaries during the last years of his life where we find many reflections on memory. *Muzhik Marei* is a reminiscence about a compassionate peasant based on an episode from his own childhood.[1] In a 'Memento, For my whole life' of 1877, Dostoevsky made a note of four future literary projects, all of which are grounded on memory: 'to write a Russian Candide, a book about Jesus Christ', his 'reminiscences' and a 'poem Sorokoviny' (the prayers said 40 days after a person's decease).[2] All these elements found their way into *The Brothers Karamazov*. The essential goodness of the simple Russian people as the repository of the true Christian spirit is one of Zosima's main themes. The philosophical tale and the polemic with Voltaire's ideas are among the major thematic and generic components of the novel. Fictional reminiscences shape its form, the theme of remembrance fills its content, and Christ is its generative ideal. The 'Sorokoviny' theme also occurs in the novel: metaphorically in Mitya's torments (*mytarstva*); concretely, in the funeral supper for Ilyusha; and mystically, in Alyosha's vision of the feast of the resurrected in Heaven. All the novel's commemorative, resurrectional and prophetic currents are reaching for an imitation of Christ on earth. All its negations of the meaning of Christ's verbal image become imitations of the devil. Thus, the novel is organised by one system governed by one idea. The poetic integration of the novel's memory system is truly extraordinary. We cannot take any aspect of this system, we cannot even select a single significant textual fragment for analysis without pulling the whole novel along with it.

Alyosha, future saint, hagiographer, the prophetic bearer and reminder of Christ's verbal image is the fullest embodiment in *The Brothers Karamazov* of Dostoevsky's Christian ideal. However, the author's 'sorrow' and 'doubt' that he will not succeed in 'proving' to his readers the remarkableness of his hero have proved prophetic. Few readers and interpreters find him convincing. This is because, as Børtnes remarks, most modern readers have 'interpreted Aleša on the conventions of the realistic novel', but to read Alyosha in this way is like 'judging a Russian icon according to the conventions of nineteenth century realistic painting'.[3] Realism has been the dominant trend in the novel for almost two centuries and the one within which we make our critical judgments about literature. But in *The Brothers Karamazov*, continues Børtnes, 'Dostoevsky has burst the conventions of the realistic novel'. The main aim of this interpretative study has been to show that he achieved this break largely through the poetic uses of Christian memory. For the image of Alyosha has been created on the basis of the older poetic codes of hagiography, iconography, religious folklore, early passion literature and the Bible, codes and traditions which the increasing secularisation of the world has deactivated or virtually obliterated from our present volume of cultural memory. Dostoevsky re-activated these ancient codes, words and genres, in a nineteenth-century novel in order to express what were for him absolute values. Every significant revitalisation of older codes results in a set of variations which are, at the same time, a resurrection of cultural and collective memories. Codes are invariant structures, and the codes of Christianity rely above all on symbols and figural interpretation.

Mirsky rightly remarked many years ago that Dostoevsky is 'a symbolist' for whom 'all relative values were related to absolute values and received their significance, positive or negative, from the way they reflected higher values'.[4] But Dostoevsky was a symbolist of a very particular type and he located the source of absolute values within the particular symbolic system of Christianity. Moreover, as soon as we appeal to the difference between relative and absolute values, we become involved with a larger philosophical problem which Wittgenstein elucidated in his lecture on ethics, a term he used in a wider sense to include not only 'the good' but, significantly, 'the most essential part of what is generally called Aesthetics'.[5] As Wittgenstein has shown, every judgment, every statement of relative value can be converted into a mere statement of fact, but 'no statement of fact can ever be, or imply, a judgment of absolute value'. Ethics and religion are concerned with absolute values, with the attempt to express what is most important, what is intrinsically noble, sublime and good. If we attempt to say scientifically (or referentially) what Ethics is, 'nothing we could ever think or say should be *the* thing'. Language is capable only of containing and conveying facts, '*natural* meaning and sense'. But 'Ethics, if it is anything, is supernatural'. Whenever we wish to express absolute values we constantly resort to similes, which is to say, we are compelled to use language symbolically. All 'ethical and religious expressions' seem to be 'just *similes*', allegories (Christ is like the sun, the Word is like a corn of wheat, the roots of our feelings lie in other worlds). But whenever we attempt to designate the fact behind the simile, we find that 'there are no such facts' and our similes seem to be nonsense. And there never will be any propositions adequate to describe the absolute values contained in religious expressions because 'their nonsensicality' is 'their very essence'. What is most important about the world (absolute values) lies beyond the world, and 'beyond significant language'. And so it is that 'the tendency of all men who ever tried to write or talk Ethics or Religion was to run against the boundaries of language'. Christianity is a system of memory thrusting against the limits of language, it expresses its meanings primarily through symbols. Christ spoke mainly in parables, similes and metaphors, one of which Dostoevsky chose for the Epigraph to his last novel. So, in the light of Wittgenstein's arguments, were we to excise the Christian symbolic system embedded in *The Brothers Karamazov*, we would still retain a dramatic description of a case of parricide with all the physical and psychological details of the crime, the pain and mayhem it caused, as well as a representation of the characters' ideas, value judgments, and so on. But in the end all we would have would be an assemblage of 'facts, facts and facts but not Ethics'. Nothing in this description would contain an absolute ethical proposition or judgment as to why we should not commit parricide and why we should be our brother's keeper. Thus, when Ivan says, in the positivist ideological idiom of his time, that he wants only to stick to facts, he is hopelessly lost in the realm of relative values. And when Ivan insists on logical explanations, Alyosha can only remind him to love in spite of logic. And when he protests against the suffering in the world, Alyosha can only invoke Christ's unique redemptive sacrifice. But Ivan, by sticking to positivism, rationalism and halfheartedly preaching nihilism, has cut himself off from that standard of absolute moral values which, in Dostoevsky's view, resides in Christ, Who gave us the model for creating the Kingdom on earth. 'The symbols of Christianity are wonderful beyond words', said Wittgenstein, but one cannot make a philosophical system out of them.[6] They are not reducible to facts or susceptible to refutation by logic. Thus, we could say that Ivan is defeated just as much by the symbolism of the novel as by its rhetoric and causally determined denouements. In this view, the fundamental relationship in Dostoevsky's poetics is not between cause and effect, but between the symbol and the symbolised.

The Brothers Karamazov is permeated with biblical symbols which contain an infinitude of meanings and associations. A symbol is 'a kind and not a single thing', it contains the 'generative law' of its own individual representations.[7] A general law can never be fully realised; it remains a potentiality which endlessly points to the indefinite future. The ideal symbol which generates the whole novel is Christ. The presence of so many variations on this symbol, negative and positive, attests to the richness of Dostoevsky's conception of Christ. Moreover, a novel whose generative model is based on the Christian symbolic system continuously implies someone who interprets the symbolism. This is why none of our readings will ever say *the* definitive thing about Dostoevsky's last novel. At the same time these symbols are very resistant to subversion or reduction into something radically different from what they signify. As we have seen, even when mocked, parodied or denied they keep reasserting their genuine original life. This is why they served Dostoevsky so well. The power which his art continues to exert depends largely on the enduring attraction of symbols and their inexhaustible capacity for generating variations. Dostoevsky's mastery lies not in having created the symbols, or the associations generated by them, but in the way he put them into his images of thinking, speaking, feeling and acting persons who have themselves become symbols which are still expanding. This is one sense in which a great artistic work transcends its author.

Dostoevsky has often been called a prophet. When people say this, they usually have in mind his extraordinary gift for detecting the destructive potential of those emerging world views which led to modern totalitarianism. Our study of poetic memory in *The Brothers Karamazov* suggests that this sense of prophecy we ascribe to Dostoevsky has also something to do with the prominence of prefiguration and figural interpretation as the fundamental structuring principles of his art. True, many of the novel's discourses reflect Dostoevsky's ideological preoccupations and polemics with his contemporaries about the future of Russia. Still, whatever Dostoevsky's publicistic aims may have been, when it came to his creative literary work, he never forgot that he was first and foremost an artist. Thus, however important prophecy is ideologically, from the point of view of poetic memory, the pair prefiguration/fulfilment is hierarchically more important. Since the figural patterns are heavily invested with symbols, they give rise to innumerable prefigurations within the novel, prefigurations of the murder, Ivan's nightmare, Smerdyakov's suicide, Alyosha's last speech, the Kingdom, and this is why this study has repeatedly returned to those scenes and images. These figural patterns form parallels based on similar symbolic motifs which are consistently fused with similar ideational content. The novel's hidden prefigurative meanings can only be understood after we have read the novel and are able to link the foreshadowing parts with their correlative fulfilments. This involves us in a dialogic activity in the process of giving meaning to the text. It is our memory acts of association, recognition and retrospection which bridge the correlative parts and supply our understanding with a sense of spiritual fulfilment. Every memory is a prophecy, every prophecy a memory. The figural patterns are the most important poetic structures in *The Brothers Karamazov*.

Prefiguration rests not only on our memory of the text's own fictional content, but also on cultural memory. The archaic definition of memory is: 'A ceremony of commemoration: a service for the dead'. *The Brothers Karamazov* is Dostoevsky's novel of commemoration in the fullest sense. It memorialises the fathers, carnal and spiritual (Fyodor, Snegirov and Zosima), the forefathers (the saints and elders of legend) and God the Father. 'Culture', said Ivanov, 'is the cult of the departed, and Eternal Memory is the soul of its life, congregational [*sobornoi*] for the most part and based on tradition'.[8] Dostoevsky brought his text together with tradition through figural interpretation. In *The Brothers Karamazov*, the soul of eternal memory receives its most condensed expression in the Epigraph where Christ prophesies two possibilities: if the corn of wheat does not fall to earth and die, 'it abideth alone'; if it does, then 'it bringeth forth much fruit'. On this opposition the novel's dramatic enactment of the *pro* and *contra* was formed. Ivan's Legend and nightmare devil are fulfilments of the first possibility; Alyosha's Life of Zosima and dream vision are fulfilments of the second. Each brother describes a passion motif which is either fulfilled (Mitya and Alyosha), truncated (Smerdyakov) or half accomplished (Ivan). Thus the whole novel enacts a progressive metaphorical fulfilment of the Epigraph which is the master prefiguration of *The Brothers Karamazov*.

Ivan's Legend is a prefiguration projected into the past of the atheistic socialist utopia of his contemporaries which opens onto the nightmarish parody of the universe in the devil's vision. The novel closes, though, with an image of Christ's second possibility where the theme of resurrection sounds in full symphony in a scene configured into an imitation of Christ with Alyosha founding his new 'church' of twelve boys. Affirming the resurrection for all, Alyosha reaffirms Christ's words in the Epigraph. The boys shout in chorus the refrain of the funeral service, 'eternal memory'. This novel suggests that 'eternal memory' is equivalent to 'eternal life'. In *The Brothers Karamazov* this idea describes a great circle from the Epilogue to the Epigraph and back again. The final scene combines a fulfilment of Markel's vision of 'paradise on earth' and of Alyosha's dream of 'the true Kingdom of Christ'. At the same time it is a prefiguration of another fulfilment to come, the Second Coming and the second novel in an anagogical sense. Alyosha designates his commemorative speech as a memory for the future. It opens up the novel's perspective onto the immediate future of the brothers, the long-range future of the boys and time-transcending eternity since it is a prefiguration of the Kingdom and eternal life. The novel stands as an organic and artistically complete whole on its own. And yet it remains open as well. In the concluding words to her study, Perlina justly remarks that 'the concept of The Word is all-encompassing and unfinalized by its essence. It continually evokes new responses and echoes in the unlimited future. In this sense' the novel 'need not and must not be completed'.[9] In the new context of a nineteenth-century Russian novel, we are reunited through poetic memory with the ancient biblical texts and with what Dostoevsky believed to be their eternal truths. Memory is a divine gift for, in Ivanov's words: 'By memory we are reunited with the Beginning and with the Word which was in the Beginning'. Such was the overriding aim of the author of *The Brothers Karamazov*.

Memory is a going back to the experience (texts) of the past. The fictitious present of *The Brothers Karamazov* is gone. The 'present moment' of the author–narrator, which was thirteen years later for Dostoevsky, is also gone. For us, they go back over one hundred years. By continuing the dialogue about *The Brothers Karamazov*, we keep the memory of Dostoevsky's art alive.

Memory is also a bringing back, for the present, but most of all for the sake of creating a programme for the future. Since *The Brothers Karamazov* is Dostoevsky's great dialogue on the future of Russia and humanity, it is also addressed to history, to the ages to come. The dialogue of *The Brothers Karamazov* represents an open system because it opens onto two radically different perspectives of the unbounded future. The fates of the brothers are unresolved and so are their opposed beliefs, so is the *pro* and *contra*. The novel also defeats any attempt at absolute closure because of its prevailing symbolism. Most of all, the novel's open-endedness has to do with the very nature of the Word as a representative of eternal memory in its continuously creative interaction with the world. Ideas and trends may come and go, events recede into the past, but the Word can never die, not only because of its unfinalisable essence, but also because, for Dostoevsky, the Word has still not been fully uttered. We are all 'unfinished', said Dostoevsky, 'transitional', but transitional *to* something. The definitive culminating event is yet to come. In memory lies the seed of a 'latent, still unuttered' Word yet to be said, the germ of a final consummation of all events in the future. In these various senses *The Brothers Karamazov* remains open, perhaps indefinitely extensible. If it is open, it is open to the future, to its future readers and interpreters, to its continuing life in the future.

Notes

1. MEMORY AND POETICS

1 Leonid Grossman, 'Put' Dostoevskogo', *Tvorchestvo Dostoevskogo: Sbornik statei i materialov*, ed. L. P. Grossman (Chicago, 1970), 83–108 (p. 108).

2 Mikhail Bakhtin, *Problems of Dostoevsky's Poetics*, ed. and trans. Caryl Emerson (Minneapolis, 1984), 121. Here and below I have slightly altered Emerson's translation.

3 My exposition combines several ideas taken from the following papers of Roman Jakobson: 'Two Aspects of Language and Two Types of Aphasic Disturbances', *Selected Writings* (hereafter abbreviated as *SW*) II (The Hague, 1971), 239–59; 'Quest for the Essence of Language', *SW*, II (The Hague, 1971), 345–59; 'Linguistics and Poetics', *SW*, III (The Hague, 1981), 18–51.

4 See William James, *The Principles of Psychology* (Cambridge, Massachusetts, 1983), 317.

5 My account is largely based on the following two articles whose ideas I have conflated for ease of exposition: Iu. Lotman and B. Uspensky, 'O semioticheskom mekhanizme kul'tury', *Trudy po znakovym sistemam*, v (Tartu, 1971), 144–66; and Iury M. Lotman, 'Pamiat' v kul'turologicheskom osveshchenii', *Wiener Slawistischer Almanach*, 16 (Vienna, 1985), 5–9.

6 For a persuasive attack on theories of 'evolution' and 'progress' in literary art, see O. Mandel'shtam, 'O prirode slova', *Proza* (Ann Arbor, Michigan, 1983), 55–72 (pp. 57–8).

7 Maurice Halbwachs, *The Collective Memory*, trans. Francis J. Ditter, Jr and Vida Yazdi Ditter (New York, 1980), 33.

8 Mikhail Bakhtin, *Problems*, 202.

9 *Ibid.*, 106, 121.

10 See Frances A. Yates, *The Art of Memory* (Penguin Books, 1978).

11 Lotman and Uspensky, 'O semioticheskom mekhanizme kul'tury', p. 149.

12 Sigurd Fasting, 'Transformacija "filantropičeskix" ėpizodov u Dostoevskogo', *International Dostoevsky Studies*, 1 (1980), 65–72 (pp. 70–1).

13 Nina Perlina, *Varieties of Poetic Utterance: Quotation in The Brothers Karamazov* (Lanham, 1985), 72.

14 Just here a problem arises for many modern readers. As Lotman points out, the memory of the genre does not in itself guarantee full intelligibility. Our age has a 'different volume of cultural memory'. The recent extensive commentaries to *The Brothers Karamazov* testify to Lotman's qualification. Now, in the late twentieth century, interpretation faces a difficulty owing to the decreasing familiarity with the Bible, not to speak of the virtual ignorance of saints' lives and their peculiar poetics. It was a difficulty already acutely felt by Dostoevsky: 'No one knows the Bible anymore', he complains in his Notes (15,206). Nowadays the Bible is read differently, often being treated as a work of literary art or as a quasi-historical, cultural document rather than a repository of truth and revelation. Even so, the fact that Dostoevsky's last novel has become a classic of world literature sufficiently confirms Bakhtin's and Lotman's arguments about the enduring nature of cultural invariants.

15 See Nina Perlina, *Varieties of Poetic Utterance*, and Victor Terras's 'Introduction' in *A Karamazov Companion* (Madison, Wisconsin, 1981), 3–38.

16 Halbwachs, *The Collective Memory*, 51–2.

17 I. A. Richards, *Principles of Literary Criticism* (London and Henley, 1976), 81.

18 Ludwig Wittgenstein, *Philosophical Investigations I*, trans. G. E. M. Anscombe (Oxford, 1958), 110.

19 *Ibid.*, 231.

20 Halbwachs, *The Collective Memory*, 33. Not surprisingly, Halbwachs rejects free will and finds that every human thought or act 'is always governed by the law of causality', p. 49.

21 *Ibid.*, 23.

22 Bakhtin, *Problems*, 28–9.

23 A. R. Luria, 'Memory', *The Working Brain* (Penguin Books, 1973), 285.

2. THE FICTIONAL NARRATOR

1 F. K. Stanzel, *A Theory of Narrative*, trans. Charlotte Goedsche (Cambridge, 1984), 14.

2 Roman Jakobson, 'Linguistics and Poetics', *SW*, III (The Hague, 1981), 18–51 (pp. 24, 26).

3 This is what Stanzel calls the 'primal motivation of all narration'. *A Theory of Narrative*, 17.

4 Roman Jakobson, 'Linguistics and Poetics', 22.

5 The fact that the introduction is an authorial address to the reader has led some critics to believe that the 'author' here is Dostoevsky himself. According to Vetlovskaia this is because Dostoevsky and his narrator 'share the same ideological orientation'. Certainly one is more aware of Dostoevsky *qua* author just at this point, but there is an unbreachable boundary between him and his narrator nonetheless, and that is the boundary drawn by mediation. Vetlovskaia finds that the boundary here between Dostoevsky and the narrator is 'effaced'. She argues that 'either the author adopts the turns of speech of his future narrator, or the author of this introduction and the fictitious narrator are the same person' (*Poetika*, 21). However, once an author adopts another's 'turns of speech', he is already involved in a mimesis of another's image which has to be created from his imagination. This is particularly so since the 'author' is not telling his autobiography. Furthermore, as soon as the 'author' begins telling his story, any illusion of identity between him and Dostoevsky is quickly dispelled, since it is abundantly clear that the Dostoevsky we know from history and the rather naive provincial narrator cannot be the same person. Finally, the narrator who proceeds to tell the story carries on as if he and the 'author' were the same person, and he reminds us of this identity subsequently. Belknap, arguing from a different perspective, also concludes that the author of the foreword 'is not Dostoevskij, but the fictional character who tells the story'. Robert L. Belknap, *The Structure of The Brothers Karamazov* (The Hague, 1967), 108.

6 Stanzel, *A Theory of Narrative*, 201, 205.

7 A. Mendilow, *Time and the Novel* (New York, 1965), 106–7.

8 K. Hamburger, *The Logic of Literature*, trans. M. J. Rose (Bloomington, Indiana, 1973), 70–1, 81.

9 Stanzel, *A Theory of Narrative*, 205.

10 Vetlovskaia, *Poetika romana 'Brat'ja Karamazovy'* (Leningrad, 1977), 13–51.

11 Robert L. Belknap, *The Structure of The Brothers Karamazov*, 78.

12 N. Malcolm, 'Three Lectures on Memory', *Knowledge and Certainty* (Englewood Cliffs, New Jersey, 1964), 191.

13 Vetlovskaia, *Poetika*, 17.

14 *Ibid.*, 19.

15 M. M. Bakhtin, *Estetika slovesnogo tvorchestva* (Moscow, 1979), 94–5.

16 Stanzel, *A Theory of Narrative*, 216.

17 As Genette explains: 'A first person narrative lends itself better than any other to anticipation, by the very fact of its avowedly retrospective character, which authorises the narrator to allude to the future'. Gérard Genette, *Narrative Discourse*, trans. Jane E. Lewin (Oxford, 1980), 67.

18 The 'eccentric beginning' of the official Perkhotin's future career, he remarks, 'is still remembered in our little town, and perhaps we shall say a special word about it when we have concluded our long story about the brothers Karamazov' (14,406). It is interesting that this unrealised project was also conceived as a fictional memoir.

19 Jan M. Meijer, 'A Note on Time in *Brat'ja Karamazovy*', *Dutch Studies in Russian Literature* 2 (The Hague, 1971), 54.

20 'From the Author' was written in 1878 when Dostoevsky began the novel. Thus the idea of a sequel occurred before he wrote the novel we have. Vetlovskaia realises the importance of this for Dostoevsky's whole conception of *The Brothers Karamazov* when she concludes that 'the work's overall structure, its foundation must certainly be in place in the work as we know it – even partially visible' (*Poetika*, 162).

21 William James, *The Principles of Psychology* (Cambridge, Massachusetts, 1983), 640.

3. MEMORY AND THE SYSTEM OF ASCENDING PLOTS

1 Gessen distinguishes three 'plans', viz, the 'empirical–psychological', the 'metaphysical' and the 'mystical'. V. Ivanov also discerns three 'plans' of what he calls 'human life', viz, the 'plot', the 'psychological' and the 'mystical', and Vetlovskaia divides the novel into a 'concrete plan' and a 'general plan'. Neuhäuser differentiates 'five levels': the 'bellestristic, philosophical, polemical, allegorical' and 'ideological'. Ivanov calls the novel a 'tragedy–novel', Grossman, a 'mystery play–novel', Bitsilli, a 'drama–novel', Vetlovskaia, a 'philosophical-publicistic novel', while Bakhtin sees the Dostoevskian novel as a new genre, as the first exemplar of the 'polyphonic novel'. See Bibliography for references.

2 Aristotle, 'Poetics', *Introduction to Aristotle*, ed. Richard McKeon (New York, 1947), 624–67 (pp. 637, 640). For example, Dostoevsky's plot depicts suffering, a tragic deed done within the family, actions which arouse pity and fear, unity of time, and an action (premeditated crime) which inevitably forms a whole with a beginning, middle and end.

3 These key phrases are variously rendered in English translations. As Sandoz has shown, Ivan's phrase 'all is permitted' (*vse poszvoleno*) is a verbatim quotation from the First Epistle to the Corinthians (6:12, 10:23) which the English Bible translates as 'all things are lawful'. However, the Russian Bible does not use *zakonnyi* (lawful) but *pozvoleno* (permitted, allowed) and hence the correct translation is 'permitted'. The importance of this biblical subtext will be considered in Chapter Five. Zosima's phrase, *vse za vsekh vinovaty* is translated as 'all are responsible [or guilty] for all'. This is not strictly accurate. Dostoevsky did not use the standard *otvetstvennyi* (responsible) or *vinovyi* (guilty), but *vinovaty* which lies somewhere between 'responsible' and 'guilty'. A closer English rendition is 'all are to blame for all', or, 'we are all at fault'. Unlike 'responsible', *vinovaty* expresses one's sympathy for, and apology to, another; one is painfully aware of the suffering one has caused another. This important nuance accords with Zosima's theology of the inseparable bond between all people which urges an acknowledgment of one's own share in the world's injustice and a willingness to co-suffer (*so-stradat'*) with others.

4 See her excellent analysis of the plot in: V. E. Vetlovskaia, 'Razviazka v *Brat'iakh Karamazovykh*', *Poetika i stilistika russkoi literatury: Pamiati akademika Viktora Valdimirovicha Vinogradova* (Leningrad, 1971), 195–203 (p. 202).

5 Aristotle, 'Poetics', 635–6.

6 Mikhail Bakhtin, *Problems of Dostoevsky's Poetics*, ed. and trans. Caryl Emerson (Minneapolis, 1984), 277, 296. All citations in this chapter from Bakhtin are taken from this translation. Page numbers are indicated in brackets at the end of the sentences.

7 Vetlovskaia, 'Razviazka', 202.

8 Stanzel, *A Theory of Narrative* (Cambridge, 1984), 17–18.

9 V. E. Vetlovskaia, *Poetika romana 'Brat'ja Karamazovy'* (Leningrad, 1977), 137.

10 Erich Auerbach, *Mimesis*, trans. Willard R. Trask (Princeton, New Jersey, 1974), 48.

11 Golosovker, approaching the problem from Kantian categories, comes to a similar conclusion: 'The essence of the matter here is not in the thesis or antithesis but in their eternal duel <...> in the battle, and not the victory'. Ia. E. Golosovker, *Dostoevskii i Kant: Razmyshlenie chitatelia nad romanom 'Brat'ia Karamazovy' i traktatom 'Kritika chistogo razuma'* (Moscow, 1963), 84.

12 *Pis'ma* IV, ed. A. S. Dolinin, (Moscow-Leningrad, 1928–59), 53, 56, 65, 91, 94, 114, 139.

13 E. M. Forster, *Aspects of the Novel* (Penguin Books, 1982), 87, 88.

14 *Ibid.*, 88–9.
15 Immanuel Kant, 'Degrees of Responsibility', *Readings in the problems of Ethics*, ed. Rosalind Ekman (New York, 1965), 234–40 (p. 237).
16 Auerbach, *Mimesis*, 555.
17 Riccardo Picchio, 'The Function of Biblical Thematic Clues in the Literary Code of "Slavia Orthodoxa"', *Slavica Hierosolymitana*, 1 (Jerusalem, 1977), 1–31 (pp. 5, 9).
18 Auerbach, *Mimesis*, 317.
19 Jostein Børtnes, 'Polyphony in *The Brothers Karamazov*: Variations on a Theme', *Canadian–American Slavic Studies*, 17, no. 3 (Fall 1983), 402–11 (p. 404).

4. THE MEMORIES OF THE CHARACTERS: FORMS OF AFFIRMATIVE MEMORY

1 Bakhtin–Vološinov, *Marxism and the Philosophy of Language*, trans. Ladislav Matejka and I. R. Titunik (New York, 1973), 138–40. This type is 'very close' to quasi-direct discourse.
2 Victor Terras, *A Karamazov Companion*, 133.
3 'Picture' is in general very apropos for conveying a memory. As von Leyden points out, a recollection is 'far from being a replica' but 'is at best more like a picture or portrait'. W. von Leyden, *Remembering: A Philosophical Problem* (London, 1961), 75.
4 Jury Lotman, *Analysis of the Poetic Text*, ed. and trans. D. B. Johnson (Ann Arbor, 1976), 88.
5 Jostein Børtnes, *Visions of Glory: Studies in Early Russian Hagiography* (Oslo, 1988), 21, 63, 82.
6 The opening line reads: 'Joyful light of holy glory, Jesus Christ, son of a deathless heavenly Father holy and blessed; we have come to the setting of the sun, and seeing the light of evening we celebrate the Father, Son and Holy Ghost as God.' *The Penguin Book of Greek Verse*, ed. Constantine A. Trypanis (Penguin Books, 1971), 359–60.
7 Dostoevsky's widow wrote apropos his admiration of Raphael's Sistine Madonna: 'Fedya sees sorrow (*skorb'*) in the smile of the Madonna'. A. G. Dostoevskaia, *Vospominaniia* (Moscow, 1971), 422. In *Crime and Punishment*, Svidrigailov alludes to Raphael's masterpiece with similar associations to suffering: 'You know, the Sistine Madonna has a fantastic face, the face of a sorrowful fool-in-God (*iurodivaia*)' (6,369).
8 See Jostein Børtnes, 'To Dostoevskijstudier', *Edda*, 1968, 2–16; *Visions*, 279–80; and V. E. Vetlovskaia, *Poetika*, 161–98.

9 This topos, says Curtius, was 'especially frequent in the *vita sancti*'. Ernst Robert Curtius, *European Literature and the Latin Middle Ages* (London and Henley, 1979), 159–60.

10 Vetlovskaia, *Poetika*, 166.

11 Erich Auerbach, *Mimesis*, 12.

12 Nathan Rosen, 'Style and Structure in *The Brothers Karamazov*', *Russian Literature Triquarterly*, 1 (1971), 352–65 (p. 363).

13 Fedor Dostoevskii, *Neizdannyi Dostoevskii: Zapisnye knizkhi i tetradi: 1860–1881*, ed. V. R. Shcherbina, *Literaturnoe nasledstvo*, 83 (Moscow, 1971), 453.

14 Zosima's account is a freely paraphrased version of the original. See (15,532).

15 In Dostoevsky's words: 'It is not a sermon but a king of story, a tale about his own life'. *Pis'ma*, IV, 59.

16 As Dostoevsky remarked in a letter, 'it stands to reason that this manuscript is compositionally organised by Aleksei Karamazov in his own way'. *Pis'ma*, IV, 92.

17 *Pis'ma*, 110.

18 Nina Perlina, *Varieties*, 25. Perlina makes this observation in connection with the fact that Zosima never quotes Pushkin who, for Dostoevsky, was a paragon of poetic beauty and truth.

19 *Pis'ma*, IV, 92.

20 Jostein Børtnes, 'Polyphony in *The Brothers Karamazov*: Variations on a Theme', *Canadian–American Slavic Studies* (Fall, 1983) 402–11 (p. 409). Jacques Catteau also emphasises the Christian significance of the solar image which he calls 'un signe mystagogique'. See his interesting discussion of this symbol in Dostoevsky's works in *La Création Littéraire chez Dostoïevski* (Paris, 1978), 544–7.

21 Quoted in *Recollections of Wittgenstein*, ed. Rush Rhees (Oxford, 1984) 182–3.

22 The main theme Dostoevsky said was 'to show [in Zosima] that a pure, ideal Christian is real <...> and that Christianity is the only refuge for Russia'. For the sake of this theme, 'the whole novel is being written'. Shortly after finishing it, Dostoevsky called it the 'culminating point of the novel' (*Pis'ma*, IV, 94, 59). We can gauge some idea of the importance of this Book for Dostoevsky from his further remark: 'I pray God that I may succeed, it will be a pathetic thing <...> I tremble' (p. 91).

23 For example, Lise's best early memories are of the times she spent with Alyosha 'the most serious friend of my childhood'. And Alyosha 'in former times <...> loved to call on her, and <...> to reminisce over childhood' (14,194,195).

24 See Linda J. Ivanits, 'Folk Beliefs About the "Unclean Force" in

The Brothers Karamazov', *New Perspectives in Nineteenth-Century Russian Prose*, ed. Lauren G. Leighton and Victor Terras (Columbus, 1982), 135–46; L. M. Lotman, 'Romany Dostoevskogo i russkaja legenda', *Russkaia literatura* 15 (1972), No. 2, 129–41; Vetlovskaia, *Poetika*, 161–92.

25 Roman Jakobson, 'On Russian Fairy Tales', *SW*, IV (The Hague, 1966), 82–100 (pp. 87–91).

26 James Joyce, *Stephen Hero* (London, 1969), 216–18.

27 In Dostoevsky's text 'Guardian Angel' begins with a capital 'A' (*Angel-xranitel'*). The English translations ignore this, thus cancelling another important nuance of the author.

28 Bakhtin, *Problems*, 262, 294.

29 Elizaveta Mnatsakanjan also emphasises the importance of the connection with childhood, innocence and confession. Only she is more interested in the psychology of writing than in distinguishing memory as a poetic structure different from psychology. See her article 'Znachenie i rol' vospominaniia v xudozhestvennoi praktike. Freid – Dostoevskii – Geine', *Wiener Slawistischer Almanach*, 16 (Vienna, 1985), 37–80 (pp. 52–7).

30 The editors of the *PSS* have drawn attention to the hagiographical motifs in Grushenka's threat to 'tear' her finery, to 'disfigure' her beauty and to go 'begging for alms' (15,572).

31 See V. E. Vetlovskaia, 'Dostoevskyi i poeticheskii mir drevnei Rusi', *Trudy Otdela Drevnerusskoi literatury*, 28, 296–307 (pp. 298–300).

32 Victor Terras, *A Karamazov Companion* (Madison, Wisconsin, 1981), 406.

33 Vetlovskaia, 'Razviazka', 199.

34 Terras, *A Karamazov Companion*, 324.

35 This quotation comes from a patristic text reproduced in Roman Jakobson's article, 'One of the Speculative Anticipations', SW, II (The Hague, 1971), 369–74 (p. 374).

36 *Neizdannyi Dostoevskii: Zapisnye knizhki i tetradi 1860–1881*, ed. V. R. Shcherbina, *Literaturnoe nasledstvo*, 83 (Moscow, 1971), 617.

37 *Pis'ma*, IV, 139.

38 *Biografiia, pis'ma i zametki iz zapisnoi knizhki F. M. Dostoevskago* (St Petersburg, 1883), 368–9. Dostoevsky expressed essentially the same idea in a note of 1877: 'Florent is dying from hunger and with pride he rejects the help of an honest woman. Zola considers this a great deed [*podvig*], but there is no brotherhood in this heart <...> Take help from her and render it to others from the fulness of a grateful heart. – Then there will be paradise on earth'. *Neizdannyi Dostoevskii*, 619. Grushenka's 'onion' is a fully realised illustration of this idea in *The Brothers Karamazov*.

5. THE MEMORIES OF THE CHARACTERS: FORMS
OF NEGATIVE MEMORY

1 Richard Peace, *Dostoyevsky: An Examination of the Major Novels*
(Cambridge, 1971), 285.
2 Immanuel Kant, 'Degrees of Responsibility', 237.
3 See Krystyna Pomorska, 'Poetics of Prose', in Roman Jakobson,
Verbal Art, Verbal Sign, Verbal Time (Minneapolis, 1985), 169–77.
4 N. Rosen notes the psychological importance of this obsession as
a determining factor in Smerdyakov's epilepsy. See his 'Freud on
Dostoevsky's Epilepsy: A Revaluation', *Dostoevsky Studies* 9
(1989), 107–25 (pp. 117–19).
5 Vetlovskaia, *Poetika*, 98–9.
6 *Ibid.*, 135–41.
7 William James, *The Principles of Psychology* (Cambridge, Massachusetts, 1983), 612, 314.
8 As Dostoevsky said, Ivan 'has gone so far away from the ancient
apostolic Orthodoxy, that he truly sees a real servant of Christ' in
his Inquisitor. 'The idea is that if you distort the Christian faith,
joining it with the aims of this world, then the whole meaning of
Christianity is at once lost, the mind must fall into unbelief'
(15,198).
9 Kant, 'Degrees of Responsibility', 239, 240.
10 Ellis Sandoz, *Political Apocalypse: A Study of Dostoevsky's Grand
Inquisitor* (Baton Rouge, 1971), 134. See also Nina Perlina's
discussion of this point in *Varieties*, 98–9.
11 William James, *Principles*, 914. James also quotes the well established logical proposition that 'all negation rests on a covert
assertion of something else than the thing denied'.
12 Norman Malcolm, 'Three Lectures on Memory', 237–8.

6. FORGETTING

1 Terras, *A Karamazov Companion*, 128.
2 *Neizdannyi Dostoevskii*, 674.
3 Robert L. Belknap, 'Memory in *The Brothers Karamazov*', 31.
4 Fyodor's threat is couched in two future perfective verbs: 'I'm
going to take it down', and 'I'm going to spit on it'.
5 In Dal' we find the saying: 'An eclipse takes place because the evil
spirit conceals God's light and in the darkness tries to ensnare
Christians in his nets'.
6 A. S. Pushkin, *Sobraniye sochinenii*, vol. 2 (Moscow, 1959), 210.
7 Dostoevsky's artistic visualisation, says Bakhtin, did not go 'into

the depths of the unconscious, but into the depths and heights of consciousness' (*Problems*, 288). Here is an instance where Dostoevsky's vision goes into the depths of the unconscious.

8 St Augustine, *Confessions*, trans. Vernon J. Bourke (Washington, D.C., 1953), 288.

9 Malcolm V. Jones, '"The Legend of The Grand Inquisitor": The Suppression of the Second Temptation and Dialogue with God', *Dostoevsky Studies*, 7 (1986), 123–34 (p. 125). See also Sandoz, *Political Apocalypse*, 152.

10 K. Mochul'sky, *Dostoevskii*, 492.

11 Belknap, 'Memory in *The Brothers Karamazov*', 33.

12 Vetlovskaia, *Poetika*, 98.

13 *Ibid.*, 98. Alyosha has another memory lapse of lesser significance. At the trial he suddenly recalls that Mitya was pointing to something around his neck: 'How could I have forgotten this until just now!' (15,10) Alyosha's recollection does not save Mitya, but it provides the only moment during the trial when 'fortune smiles on Mitya'.

14 *Ibid.*, 100.

15 Plato, *Cratylus*. See Bibliography for edition.

16 For example, Alyosha's news that Smerdyakov has hung himself comes as no surprise to Ivan, the last person who saw him alive: 'But I knew he hung himself <...> Yes, he [the devil] told me. He was just now speaking to me ... ' But the devil only told Ivan that Alyosha was bringing him some 'unexpected and curious news' (15,85,84).

17 Halbwachs, *The Collective Memory*, 157.

18 Nina Perlina, *Varieties*, 132.

19 Ivan may be quoting Feuerbach's *The Essence of Christianity* and Max Stirner's *The Ego and His Own*, both works known to Dostoevsky in his youth while a member of the Petrashevsky circle. According to Feuerbach, all the attributes of the divine nature are in fact attributes of the human nature. Man is the real god. Stirner went further still when he claimed that it was not only necessary to kill God, but also Man, the ideal of humanity. See Andrzej Walicki, *A History of Russian Thought from the Enlightenment to Marxism* (Stanford, California, 1979), 315–16. See also Frank's interesting account of the influence of Feuerbach, Stirner and Belinsky on Dostoevsky in *Dostoevsky, The Seeds of Revolt* (Princeton, 1976), 182–98.

20 Bakhtin, *Problems*, 287.

7. FORETELLING

1 Ludolf Müller, 'Die Religion Dostojewskijs', *Von Dostojewskij bis Grass*, Schriftsteller vor der Gottesfrage, ed. Wolfgang Bohne, Herrenalber Texte 71 (Karlsruhe, 1986), 30–59.

2 Bakhtin, *Problems of Dostoevsky's Poetics*, 90–1.

3 Lotman and Uspensky, 'O semioticheskom mekhanizme kul'tury', 148.

4 As Kermode points out: 'All plots have something in common with prophecy, for they must appear to educe from the prime matter of the situation the forms of a future.' Frank Kermode, *The Sense of an Ending* (New York, 1979), 83.

5 Gérard Genette, *Narrative Discourse*, trans. Jane E. Lewin (Oxford, 1980), 40.

6 Robert L. Belknap, 'Memory in *The Brothers Karamazov*', 30.

7 Vetlovskaia, *Poetika*, 193–6. 'Le mouvement du roman est une spirale presque parfaite dont *trois* est le nombre d'or'. Jacques Catteau, *La création littéraire chez Dostoïevski* (Paris, 1978), 462–4.

8 'Eccentric' and 'eccentricity' are flawed but inevitable translations of *chudak* and *chudachestvo* since there are no equivalents in English. The Russian words have very positive, affectionate connotations; the root 'chud-' means 'miracle', 'marvel', 'wonder'. The author left it to Miusov to use the Western loan word *ektsentrik* as an appellation for Ivan.

9 M. Bakhtin, *Problemy poetiki Dostoevskogo*, 174.

10 Jostein Børtnes, 'The Function of Hagiography in Dostoevskij's Novels', *Scando-Slavica*, 24 (1978), 27–33 (p. 29).

11 See Auerbach's discussion on how the idea of 'creatural realism' degenerated into a devaluation of life in the late Middle Ages, *Mimesis*, 246–50.

12 F. M. Dostoevsky, *Zapisnye tetradi F. M. Dostoevskogo* (Moscow–Leningrad, 1935), 179.

13 Auerbach, *Mimesis*, 49.

14 *Ibid.*, 158, also 16, 73.

15 Erich Auerbach, 'Figura', *Scenes from the Drama of European Literature, Theory and History of Literature*, 9 (Minneapolis, 1984), 11–76 (p. 53).

16 E. M. Forster, *Aspects of the Novel*, 122–3. Not surprisingly, his remarks occur in his chapter on 'Prophecy', which he calls a 'tone of voice' possessed only by the greatest artists, among whom he places Dostoevsky.

17 A. S. Pushkin, *Sobraniye sochinenii*, vol. 2 (Moscow, 1959), 297–8.

18 The author never brings Zosima and Smerdyakov face to face,

word to word. They inhabit the same geographic and novelistic world, but totally disjoint spiritual worlds. About Smerdyakov Zosima never says a word, let alone make prophecies for him. But then Smerdyakov has no future.

19 Alexander Golubov, 'Religious Imagery in the Structure of *The Brothers Karamazov*', *Russian and Slavic Literature: 1700–1917*, ed. Richard Freeborn (Bloomington, Indiana, 1976), 113–36, (p. 125).

20 The question of Alyosha's future has proved the most contentious. We can only base our analysis on the novel we have, and in *The Brothers Karamazov*, there is no solid evidence for any permanent, radical departure from Zosima's prophecy. On the contrary. The proof that Zosima's prophecy came true up to Alyosha's thirty-third year lies in the very existence of his Life of Zosima, and in the narrator's manifest respect for his hero's manuscript which he 'now', thirteen years later, includes in his novel. Furthermore, after his great dream vision, Alyosha, affirms the narrator, 'had fallen on the earth a weak youth, but he rose up a steadfast fighter for the rest of his life' (14,328). Had Alyosha undergone some permanent, total transformation in the second novel, Dostoevsky would have irredeemably undermined the reliability of his narrator, the clear authoritativeness of Zosima's and Paisy's words, the hagiographical representation of his hero, Alyosha's Life of Zosima and the ideal represented in it, the love and respect of virtually all of the characters and the children's trust in Alyosha ('We love you, we love you!') which closes the novel and foreshadows Alyosha's creation of an open community of brotherhood 'in the world'. Thus on textual evidence alone we can reject Suvorin's oft-quoted report that Dostoevsky intended to have Alyosha become a revolutionary and regicide. (See A. S. Suvorin, *Dnevnik*, ed. M. Krichevskii (Moscow–Petrograd, 1923), 16.) We do not even need the testimony of Dostoevsky's widow who, according to Hoffman, told her that her husband's plan was to have Alyosha end up in the monastery. Vetlovskaia rejects Suvorin's remark outright: 'Nothing in the existing part of the novel supports this idea' (*Poetika*, 191). Maximilian Braun comes to the same conclusion in '*The Brothers Karamazov* as an Expository Novel', *Canadian–American Slavic Studies*, 6 (1972), 199–208, and *Dostojewskij: Das Gesamtwerk als Vielfalt und Einheit* (Göttingen, 1976), 260.

21 This is one reason why Dostoevsky's interpretation of Christianity attracted criticism and was held suspect by the official Orthodox Church, and is to this day.

22 Evelyn Birge Vitz, *PMLA*, 93, 396–408 (p. 406).

23 See Bernard Comrie's discussion of the future tense in *Tense* (Cambridge, 1985), 43–8.

24 'Lutheran protestantism', wrote Dostoevsky in 1877, is 'a protesting and only negative faith, and as soon as catholicism disappears from the earth, so will protestantism surely disappear after it because there won't be anything to protest against, it will turn into straightforward atheism and that's what it will end in' (15,556–57).

25 Jean Starobinski, 'The Struggle with Legion: A Literary Analysis of Mark 5:1–20', *New Literary History*, 4 (1973), 331–56 (p. 341). Terras also interprets these plurals as 'diabolic imagery'. See his *A Karamazov Companion*, 367–8.

26 Quoted in Ellis Sandoz, *Political Apocalypse: Dostoevsky's Grand Inquisitor* (Baton Rouge, 1971), 87.

27 Ivan's title, as the editors of the *PSS* remark (15,595), is very likely an echo from Renan's chapter on Jesus' ideas on the Kingdom of God where he writes: 'The principles of our positive science are offended by the dreams which formed part of the ideal scheme of Jesus. We know the history of the earth; cosmical revolutions of the kind expected by Jesus are only the results of geological or astronomical causes, the connection of which with spiritual things has never yet been demonstrated'. *Renan's Life of Jesus*, trans. William G. Hutchinson (London, 1898), 79. Dostoevsky is engaging in a hidden polemic with Renan whose book he condemned as 'full of unfaith'. See also E. I. Kiiko, 'Dostoevskii i Renan', *Materialy i issledovaniia*, 4, ed. G. M. Fridlender (Leningrad, 1980), 106–22.

28 See H. G. Schenk, *The Mind of the European Romantics* (Oxford, 1966); with a Preface by Isaiah Berlin.

29 D. S. Mirsky, *A History of Russian Literature: From Its Beginnings to 1900*, ed. Francis J. Whitfield (New York, 1958), 279–80.

30 Ernst Cassirer, *The Philosophy of Symbolic Forms*, vol. II (New Haven, 1955), 120. See also, Harold Fisch, *A Remembered Future* (Bloomington, Indiana, 1984).

31 M. M. Bakhtin, *The Dialogic Imagination*, ed. Michael Holquist, trans. Michael Holquist and Caryl Emerson (Austin, 1981), 158.

32 Bakhtin, *Problems*, 127.

33 In the ordination ceremony of the Orthodox Church, the newly ordained priest kisses the bishop's shoulder to the accompaniment of the credo: 'Christ is and ever will be among us'. I thank Sergei Hackel for this information.

34 Lise's wish to burn down her house – 'I want awfully to burn

down the house, Alyosha, our house' – comes with this echo behind it (15,22).

35 See Richard Peace's discussion of Smerdyakov's conversion to the 'Contemplative Sects' of Castrates and Flagellants in *Dostoyevsky*, 261–3.

36 The 'progressive flesh' (where 'flesh' translates 'miaso', 'animal meat') is a synonym for, 'cannonfodder of progress' and an allusion, as Terras notes, to Herzen's article of 1862, 'Cannonfodder of the Emancipation' (Terras, *Handbook*, 181).

37 *Neizdannyi Dostoevskii*, 675.

38 As Nina Perlina similarly puts it: 'Alyosha's speech serves as the final metaphoric transfiguration of the novel's epigraph <...> the seed of truth sown by Zosima brings forth fruit in Alyosha's soul <...> Zosima's word lovingly preserved in Alyosha, is implanted in the "virgin-soil" of the boys' consciousness, and here it will bring forth much fruit'. Nina Perlina, *Varieties*, 193.

8. THE CHRISTOCENTRIC POETIC MEMORY SYSTEM

1 M. Bakhtin, *Problemy poetiki Dostoevskogo* (Moscow, 1979), 112; also *Problems*, 97, 100.

2 Roman Jakobson, 'The Dominant', *SW*, III (The Hague, 1981), 751–6 (p. 751).

3 Leonid Grossman, 'Put' Dostoevskogo', *Tvorchestvo Dostoevskogo: Sbornik statei i materialov*, ed. L. P. Grossman, (Chicago, 1970), 83–108 (p. 100).

4 Dostoevsky viewed the classical tradition as one promoting the man–god idea. Apollo versus Christ, he wrote as late as August 1880 in his *Diary of a Writer*, represented the 'two most opposite ideas which ever existed'. In this opposition the 'man–god met the God–man' (31,169).

5 V. Komarovich, 'Dostoevskii i Geine', *Sovremennyi mir* (1916), No. 10, part II, 100–4 (pp. 100, 103–4). Komarovich quotes Dostoevsky as saying that Heine 'could not understand where irony ends and heaven begins'. See also *PSS* (15,558).

6 Antony Johae, 'Idealism and the Dialectic in *The Brothers Karamazov*', *F. M. Dostoevsky (1821–1881): A Centenary Collection*, ed. Leon Burnett (University of Essex, 1981), 109–17 (p. 116).

7 Leonid Ouspensky, *Theology of the Icon* (Crestwood, New York, 1978), 201–2.

8 As far as I know, only Müller has remarked this fact. See Ludolf Müller, *Dostojewskij* (Munich, 1982), 94.

9 Jostein Børtnes, 'Polyphony', 411.
10 Leonid Grossman, 'Put' Dostoevskogo', 99.
11 *Pisma*, IV, 114.
12 Nina Perlina, *Varieties*, 80.
13 M. Bakhtin, *Problemy poetiki Dostoevskogo*, 290–1.
14 All quotations from 'Cana of Galilee' are from (14,325–8).
15 Ouspensky, *Theology of the Icon*, 224–5.
16 S. Linnér, *Starets Zosima, A Study of the Mimesis of Virtue* (Stockholm, 1975), 175.
17 From a sixteenth- seventeenth-century manuscript reproduced in Roman Jakobson's article, 'One of the Speculative Anticipations', *SW*, II (The Hague, 1971), 370. See also Paul's vision on the road to Damascus, Acts 26:13.
18 Paul Evdokimov, *Gogol et Dostoievsky ou la descente aux enfers* (Bruges 1961), 282.
19 See Jostein Børtnes 'To Dostoevskijstudier, I. Ivan Karamazov og Storinkvisitoren. II. Aljoša og det nye liv', *Edda* 68 (1968), 1–16.
20 This interpretation of Ivan, which coincides with my own, was first put forward by Arpád Kovács in his talk given at the Dostoevsky Symposium in Ljubljana, 1989.
21 *Neizdannyi Dostoevskii*, 699.
22 See Jostein Børtnes' analysis of this poem in 'On Puškin's Response to Liturgical Poetry: "Otcy pustynniki i Ženy neporočny" and Saint Ephraim the Syrian's Penitent Prayer', *Text and Context*, Essays to honor Nils Ake Nilsson (Stockholm, 1987), 26–37.
23 These episodes are depicted in Flaubert's *La légende de Saint Julian l'Hospitalier* which was published in a translation by Turgenev in 1877. See I. S. Turgenev, *Polnoe sobranie sochinenii i pisem*, 10 (Moscow, 1982), 194–219.
24 *Three Byzantine Saints*, trans. E. Dawes and N. Baynes (Oxford, 1948).
25 Nina Perlina, 'Quotation as an element of the poetics of *The Brothers Karamazov*', (Unpublished Ph.D. thesis, Brown University, 1977), 85–6.
26 Robert Belknap, 'The Origins of Alëša Karamazov' in *American Contributions to the Sixth International Congress of Slavists*, ed. William E. Harkins, 2 (The Hague, 1968), 7–27 (p. 26).
27 From a letter to Boccaccio quoted by David Lowenthal in *The Past Is A Foreign Country* (Cambridge, 1985), 81.
28 Losev likens a symbol to a mathematical function which can be decomposed into an infinite series of representations. A. F. Losev

'Simvol i xudozhestvennoe tvorchestvo', *Izvestiia Akademii nauk SSSR, Seriia literatury i iazyka*, 30 (Moscow, 1971), 3–14.

29 It may be objected that the analogy Alyosha/Christ is being carried too far since Alyosha makes several remarks revealing his awareness that he too bears the mark of the Karamazov sensuality. But as Volynsky pointed out, 'there is not a single episode which could artistically justify his words'. (A. L. Volynskii, *Tsarstvo Karamazovykh* (St Petersburg, 1901), 155.) In an early conversation with Lise, Alyosha momentarily doubts his faith in God (14,201). Vetlovskaia's explanation may suffice: 'When unbelief has the character of a temporary doubt, it also serves authoritativeness. After all the path to truth lies through doubts <...> what is accepted without questions may be just a prejudice. Thus the doubt Alyosha suffers imparts authority to his convictions' (*Poetika*, 86). Moreover, these remarks come before Alyosha's rite of passage after which he emerged 'a firm fighter for life'.

30 Jean Starobinsky, 'The Struggle with Legion', *New Literary History*, 4 (1973), 331–56 (p. 341).

31 John Meyendorff, 'L'iconographie de la sagesse divine dans la tradition Byzantine', *Byzantine Hesychasm* (London, 1974), 259–77 (pp. 268–9).

32 Jostein Børtnes, 'The Function of Hagiography in Dostoevskij's Novels', *Scando-Slavica*, 24 (1978), 27–33 (p. 29).

33 For example, 'Lover of Man, glory to Thee', 'We glorify Thee, the only Lover of Man'; see the *Molitvoslov* (St Petersburg, 1908), 147, 246, 247, 398, 399.

34 Volynskii, *Tsarstvo Karamazovykh*, 148–9.

35 Evelyn Birge Vitz, 'La Vie de Saint Alexis: Narrative Analysis and the Quest for the Sacred Subject', *PMLA*, 93, 396–408.

9. AFTERWORD

1 *PSS*, 22 (Leningrad, 1981), 46–50, 154. See also Robert Louis Jackson, *The Art of Dostoevsky, Deliriums and Nocturnes* (Princeton, New Jersey, 1981), 20–33.

2 Quoted by Konstantin Mochul'skii in *Dostoevskii* (Paris, 1980), 448.

3 Jostein Børtnes, *Visions of Glory* (Oslo, 1988), 280.

4 D. S. Mirsky, *A History of Russian Literature: From Earliest Times to the Death of Dostoevsky (1881)* (London, 1927), 345.

5 Ludwig Wittgenstein, 'A Lecture on Ethics', *Philosophical Review*, 74 (1965), 3–12.

6 *Recollections of Wittgenstein*, ed. Rush Rhees (Oxford, 1984), 86. Interestingly, Wittgenstein placed *The Brothers Karamazov* among the highest artistic achievements in literature.

7 See Roman Jakobson's discussion of C. S. Pierce's ideas in 'Quest for the Essence of Language', *SW*, II (The Hague, 1971), 345–59 (p. 358).

8 Viacheslav Ivanov, *Po zvezdam*, Bradda Rarity Reprints, 25 (Letchworth, 1971), 393–4.

9 Nina Perlina, *Varieties*, 193.

Bibliography

This bibliography contains all sources cited in the text and notes as well as other selected works consulted in the writing of this study. Works published after 1988 could not be included.

PRIMARY SOURCES

Dostoevskii, F. M., *Brat'ia Karamazovy, Polnoe sobranie sochinenii v tridtsati tomax*, vols. 14 and 15 (Leningrad, 1976).

Dnevnik pisatelia, Polnoe sobranie sochinenii v tridtsati tomax, vols. 21–7 (Leningrad, 1980–4).

Biografiia, pis'ma i zametki iz zapisnoi knizhki F. M. Dostoevskago (St Petersburg, 1883).

Pis'ma, ed. A. S. Dolinin, 4 vols (Moscow–Leningrad, 1928–59).

Zapisnye tetradi F. M. Dostoevskogo (Moscow–Leningrad, 1935).

Materialy i issledovaniia, ed. A. S. Dolinin (Leningrad, 1935).

Neizdannyi Dostoevskii: Zapisnye knizhki i tetradi 1860–1881, ed. V. R. Shcherbina, Literaturnoe nasledstvo, 83 (Moscow, 1971).

Dostoevskaia, A. G., *Vospominaniia* (Moscow, 1971).

Bible, Russian Testament, *Gospoda nashego Iisusa Khrista Novyi zavet* 2nd edn (St Petersburg, 1823).

Kniga xvalenii ili Psaltir', 3rd edn (St Petersburg, 1822).

Molitvoslov (St Petersburg, 1908).

Dal', Vladimir. *Tolkovyi slovar' zhivogo velikorusskago iazkya*, 4 vols, 4th edn, ed. I. A. Boduen-de-Courtene (St Petersburg–Moscow, 1912).

Dostoevsky, Fyodor, *The Diary of a Writer*, 2 vols, trans. and ed. Boris Brasol, (New York, 1949).

The Brothers Karamazov, trans. David Magarshack (Penguin Books, 1958).

The Brothers Karamazov: The Garnett Translation, Revised by Ralph E. Matlaw: Backgrounds and Sources, Essays in Criticism, ed. Ralph E. Matlaw (New York, 1976).

Terras, Victor, *A Karamazov Companion: Commentary on the Genesis, Language and Style of Dostoevsky's Novel* (Madison, Wisconsin, 1981).
Three Byzantine Saints, trans. E. Dawes and N. Baynes (Oxford, 1948).

SECONDARY SOURCES

Abrams, Meyer Howard, *The Mirror and the Lamp* (Oxford, 1974).
Allain, Louis, *Dostoïevski et Dieu: la morsure du divin* (Lille, 1981).
Allen, Gay Wilson, *American Prosody* (New York, 1935).
Andreyev, Nikolay, 'Literature in the Muscovite Period (1300–1700)', *An Introduction to Russian Language and Literature*, ed. Robert Auty and Dimitri Obolensky (Cambridge, 1980), 90–110.
Annenskii, Innokentii, *Knigi otrazhenii* (Moscow, 1979).
Antonovich, M. A., *Izbrannye stat'i* (Leningrad, 1938).
Aristotle, 'On Memory and Reminiscence', *The Basic Works of Aristotle*, ed. R. McKeon (New York, 1941).
'Poetics', *Introduction to Aristotle*, ed. Richard McKeon (New York, 1947).
Arseniev, Nicholas, *Russian Piety*, trans. Asheleigh Moorhouse (London, 1964).
Auerbach, Erich, *Mimesis*, trans. Willard R. Trask (Princeton, 1974).
'Figura', *Scenes from the Drama of European Literature, Theory and History of Literature*, 9, (Minneapolis, 1984).
St Augustine, *Confessions*, trans. Vernon J. Bourke (Washington D.C., 1953).
Bakhtin, Mikhail, *Problemy tvorchestva Dostoevskogo* (Leningrad, 1929).
Voprosy literatury i estetiki (Moscow, 1975).
Problemy poetiki Dostoevskogo, 4th edn (Moscow, 1979).
Estetika slovesnogo tvorchestva (Moscow, 1979).
The Dialogic Imagination, ed. Michael Holquist, trans. Caryl Emerson and Michael Holquist (Austin, 1981).
Problems of Dostoevsky's Poetics, ed. and trans. Caryl Emerson (Minneapolis, 1984)
Bakhtin–Voloshinov, see Vološinov.
Banfield, Ann, *Unspeakable Sentences: Narration and Representation in the Language of Fiction* (Boston, 1982).
Beckwith, John, *Early Christian and Byzantine Art* (Penguin Books, 1979).
Belknap, Robert L., *The Structure of The Brothers Karamazov* (The Hague, 1967).
'The Origins of Alësa Karamazov', *American Contributions to the Sixth International Congress of Slavists*, 2, ed. William E. Harkins (The Hague, 1968), 7–28.

'The Sources of Mitja Karamazov', *American Contributions to the Seventh International Congress of Slavists*, vol. II, ed. Victor Terras (The Hague, 1973), 39–51.

'Memory in *The Brothers Karamazov*', *American Contributions to the Eighth International Congress of Slavists*, vol. II, ed. Victor Terras (Columbus, Ohio, 1978), 24–41.

Belyi, Andrei, *Tragediia tvorchestva: Dostoevskii i Tolstoi* (Moscow, 1911).

Bem, A. L., '*Faust* v tvorchestve Dostoevskogo', Fascicle 5, *Russkii Svobodnyi Universitet v Prage: Zapiski nauchno-issledovatel'skogo ob"edineniia* (Prague, 1973), 109–43.

'*Skupoi rytsar'* v tvorchestve Dostoevskogo', *O Dostoevskom: sbornik statei*, 3 (Prague, 1936), 115–17.

Berdiaev, Nikolai, *Mirosozertsanie Dostoevskogo* (Prague, 1923).

Besançon, Alain, *The Rise of the Gulag: Intellectual Origins of Leninism*, trans. Sarah Matthews (Oxford, 1981).

Bitsilli, P. M., 'Pochemu Dostoevskii ne napisal "Zhitia velikogo greshnika"', *O Dostoevskom: sbornik statei* 2, ed. A. L. Bem (Prague, 1933), 25–30.

'K voprosu o vnutrennei forme romana Dostoevskogo', *O Dostoevskom: Stat'i*, ed. Donald Fanger, Brown University Slavic Reprints, 4 (Providence, 1966), 1–72.

Blagoi, D. D., 'Put' Aleshi Karamazova', *Izvestiia AN SSSR*, (1974), 8–26.

Bocharov, S. G. 'O dvukh pushkinskikh reministsentsiiakh v *Brat'iakh Karamazovykh*', *Dostoevskii: Materialy i issledovaniia*, 2 (Leningrad, 1976), 145–53.

Both, Wayne C., *The Rhetoric of Fiction*, 2nd edn (Chicago, 1983).

Børtnes, Jostein, 'To Dostoevskijstudier: I. Ivan Karamazov og Storinkvisitoren. II. Aljoša og det nye liv', *Edda* 68 (1968), 1–16.

'The Function of Hagiography in Dostoevskij's Novels', *Scando-Slavica*, 24 (1978), 27–33.

'Polyphony in *The Brothers Karamazov*: Variations on a Theme', *Canadian–American Slavic Studies*, 17 (Fall, 1983), 402–11.

'On Puškin's Response to Liturgical Poetry: "Otcy pustynniki i Ženy neporočny" and Saint Ephraim the Syrian's Penitent Prayer', *Text and Context*, Essays to honor Nils Ake Nilsson (Stockholm, 1987), 26–37.

Visions of Glory (Oslo, 1988).

Braun, Maximilian '*The Brothers Karamazov* as an Expository Novel', *Canadian–American Slavic Studies*, 6 (Summer, 1972), 199–208.

Dostojewskij: Das Gesamtwerk als Vielfalt und Einheit (Gottingen, 1976).

Brose, Margaret, 'Leopardi's "L'Infinito" and the Language of the Romantic Sublime', *Poetics Today*, 4:1 (1983), 47–71.

Bulgakov, S. N., 'Ivan Karamazov kak filosofskii tip', *Ot marksizma k idealizmu* (St Petersburg, 1903), 83–112.

Carr, Edward Hallett, *Dostoevsky: 1821–1881* (London, 1931).

Cassirer, Ernst, *The Philosophy of Symbolic Forms*, vol. II (New Haven, 1955).

Catteau, Jacques, *La Création Littéraire chez Dostoïevski* (Paris, 1978).

'The Paradox of the Legend of the Grand Inquisitor in *The Brothers Karamazov*', *Dostoevsky: New Perspectives*, ed. Robert Louis Jackson (Englewood Cliffs, N.J., 1984).

Chizhevski, D., 'Schiller und die Brüder Karamazoff', *Zeitschrift für Slavische Philologie*, 6 (Leipzig, 1929), 1–42.

'The Theme of the Double in Dostoevsky', *Dostoevsky: A Collection of Critical Essays*, ed. René Wellek (Englewood Cliffs, N.J., 1962), 112–29.

Comrie, Bernard, *Tense* (Cambridge, 1985).

Curtius, Ernst Robert, *European Literature and the Latin Middle Ages* (London and Henley, 1979).

Danow, David K., 'The Deconstruction of an Idea (*Crime and Punishment* and *The Brothers Karamazov*)', *Dostoevsky Studies*, 6 (1985), 91–102.

Doležel, Lubomír, *Narrative Modes in Czech Literature* (Toronto, 1973).

Dolinin, A. S., 'K istorii sozdaniia *Brat'ev Karamazovykh*', *F. M. Dostoevskii: Materialy i issledovaniia*, ed. A. S. Dolinin (Leningrad, 1935), 9–80.

Durylin, Sergei, 'Ob odnom simvole u Dostoevskogo: Opyt tematischeskogo obzora', *Dostoevskii* (Moscow, 1928), 163–98.

Evdokimov, Paul, *Gogol et Dostoïevsky ou la descente aux enfers* (Bruges, 1961).

Fanger, Donald, *Dostoevsky and Romantic Realism* (Chicago, 1974).

Fasting, Sigurd, 'Transformacija filantropičeskix' épizodov u Dostoevskogo', *International Dostoevsky Studies*, 1 (1980), 65–72.

Fedorov, N. F., *Filosofiia obshchego dela* (Moscow, 1906).

Fedotov, G. P., ed., *A Treasury of Russian Spirituality* (New York, 1950).

Sviatye drevnei Rusi (Paris, 1985).

Finley, M. I., 'Myth, Memory and History, History and Theory', *Studies in the Philosophy of History*, 4 (1965), 281–302.

Fisch, Harold, *A Remembered Future* (Bloomington, Indiana, 1984).

Forster, E. M., *Aspects of the Novel* (Penguin Books, 1982).

Frank, Joseph, *Dostoevsky: The Seeds of Revolt, 1821–1849* (Princeton, 1976).

Dostoevsky: The Years of Ordeal, 1850–1859 (Princeton, 1983).

Dostoevsky: The Stir of Liberation, 1860–1865 (Princeton, 1986).

Freud, Sigm., 'Dostojewski und die Vatertötung, *Gesammelte Werke: Werke aus den Jahren 1925–31*, 14 (London, 1948), 399–418.

Fridlender, Georgii, 'Ot Podrostka k Brat'iam Karamazovym', *Dostoevsky Studies*, 7 (1986), 3–10.

Frye, Northrop, *The Great Code: The Bible and Literature* (London, 1982).

Genette, Gérard, *Narrative Discourse*, trans. Jane E. Lewin (Oxford, 1980).

Gerigk, Horst-Jürgen, 'Der Mörder Smerdjakow. Bemerkungen zu Dostojewskijs Typologie der Kriminellen Persönlichkeit', *Dostoevsky Studies*, 7 (1986), 107–122.

Gessen, S. I., 'Tragediia dobra v 'Brat'iax Karamazovykh' Dostoevskogo', in *O Dostoevskom: Stat'i*, ed. Donald Fanger (Providence, 1966), 197–229.

Gibson, A. Boyce, *The Religion of Dostoevsky* (London, 1973).

Goethe, *Faust*, ed. Erich Trunz, (Hamburg, 1962).

Golosovker, Ia. E., *Dostoevskii i Kant: Razmyshlenie chitatelia nad romanom 'Brat'ia Karamazovy' i traktatom 'Kritika chistogo razuma'* (Moscow, 1963).

Golubov, Alexander, 'Religious Imagery in the Structure of *The Brothers Karamazov*', *Russian and Slavic Literature: 1700–1917*, ed. Richard Freeborn (Bloomington, Indiana, 1976), 113–36.

Gornostaev, A. K., *Rai na zemle:k ideologii tvorchestva F. M. Dostoevskogo* (Harbin, 1929).

The Penguin Book of Greek Verse, ed. Constantine A. Trypanis (Penguin Books, 1971).

Grossman, Leonid, 'Put' Dostoevskogo', *Tvorchestvo Dostoevskogo, Sbornik statei i materialov*, ed. L. P. Grossman, Russian Language Specialties (Chicago, 1970), 83–108.

Guardini, Romano, *Religiöse Gestalten in Dostojewskijs Werk* (Munich, 1947).

Hackel Sergei, 'F. M. Dostoevsky (1821–1881): Prophet Manqué', *Dostoevsky Studies*, 3 (1982), 5–25.

'The religious dimension: vision or evasion? Zosima's discourse in *The Brothers Karamazov*', *New Essays on Dostoevsky*, ed. M. V. Jones and G. Terry (Cambridge, 1983), 139–68.

Halbwachs, Maurice, *The Collective Memory*, trans. Francis J. Ditter, Jr. and Vida Yazdi Ditter (New York, 1980).

Hamburger, K., *The Logic of Literature*, trans. M. J. Rose (Bloomington, Indiana, 1973).

Hoffmann, N., *Th. M. Dostojewsky: Eine biographische Studie* (Berlin, 1899).

Holquist, Michael, *Dostoevsky and the Novel* (Princeton, 1977).

Hume, David, *A Treatise of Human Nature* (Penguin Classics, 1985).

Ivanits, Linda J., 'Folk Beliefs About the Unclean Force in *The Brothers Karamazov*', *New Perspectives in Nineteenth-Century Russian Prose*, ed. Lauren G. Leighton and Victor Terras (Columbus, 1982), 135–46.

Ivanov, Viacheslav, 'Dostoevskii i roman-tragediia', *Borozdi i mezhi* (Moscow, 1916).

Po zvezdam, Bradda Rarity Reprints, 25 (Letchworth, 1971).

Jackson, Robert Louis, *Dostoevsky's Quest for Form: A Study of His Philosophy of Art*, 2nd ed. (New Haven and London, 1966).

'Vynesenie prigovora Fedoru Pavlovichu Karamazovu', *Dostoevskii: Materialu i issledovaniia*, 2, (Leningrad, 1976), 137–44.

The Art of Dostoevsky, Deliriums and Nocturnes (Princeton, 1981).

Jakobson, Roman, *SW = Selected Writings*.

'On Russian Fairy Tales', *SW*, iv (The Hague, 1966), 82–100.

'One of the Speculative Anticipations', *SW*, ii (The Hague, 1971), 369–74.

'Two Aspects of Language and Two Types of Aphasic Disturbances', *SW*, ii (The Hague, 1971), 239–59.

'Quest for the Essence of Language', *SW*, ii (The Hague, 1971), 345–59.

'Linguistics and Poetics', *SW*, iii, ed. Stephen Rudy (The Hague, 1981), 18–51.

'Poetry of Grammar and Grammar of Poetry', *SW*, iii (The Hague, 1981), 87–97.

'The Dominant', *SW*, iii (The Hague, 1981), 751–6.

Verbal Art, Verbal Sign, Verbal Time, ed. Krystyna Pomorska and Stephen Rudy (Minneapolis, 1985).

James, William, *The Principles of Psychology* (London, 1983).

Johae, Antony, 'Idealism and the Dialectic in *The Brothers Karamazov*', *F. M. Dostoevsky (1821–1881): A Centenary Collection*, ed. Leon Burnett (University of Essex, 1981), 109–17.

Jones, John, *Dostoevsky* (Oxford, 1983).

Jones, Malcolm V., *Dostoyevsky: The Novel of Discord* (London, 1976).

'"The Legend of the Grand Inquisitor": The Suppression of the Second Temptation and Dialogue with God', *Dostoevsky Studies*, 7 (1986), 123–34.

Joyce, James, *Stephen Hero* (London, 1969).

Kant, Immanuel, 'Degrees of Responsibility', *Readings in the Problem of Ethics* ed. Rosalind Ekman (New York, 1965), 234–40.

Kelly, Aileen, 'Dostoevskii and the Divided Conscience', *Slavic Review*, 47, no. 2 (Summer, 1988), 239–60.

Kermode, Frank, *The Sense of an Ending: Studies in the Theory of Fiction* (New York, 1979).

The Genesis of Secrecy: On the Interpretation of Narrative (Cambridge, Massachusetts, 1980).

Kiiko, E. I., 'Iz istorii sozdaniia *Brat' ev Karamazovykh*: Ivan i Smerdiakov', *Dostoevskii: Materialy i issledovaniia*, 2 (Leningrad, 1976), 125–9.

'Dostoevskii i Renan', *Materialy i issledovaniia*, 4, ed. G. M. Fridlender (Leningrad, 1980), 106–22.

Kjetsaa, Geir, *Dostoevsky and his New Testament* (Oslo, 1984).

Fyodor Dostoyevsky: A Writer's Life, trans. Siri Hustvedt and Dvid McDuff (New York, 1987).

Kliuchevskii, V. O., *Drevnerusskiia zhitiia sviatykh kak istoricheskii istochnik* (Moscow, 1871).

Komarovich, V. L., 'Dostoevskii i Geine', *Sovremennyi mir* (1916), No 10, 100–4.

Die Urgestalt der Brüder Karamasoff (Munich, 1928).

Kovács, Arpád, 'The Narrative Model of the Novel of "Awakening": Dostoevsky' *Acta Litteraria Academiae Scientiarum Hungaricae* 25 (1983), 359–73.

Lapshin, I. I., 'Kak slozhilas' legenda o Velikom Inkvizitore', *O Dostoevskom: sbornik statei*, 1, ed. A. L. Bem (Prague, 1929), 125–39.

Lawrence, D. H., 'Preface to Dostoevsky's *The Grand Inquisitor*', *Dostoevsky: A Collection of Critical Essays*, ed. René Wellek (Englewood Cliffs, N.J., 1962), 90–7.

Likhachev, D. S., *Chelovek v literature drevnei Rusi* (Moscow-Leningrad, 1958).

'"Predislovnyi rasskaz" Dostoevskogo', *Poetika i stilistika russkoi literatury: Pamiati akademika Vitora Vladimirovicha Vinogradova* (Leningrad, 1971), 189–94.

'"Nebrezhenie slovom" u Dostoevskogo', *Materialy i issledovaniia* 2 (Leningrad, 1976), 30–41.

Linnér, Sven, *Starets Zosima in 'The Brothers Karamazov': A Study in the Mimesis of Virtue* (Stockholm, 1975).

Locke, J., *An Essay Concerning Human Understanding* (Oxford, 1975).

Lord, Robert, *Dostoevsky: Essays and Perspectives* (London, 1970).

Losev, A. F., 'Simvol i xudozhestvennoe tvorchestvo', *Izvestiia Akademii nauk SSSR*, Seriia literatury i iazyka 30 (1971), 3–14.

Lossky, V., *The Mystical Theology of the Eastern Church* (London, 1957).

The Vision of God, trans. A. Moorhouse (London, 1963).

In the Image and Likeness of God, ed. J. H. Erickson and T. E. Bird (London, 1975).

Lotman, L. M., 'Romany Dostoevskogo i russkaja legenda', *Russkaja literatura*, 15 (1972), 2, 129–41.

Lotman, Y., *Analysis of the Poetic Text*, ed. and trans. D. B. Johnson (Ann Arbor, 1976).

'Pamiat' v kul'turologicheskom osveshchenii', *Wiener Slawistischer Almanach*, 16 (Vienna, 1985), 5–9.

Lotman, Iu. and Uspensky, B., 'O semioticheskom mekhanizme kul'tury', *Trudy po znakovym sistemam*, v (Tartu, 1971), 144–66.

Lowenthal, David, *The Past is a Foreign Country* (Cambridge, 1985).

Lukács, Georg, 'Dostoevsky', *Dostoevsky: A Collection of Critical Essays*, ed. René Wellek (Englewood Cliffs, N.J., 1962), 146–58.

Luria, A. R., *The Working Brain* (Penguin Books, 1973).

Lyngstad, A. H., *Dostoevskij and Schiller* (The Hague, 1977).

Malcolm, N., 'Three Lectures on Memory', *Knowledge and Certainty* (Englewood Cliffs, N.J., 1964).

Mandel'shtam, O., 'O prirode slova', *Proza* (Ann Arbor, Michigan, 1983).

Mathewson, Jr., Rufus, W., *The Positive Hero in Russian Literature* (Stanford, California, 1975).

Matlaw, Ralph E., *'The Brothers Karamazov': Novelistic Technique* (The Hague, 1957).

'Recurrent Imagery in Dostoevskij', *Harvard Slavic Studies* 3 (The Hague, 1957), 201–25.

Medieval Russia's Epics, Chronicles, and Tales, ed. Serge A. Zenkovsky (New York, 1963).

Meijer, Jan M., 'The Author of *Brat'ja Karamazovy*', *Dutch Studies in Russian Literature: The Brothers Karamazov by F. M. Dostoevskij* (The Hague, 1971), 7–46.

'A Note on Time in *Brat'ja Karamazovy*', *Dutch Studies in Russian Literature: The Brothers Karamazov by F. M. Dostoevskij* (The Hague, 1971), 47–62.

Mendilow, A., *Time and the Novel* (New York, 1965).

Merezhkovsky, D. S., *L. Tolstoi i Dostoevskii: Khristos i antikhrist v russkoi literature*, I (St Petersburg, 1901).

Meyendorff, John, 'L'iconographic de la sagesse divine dans la tradition Byzantine', *Byzantine Hesychasm* (London, 1974), 259–77.

Miller, Robin Feuer, *Dostoevsky and 'The Idiot'* (Cambridge, Massachusetts; London, 1981).

Milosz, Czeslaw, 'Dostoevsky and Swedenborg', *Emperor of the Earth* (Berkeley, 1981), 120–43.

Mirsky, D. S., *A History of Russian Literature: From Earliest Times to the Death of Dostoevsky (1881)* (London, 1927).

Mnatsakanjan, Elizaveta, 'Znachenie i rol' vospominaniia v xudozhestvennoi praktike. Freid – Dostoevskii – Geine', *Wiener Slawistischer Almanach*, 16 (Vienna, 1985), 37–80.

Mochul'skii, K., *Dostoevskii* (Paris, 1980).

Moser, Charles A., 'The Brothers Karamazov as a Novel of the 1860s', *Dostoevsky Studies*, 7 (1986), 73–80.

Müller, Ludolf, *Dostojewskij* (Munich, 1982).

'Die Religion Dostojewskijs', *Von Dostojewskij bis Grass*, Schriftsteller vor der Gottesfrage, ed. Wolfgang Bohne, Herrenalber Texte 71 (Karlsruhe, 1986), 30–59.

Neuhäuser, Rudolf, '*The Brothers Karamazov*. A Contemporary Reading of Book VI, "A Russian Monk"', *Dostoevsky Studies*, 7 (1986), 135–51.

Obolensky, Dimitri, 'Early Russian Literature (1000–1399)', *An Introduction to Russian Language and Literature*, ed. Robert Auty and Dimitri Obolensky (Cambridge, 1980), 56–89.

Onasch, Konrad, *Der verschwiegene Christus: Versuch uber die Poetisierung des Christentums in der Dichtung F. M. Dostojewskis* (Berlin, 1976).

Ouspensky, Leonid, *Theology of the Icon* (Crestwood, New York, 1978).

Parfeny (monk), *Skazenie o stranstvii i puteshestvii po Rossii, Turtsii i Sviatoi Zemle* (Moscow, 1856).

Peace, Richard, *Dostoyevsky: An Examination of the Major Novels* (Cambridge, 1971).

Perlina, Nina, 'Quotation as an Element of the Poetics of *The Brothers Karamazov*' (unpublished Ph.D. thesis, Brown University, 1977). *Varieties of Poetic Utterance: Quotation in The Brothers Karamazov* (Lanham, 1985).

Picchio, Riccardo, 'The Function of Biblical Thematic Clues in the Literary Code of "Slavia Orthodoxa"', *Slavica Hierosolymitana*, 1 (Jerusalem, 1977), 1–31.

Piretto, Gian Piero, 'Staraia Russa and Petersburg: Provincial Realities and Metropolitan Reminiscences in *The Brothers Karamazov*', *Dostoevsky Studies*, 7 (1986), 81–6.

Plato, 'Theaetetus', 'Cratylus', *The Dialogues of Plato*, trans. B. Jowett, 11th edn, 2 vols (New York, 1937).

Pletnev, R., 'Serdtsem mudrye': (O "startsakh" u Dostoevskogo)', *O Dostoevskom*, 2, ed. A. Bem (Prague, 1933), 73–92.

'Ob iskushenii Xrista v pustyne i Dostoevskom" *RLJ*, xxxvi, Nos. 123–4 (1982), 66–74.

Pomerants, Grigorii, '"Evklidovskii" i "neevklidovskii" razum v tvorchestve Dostoevskogo', *Kontinent*, 3 (1975), 109–50.

Pomorska, Krystyna, 'Poetics of Prose', in Roman Jakobson, *Verbal Art, Verbal Sign, Verbal Time* (Minneapolis, 1985), 169–77.

Proust, Marcel, *A la recherche du temps perdu*, vol. III, ed. Pierre Clarac and André Ferré (Paris, 1954).

Pumpianskii, L. V., *Dostoevskii i antichnost'*, Studien und Texte I (Bremen, 1973).

Pushkin, A. S., *Sobranie sochinenii*, vol. II (Moscow, 1959).

Renan, Ernst, *Renan's Life of Jesus*, trans. William G. Hutchinson (London, 1898).

Rice, James L., *Dostoevsky and the Healing Art* (Ann Arbor, 1985).

Richards, I. A., *Principles of Literary Criticism* (London and Henley, 1976).

Rosen, Nathan, 'Style and Structure in *The Brothers Karamazov*: The Grand Inquisitor and the Russian Monk', *Russian Literature Triquarterly* I (1971), 352–65.

'Why Dmitrii Karamazov Did Not Kill His Father', *Canadian–American Slavic Studies* 6 (Summer, 1972), 209–94.

'Freud on Dostoevsky's Epilepsy: A Revaluation', *Dostoevsky Studies*, 9 (1989), 107–25.

Rozanov, V. V., *Legenda o Velikom Inkvizitore F. M. Dostoevskogo:opyty kriticheskogo kommentariia* (St Petersburg, 1906).

Sandoz, Ellis, *Political Apocalypse: Dostoevsky's Grand Inquisitor* (Baton Rouge, 1971).

Schenk, H. G., *The Mind of the European Romantics* (Oxford, 1966).

Seeley, Frank Friedeberg, 'Ivan Karamazov', *New Essays on Dostoevsky*, ed. Malcolm V. Jones and Garth M. Terry (Cambridge, 1983), 121–6.

'Smerdiakov', *Dostoevsky Studies*, 7 (1986), 99–105.

Setchkarev, V., 'From the Golden to the Silver Age (1820–1917)', *An Introduction to Russian Language and Literature* ed. Robert Auty and Dimitri Obolensky (Cambridge, 1980), 133–84.

Solov'ev, V. S., 'Tri rechi v pamiat' Dostoevskogo (1881–1883)', *Sobranie sochinenii V. S. Solov'eva*, 3 (St Petersburg, 1901), 169–205.

Stankiewicz, Edward, 'Linguistics, Poetics, and the Literary Genres', *New Directions in Linguistics and Semiotics*, ed. J. E. Copeland (Houston, 1984), 155–78.

Stanzel, F. K., *A Theory of Narrative*, trans. Charlotte Goedsche (Cambridge, 1984).

Starobinski, Jean, 'The Struggle with Legion: A Literary Analysis of Mark 5:1–20', *New Literary History*, 4, 1973, 331–56.

Suvorin, A. S., *Dnevnik*, ed. M. Krichevskii (Moscow–Petrograd, 1923).

Terras, Victor, 'Turgenev and the Devil in *The Brothers Karamazov*', *Canadian–American Slavic Studies* 6 (Summer, 1972), 265–71.

'The Art of Fiction as a Theme in *The Brothers Karamazov*,

Dostoevsky: New Perspectives, ed. Robert Louis Jackson (Englewood Cliffs, N.J., 1984).

Thompson, Diane Ella Oenning, '*The Brothers Karamazov* and the Poetics of Memory' (unpublished Ph.D. thesis, University of Cambridge, 1985).

'Poetic Transformations of Scientific Facts in *Brat'ja Karamazovy*' *Dostoevsky Studies*, 8 (1987), 73–85.

Tikhonravov, N., 'Khozhdenie Bogoroditsy po mukam', *Pamiatniki otrechennoi russkoi literatury*, 2 (Moscow, 1863), 23–30.

Todd, William Mills III, '*The Brothers Karamazov* and the Poetics of Serial Publication', *Dostoevsky Studies*, 7 (1986), 87–97.

Todorov, T., *The Poetics of Prose* (Oxford, 1977).

Tracy, David, 'Metaphor and Religion: The Test Case of Christian Texts', *On Metaphor* ed. Sheldon Sacks (Chicago, 1979), 89–104.

Traversi, Derek, 'Dostoevsky', *Dostoevsky: A Collection of Critical Essays*, ed. René Wellek (Englewood Cliffs, N.J., 1962), 159–71.

Troncale, Joseph Charles, 'Dostoevsky's use of Scripture in *The Brothers Karamazov*' (unpublished Ph.D. thesis, Cornell University, 1979).

Trubetzkoy, N. S., *Dostoevskij als Künstler* (The Hague, 1964).

Turgenev, I. S., *Polnoe sobranie sochinenii i pis'em v tridtsati tomax*, 10 (Moscow, 1982).

Tynianov, Iu., *Problema stikhotvornogo iazyka: stat'i* (Moscow, 1965).

Van der Eng, Jan, '"Suspense" v *Brat'jax Karamazov*', *Dutch Studies in Russian Literature: The Brothers Karamazov by F. M. Dostoevskij* (The Hague, 1971), 63–148.

'A Note on Comic Relief in *The Brothers Karamazov*', *Dutch Studies in Russian Literature: The Brothers Karamazov by F. M. Dostoevskij* (The Hague, 1971), 149–62.

Vetlovskaia, V. E., 'Razviazka v *Brat'yakh Karamazovykh*', *Poetika i stilistika russkoi literatury: Pamiati akademika Viktora Vladimirovicha Vinogradova* (Leningrad, 1971), 195–203.

'Simbolika chisel v *Brat'iax Karamazovykh*', *Drevnerusskaia literaturai: ee traditsii v russkoi literature XVII–XIX vv.* (Leningrad, 1971), 143–61.

'Dostoevskii i poeticheskii mir drevnei Rusi: (Literaturnye i fol'klornye istochniki Brat'ev Karamazovykh)', *Trudy Otdela Drevnerusskoi Literatury* 28, ed. D. S. Likhachev (Leningrad, 1974), 296–307.

Poetika romana 'Brat'ja Karamazovy' (Leningrad, 1977).

'Pater Seraphicus', *Dostoevskii: Materialy i issledovaniia* 5, ed. G. M. Fridlender, (Leningrad, 1983), 163–78.

Vitz, Evelyn Birge, 'La Vie de Saint Alexis: Narrative Analysis and the Quest for the Sacred Subject', *PMLA* 93, 396–408.

Vivas, Eliseo, 'The Two Dimensions of Reality in *The Brothers Karamazov, Dostoevsky: A Collection of Critical Essays*, ed. René Wellek (Englewood Cliffs, N.J., 1962), 71–89.

Vološinov, V. N., *Marxism and the Philosophy of Language*, trans. Ladislav Makejka and I. R. Titunik (London, 1973).

Volynskii, A. L., *Tsarstvo Karamazovykh* (St Petersburg, 1901).

Von Leyden, W., *Remembering: A Philosophical Problem* (London, 1961).

Walicki, Andrzej, *A History of Russian Thought from the Enlightenment to Marxism*, trans. Hilda Andrews-Rusiecka (Stanford, California, 1979).

Ware, Timothy, *The Orthodox Church* (Pelican Books, 1986).

Wasiolek, Edward, *Dostoevsky: The Major Fiction* (Cambridge, Massachusetts, 1973).

Wellek, René, 'Introduction: A History of Dostoevsky Criticism', *Dostoevsky: A Collection of Critical Essays*, ed. René Wellek (Englewood Cliffs, N.J., 1962), 1–15.

'Bakhtin's View of Dostoevsky: "Polyphony" and "Carnivalesque"', *Dostoevsky Studies* 1 (1980), 31–9.

Weyl, Hermann, *Symmetry* (Princeton, 1952).

Wittgenstein, Ludwig, *Philosophical Investigations I*, trans. G. E. M. Anscombe (Oxford, 1958).

'A Lecture on Ethics', *Philosophical Review*, 74 (1965), 3–12.

Recollections of Wittgenstein, ed. Rush Rhees (Oxford, 1984).

Yates, Frances A., *The Art of Memory* (Penguin Books, 1978).

Zen'kovskii, V. V., 'Fiodor Pavlovich Karamazov', *O Dostoevskom: sbornik statei*, II, ed. A. L. Bem (Prague, 1929–36), 93–114.

'Dostoevsky's Religious and Philosophical Views', *Dostoevsky: A Collection of Critical Essays*, ed. René Wellek (Englewood Cliffs, N.J., 1962), 130–45.

Ziolkowski, Theodore, *Fictional Transfigurations of Jesus* (Princeton, 1972).

Index

This index does not contain the names of the fictional characters. Individual works by Dostoevsky are listed alphabetically.

356

NOTTINGHAM UNIVERSITY LIBRARY

CAMBRIDGE STUDIES IN RUSSIAN LITERATURE
General editor MALCOLM JONES
Editorial board: ANTHONY CROSS, CARYL EMERSON,
HENRY GIFFORD, G. S SMITH, VICTOR TERRAS